AMERICAN CULTURES:
Readings in Social and Cultural History

By A. J. Smith, III

Acknowledgements: I would like to formally acknowledge all of the un-named people who led unheralded lives of quietly determined struggle.

Third Edition
©1999, 2004 by Al Smith
All rights reserved. Published 2006
ISBN 978-1-4357-0160-1
Printed in the United States of America

Library of Congress Cataloging in Publication Data

Smith, Albert 1957 –
American Cultures: Readings in Social and Cultural History

This book is dedicated to my friends who still try to think the best of me – even when I feel the worst…

TABLE OF CONTENTS

African Americans

Asian Americans

Latino Americans

PREFACE

......But, on the other hand, there is the idea called "freedom". At the center of all questions in a free society stands the individual need for identity and self-determination.

This book investigates the question of why so much social disparity exists between different ethnic and cultural groups in American history. By extension, what is looked for here is why such differences of opportunity persist. The results that are sought in writing this book involve what to do about the future of individual, cultural, and ethnic diversity in the United States of America. Identifications of race persist as different from definitions of American. Regardless of the benefits, the historic costs of inclusion in that definition are variable. Gender and social class are perpetually contentious issues, but even more central is the relationship of cultural diversity to American social institutions. Why and how do cultural diversity and social institutions mutually effect each other, and what are the practical results of social change? This is the heart of the role of the individual in society. People are concerned about how to better their condition. Therefore, any historic examination of American society and culture should be aimed at activism and social transformation.

History as a discipline has its own set of contexts. At times history has served to legitimize nationalism, colonialism, slavery, genocide, sexism, class-ism, and other identities of power and privilege. Only relatively recently have revisionist historians moved to a premise of intellectual activism and social transformation. Applied social science was the result. The concept that the skills and knowledge of social sciences had applications for the solution of human problems meant a new commitment to social responsibility. Post revisionists of the last few decades have drifted away from the sometimes strident and occasionally exclusionary excesses of the early revisionists. However, an additional casualty of attempts at a balanced approach has been the commitment to activism and social transformation. This anthology attempts both a balanced portrayal of American society and culture, while also strongly advocating intellectual activism as a tool toward social transformation.

An anthology, such as this, can offer balance by providing for original voices to be heard on their own terms. Each document is "as is" – in the spelling, grammar and idiom of the original writers. To be sure, as in American history, each inclusion occurs at the exclusion of others, partly as a concession to space. However, each inclusion represents the beginnings of a dialog in which the reader is invited to participate. And, each article or document has been selected to include the widest range of cultural and social input. Efforts toward activism and social transformation require critical thought to be based on broad sources of information. But, also the tools of critical thought themselves must be sharpened toward the challenges of the future. These intellectual tools are a major feature of this anthology. Intellectual activism is a process of interactive education implying thought and deed. It is not enough to simply reflect. Nor is thoughtless action productive of social transformation. Applied social science requires participation in a process of both critical thought and socially responsible action. This anthology invites the reader to use the articles and documents interactively with each other and with the exercises in critical thought as the beginnings of a process of activism and social transformation.

At the nexus of these social and cultural questions of American history is the concept of identity. Cultural identity is a prime source of personal authority and self-determination. In a social context, identity forms the basis for power and privilege. From where does an individual identity originate? How is identity perpetuated? How is it shared? To what degree can there really be a national identity, whether it be considered social, cultural, or ethnic? Because if identity cannot be shared equally by all members of a Nation, then to what degree can the Nation expect individuals to participate in the common goal that Nationality represents? If you are non-white, an immigrant, a woman, gay or lesbian, disabled, or a host of other institutionally defined diverse groups, the question simply put becomes, what's in it for me? Historically and presently, the answer has been shades of "less than" or "nothing."

We are all looking at a twenty-first century world, with twenty-first century problems that must be faced collectively. A century ago, the sense of collective commitment to a clearer set of common goals was based on an even narrower concept of American identity. At that time, far more diverse elements of American society were optimistic about their ability to become American and share fully in that collective identity. Now, a century later, many of those illusions have been shattered. We are a melting pot that didn't. Many cultural groups have found their access to the American dream to be socially limited by sets of formal and informal institutions. Yet people still come to America. Why, and what can we do to preserve individual, cultural opportunity while sharing in the social commitment of national identity is the subject of this book.

Born here, I have lived in this United States of America, as a marginalized citizen preoccupied with the question why. My cultural and ethnic identity has sustained me even as my social identity has been redefined, largely by institutional forces beyond my control. I have lived long enough to be colored, Negro, Black, Afro-American (a hair style), and African-American. I am often asked – quite genuinely – why I am not satisfied with simply being an American. This is because while the above names were labels put on me by formal government institutions, other, more informal labels like coon, jig, Nigger, jungle bunny, spear chucker, and Alabama porch monkey, were consistent reminders of my otherness. To me, the Confederate flag – the "stars and bars" still popular in many parts of the U.S. – can never be a symbol of anything but a history of hate. More recently, I have been labeled an urban problem, an ethnic minority, a member of an underrepresented group, a member of an over-entitled group, and so on. I am not satisfied with being simply an American because rarely am I treated simply as an American, much less as an individual. I become, instead, an object, interchangeable with others of my type.

But, where I have been marginalized socially, I have thrived culturally, and ethnically. At times when I am reminded of my inability to share purely in the social identity of American, my sanctuary has been my cultural and ethnic identity. There is great strength in separateness, but it is the strength of a person or a people, not the strength of a Nation. Many like me, who see their identity as an American to be less than that of others, feel denied. Each of us has something powerful to contribute. In being denied full American identity, many will deny America the individual and collective power of their diversity. America, in denying us will eventually lose the value of our potential. Who and what an American is results from the individuals position between personal culture and the institutions of society. This book is about the value and persistence of diversity. It was written for we who will not deny ourselves and who still struggle to be American in a Nation that often denies us. And, this book was written for those who still ask why I am not satisfied with simply being an American.

INTRODUCTION

AMERICAN SOCIAL AND CULTURAL HISTORY

American history is a history of diversity. It is an ongoing social and cultural experiment involving those who consider themselves indigenous with they who are considered immigrant. This cultural synthesis is controlled by social institutions that themselves must evolve in response to the possible inclusion of the other, the newcomer, the outsider. Ever since Europeans have used the name America, there have been problems of inclusion, and exclusion. But, who is an American? The consistent denial by original European immigrants of a role for either indigenous Native Americans or imported Africans in the American experience was just a beginning. Gender, religion, and class joined ethnicity as reasons for exclusion from the society and culture of power and privilege that were, and are fundamental to American identity. American history is the story of the struggles for inclusion, identity, and self-determination. Individuals and groups continued contributing, and demanding a part in a national cultural identity, regardless being of marginal social status.

A new American society and culture was formed and reformed as colony expanded into nation, and nation into world power. At each historic juncture – each point in time – America has redefined both its culture and social institutions based on who was encountered, embraced, or denied. Since the Declaration of Independence, American culture and society has been philosophically based on freedom and self-determination. Yet, when economic and political leaders sat down to form the philosophies of revolution into the formal institutions of society, the Constitution that was produced was a document of exclusion. Social institutions of the new United States of America placed clear limits on inclusion of diversity in the culture of the United States of America. "We the people" meant the class of wealthy White male property owners, who for the most part were products of the Protestant faith, if not ethic. Outside of Constitution Hall, America was always a rainbow of diversity. The Nation encompassed (if not embraced) men and women of a wide variety of cultural and ethnic origins, bringing a diversity of aspirations and aptitudes. It becomes far more relevant to ask not what American Culture is, but to ask what does it mean to be an American.

Just as the formal institutions of the United States governed the opportunities of the diverse American cultures, so also did the informal institutions of America impose limits. In the end, many individuals found personally cultivated networks of culture to be the foundation of opportunity. For those unmentioned, overlooked, or expressly denied by the formal and informal social institutions of the United States of America, culture was (and sometimes still is) the sole basis for opportunity.

American history and thus American social identity has mostly been the product of the same institutional influences of power and privilege. In the earliest incarnations, U.S history was the written record made by the class of wealthy White male property owning

Protestants. It should not be surprising that this record, like the Constitution, served primarily its authors. Fortified with both a clearly defined social role of power and privilege linked to a clearly articulated cultural identity infused with a sense of superiority, it is no wonder that the Nation and the discipline of history have remained controlled by a few instead of the many. In recent times, however, new interpretations of history have significantly revised the discipline and broadened the definition of American identity. The most significant aspect of revisionist history is an inclusive quality that enriches the range of human possibility.

Just what it means to be an American for many – such as myself – is still a question without a satisfactory answer. Who I am is part the result of the past. This cultural identity is in layers, personal, familial, and ethnically historic. However, a portion of my identity is the product of who I am seen to be. This social identity is composed of how formal and informal institutions characterize me. My full identity as an American results from the options I exercise between the two. My identity as an American is both social and cultural. To be an American is to have many options and many limitations. America's past, present and future histories are the results of those who employ the most of the options against limitation.

This is a fundamentally American expression in culture and character.

This anthology is interdisciplinary, because the real world is. This text is multicultural, because the real world is. This book takes the position that intellectual activity must result in activism, because that is how the real people change the real world for the better. Social transformation does not just happen mysteriously through luck, but must be the result of work. And, for a society to be a success by any criteria, it must actively embrace the efforts of all diverse individual resources. This is an American social and cultural history anthology. However, history means nothing unless it serves individuals in the context of society.

American history is defined by the relationship between society and culture – between institutions and individuals. American society is defined by its institutions. Culture in American history is defined by individuals, some real, some totally imagined, most a blend of the two. Almost all of the individuals who have been used by historians to define American culture in history books have been male and white. Based on these examples, American culture is often considered to be a relatively uniform and nationally shared phenomenon from which sub-cultures may deviate, but nevertheless orbit. This is a trick of perspective, and a curse on multicultural studies. The word "sub-cultures" itself, like "minorities" suggests inferior status. American institutions treat individuals as if they represent groups. Culture, in the most basic analysis, is the fundamental set of conscious and unconscious assumptions that govern an individual persons set of responses to the environment. For people, the environment is largely made of the formal and informal social institutions structured to govern our collective group behavior. And here is the trick of perspective. Any shared American culture must result from individual responses to collective institutions. And our social institutions evolve through interactions with individuals. We remain individual, but necessarily must each respond to similar institutions. Culture serves the individual. Society serves groups. This interplay between social institutions and individual culture produces the events of American history.

This text is an interdisciplinary experience into American social, cultural, and ethnic history. Readings and documents are drawn from many sources in the making of this text. Although this is primarily a history book, many disciplines contribute to its wholeness. Scholarly authors are found alongside literary giants or government officials. Heroes, poets, and common people share their perspectives next to political activists and academics. This is important. What we in the United States call America and American history is really the written account of many. Like on the dollar bill: E Pluribus Unum – the many into one, a kind of plural unity. If you ask a Guatemalan, a Canadian, or a Brazilian what they would call themselves other than those national political titles, they would call themselves Americans – North, South, and Central -- but still Americans. So too within the United States, the answers to what it means to be an American differs. It may be Italian, or Lakota, Basque, or African, Mexican, or Japanese, Dine, Filipino, or Irish -- all hyphenated Americans. Fear not, there is a clear answer to the question of what it means to be an American. The issue is that there are many voices answering. Some of the voices are from the past, but all speak to a continuing future as Americans. Some voices have been heard over others. Some have scarcely been heard at all. Yet all are significant in the making of American society and culture.

Just as there can be no single answer to the question of what it means to be an American, so too there can be no single way of seeking that answer. Instead, there are many disciplines, many cultures, and many people.

There are probably hundreds of thousands of particular names, dates, and events in American history. In fact, there are far, far too many particulars for any investigator or text to encompass. The only reasonable course is to learn concepts instead of raw rambling totals of fact. History is a chain of causes and effects and not just names, dates, and events. Looking at history as a process generates problem-solving skills that are valuable to students and citizens. By examining historic limitations and opportunities for social and cultural change, the processes influencing present and future events becomes clearer, and sets of possibilities revealed. This is an issue oriented applied approach of intellectual activism. In this way, new facts can be critically analyzed as they arise. The individual in American society becomes more powerful in a number of ways and for a number of purposes.

Exercises and selections in this interdisciplinary anthology are conceptual doorways to intellectual activism and critical thought. It is not so important what you know as it is the many ways you can know.

The theoretical orientations of this anthology come primarily from methodologies of both history and anthropology. A theoretical orientation is a point of view that provides the intellectual tools for problem solving. Theoretical orientations become vantage points from which American society and culture can be viewed. Observations will inevitably lead to judgments. Clear criteria for judgment must be set. Interdisciplinary sets of criteria – or theoretical orientations – insure an inclusive interpretation of American history. Historical and anthropological theory provides the interdisciplinary criteria for these analyses of American society and culture.

Institutions of American society have suffered from short-term perspectives that deliver short term and often ultimately ineffective solutions. We study history because all that is now has a history, and all that is now will become history. We exist now and historically as cultural beings. Our foremost tool is culture. Culture has been our way of dealing with the natural environment for so long that we exist, thrive, and prosper mostly through cultural and social behavior. Foremost among human intellectual tools for analyzing culture is the discipline of anthropology. Theoretical orientations in this text will shift between those of history and anthropology as needed.

Adopting a historical perspective proves valuable because what American culture is now, is not what it was, or what it will become. History means change over time. What it has meant to be (or to become) an American is a matter of historic context and interpretation of significance. In the late 1960s an evenings' dinner option for "average" Americans would never have included the possibility of a Vietnamese restaurant. Americans were killing and being killed by those people. One hundred years ago, the Monica Lewinsky affair would have made little impact on an American president. And because press of earlier eras mostly turned a blind eye to such things private presidential affairs usually had even less impact on the American people. Dr. King, the Kennedys, Waco, Columbine High School in Littleton, Colorado, The Murrah Building in Oklahoma City, 9/11, Operation Iraqi Freedom and the list goes on...The fundamental understanding of the American identity has – and continues to be – forever changed by such historic events.

And historian's perspectives vary. Each cloaks their interpretation of the meaning of the facts with the mantle of academic certainty, but many accounts are just that – interpretations. We rely as heavily as possible on original written sources of information – on primary source documents. Those are (mostly) the facts. But, history is only the partial written account of past events. All events were not rigorously recorded. Of the events that were, first person (original source) accounts often differ - sometimes dramatically - from one another. Rarely do two people see the same thing in the same way. Each eyewitness has a different perspective, as well as an individual background, and a different interpretation of events. Add to this the interpretations of historical significance of facts rendered secondarily by distant and supposedly objective scholars, who themselves are not without an agenda...well, you see. Though we must strive for it, total objectivity is a sham and a physical impossibility. To understand this is essential to the realization of the effects of history on culture. But it is also fundamental to deciphering the effects of culture on history. Historians are people, and as such are products of our own history and culture. Bound by our own time and beliefs, we cannot help from investing ourselves in our work. Always, it is like the old story about the three blind men describing the elephant. We never know it was gray.

The best that can humanly be done is to compare subjective realities to approximate objective reality. This is the interdisciplinary approach. This is where anthropology comes in. Anthropologists investigate and compare cultures. Like historians, anthropologists are human; however anthropologists are also involved in a discipline that consistently makes them aware of cultural influences on objectivity. At the core of anthropological inquiry rests a multidisciplinary assumption. The idea – or theoretical orientation – that there are many valuable tools available from the diverse perspectives of human inquiry. Human experience is far too complex to be evaluated on the basis of one situation, motivation, or event. A diverse amount of disciplines must be brought to bear on any individual or historic context. Anthropology fills that need to explain the "Why?" of the human social & cultural adventure. Art, biology, technology, philosophy, theology, and many more disciplines are tools to investigate any subject. Anthropologists are by training, education and experience, interdisciplinary thinkers. This theoretical orientation is comparative and integrative. Even the most cursory observations of America reveal a wide range of influences affecting American culture and society. Apart from fairly overt particulars of historical events, there is an ever subtle and often more complex cultural dynamic to American life. There are the questions: Why and How? Anthropology is adept at asking the kinds of questions that produces answers explaining why America is the way it is – of why and how we became who we are – and of who we are likely to become.

Anthropology also offers a key model for investigating the question of what it means to be an American. Cultural anthropology has within it a spirited debate over what influences social and cultural change the most. This argument can be summed up by the statement: "nature versus nurture." On one hand, we are the products of our background – our nature – and those influences determine our reality. On the other hand, we are the result of our environment – of how we are nurtured – and we can learn to be anything we want. It is clear that both influences are important factors. The disagreement is over which influence determines our behavior. If we apply these concepts to society and culture, we may have one of the foremost tools for understanding what it means to be an American. Are we who we are because of our social background (nature), or are we who we are because of what we cultivate through culture (nurture)? In this book, it is the interplay between the nature of society versus the nurturing influence of culture that produces what it means to be an American.

What American anthropology has missed is the concept from history that events which have transpired have done so from within their own temporal context. That persons, places, and things were at one moment in time the unique creations of human agency. History recognizes the moment of decision. The moment when through intimidation or inspiration, the individual decides on change or decides to resist change. History is change over time. Any historic moment in time has its own context that makes it unique and human. Persons who viewed places and took note of things from their own perspectives acted creatively or otherwise in specific ways and generating specific events in time. But historians often wear only one set of glasses and seek single sets of causes for events.

What history has often missed is the anthropological concept that there are many senses to be used in deciding what something is, or why and how it became that way. It is often absurd and always entertaining to the average citizen that a "nationalist" historian will argue so strongly against the view of, say a "revisionist" historian. It is clear to the average citizen that nationalism has its place among many aspects of daily life and that (maybe all) history is in need of some revision.

Anthropology's interdisciplinary network approach and history's cause-action-effect linear approach balance and invigorate one another. The failures and successes of human history studied from the anthropological realizations of why those events may have occurred provide the intellectual tools/weapons for social transformation and activism.

The challenge is to cultivate a community of learning that embraces as much as possible of the human/American experience. To generate a new eclectic renaissance perspective that operates in fluid process, and is not overly mired in static particulars. It is the type of liberal arts education that is fit for the twenty-first century. The accelerated and potentially volatile nature of current American society demands the cultivation of a broad understanding of cultural reality and social diversity. On the individual level, the social goal is to build an organic network of opportunities, clearly understanding the functions and potential dysfunction(s) of American society. Many purely academic traditions are static and artificially isolate subject matter that must be integrated and active in real world environments. Like the many inventions that historically went into the development of a modern automobile. If we consider the parts separately, and in isolation, it's nearly impossible to tell how they unite to get you down the road. In social science, an interdisciplinary approach develops an individual's skill at cultivating an understanding of how to influence their situation in positive ways.

INTELLECTUAL ACTIVISM, SOCIAL TRANSFORMATION, & SELF-DETERMINATION

The central emphasis here is critical thought, intellectual activism, and social transformation. The idea that society can improve through planned concerted social action. This is not a new concept. The political philosophy: "of, by, and for the people" is the foundation of American social institutions. The idea that democracy should be in balance with federal and republican principles for the betterment of all is still progressive intellectual currency. Democracy is still radical. But, the belief that government should work for the citizen (or at least stay out of the way) is a major historic social transformation that is in large part responsible for birthing a common American culture. America – before and since it was called that – has always been about social transformation.

It may well be central to the human cultural experience that we seek, collectively and individually, to better our lot. But, it must be asked: from the limitations of what (cultural or social) perspective? By what criteria do we evaluate ourselves? Intellectual activism is thought interacting with deed. It means a process of individual and collective self-evaluation. Differing concepts of progress and what is better for the common good are set against equally variable and diverse visions of individual good. Sometimes American social transformations have been the result of intellectual activism. Most often they have not. Historically in America, moral relativism in its excess gives way to cultural absolutism, only to see excess absolutism to retreat, in turn before relativism. A socially active role requires equilibrium. Critical thought is the primary form of balanced intellectual activism. Honest and ongoing self-critique linked to the analysis of what is going on socially opens the door to effective intellectual activism. The stakes are the state of the human condition in America.

We could move through life "fat, dumb, and happy" as my Texas/Oklahoma grandfather would say, or we could at least try to do something about our own condition. Does history really repeat itself? Of course not. There are recurring events to be sure. But, these are symptoms of underlying social and cultural issues that have not been fully resolved. All too often, the American social response to events is reactive and focused on symptoms, not underlying or inherent causes. Responding after the fact with outpourings of concern, sympathy, or indignant outrage, bureaucratic officials representing formal social institutions pass the buck, or – if it's an election year – throw public dollars and rhetoric at problems. Private citizens, ever focused on servicing social needs, frequently respond viscerally and reactively. Mollified, tranquilized and isolated by social/cultural circumstance, most citizens' pursuit of intellectually active social transformation is limited. Seemingly recurring events are like coughs and fevers of an organism called America of which we are all a part. It is as if American society catches pneumonia, and is treated with cough syrup. For cancer, a band-aid. Thus many problems of a social nature persist to the point of crisis. This text is concerned with a deeper diagnosis of the health of the American condition in reference to culture and society. Intellectual activism is a proactive – not reactive – position. The Civil Rights movement, the NRA, the Feminist movement, and the Ku Klux Klan are all America. So is the Museum of Tolerance and the Southern Poverty Law Center.

American history includes these and a host of quite conscious, intellectually active, and socially transformative phenomenon. Yes, Thomas Jefferson wrote the Declaration of Independence and owned slaves -- a living contradiction between culture and society. Enslaved Africans and Indian wars - we have our own holocausts.

The route of self-determination is open. Any individual can decide to change the conditions of her/his own life. Seek social transformation. Knowledge is not an ivory tower antiseptic activity of intellectual elites. Knowledge is transformative. This text involves intellectual activism and social transformation. By studying the intellectual activism and social transformations of America, new avenues of personal change and growth become realities. In American history, the individual has always been at the nexus (junction) between two realities – society and culture. Some level of conformity is an unavoidable part of a social existence. However, all things can be both limiting and enriching. Any direction mitigates or eliminates others. This is especially true of the relationship of the individual (representative of culture, ethnicity, class, gender, etc.) to society. Partly because social institutions are group oriented, the needs of the individual are discounted, overlooked, purposefully ignored. So individual identity only becomes socially effective when the individual affiliates with a group – when one becomes many. When society fails the individual, the individual relies on culture. This is why diversity in America persists. This is America. The life of the individual American is a struggle between the social demand for a single unified America and the interplay of individual diverse culture.

Anthropology centers on Culture (with a capital "C") and human diversity. Immigration, emigration and in-migration have provided for astonishing and more than occasionally disturbing amounts of American cultural diversity. The theoretical orientations of anthropology contain the tools for analysis not only of Culture – the singular, but also of cultures – the plural. Perhaps the most significant aspects of American history have been the challenges of human diversity and human rights. Although America is clearly not a melting pot, nevertheless, out of this dynamic has come a distinct American culture, singular and unique. And because of the continuing influences of diversity in culture and society, American culture is far from static.

Always in America there has been culture(s). Apart from agency, culture and change are the consistent essential factors in the human experience. Undeniably, throughout history many geographic locations within and outside of the Americas have been host to dramatic social and cultural changes. However, the brief history of the United States of America can be seen as one of the most unique and sometimes bizarre experiments in human social and cultural diversity in any historic age. The United States of America was given birth by social and cultural diversity. America has both accepted and restricted vast amounts of immigrants from every corner of the world. Always the offer to the diverse peoples of the world was an opportunity for self-determination. Many craved the ability to undergo a social transformation, become Americans, and to improve their individual and collective conditions. Always – at least initially – the United States was to benefit also.

The social and political foundation of the United States of America is – as will be shown – intellectual activism and social transformation. The radically aggressive social institutions and cultural values of we who ethnocentrically call ourselves Americans have resulted in a historically lightning swift movement to continental, hemispherical and global significance. A peculiar facet of the American cultural and historic experience is that we assume change means progress – and that progress is always for the better. So far, many indications clearly show that we have fallen prey to fallacy. Historic data reveals change as inevitable, but progress requires copious quantities of vision and effort. A whole era of American Progressives met with mixed success partly because of such unquestioned assumptions. Intellectual activism continually requires analytic self-assessment. One need only examine the headlines to see that we have not always changed for the better. If we as Americans are going to unavoidably change, then we owe it to those who come after us – to the victims of our progress – to get it right.

Anthropologic research has demonstrated that cultural (and biologic) diversity may well provide for the widest range of opportunities for survival and prosperity. Cultural and individual diversity (AKA freedom) offer the broadest possible base for positive social change. However, America's history of social intolerance to diversity and cultural difference has also become one of the single greatest potential threats to the prosperity of the Nation (and perhaps human survival as a species). This is especially true in the case of the American failure to celebrate (not just tolerate) ethnic diversity. We have created social institutions to control our prosperity. Many of those institutions also have controlled the specific prosperity of select groups of our society as a whole. American institutions treat diverse groups differently. There is institutional racism. Gender, class, ethnicity, nationality, and culture have all become reasons for formal and informal discrimination. Human potential becomes limited when social institutions fail to celebrate diversity. American potential is denied when American institutions limit the contributions of cultural diversity. The richness and vitality of what it means to be an American is rendered bland and colorless. All Americans suffer the loss of opportunities to survive and thrive when any single aspect of American culture is denied. Each stereotype dehumanizes us all.

Between ethnic groups in the United States, there continues to be fear, oppression, and violence based on the American mythology of racism. Class conflict is a reality. Gender and age discrimination thrives. And then, consider the relationship between the Nations of the world. No need to reference any specific headline, the nature and frequency of incident guarantees the reader my example.

"Just because that's the way it is" was the perennially disappointing answer I would get. You see, I was one of those annoying kids that kept asking why. Then, when I got an answer, my response would usually be: "but why?" Why do people get scared? Why are there poor people? Why is there war? Why do some people that I don't even know like (or dislike) me just because of the way I look, dress, or act? There was never a satisfactory answer. I continue asking. I have added such questions as how? or when?, and others. As an older annoying kid, I realize that there is no one answer. We lump our reasons why together. Glib and trite reasons under the umbrellas of culture, society, race, class, gender, and a host of other abstract groupings are used to explain individual circumstances. At a point, they are no more informative than "just because that's the way it is" was. Though we are part of groups, we are not stereotypic representatives of our group. Group answers to individual questions are more than imprecise conveniences. These group answers become shared perspectives. While the ultimate reality is that we are all individuals, our social institutions are group institutions. The truth of the human (American) situation is that individual problems, goals, aspirations, and assets are shared through social context. We thrive as individuals by being organized socially. We are all in this together.

But, on the other hand, We are all in this alone. There is the idea called "freedom". At the center of all questions stands the individual need for identity, self-worth, and self-determination. When balanced against the day-to-day social realities of American power and privilege, the cultivation of individual culture often becomes the sole bulwark for survival.

Herein lays a certain responsibility. It is the responsibility of the one to the many, and of the many to the one. Group identity works both for and against the individual. No more factious and visceral a battle cry is there than "you don't really know how it is to be" Black, or a Woman, or Gay, or Poor. In truth, no one really knows what it is to be anyone else. American culture and society is made of elements of shared individual experience. What must not be forgotten is that what are being shared are similar, yet individual experiences.

The original documents of American social and cultural history are in conflict with many aspects of modern post revisionist, "politically correct" America. Old decisions are gone. No longer should we be "us" or "them". The names have changed but the song remains the same. Beware. Often, the new "PC" merely trains us to demote individual genius and flawed success in favor of conformity to new dividing lines. The dynamic tension between culture and society remain, with the individual citizen at the center.

From intellectually diverse sources come metaphors for the value of diversity. Biologically, we, as a human race, exist due to our diversity. Wholeness and vitality are products of dynamic interactions between apparent contradictions. The Male principle has value only because of Female principle, and poverty only has meaning in the face of wealth. Human diversity is human potential. Our differences are enriching opportunities that drive social and cultural change. Intellectual activists see diversity of all types as sources of social transformation.

In American history, many turning points have occurred -- some for the better, some for the worse. How are better and worse to be defined? Better and worse are defined by the transformations effected in social institutions by the continuous interactions with cultures, ethnicity, gender, & class. Better is a transformation to the benefit of the lowest/weakest/most (see Thanksgiving). How to define worse? That social transformation that limits, excludes, denies, or oppresses. This is not a liberal or conservative political position. This definition of better or worse - like in a marriage - embraces self-determination – the primary sense of freedom that this nation professes to be founded upon. It is the "bottom line" of day to day existence and potential for all Americans.

What does it mean to be an American? Is it a type, a hyphen, an image, a myth, an acronym like WASPM?

ON MULTICULTURALISM & INTERDISCIPLINARY BIAS:
Moving Beyond "Tolerance"

Intellectual liberals argue for multiculturalism from a context of inclusiveness. To an intellectual liberal – a real liberal – argument and critical analysis proceeds from an assumption of minority status. The struggle is to provide a diversity of viewpoints, experiences, and solutions to human needs. Multiculturalists do not exclude or omit.

Those who label themselves intellectual conservatives and the extremists among them who fashion themselves anti multiculturalists (Bloom, Bork, Lawler, Thornton & Jacoby) argue their cases from within a context of exclusion. Conservative intellectual argument all too often proceeds from a reactionary assumption. Seeing themselves in a possible minority status, their responses are often filiopietist, threatened, and ethnocentrically defensive, if not outright reactive. Intellectual conservatism limits inquiry and denies active participation in social growth and change. Indeed, change seems to be a threat, even though – ironically – change is the only human constant. Civilizations ebb and flow away, people are born, mature, live, and die. All changes.

In seeking a balance between the unnecessary duality of the liberal versus the conservative critique, the common citizen needs a wide exposure to both concepts and situations that define and demand continuing re-definition of what human social and cultural experience embraces. While this text places itself squarely within the liberal intellectual tradition, the current state of liberal critique and pedagogy are not above objective analysis – at least as objective an analysis as is possible. Liberal intellectual critique has all too often become prey to fashion and reductionist fad. An instant rejection of all things European, Judeo-Christian, and Y chromosome does no service to broadening inclusion or deepening intellectual debate. If there is one thing that multiculturalism has shown to be true, it is that no group can realistically elevate itself by standing on the neck of others. Far too many shallow liberal analyses of intellectual conservatism see excluding conservatism as establishing liberalism. Neither of those points of view are multicultural or interdisciplinary. It must be all right to be different.

Conservative intellectual critics often assert that the academic world should hold itself aloof from activism. For them the campus should not be a proving ground for deeds, but only for thoughts. Modern conservative educators state that the academic world should be a kind of ivory tower of pure reason in which the great educators supposedly lived. (Socrates is often used as a model. This conservative pietist illusion fades when one realizes that historically Socrates died as a social activist). The cruel reality to this conservative pseudo-objective fantasy is that all deeds begin as thoughts. On a social level, it becomes absolutely essential for human prosperity to have those deed-generating thoughts and ideas to be as rational and inclusive as possible.

College and the university are some of the most socially transforming institutions of American society. They are also instruments of individual change. Conservatives and liberals both agree on this. Asserting that the goals and identity of the individual have great social value, this text places the individual and self-determination in the center of the university. The common good is never really served otherwise, only the majority or the controlling minority. History shows that (for better or worse) the lack of self-determination results in marginalization, dominance, and oppression.

Examine the dialog between intellectual conservative and liberal, both make some good points. They both overlook a host of diversity issues. Both ignore the potential brought to the table by individual diversity, focusing instead only on the collective. It is also a peculiar American irony that American culture elevates the individual, while American social institutions function only through group identity and political organization.

Interdisciplinary bias refers to this text's theoretical orientation that historically, the many disciplines of academia -- similar to the many peoples of American society – have been kept artificially separated. As in the nature of people in real-world American society, intellectual disciplines must interrelate and co-function in order to remain vital, active, and productive.

Featuring works generated from a diversity of disciplines demands not only critical thought, but also insists on a certain intellectual activism on the part of the reader. In order to reconcile the differing disciplines represented, the reader must move beyond thought to action. In actively examining the pieces in this anthology, analyzing their relative perspectives, and evaluating their significance, the reader will unavoidably glimpse new aspects of the truths of what it means to be an American.

This evaluation invites the readers to acknowledge realities different from their own. The real challenge is to move beyond acknowledgement to tolerance. But tolerance suggests the mere suspension of discomfort in the presence of the "other", who will be "put up with" until "normalcy" returns. The task, then, is to stride beyond tolerance, which implies distant (and distasteful) resignation to diversity, to acceptance. Accepting diversity develops the embrace of the "other" as an opportunity for growth. Advancing beyond acceptance will require casting off notions of "otherness" and separation implicit in group identities. When each individual in a social context ceases to be perceived as a representative of their group, the celebration of uniqueness occurs. People can be valued for who, not what, they are. Celebration of diversity – the final step – involves the realization of individual worth.

HISTORY, RACE, CULTURE, SOCIETY, ETHNICITY, & CLASS

DEFINITIONS

Terms like race, ethnicity, and nationality are often used interchangeably by media. Those terms as well as others by which we define ourselves are quite important. And – perhaps more seriously in the social context – terms by which others define us are frequently decisive factors in how we all get along. Labels are the center of our relationships. Individual and collective identity hinge on what we assume those terms to mean. This assumption of meaning affects everyone's daily reality. It becomes essential to understanding ourselves socially and culturally to know what we call ourselves and why. There are the many well-known derogatory and offensive stereotypes, but what is important here are the terms that are socially acceptable and politically correct. The misuse and misunderstanding of these few key terms can and has distorted human relationships on a historic scale.

HISTORY

History is the incomplete written record or oral tradition of the experiences of humans through the contexts of time. While there are many types of history – such as political, economic, technological, or social history – all are dependant on documents and their interpretation. History, like language, is very plastic. Historians have been both under and have cast the spell of history for various reasons and diverse ends. An important anthropological fact here is that individual historians are products of unique interactions between their predisposition and historic context (environment through time).

All of the following definitions are historically dependent. That is to say that their specifics have all changed over time depending on the factors of their historic context.

SOCIETY

A society is an artificial construction of a collection of formal and informal institutions that govern group behavior. At their best these social institutions, as instruments of order and control, seek to do the most good for the majority. This means that by their very nature, formal and informal social institutions mitigate, reject, or ignore minority concerns. This also means that social institutions are characteristically reactive. Proactive behavior in social institutions is limited by bureaucratic development. The more formal and bureaucratic the social institution, the more reactive it will be. The more bureaucratic the social institution, the more its proactive potential will be focused on self-maintenance and defense. This appears to be a progressive feature of formal social institutions.

CULTURE

Culture is the set of conscious and unconscious individual beliefs and assumptions about the way in which world works that governs individual behavior. As the word infers, culture can be the product of cultivation on the conscious level. This means that culture is plastic and changeable, organic and vital. There are many cultures. Elements of culture are both shared and personal. Culture is always ahead of social institutions (until historically recently). Although culture is not fully proactive, culture remains as the intimate and personal tool for individual day to day problem solving. As people in America confront the changing issues of life, they react through culture far more rapidly than either formal or informal social institutions can. Culture changes whether we will it or not.

COMMUNITY

Communities in America are formed from the interactions of culture and society. When individuals are united into groups by complimentary internal (cultural) and external (social) influences, the groups of people can be identified as communities. Such a group of people who share common assumptions about the way the world works, and who are identified within a social context, need not be physically in contact, or segregated in order to feel a sense of community. Always, very few members of such a group share every aspect of cultural belief, or of social role. Commonalities exist, but members of a community retain individuality.

(**Note:** Keep in mind that the verb: govern, implies both the promotion and limitation of freedom.)

RACE

Biologically, there is only one race – human. All other categories of race are artificial social constructs of classification based on visual differences, cultural expressions, political necessity, and economic priority. What is commonly called race is really racism. The history of the concept of race parallels the development of the American identity. The hierarchical classification of the ethnicities of the world is a by-product of the same European intellectual influences that generated colonialism in general, and the formative philosophies of the United States in particular.

RACISM (also called ethnocentrism)

Racism exists when a labeled group is disadvantaged socially based on the artificial classifications of race by another group in possession of unearned power and privilege to do so.*

ETHNICITY

Ethnicity refers to heritage or culture expressed over time. The cultural history of a group of people produces differences in populations that give rise – both culturally and biologically – to ethnicity.

CLASS

Class is the stratified level of economic opportunity within a culture or society. Class differences – differences in opportunity and access – may be based on racism, ethnicity, gender, education, age, disability or a host of other recognized group classifications.

GENDER

Gender refers to the social roles and rules of behavior attributed to biological sex. Gender is not sex, but is instead what it means to "be a man." or to "act like a lady" in any particular society. Gender issues are historically intertwined with issues of race and class in American social and cultural history. Gender is public performance for which society rewards or punishes individuals based on a historically shifting set of social norms. For the purposes of this discussion, the term gender will include gender orientation as in the case of gay, lesbian, bisexual and trans-gendered people.

NATIONALITY
Nationality is a political description of place of birth or naturalization.

In addition there are some concepts that are useful in the discussion of American social and cultural history.

PUSH FACTOR
Push factors cause individuals or groups to relocate from one place to another.

PULL FACTOR
Pull factors draw individuals or groups to a specific location.

DIASPORA
Diaspora refers to the (often forced) dispersal of populations from a specific location to several locations throughout the world.

IMMIGRATION
Immigrants are individuals or groups that come into a place.

EMIGRATION
Emigrants are individuals or groups that leave from a place.

IN-MIGRATION
In-migrants are individuals or groups that move from one place to another within a country, state, or nation.

SOJOURNER
A sojourner is a person (or persons) who crosses regional or national boundaries (frequently for social and economic benefit) with specific intent to return to their place of origin.

REFUGEE
A person or group of people fleeing from specific organized social systems of oppression, war, and/or genocide, and seeking sanctuary outside the political reach of those systems.

*The American obsession with race and racism is a historic artifact of the society. The suffix "ism", added to almost any word suggests the ability or desire to exercise influence, control or power - race as a metaphor in the finest sense of Joseph Campbell.

ON DIVERSITY

While there is no finite definition of cultural or ethnic diversity, this text uses the classifications of ethnicity developed at University of California at Berkeley for their utility and discreetness. U C Berkeley's American Cultures Department identifies Indigenous Native Americans, European Americans, African Americans, Asian Americans, and Latin Americans as the five essential cultural groups in U.S. history. Important to remember when looking at these five ethnic groups is the stunning amount of cultural diversity _within_ each group.

Diversity becomes most important in history as the complex interaction between groups, their culture and American social institutions. At each coming together of an immigrant or indigenous group and American formal and informal social institutions, a transformation of both has occurred. These social transformations have continually remade America.

Most people's understanding of diversity is couched solely in ethnic terms. This is not a satisfactory definition. Under the question "what is diversity?" it is more useful to consider:
* **ideology * religion * social-economic class * gender * gender orientation * disability * culture * ethnicity * political principles * educational background * age * language & dialect * learning**

styles * intellectual opinion * visceral response & individual temperament * personal experience…and the list is legion.

Diversity then, is both social and cultural fact and biologic fiction. In the rest of the text, look for the five groups recognized by UC Berkeley, and the range of diversity within those groups.

The entire relevant reason for the study of history and for the ongoing investigation of the human adventure is intellectual activism and social transformation. This is a cross-cultural comparative approach that tracks change through time. This anthology of time, change and culture will evolve in two stages. The first is a chronological historical presentation of documents, essays, and accounts that make up formal and informal American social institutions and the American ideal. The second section examines American realities through manifestations of American cultural diversity. Five of the cultural diversity segments are ethnically centered, while the final two investigate class and gender.

Be advised that there are many, many aspects of the American social and cultural history that are not directly addressed. Concepts of assimilation and acculturation are set aside to focus instead on the interactions between culture, the individual, and society. There are no topical discussions of technology, or drugs, or abortion, or a host of other aspects of American society and culture. But, there are concepts and principles of investigation that are applicable to those and many more facets of American society and culture. This is the beginning of a process of critical thought to be applied to any, and every, area of inquiry.

AMERICAN SOCIAL INSTUTIONS - FORMAL

KEY CONCEPTS

There is a real and an ideal about the United States of America. "We the People" was not. Formal social institutions are hierarchical, and rigidly codified. As such, they produce many documents – not all of which are actually read regularly by those who they represent or govern. "We the People" are rarely fully aware of what is done in our names, and those who govern are rarely aware of what goes on in the lives of the People. Assumptions and myths evolve socially and culturally. In the following writings and critiques, examine the literal meanings of the words in these documents. Investigate the historic context in which the words were put down. What do these documents mean to our understanding of race, gender, class, political economy, and human rights? How do the documents result in (or from) formal social institutions of the United States? Research the authoring personalities, especially those thought to be familiar. What was the context of their lives? Compare their words with the social and cultural realities of their time. What events and interactions with formal social institutions conditioned their understanding of the world? Contrast each against the other and evaluate the significance of each document to modern formal and informal institutions.

A Priest's Account of the "Discovery" and Colonization of the Indies
(Translated by Professor John Ulloa).

Of all in the infinite universe, these people are those most without guile, wickedness, or duplicity, those most obedient and ever faithful to their native masters and to the Spanish Christians they now serve. They are naturally humble, patient, and of peaceful nature, holding no grudge, and, being not excitable or quarrelsome, they remain free from embroilment. These people are more devoid of rancor, hatred, or vengeance than any people in the world. Because of this, they are less able to endure heavy labors and soon sicken and die, no matter the malady. Sons of our nobility, brought up enjoying life's refinements, are no more delicate than Indians of even the lowliest rank of laborer. They are also a poor people, who have little and also have little desire for worldly goods. For this reason they are neither arrogant, nor bitter or greedy. The meals they partake are as parsimonious, and poor as that of the Holy Fathers in the desert. In their dress they are nearly naked, with only their nether regions covered. When the cover their shoulders, it is with a square of native fabric of not more than two yards in size. They have not the beds that we would recognize, but sleep on matting or a net they call hamacas. They are very clean of body, and have alert, intelligent minds that are both docile and open to doctrine, to virtuous customs, eager to accept holy Catholic faith and godly behavior. When they hear the tidings of our Faith, they become so insistent on knowing more and on receiving the sacraments of the Church and observing the divine cult that the missionaries here need to be gifted by God with the virtue of patience so as to be able to cope with such eagerness. Many of the secular Spaniards who have been here for some years say that the Indians are undeniably good and if they could be brought to God they would be among the most fortunate in the world....

It is most unfortunate that the most common treatment that the Indians have received from the Spaniards who call themselves Christian has been to attempt to wipe them from the earth by waging unjust, cruel, and bloody wars. And, when they have slain all of those native rulers and young men who have fought for their lives and freedom, then the Spaniards enslave the remaining women and children subjecting them to the most bitter kinds or servitude. Using the most infernal and tyrannical methods, they debase and make weak countless members of Indian nations.

The Spaniards give the desire to acquire gold and riches, and the aim of rising to high estate in as brief a time as possible as the reasons for killing and destroying so many native souls. All should keep mindful of the insatiable greed and ambition, unexcelled by any in the world, that causes the villainies of the Spaniards. Also that the lands are of such value, and the native people so meek, that our Spaniards have no more consideration of the Indians than if they were beasts. I say these things from my own knowledge of what I have witnessed. I should not even say "beasts" for, by God, the Spaniards have treated beasts with at least some respect. I should say that they have treated the Indians like excrement on public squares...

A noteworthy set of outrages was committed against a cacique, a very important noble, named Hatuey, who had brought many of his people in flight from inhuman acts of the Christians to Cuba from Hispaniola. When he was told by certain Indians that the Christians were now coming to Cuba, he gathered as many of his followers as he could and said to them: "Now you must know that they are saying the Christians are coming here, and you know by experience how they put So and So and So and So, and other nobles to an end. And now they are coming from Haiti (which is Hispaniola) to do the same here. Do you know why they do this?" The Indians replied: "No, we do not know. It may be that they are wicked and cruel by nature." But, he told them: "No they do not act because of that, but because they have a God they greatly worship and they want us to worship that God, and that is why they struggle with us and subject us and kill us." . . .

Religion

He had a basket full of gold and jewels and he said: "You see their God here, this is the God of the Christians. If you agree to it, let us dance for this God, who knows, it may please the God of the Christians and then they will do us no harm." And his followers all said together, "Yes, that is good, that is good!" And they danced around the basket of gold until they all fell down exhausted. Then their chief, the cacique Hatuey, said to them: "See here, if we keep this basket of gold they will take it from us and will end up by killing us. So let is cast away the basket into the river." They all agreed to do this, and they hurled the basket of gold into the river that was nearby.

This cacique, Hatuey, was constantly fleeing before the Christians from the time that they arrived on the island of Cuba, knowing them and knowing of what they were capable. Now and then the Christians encountered him and he defended himself, but they finally killed him. And they did this for the sole reason that he had fled from the cruelty and wickedness of the Christians and had defended himself against them. And when they had finally captured him with as many of his followers as they could, they burned all of them at the stake.

When they tied him to the stake, the cacique Hatuey was told by a Franciscan friar something about the God of the Christians and of the Articles of the Faith. And he was told what he could do in the brief time that remained to him, in order to be saved and go into Heaven. The cacique, who had never heard any of this before, and was told he would go to the Inferno, where, if he did not adopt the Christian Faith, he would suffer eternal torment. The cacique asked the Franciscan friar if Christians all went to Heaven. When told they did, he said he would prefer to go to Hell. Such is the fame and honor that God and our Faith have earned through the Christians who have thus far gone out to the Indies...

...And the Christians, with their horses and swords and pikes began to carry out massacres and strange cruelties against them. They attacked the towns and spared neither the children nor the aged nor pregnant women nor women in childbed, not only stabbing them and dismembering them with but cutting them to pieces as if dealing with sheep in the slaughterhouse. They laid bets as to who, with one stroke of the sword, could split a man in two or could cut off his head or spill out his entrails with a single stroke of the pike. They took infants from their mothers' breasts, snatching them by the legs and pitching them headfirst against the crags or snatched them by the arms and threw them into the rivers, roaring with laughter and saying bas the babies fell into the water, "Boil there, you offspring of the devil!" Other infants they put to the sword along with their mothers and anyone else who happened to be nearby.

They made some low wide gallows on which the hanged victim's feet almost touched the ground, stringing up their victims in lots of thirteen, in memory of Our Redeemer and His twelve apostles, then set burning wood at their feet and thus burned them alive. To others they attached straw or wrapped their whole bodies in straw and set them afire. With still others, all those they wanted to capture alive, they cut off their hands and hung them round the victim's neck, saying, "Go now, carry the message," meaning, Take the news to the Indians who have fled to the mountains.

They usually dealt with the chieftains and nobles in the following way: they made a grid of rods which they placed on forked sticks, then lashed the victims to the grid and lighted a smoldering fire underneath, so that little by little, as those captives screamed in despair and torment, their souls would leave them. I once saw this, when there were four or five nobles lashed on grids and burning; I seem even to recall that there were two or three pairs of grids where others were burning, and because they uttered such loud screams that they disturbed the captain's sleep, he ordered them to be strangled. And the constable, who was worse than an executioner, did not want to obey that order (and I know the name of that constable and know his relatives in Seville), but instead put a stick over the victims' tongues, so they could not make a sound, and he stirred up the fire, but not too much, so that they roasted slowly, as he liked.

I saw all these things I have described, and countless others. And because all the people who could do so fled to the mountains to escape these inhuman, ruthless, and ferocious acts, the Spanish captains, enemies of the human race, pursued them with the fierce dogs they kept which attacked the Indians, tearing them to pieces and devouring them. And because on few and far between occasions, the Indians justifiably killed some Christians, the Spaniards made a rule among themselves that for every Christian slain by the Indians, they would slay a hundred Indians.

Source: De las Casas, Bartolome. The Devastation of the Indies. The Crossroad Publishing Company. English Translation Copyright 1974.

The Difference Between Servants and Slaves in 1722 Virginia

Their servants they distinguish by the names of slaves for life, and servants for a time. Slaves are the Negroes and their posterity, following the condition of the mother, according to the maxim, partus frequitur ventrm. They are called slaves, in respect of the time of their servitude, because it is for life.

Servants, are those which serve only for a few years, according to the time of their indenture, or the custom of the country. The custom of the country takes place upon such as have no indentures. The law in this case is, that if such servants be under nineteen years of age, they must be brought into court to have their age adjudged; and from the age they are judged to be of, they must serve until they reach four and twenty; but if they be adjudged upwards of nineteen, they are then only to be servants for the term of five years.

The male servants, and slaves of both sexes, are employed together in tilling and manuring the ground, in sowing and planting tobacco, corn, &c. Some distinction indeed is made between them in their clothes, and food;

but the work of both is no other than what the overseers, the freemen, and the planters themselves do.

Sufficient distinction is also made between the female servants, and slaves; for a white woman is rarely or never put to work in the ground, if she be good for anything else; and to discourage all planters from using any women so, their law makes female servants working in the ground tithables, while it suffers all other white women to be absolutely exempted; whereas, on the other hand, it is a common thing to work a woman slave out of doors, nor does the law make any distinction in her taxes, whether her work be abroad or at home.

Source: Beverly, Robert. The History of Virginia in Four Parts. (London, 1722).

The Declaration of Independence (preamble)

Action of Second Continental Congress, July 4, 1776 representing the unanimous Declaration of the thirteen United States of America

When in the Course of human events, it becomes necessary for one people to dissolve the political bands which have connected them with another, and to assume among the powers of the earth, the separate and equal station to which the Laws of Nature and of Nature's God entitle them, a decent respect to the opinions of mankind requires that they should declare the causes which impel them to the separation.

We hold these truths to be self-evident, that all men are created equal, that they are endowed by their Creator with certain unalienable Rights, that among these are Life, Liberty and the pursuit of Happiness.--That to secure these rights, Governments are instituted among Men, deriving their just powers from the consent of the governed, --That whenever any Form of Government becomes destructive of these ends, it is the Right of the People to alter or to abolish it, and to institute new Government, laying its foundation on such principles and organizing its powers in such form, as to them shall seem most likely to effect their Safety and Happiness. Prudence, indeed, will dictate that Governments long established should not be changed for light and transient causes; and accordingly all experience hath shewn, that mankind are more disposed to suffer, while evils are sufferable, than to right themselves by abolishing the forms to which they are accustomed. But when a long train of abuses and usurpations, pursuing invariably the same Object evinces a design to reduce them under absolute Despotism, it is their right, it is their duty, to throw off such Government, and to provide new Guards for their future security.--Such has been the patient sufferance of these Colonies; and such is now the necessity which constrains them to alter their former Systems of Government. The history of the present King of Great Britain is a history of repeated injuries and usurpations, all having in direct object the establishment of an absolute Tyranny over these States. To prove this, let Facts be submitted to a candid world.

(This is an excerpted portion from the full document. The remainder lists and articulates the grievances the colonial Americans had against the English government which justified revolt – among these are taxation without representation. But although Thomas Jefferson originally listed slavery as an evil forced on the colonies by the English, his fellow colonists edited that part out in the final draft. It is the document that Americans often quote, but frequently have never read. You should read it.)

Source (complete): Jefferson, Thomas. <u>The Declaration of Independence</u>. 1776.

The Constitution of the United States

Preamble

We the people of the United States, in order to form a more perfect union, establish justice, insure domestic tranquility, provide for the common defense, promote the general welfare, and secure the blessings of liberty to ourselves and our posterity, do ordain and establish this Constitution for the United States of America.

Article. I.

Section. 1.

All legislative Powers herein granted shall be vested in a Congress of the United States, which shall consist of a Senate and House of Representatives.

Section. 2.

The House of Representatives shall be composed of Members chosen every second Year by the People of the several States, and the Electors in each State shall have the Qualifications requisite for Electors of the most numerous Branch of the State Legislature.

No Person shall be a Representative who shall not have attained to the Age of twenty five Years, and been seven Years a Citizen of the United States, and who shall not, when elected, be an Inhabitant of that State in which he shall be chosen.

Representatives and direct Taxes shall be apportioned among the several States which may be included within this Union, according to their respective Numbers, which shall be determined by adding to the whole Number of free Persons, including those bound to Service for a Term of Years, and excluding Indians not taxed, three fifths of all other Persons. The actual Enumeration shall be made within three Years after the first Meeting of the Congress of the United States, and within every subsequent Term of ten Years, in such Manner as they shall by Law direct. The Number of Representatives shall not exceed one for every thirty Thousand, but each State shall have at Least one Representative; and until such enumeration shall be made, the State of New Hampshire shall be entitled to choose three, Massachusetts eight, Rhode-Island and Providence Plantations one, Connecticut five, New-York six, New Jersey four, Pennsylvania eight, Delaware one, Maryland six, Virginia ten, North Carolina five, South Carolina five, and Georgia three.

When vacancies happen in the Representation from any State, the Executive Authority thereof shall issue Writs of Election to fill such Vacancies.

The House of Representatives shall choose their Speaker and other Officers; and shall have the sole Power of Impeachment.

Section. 3.

The Senate of the United States shall be composed of two Senators from each State, chosen by the Legislature thereof for six Years; and each Senator shall have one Vote.

Immediately after they shall be assembled in Consequence of the first Election, they shall be divided as equally as may be into three Classes. The Seats of the Senators of the first Class shall be vacated at the Expiration of the second Year, of the second Class at the Expiration of the fourth Year, and of the third Class at the Expiration of the sixth Year, so that one third may be chosen every second Year; ...

(This is an excerpted portion from the full document. The remainder delineates the structure of government and delegates powers to the various institutions created – among these are treasury, taxation, and formation of a military. It is the document that Americans often quote, but frequently have never read. You should read it.)

Source (complete): Madison, James, et al., <u>The Constitution of the United States of America</u>. 1787.

The Bill of Rights

Of the Constitution of the United States

The Conventions of a number of the States having, at the time of adopting the Constitution, expressed a desire, in order to prevent misconstruction or abuse of its powers, that further declaratory and restrictive clauses should be added, and as extending the ground of public confidence in the Government will best insure the beneficent ends of its institution;

Resolved, by the Senate and House of Representatives of the United States of America, in Congress assembled, two-thirds of both Houses concurring, that the following articles be proposed to the Legislatures of the several States, as amendments to the Constitution of the United States; all or any of which articles, when ratified by three-fourths of the said Legislatures, to be valid to all intents and purposes as part of the said Constitution, namely:

Amendment I
Congress shall make no law respecting an establishment of religion, or prohibiting the free exercise thereof; or abridging the freedom of speech, or of the press; or the right of the people peaceably to assemble, and to petition the government for a redress of grievances.

Amendment II
A well regulated militia, being necessary to the security of a free state, the right of the people to keep and bear arms, shall not be infringed.

Amendment III
No soldier shall, in time of peace be quartered in any house, without the consent of the owner, nor in time of war, but in a manner to be prescribed by law.

Amendment IV

The right of the people to be secure in their persons, houses, papers, and effects, against unreasonable searches and seizures, shall not be violated, and no warrants shall issue, but upon probable cause, supported by oath or affirmation, and particularly describing the place to be searched, and the persons or things to be seized.

Amendment V

No person shall be held to answer for a capital, or otherwise infamous crime, unless on a presentment or indictment of a grand jury, except in cases arising in the land or naval forces, or in the militia, when in actual service in time of war or public danger; nor shall any person be subject for the same offense to be twice put in jeopardy of life or limb; nor shall be compelled in any criminal case to be a witness against himself, nor be deprived of life, liberty, or property, without due process of law; nor shall private property be taken for public use, without just compensation.

Amendment VI

In all criminal prosecutions, the accused shall enjoy the right to a speedy and public trial, by an impartial jury of the state and district wherein the crime shall have been committed, which district shall have been previously ascertained by law, and to be informed of the nature and cause of the accusation; to be confronted with the witnesses against him; to have compulsory process for obtaining witnesses in his favor, and to have the assistance of counsel for his defense.

Amendment VII

In suits at common law, where the value in controversy shall exceed twenty dollars, the right of trial by jury shall be preserved, and no fact tried by a jury, shall be otherwise reexamined in any court of the United States, than according to the rules of the common law.

Amendment VIII

Excessive bail shall not be required, nor excessive fines imposed, nor cruel and unusual punishments inflicted.

Amendment IX

The enumeration in the Constitution, of certain rights, shall not be construed to deny or disparage others retained by the people.

Amendment X

The powers not delegated to the United States by the Constitution, nor prohibited by it to the states, are reserved to the states respectively, or to the people.

Source: The United States Congress. The Bill Of Rights. 1787.

The 13th, 14th, and 15th Amendments to the Constitution

Amendment XIII

(1865)

Section 1. Neither slavery nor involuntary servitude, except as a punishment for crime whereof the party shall have been duly convicted, shall exist within the United States, or any place subject to their jurisdiction.

Section 2. Congress shall have power to enforce this article by appropriate legislation.

Amendment XIV

(1868)

Section 1. All persons born or naturalized in the United States, and subject to the jurisdiction thereof, are citizens of the United States and of the state wherein they reside. No state shall make or enforce any law which shall abridge the privileges or immunities of citizens of the United States; nor shall any state deprive any person of life, liberty, or property, without due process of law; nor deny to any person within its jurisdiction the equal protection of the laws.

Section 2. Representatives shall be apportioned among the several states according to their respective numbers, counting the whole number of persons in each state, excluding Indians not taxed. But when the right to vote at any election for the choice of electors for President and Vice President of the United States, Representatives in Congress, the executive and judicial officers of a state, or the members of the legislature thereof, is denied to any of the male inhabitants of such state, being twenty-one years of age, and citizens of the United States, or in any way abridged, except for participation in rebellion, or other crime, the basis of representation therein shall be reduced in the proportion which the number of such male citizens shall bear to the whole number of male citizens twenty-one years of age in such state.

Section 3. No person shall be a Senator or Representative in Congress, or elector of President and Vice President, or hold any office, civil or military, under the United States, or under any state, who, having previously taken an oath, as a member of Congress, or as an officer of the United States, or as a member of any state legislature, or as an executive or judicial officer of any state, to support the Constitution of the United States, shall have engaged in insurrection or rebellion against the same, or given aid or comfort to the enemies thereof. But Congress may by a vote of two-thirds of each House, remove such disability.

Section 4. The validity of the public debt of the United States, authorized by law, including debts incurred for payment of pensions and bounties for services in suppressing insurrection or rebellion, shall not be questioned. But neither the United States nor any state shall assume or pay any debt or obligation incurred in aid of insurrection or rebellion against the United States, or any claim for the loss or emancipation of any slave;

but all such debts, obligations and claims shall be held illegal and void.

Section 5. The Congress shall have power to enforce, by appropriate legislation, the provisions of this article.

Amendment XV

(1870)

Section 1. The right of citizens of the United States to vote shall not be denied or abridged by the United States or by any state on account of race, color, or previous condition of servitude.

Section 2. The Congress shall have power to enforce this article by appropriate legislation.

Source: The United States Congress. The 13th, 14th, and 15th Amendments to the Constitution of the United States.

Manifest Destiny and Mexico

I am in favor of now elevating this question of the reception of Texas into the Union... up to its proper level of a high and broad nationality, it surely is to be found, found abundantly, in the manner in which other nations have undertaken to intrude themselves into it... in a spirit of hostile interference against us, for the avowed object of thwarting our policy and hampering our power, limiting our greatness and checking the fulfillment of our manifest destiny to overspread the continent allotted by Providence for the free development of our yearly multiplying millions....

It is wholly untrue, and unjust to ourselves, the pretense that the Annexation [of Texas] has been a measure of spoliation, un-rightful and unrighteous of military conquest... of aggrandizement at the expense of justice.... This view of the question is wholly unfounded....

California will, probably, next fall away from [Mexico]....
Imbecile and distracted, Mexico never can exert any
real governmental authority over such a country.... The
Anglo-Saxon foot is already on [California's] borders.
Already the advance guard of the irresistible army of
Anglo-Saxon emigration has begun to pour down upon
it, armed with the plow and the rifle, and marking its trail
with schools and colleges, courts and representative
halls, mills and meetinghouses....

[All this] in the natural flow of events, the spontaneous
workings of principles....

And [the Californians] will have a right to independence
to self-government   to the possession of the homes
conquered from the wilderness by their own labors and
dangers, sufferings and sacrifices   a better and a truer
right than the artificial title of sovereignty in Mexico a
thousand miles away....The day is not distant when the
Empires of the Atlantic and the Pacific would again flow
together into one....

Source: O'Sullivan John L. "Annexation of Texas." The
Democratic Review . 1845.

A Proclamation Against Annexation of Mexican Territories By the United States

PROCLAMATION
Be it known: That the general congress has decreed,
and the executive sanctioned, the following:

The national congress of the Mexican Republic,
considering:

That the congress of the United States of the North has,
by a decree, which its executive sanctioned, resolved to

incorporate the territory of Texas with the American union;

That this manner of appropriating to itself territories upon which other nations have rights, introduces a monstrous novelty, endangering the peace of the world, and violating the sovereignty of nations;

That this usurpation, now consummated to the prejudice of Mexico, has been in insidious preparation for a long time; at the same time that the most cordial friendship was proclaimed, and that on the part of this republic, the existing treaties between it and those states were respected scrupulously and legally;

That the said annexation of Texas to the U. States tramples on the conservative principles of society, attacks all the rights that Mexico has to that territory, is an insult to her dignity as a sovereign nation, and threatens her independence and political existence;

That the law of the United States, in reference to the annexation of Texas to the United States, does in nowise destroy the rights that Mexico has, and will enforce, upon that department; That the United States, having trampled on the principles which served as a basis to the treaties of friendship, commerce and navigation, and more especially to those of boundaries fixed with precision, even previous to 1832, they are considered as inviolate by that nation.

And, finally, that the unjust spoliation of which they wish to make the Mexican nation the victim, gives her the clear right to use all her resources and power to resist, to the last moment, said annexation;

IT IS DECREED

1st. The Mexican nation calls upon all her children to the defense of her national independence, threatened by the usurpation of Texas, which is intended to be realized by the decree of annexation passed by the congress, and sanctioned by the president, of the United States of the north.

2d. In consequence, the government will call to arms all the forces of the army, according to the authority granted it by the existing laws; and for the preservation of public order, for the support of her institutions, and in case of necessity, to serve as the reserve to the army, the government, according to the powers given to it on the 9th December 1844, will raise the corps specified by said decree, under the name of "Defenders of the Independence and of the Laws."

JOSÉ JOAQUIN DE HERRERA (acting President of the Republic of Mexico).

Source: De Herrera, Jose Joaquin. Palace of the National Government. City of Mexico, June 4, 1845.

Racism and the Law

The appellant, a free white citizen of this State, was convicted of murder upon the testimony of Chinese witnesses.

The point involved in this case is the admissibility of such evidence.

The 394th section of the Act Concerning Civil Cases provides that no Indian or Negro shall be allowed to testify as a witness in any action or proceeding in which a white person is a party.

The 14th section of the Act of April 16th, 1850, regulating Criminal Proceedings, provides that "No black or mulatto person, or Indian, shall be allowed to give evidence in favor of, or against a white man."

The true point at which we are anxious to arrive is, the legal signification of the words, "black, mulatto, Indian, and white person, " and whether the Legislature adopted them as generic terms, or intended to limit their application to specific types of the human species. . . .

The Act of Congress, in defining that description of aliens may become naturalized citizens, provides that every "free white citizen," etc. . .

If the term "white," as used in the Constitution, was not understood in its generic sense as including the Caucasian race, and necessarily excluding all others, where was the necessary of providing for the admission of Indians to the privilege of voting, by special legislation?

We are of the opinion that the words "white," "Negro," "mulatto," "Indian," and "black person," wherever they occur in our Constitution and laws, must be taken in their generic sense, and that, even admitting the Indian of this continent is not of the Mongolian type, that the words "black person," in the 14th section, must be taken as contradistinguished from white, and necessary excludes all races other than the Caucasian.

We have carefully considered all the consequences resulting from a different rule of construction, and are satisfied that even in a doubtful case, we would be impelled to this decision on ground of public policy.

The same rule which would admit them to testify, would admit them to all the equal rights of citizenship, and we might soon see them at the polls, in the jury box, upon the bench, and in our legislative halls.

This is not a speculation which exists in the excited and overheated imagination of the patriot and statesman, but it is an actual and present danger.

The anomalous spectacle of a distinct people, living in our community, recognizing no laws of this State, except through necessity, bringing with them their prejudices and national feuds, in which they indulge in open violation of law; whose mendacity is proverbial; a race of people whom nature has marked as inferior, and who are incapable of progress or intellectual development beyond a certain point, as their history has shown; differing in language, opinions, color, and physical conformation; between whom and ourselves nature has placed an impassable difference, is now presented, and for them is claims, not only the right to swear away the life of a citizen, but the further privilege of participating with us in administering the affairs of our Government.

These facts were before the Legislature that framed this Act, and have been known as matters of public history to every subsequent Legislature.

There can be no doubt as to the intention of Legislature, and that if it had ever been anticipated that this class of people were not embraced in the prohibition, then such specific words would have been employed as would have put the matter beyond any possible controversy.

For these reasons, we are of opinion that the testimony was inadmissible.

The judgment is reversed and the cause remanded.
Source: The People v George W. Hall. California Supreme Court, Mr. Ch. J. Murray delivering the opinion. October term 1854.

Against Imperialism

From the speech of Senator George F. Hoar, to the Massachusetts Club, July 29, 1898, as reported in Boston Journal.

It is impossible with our eyes on this constantly changing kaleidoscope to predict with certainty how we are to solve the difficult problems that are coming upon us at the end of this war with Spain. But of this you may be sure, that the vote of every person who now has legislative responsibility in either House of Congress, by the choice of the Republicans of Massachusetts, or is likely to have such responsibility hereafter, will be cast in accordance with the opinion of Massachusetts. Her opinion on such questions are the fruit of nearly 300 years of a great and honorable history. She will not depart from the Declaration of Independence. She will not depart from the doctrines of liberty laid down in her own Constitution. She will not consent to be the ruler over vassal States or subject peoples. She will enter upon no mad career of empire in distant seas. She will not seek to force her trade upon unwilling peoples at the cannon's mouth. She will not exact tribute or revenues from men who have no voice in regard to them. She will not consent to enter with the powers of Europe into any partnership, alliance or contest for the plunder of China or the division of Africa, or for the subjugation of eastern archipelagoes, or for compelling unwilling peoples to trade with her. If the American flag appear in the East, it will be as the emblem of their liberty and not of our dominion. She will desire to meet the great responsibilities which the end of this war seems likely to bring to the American people solely in the interests of the provinces we may deliver from Spain and not for our own. The power of the United States is to be exerted through example and influence, and not by force.

It will be a sad thing for the country, it will be a sad thing for mankind, if the people of the United States come to abandon their fundamental doctrine. We are giving it a hard strain in our dealing with the negro at the South. We are giving it a hard strain in our dealing with the great problem of immigration. But it cannot stand if this country undertake also to exercise dominion over conquered islands, over vassal States, over subject races; if in addition to the differences of race and the differences of education we attempt to govern great masses of people, aliens in birth, of strange language, of different religions. If we do it, our spirit will not, I am afraid -- God grant that I may be wrong -- the American spirit will not enter into and possess them, but their spirit will enter into and possess us.

The best thing we could hope in such case is that we shall succeed only as England has succeeded with those of her colonies whom she admits to no considerable self-government. It is much more likely that we may fail as Spain has failed. Let us wait until the Negro throughout the South can cast his vote and have it counted in freedom and in honor. Let us wait until the poor immigrant can come into the northern port and be received as a brother and as an equal, without being used as an instrument to debase the elections in New York or Baltimore or Chicago.

Mr. Gladstone, in his famous comparison of England and the United States, in which he expresses his admiration for our Constitution, says also: "In England inequality lies at the very base of the social structure. Equality combined with liberty was the groundwork of the social creed of the American colonies." An aristocracy or a monarchy may govern subject States. It never was done and never will be done successfully by a democracy or a republic.

Source: Hoar, George F. "The Opinion of Massachusetts on 'Imperialism.'" (Boston: Anti-Imperialist Committee of Correspondence, 1898).
Additional Source: Hoar, George F. "Against Imperialism." Congressional Record, 57th Congress, 1st Session(1902).

The Corollary to the Monroe Doctrine
Excerpted from Roosevelt's Annual Messages
December 6, 1904, and on December 5, 1905.

...It is not true that the United States feels any land hunger or entertains any projects as regards the other nations of the Western Hemisphere save such as are for their welfare. All that this country desires is to see the neighboring countries stable, orderly, and prosperous. Any country whose people conduct themselves well can count upon our hearty friendship. If a nation shows that it knows how to act with reasonable efficiency and decency in social and political matters, if it keeps order and pays its obligations, it need fear no interference from the United States. Chronic wrongdoing, or an impotence which results in a general loosening of the ties of civilized society, may in America, as elsewhere, ultimately require intervention by some civilized nation, and in the Western Hemisphere the adherence of the United States to the Monroe Doctrine may force the United States, however reluctantly, in flagrant cases of such wrongdoing or impotence, to the exercise of an international police power. If every country washed by the Caribbean Sea would show the progress in stable and just civilization which with the aid of the Platt amendment Cuba has shown since our troops left the island, and which so many of the republics in both Americas are constantly and brilliantly showing, all question of interference by this Nation with their affairs would be at an end. Our interests and those of our southern neighbors are in reality identical. They have great natural riches, and if within their borders the law reign of law and justice obtains, prosperity is sure to come to them. While they thus obey the primary laws of civilized society they may rest assured that they will be treated by us in a spirit of cordial and helpful sympathy. We would interfere with them only in the last resort, and then only if it became evident that their inability or unwillingness to do justice at home and abroad had violated the rights of the United States or had invited foreign aggression to the detriment of the entire body of American nations. It is a mere truism to say that every nation, whether in America or anywhere else, which desires to maintain its freedom, its independence, must ultimately realize that the right of such independence can not be separated from the responsibility of making good use of it.

In asserting the Monroe Doctrine, in taking such steps as we have taken in regard to Cuba, Venezuela, and Panama, and in endeavoring to circumscribe the theater of war in the Far East, and to secure the open door in China, we have acted in our own interest as well as in the interest of humanity at large. There are, however, cases in which, while our own interests are not greatly involved, strong appeal is made to our sympathies... But in extreme cases action may be justifiable and proper. What form the action shall take must depend upon the circumstances of the case; that is, upon the degree of the atrocity and upon our power to remedy it. The cases in which we could interfere by force of arms as we interfered to put a stop to intolerable conditions in Cuba are necessarily very few.

And on December 5, 1905:

... It must be understood that under no circumstances will the United States use the Monroe Doctrine as a cloak for territorial aggression. We desire peace with all the world, but perhaps most of all with the other peoples of the American Continent. There are, of course, limits to the wrongs which any self-respecting nation can endure. It is always possible that wrong actions toward this Nation, or toward citizens of this Nation, in some State unable to keep order among its own people , unable to secure justice from outsiders, and unwilling to do justice to those outsiders who treat it well, may result in our having take action to protect our rights; but such action will not be taken with a view to territorial aggression, and it will be taken at all only with extreme reluctance and when it has become evident that every other resource has been exhausted.

Moreover, we must make it evident that we do not intend to permit the Monroe Doctrine to be used by any nation on this Continent as a shield to protect it from the consequences of its own misdeeds against foreign nations. If a republic to the south of us commits a tort against a foreign nation, such as an outrage against a citizen of that nation, then the Monroe Doctrine does not force us to interfere to prevent punishment of the tort, save to see that the punishment does not assume the form of territorial occupation in any shape. The case is more difficult when it refers to a contractual obligation. Our own Government has always refused to enforce such contractual obligations on behalf of its citizens by an appeal to arms. It is much to be wished that all foreign governments would take the same view. But they do not; and in consequence we are liable at any time to be brought face to face with disagreeable alternatives. On the one hand, this country would certainly decline to go to war to prevent a foreign government from collecting a just debt; on the other hand, it is very inadvisable to permit any foreign power to take possession, even temporarily , of the custom houses of an American Republic in order to enforce the payment of its obligations; for such temporary occupation might turn into a permanent occupation. The only escape from these alternatives may at any time be that we must ourselves undertake to bring about some arrangement by which so much as possible of a just obligation shall be paid. It is far better that this country should put through such an arrangement, rather than allow any foreign country to undertake it. To do so insures the defaulting republic from having to pay debt of an improper character under duress, while it also insures honest creditors of the republic from being passed by in the interest of dishonest or grasping creditors. Moreover, for the United States to take such a position offers the only possible way of insuring us against a clash with some foreign power. The position is, therefore, in the interest of peace as well as in the interest of justice. It is of benefit to our people; it is of benefit to foreign peoples; and most of all it is really of benefit to the country concerned...

Source: Roosevelt, Theodore. "The Corollary to the Monroe Doctrine." Annual Message to the United States Congress, December 1904 and December 1905.

Immigration: Opposing Viewpoints

Until the late nineteenth century, U.S. policy regarding immigration remained largely true to George Washington ' s assertion that the "bosom of America is open to receive not only the opulent and respected stranger, but the oppressed and persecuted of all nations and religions, whom we shall welcome to a participation of all our rights and privileges." The exceptions were the Alien and Sedition acts passed by Congress in 1798 authorizing the refusal of entry or the deportation of people who might endanger the security of the United States. However, these acts lapsed after only two years.

The tremendous influx of immigrants in the mid-eighteenth century, however, made many Americans extremely nervous, particularly when large groups began to arrive from non-northern European nations. Those Americans concerned about immigration in the mid-nineteenth century worried primarily about competition for jobs and resources and moral and political corruption from people whose' religious and personal values were extremely different from those of the mostly white Anglo-Saxon Protestants (WASP) who peopled the United States. Movements of various kinds attempted to restrict the opportunities of immigrants and even to get Congress to restrict or eliminate their entrance to the country. In 1875 those concerned about the evils they associated with immigrants were able to get the first restrictive legislation passed. It prohibited the immigration of convicts and prostitutes. In 1882, Congress further barred "idiots, lunatics, and persons likely to become public charges." More important, in that same year Congress passed the first law discriminating against immigrants on the basis of their race. They forbade the further immigration of Chinese laborers.

Americans had tolerated the Chinese, who first arrived at the time of the Gold Rush, as long as they were only a small number of alien workers. But when it appeared that their numbers were increasing rapidly, that they might pose a threat to the jobs and wages of "native" Americans, and that eventually they were going to want the benefits of citizenship, many Americans-particularly in California where the Chinese were settling-began a movement to restrict or even forbid Chinese from entering the United States. Their activism resulted in the passing of the 1882 Chinese Exclusion Act, forbidding the immigration of Chinese laborers to America and forbidding the naturalization of any Chinese.

On the East Coast, Americans objected to the new waves of southern and eastern European and Near Eastern immigrants. Many of these people-Italians, Jews, Poles, Greeks, Russians, and others-had dark skins, spoke foreign languages, and were non-Protestant (most were Catholics and Jews). Between 1880 and 1920, nearly 24 million foreigners entered the United States, the majority of them from these "undesirable" groups. The dominant American classes-mainly WASP-were alarmed. They feared that these people would lower wages, corrupt the " American race," and overwhelm American society with their unassimilable foreign ways. People from both the working and the moneyed classes lobbied to restrict the immigration of these undesirables. They first achieved restrictions of certain types of laborers, including European contract laborers and Korean and Japanese workers. They were able to add additional restrictions based on undesirable characteristics, including mental diseases, pauperism, anarchic political philosophies, certain physical diseases, and illiteracy. This last trait was a matter of controversy for more than twenty years, as groups such as the Immigration Restriction League battled to make literacy a requirement for the admission of male immigrants. (Many restrictionists viewed children and females as "accessories" to the more important males, who would be the ones potentially participating in the work force, in politics, and in other important aspects of American life.)

The culmination of the immigration restriction efforts came in 1921 when the first Quota Law was enacted. Like the Chinese Exclusion Act, it restricted immigration based on national origin. While it did not exclude any nationality, it put strict limits on the number of people who could enter the United States from any particular foreign country. Essentially, the quotas were based on a percentage of each nationality's population in the United States in 1910. Once people realized, however, that the great waves of 1890 to 1910 had already allowed large numbers of "undesirables" into the United States, they revised the law with the 1924 National Origins Quota System Act, which based its limitations on the 1890 census. This ensured that the largest number of new immigrants after 1924 would come from the less threatening northern and western European countries.

Since 1924, many other immigration laws have been passed. Notably, a law repealing the Chinese Exclusion Act was passed in 1943, and the National Origins Quota System Act was replaced in 1965. Today, immigration into the United States is largely determined by the 1965 act, which established numerical ceilings for each of the world's hemispheres: 120,000 immigrants are allowed from the Western Hemisphere and 170,000 from the Eastern Hemisphere. Although entrance is on a first come, first served basis, the law also established a hierarchy of preferences (relatives, 74 percent; scientists and artists, 1 percent; skilled and unskilled labor, 10 percent; and refugees, 6 percent).

To many people it seems ironic that in America, a nation built on the toil of immigrants, the debate over who should be allowed to populate it remains such a controversial issue. ~

Source: O'Neill, Teresa, ed. Immigration: Opposing Viewpoints. San Diego: Greenhaven Press, Inc., 1992.

The Civil Rights Acts

The Civil Rights Acts of 1964, 1965, and 1968 are what most consider to be the "civil rights acts." However, civil rights laws go back to the U.S. Constitution and Bill of Rights. The issues in the 1960's were: Who holds these rights?, Who enforces them?, and How are rights that are denied to be enforced? Therefore, the Civil Rights Acts also have become known as Affirmative Action. They were passed in the aftermath of the assassinations of President Kennedy, Malcolm X, and Martin Luther King. The Acts are summarized here (the 1964 Act is 60 pages long, for instance), but full text is available at any full service public library, or on the internet.

The numerous sections of the **1964 Civil Rights Act** aimed at ending many social injustices faced by people of color. The long list included (but was not limited to): ending voter discrimination, funding school desegregation, empowering the Federal Civil Rights Commission another four years, identifying and eliminating the use of federal funds for discriminatory schools or programs, ending employment and union discriminatory practices, keeping civil rights cases in federal courts instead of state or local courts, and the right to a jury trial for discrimination cases involving the act.

The Voting Rights Act of 1965 created and institutionalized federal registrars, under the direct control of the Attorney General. This replaced state officials who had generally proven to be discriminatory in their treatment of (especially Black) voters. In many places in the South, as well as in the North, fewer than 50% of the adult population had voted in the previous general election. This had been due to Jim Crow voter restrictions like Grandfather Laws, Poll Tax, and Literacy requirements that had been in place since the failure of post Civil War Reconstruction. Such tests and requirements (that other Americans did not face) were outlawed, and federal registrars were given the power to register Black citizens to vote. Thus, the Voting Rights Act re-issued to Black Americans in particular, the same rights originally guaranteed by the 14th, and 15th Amendments to the Constitution after the Civil War of a century before.

The Civil Rights Act of 1968 is known as the Fair Housing Act. Immediately following the assassination of Martin Luther King, Jr., the act attempted to eliminate discriminatory renting, leasing and home sales. The Act covers most transactions, and forbids landlords from refusing to sell or rent not just on the basis of race, but also on the basis of ethnicity, religion, and/or gender. Multi-family dwellings (up to three rental units) and owners of three or fewer rental houses who rent without a real estate agent and who do not indicate racial preference in advertising are exempted from this Act, however. "Redlining" (refusing to approve mortgages for Blacks to move into White neighborhoods) by banks, savings and loans, and realtors was prohibited. Also, "blockbusting" – a system of moving Black families into a neighborhood for the purposes of causing racial friction and economic fear among white homeowners – was outlawed by the Act.

Sources: The United States Congress. The Civil Rights Act, 1964. 78 U.S. Statutes At Large 241 ff. Public Law 88-352.

The United States Congress. The Voting Rights Act, 1965.

The United States Congress. The Civil Rights Act, 1968.

The Kerner Report of the National Advisory Commission on Civil Disorders (Race Riots)

Summary of Report

INTRODUCTION:

The summer of 1967 again brought racial disorders to American cities, and with them shock, fear and bewilderment to the nation.

The worst came during a two-week period in July, first in Newark and then in Detroit. Each set off a chain reaction in neighboring communities.

On July 28, 1967, the President of the United States established this Commission and directed us to answer three basic questions:

What Happened?

Why did it happen?

What can be done to prevent it from happening again?

To respond to these questions, we have undertaken a broad range of studies and investigations. We have visited the riot cities; we have heard many witnesses; we have sought the counsel of experts across the country.

This is our basic conclusion: Our nation is moving toward two societies, one black, one white—separate and unequal.

Reaction to last summer's disorders has quickened the movement and deepened the division. Discrimination and segregation have long permeated much of American life; they now threaten the future of every American.

This deepening racial division is not inevitable. The movement apart can be reversed. Choice is still possible. Our principal task is to define that choice and to press for a national resolution.

To pursue our present course will involve the continuing polarization of the American community and, ultimately, the destruction of basic democratic values.

The alternative is not blind repression or capitulation to lawlessness. It is the realization of common opportunities for all within a single society.

This alternative will require a commitment to national action—compassionate, massive and sustained, backed by the resources of the most powerful and the richest nation on this earth. From every American it will require new attitudes, new understanding, and, above all, new will.

The vital needs of the nation must be met; hard choices must be made, and, if necessary, new taxes enacted.

Violence cannot build a better society. Disruption and disorder nourish repression, not justice. They strike at the freedom of every citizen. The community cannot—it will not—tolerate coercion and mob rule.

Violence and destruction must be ended—in the streets of the ghetto and in the lives of people.

Segregation and poverty have created in the racial ghetto a destructive environment totally unknown to most white Americans.

What white Americans have never fully understood but what the Negro can never forget—is that white society is deeply implicated in the ghetto. White institutions created it, white institutions maintain it, and white society condones it.

It is time now to turn with all the purpose at our command to the major unfinished business of this nation. It is time to adopt strategies for action that will produce quick and visible progress. It is time to make good the promises of American democracy to all citizens—urban and rural, white and black, Spanish-surname, American Indian, and every minority group.

Our recommendations embrace three basic principles:

*To mount programs on a scale equal to the dimension of the problems;
*To aim these programs for high impact in the immediate future in order to close the gap between promise and performance;
*To undertake new initiatives and experiments that can change the system of failure and frustration that now dominates the ghetto and weakens our society.

These programs will require unprecedented levels of funding and performance, but they neither probe deeper nor demand more than the problems which called them forth. There can be no higher priority for national action and no higher claim on the nation's conscience.

We issue this Report now, four months before the date called for by the President. Much remains that can be learned. Continued study is essential.

As Commissioners we have worked together with a sense of the greatest urgency and have sought to compose whatever differences exist among us. Some differences remain. But the gravity of the problem and the pressing need for action are too clear to allow further delay in the issuance of this Report.

PART 1—WHAT HAPPENED?

Chapter 1—Profiles of Disorder

The report contains profiles of a selection of the disorders that took place during the summer of 1967. These profiles are designed to indicate how the disorders happened, who participated in them, and how local officials, police forces, and the National Guard responded. Illustrative excerpts follow:

NEWARK

. . . It was decided to attempt to channel the energies of the people into a nonviolent protest. While Lofton promised the crowd that a full investigation would be made of the Smith incident, the other Negro leaders began urging those on the scene to form a line of march toward the city hall.

Some persons joined the line of march. Others milled about in the narrow street. From the dark grounds of the housing project came a barrage of rocks. Some of them fell among the crowd. Others hit persons in the line of march. Many smashed the windows of the police station. The rock throwing, it was believed, was the work of youngsters; approximately 2,500 children lived in the housing project.

Almost at the same time, an old car was set afire in a parking lot. The line of march began to disintegrate. The police, their heads protected by World War I-type helmets, . . .

*Although almost all cities had some sort of formal grievance mechanism for handling citizen complaints, this typically was regarded by Negroes as ineffective and was generally ignored.

* although specific grievances varied from city to city, at least 12 deeply held grievances can be identified and ranked into three levels of relative intensity:

First Level of Intensity
Police practices
Unemployment and underemployment
Inadequate housing

Second Level of Intensity
Inadequate education
Poor recreation facilities and programs
Ineffectiveness of the political structure and grievance mechanisms

Third Level of Intensity
Disrespectful white attitudes
Discriminatory administration of justice
Inadequacy of federal programs
Inadequacy of municipal services
Discriminatory consumer and credit practices
Inadequate welfare programs

*The results of a three-city survey of various federal programs—manpower, education, housing, welfare and community action—indicate that, despite substantial expenditures, the number of persons assisted constituted only a fraction of those in need.

The background of disorder is often as complex and difficult to analyze as the disorder itself. But we find that certain general conclusions can be drawn:

* Social and economic conditions in the riot cities constituted a clear pattern of sever disadvantage for Negroes compared with whites, whether the Negroes lived in the area where the riot took place or outside it. Negroes had completed fewer years of education and fewer had attended high school. Negroes were twice as likely to be unemployed and three times as likely to be in unskilled and service jobs. Negroes averaged 70 percent of the income earned by whites and were ore than twice as likely to be living in poverty. Although housing cost Negroes relatively more, they had worse

housing—three times as likely to be overcrowded and substandard. When compared to white suburbs, the relative disadvantage is even more pronounced.

A study of the aftermath of disorder leads to disturbing conclusions. We find that, despite the institution of some post riot programs:

* Little basic change in the conditions underlying the outbreak of disorder has taken place. Actions to ameliorate Negro grievances have been limited and sporadic; with but few exceptions, they have not significantly reduced tensions.
* In several cities, the principal official response has been to train and equip the police with more sophisticated weapons. In several cities, increasing polarization is evident, with continuing breakdown of interracial communication, and growth of white segregationist or black separatist groups.

Chapter 3—Organized Activity

The President directed the Commission to investigate "to, what extent, if any, there has been planning or organization in any of the riots."

To carry out this part of the President's charge, the Commission established a special investigative staff supplementing the field teams that made the general examination of the riots in 23 cities. The unit examined data collected by federal agencies and congressional committees, including thousands of documents supplied by the Federal Bureau of Investigation, gathered and evaluated information from local and state law enforcement agencies and officials, and conducted its own field investigation in selected cities.

On the basis of all the information collected, the Commission concludes that:

The urban disorders of the summer of 1967 were not cause by, nor were they the consequence of, any organized plan or "conspiracy."

Specifically, the Commission has found no evidence that all or any of the disorders or the incidents that led to them were planned or directed by any organization or group, international, national or local.

Militant organizations, local and national, and individual agitators, who repeatedly forecast and called for violence, were active in the spring and summer of 1967. We believe that they sought to encourage violence, and that they helped to create and atmosphere that contributed to the outbreak of disorder.

We recognize that the continuation of disorders and the polarization of the races would provide fertile ground for organized exploitation in the future.

Investigations of organized activity are continuing at all levels of government, including committees of Congress. These investigations relate not only to the disorders of 1967 but also to the actions of groups and individuals, particularly in schools and colleges, during this last fall and winter. The Commission has cooperated in these investigations. They should continue.

PART II—WHY DID IT HAPPEN?

Chapter 4—The Basic Causes

In addressing the question "Why did it happen?" we shift our focus from the local to the national scene, from the particular events of the summer of 1967 to the factors within the society at large that created a mood of violence among many urban Negroes.

These factors are complex and interacting; they vary significantly in their effect from city to city and from year to year; and the consequences of one disorder, generating new grievances and new demands, become the causes of the next. Thus was created the "thicket of tension, a conflicting evidence and extreme opinions" cited by the President.

Despite these complexities, certain fundamental matters are clear. Of these, the most fundamental is the racial attitude and behavior of white Americans toward black Americans.

Race prejudice has shaped our history decisively; it now threatens to affect our future.

White racism is essentially responsible for the explosive mixture which has been accumulating in our cities since the end of World War II. Among the ingredients of this mixture are:

*Pervasive discrimination and segregation in employment, education and housing, which have resulted in the continuing exclusion of great numbers of Negroes from the benefits of economic progress.
*Black in-migration and white exodus, which have produced the massive and growing concentrations of impoverished Negroes in our major cities, creating a growing crisis of deteriorating facilities and services and unmet human needs.
*The black ghettos where segregation and poverty converge on the young to destroy opportunity and enforce failure. Crime, drug addiction, dependency on welfare, and bitterness and resentment against society in general and white society in particular are the result.

At the same time, most whites and some Negroes outside the ghetto have prospered to a degree unparalleled in the history of civilization. Through television and other media, this affluence has been flaunted before the eyes of the Negro poor and the jobless ghetto youth.

Yet these facts alone cannot be said to have caused the disorders. Recently, other powerful ingredients have begun to catalyze the mixture:

* Frustrated hopes are the residue of the unfulfilled expectations aroused by the great judicial and legislative victories of the Civil Rights Movement and the dramatic struggle for equal rights in the South.
* A climate that tends toward approval and encouragement of violence as a form of protest has been created by white terrorism directed against nonviolent protest; by the open defiance of law and federal authority by state and local officials resisting desegregation; and by some protest groups engaging in civil disobedience who turn their backs on nonviolence, go beyond the constitutionally protected rights of petition and free assembly, and resort to violence to attempt to compel alteration of laws and policies with which they disagree.
* The frustrations of powerlessness have led some Negroes to the conviction that there is no effective alternative to violence as a means of achieving redress of grievances, and of "moving the system." These frustrations are reflected in alienation and hostility toward the institutions of law and government and the white society which controls them, and in the reach toward racial consciousness and solidarity reflected in the slogan "Black Power."
* an new mood has sprung up among Negroes, particularly among the young, in which self-esteem and

enhanced racial pride are replacing apathy and submission to "the system."

* The police are not merely a "spark" factor. To some Negroes police have come to symbolize white power, white racism and white repression. And the fact is that many police do reflect and express these white attitudes. The atmosphere of hostility and cynicism is reinforced by a widespread belief among Negroes in the existence of police brutality and in a "double standard" of justice and protection—one for Negroes and one for whites.

To this point, we have attempted to identify the prime components of the "explosive mixture." In the chapters that follow we seek to analyze them in the perspective of history. Their meaning, however, is clear:

In the summer of 1967, we have seen in our cities a chain reaction of racial violence. If we are heedless, none of us shall escape the consequences.

Chapter 5—Rejection and Protest: An Historical Sketch

The causes of recent racial disorders are embedded in a tangle of issues and circumstances— social, economic, political and psychological which arise out of the historic pattern of Negro-white relations in America.

In this chapter we trace the pattern, identify the recurrent themes of Negro protest and, most importantly, provide a perspective on the protest activities of the present era.

We describe the Negro's experience in America and the development of slavery as an institution. We show his persistent striving for equality in the face of rigidly maintained social, economic and educational barriers, and repeated mob violence. We portray the ebb and flow of the doctrinal tides—accommodation, separatism, and self-help—and their relationship to the current theme of Black Power. We conclude:

The Black Power advocates of today consciously feel that they are the most militant group in the Negro protest movement. Yet they have retreated from a direct confrontation with American society on the issue of integration and, by preaching separatism, unconsciously function as an accommodation to white racism. Much of their economic program, as well as their interest in Negro history, self-help, racial solidarity and separation, is reminiscent of Booker T. Washington. The rhetoric is different, but the ideas are remarkably similar.

Chapter 6—The Formation Of the Racial Ghettos1

Throughout the 10th century the Negro population of the United States has been moving steadily from rural areas to urban and from South to North and West. In 1910, 91 percent of the nation's 9.8 million Negroes lived in the South and only 27 percent of American Negroes lived in cities of 2,500 persons or more. Between 1910 and 1966 the total Negro population more than doubled, reaching 21.5 million, and the number living in metropolitan areas rose more than fivefold (from 2.6 million to 14.8 million). . . .

* Elements of the news media failed to portray accurately the scale and character of the violence that

---

[1] The term "ghetto" as used in this report refers to an area within a city characterized by poverty and acute social disorganization, and inhabited by members of a racial or ethnic group under conditions of involuntary segregation.

occurred last summer. The overall effect was, we believe, an exaggeration of both mood and event.

* Important segments of the media failed to report adequately on the causes and consequences of civil disorders and on the underlying problems of race relations. They have not communicated to the majority of their audience—which is white—a sense of the degradation, misery and hopelessness of life in the ghetto.

These failings must be corrected, and the improvement must come from within the industry. Freedom of the press is not the issue. Any effort to impose governmental restrictions would be inconsistent with fundamental constitutional precepts.

We have seen evidence that the news media are becoming aware of and concerned about their performance in this field. As that concern grows, coverage will improve. But much more must be done, and it must be done soon.

The Commission recommends that the media:

*Expand coverage of the Negro community and of race problems through permanent assignment of reporters familiar with urban and racial affairs, and through establishment of more and better links with the Negro community.

* Integrate Negroes and Negro activities into all aspects of coverage and content, including newspaper articles and television programming. The news media must publish newspapers and produce programs that recognize the existence and activities of Negroes as a group within the community and as a part of the larger community.

* Recruit more Negroes into journalism and broadcasting and promote those who are qualified to

positions of significant responsibility. Recruitment should begin in high schools and continue through college; where necessary, aid for training should be provided.

* Improve coordination with police in reporting riot news through advance planning, and cooperate with the police in the designation of police information officers, establishment of information centers, and development of mutually acceptable guidelines for riot reporting and the conduct of media personnel.

* Accelerate efforts to ensure accurate and responsible reporting of pot and racial news, through adoption by all news gathering organizations of stringent internal staff guidelines.

* Cooperate in the establishment of a privately organized and funded Institute of Urban Communications to train and educate journalists in urban affairs, recruit and train more Negro journalists, develop methods for improving police-press relations, review coverage of riots and racial issues, and support continuing research in the urban field.

Chapter 16—The Future of the Cities

By 1985, the Negro population in central cities is expected to increase by 72 percent to approximately 20.8 million. Coupled with the continued exodus of white families to the suburbs, this growth will produce majority Negro populations in many of the nation's largest cities.

The future of these cities, and of their burgeoning Negro populations, is grim. Most new employment opportunities are being created in suburbs and outlying areas. This trend will continue unless important changes in public policy are made.

In prospect, therefore, is further deterioration of already inadequate municipal tax bases in the face of increasing demands for public services, and continuing unemployment and poverty among the urban Negro population:

Three choices are open to the nation:

* We can maintain present policies, continuing both the proportion of the nation's resources now allocated to programs for the unemployed and the disadvantaged, and the inadequate and failing effort to achieve an integrated society.
* We can adopt a policy of "enrichment" aimed at improving dramatically the quality of ghetto life while abandoning integration as a goal.
* We can pursue integration by combining ghetto "enrichment" with policies which will encourage Negro movement out of central city areas.

The first choice, continuance of present policies, has ominous consequences for our society. The share of the nation's resources now allocated to programs for the disadvantaged is insufficient to arrest the deterioration of life in central city ghettos. Under such conditions, a rising proportion of Negroes may come to see in the deprivation and segregation they experience, a justification for violent protest, or for extending support to now isolated extremists who advocate civil disruption. Large-scale and continuing violence could result, followed by white retaliation, and, ultimately, the separation of the two communities in a garrison state.

Even if violence does not occur, the consequences are unacceptable. Development of a racially integrated society, extraordinarily difficult today, will be virtually impossible when the present black ghetto population of 12.5 million has grown to almost 21 million.

To continue present policies is to make permanent the division of our country into two societies;

one, largely Negro and poor, located in the central cities; the other, predominantly white and affluent, located in the suburbs and in outlying areas.

The second choice, ghetto enrichment coupled with abandonment of integration, is also unacceptable. It is another way of choosing a permanently divided country. Moreover, equality cannot be achieved under conditions of nearly complete separation. In a country where the economy, and particularly the resources of employment, are predominantly white, a policy of separation can only relegate Negroes to a permanently inferior economic status.

We believe that the only possible choice for America is the third—a policy which combines ghetto enrichment with programs designed to encourage integration of substantial numbers of Negroes into the society outside the ghetto.

Enrichment must be an important adjunct to integration, for no matter how ambitious or energetic the program, few Negroes now living in central cities can be quickly integrated. In the meantime, large-scale improvement in the quality of ghetto life is essential.

But this can be no more than an interim strategy. Programs must be developed which will permit substantial Negro movement out of the ghettos. The primary goal must be a single society, in which every citizen will be free to live and work according to his capabilities and desires, not his color.

Chapter 17—Recommendations for National Action

INTRODUCTION

No American—white or black—can escape the consequences of the continuing social and economic decay of our major cities.

Only a commitment to national action on an unprecedented scale can shape a future compatible with the historic ideals of American society.

The great productivity of our economy, and a federal revenue system which is highly responsive to economic growth, can provide the resources.

The major need is to generate new will—the will to tax ourselves to the extent necessary, to meet the vital needs of the nation.

We have set forth goals and proposed strategies to reach those goals. We discuss and recommend programs not to commit each of us to specific parts of such programs but to illustrate the type and dimension of action needed.

The major goal is the creation of a true union—a single society and a single American identity. Toward that goal, we propose the following objectives for national action:

*Opening up opportunities to those who are restricted by racial segregation and discrimination, and eliminating all barriers to their choice of jobs, education and housing.

*Removing the frustration of powerlessness among the disadvantaged by providing the means for them to deal with the problems that affect their own lives and by increasing the capacity of our public and private institutions to respond to these problems.

*Increasing communication across racial lines to destroy stereotypes, to halt polarization, end distrust and hostility, and create common ground for efforts toward public order and social justice.

We propose these aims to fulfill our pledge of equality and to meet the fundamental needs of a democratic and civilized society—domestic peace and social justice.

EMPLOYMENT

Pervasive unemployment and underemployment are the most persistent and serious grievances in minority areas. They are inextricably linked to the problem of civil disorder.

Despite growing federal expenditures for manpower development and training programs, and sustained general economic prosperity and increasing demands for skilled workers, about two million—white and nonwhite—are permanently unemployed. About ten million are underemployed, of whom 6.5 million work full time for wages below the poverty line.

The 500,000 "hard-core" unemployed in the central cities who lack a basic education and are unable to hold a steady job are made up in large part of Negro males between the . . .

* Expansion and modification of the below-market interest rate program to enlarge the interest subsidy to all sponsors and provide interest-free loans to nonprofit sponsors to cover pre-construction costs, and permit sale of projects to nonprofit corporations, cooperatives, or condominiums.

* Creation of an ownership supplement program similar to present rent supplements, to make home ownership possible for low-income families.

* Federal writedown of interest rates on loans to private builders constructing moderate rent housing.

* Expansion of the public housing program, with emphasis on small units on scattered sites, and leasing and "turnkey" programs.

* Expansion of the Model Cities program.

* Expansion and reorientation of the urban renewal program to give priority to projects directly assisting low-income households to obtain adequate housing.

CONCLUSION

One of the first witnesses to be invited to appear before this Commission was Dr. Kenneth B. Clark, a distinguished and perceptive scholar. Referring to the reports of earlier riot commissions, he said:

I read that report. . . of the 1919 riot in Chicago, and it is as if I were reading the report of the investigating committee on the Harlem riot of '35, the report of the investigating committee on the Harlem riot of '43, the report of the McCone Commission on the Watts riot.

I must again in candor say to you members of this Commission—it is a kind of Alice in Wonderland—with the same moving picture re-shown over and over again, the same analysis, the same recommendations, and the same inaction.

These words come to our minds as we conclude this report.

We have provided an honest beginning. We have learned much. But we have uncovered no startling truths, no unique insights, no simple solutions. The destruction and the bitterness of racial disorder, the harsh polemics of black revolt and white repression have been seen and heard before in this country.

It is time now to end the destruction and the violence, not only in the streets of the ghetto but in the lives of the people.

Source: Report of the National Advisory Commission on Civil Disorders. New York: Bantam Books, 1968, excerpts from pp. 1-29.

COINTELPRO: The FBI's Covert Action Programs Against American Citizens

I. Introduction and Summary

COINTELPRO is the FBI acronym for a series of covert action programs directed against domestic groups. In these programs, the Bureau went beyond the collection of intelligence to secret action defined to "disrupt" and "neutralize" target groups and individuals. The techniques were adopted wholesale from wartime counterintelligence, and ranged from the trivial (mailing reprints of Reader's Digest articles to college administrators) to the degrading (sending anonymous poison-pen letters intended to break up marriages) and the dangerous (encouraging gang warfare and falsely labeling members of a violent group as police informers).

This report is based on a staff study of more than 20,000 pages of Bureau documents, depositions of many of the Bureau agents involved in the programs, and interviews of several COINTELPRO targets. The examples selected for discussion necessarily represent a small percentage of the more than 2,000 approved COINTELPRO actions. Nevertheless, the cases demonstrate the consequences of a Government agency's decision to take the law into its own hands for the "greater good" of the country.

COINTELPRO began in 1956, in part because of frustration with Supreme Court rulings limiting the Government's power to proceed overtly against dissident groups; it ended in 1971 with the threat of public exposure.

1, In the intervening 15 years, the Bureau conducted a sophisticated vigilante operation aimed squarely at preventing the exercise of First Amendment rights of speech and association, on the theory that preventing the growth of dangerous groups and the propagation of dangerous ideas would protect the national security and deter violence.

2, Many of the techniques used would be intolerable in a democratic society even if all of the targets had been involved in violent activity, but COINTELPRO went far beyond that. The unexpressed major premise of the programs was that a law enforcement agency has the duty to do whatever is necessary to combat perceived threats to the existing social and political order.

A. "Counterintelligence Program": A Misnomer for Domestic Covert Action.

COINTELPRO is an acronym for "counterintelligence program." Counterintelligence is defined as those actions by an intelligence agency intended to protect its own security and to undermine hostile intelligence operations. Under COINTELPRO certain techniques the Bureau had used against hostile foreign agents were adopted for use against perceived domestic threats to the established political and social order. The formal programs which incorporated these techniques were, therefore, also called "counterintelligence." "Covert action" is, however, a more accurate term for the Bureau's programs directed against American citizens. "Covert action" is the label applied to clandestine activities intended to influence political choices and social values.

B. Who Were the Targets?

1. The Five Targeted Groups

The Bureau's covert action programs were aimed at five perceived threats to domestic tranquility: the "Communist Party, USA" program (1956-71) ; the "Socialist Workers Party" program (1961-69) ; the "White Hate Group" program (1964-71) ; the "Black

Nationalist-Hate Group" program (1967-71) ; and the "New Left" program (1968-71).

2. Labels Without Meaning

The Bureau's titles for its programs should not be accepted uncritically. They imply a precision of definition and of targeting which did not exist.

Even the names of the later programs had no clear definition. The Black Nationalist program, according to its supervisor, included "a great number of organizations that you might not today characterize as black nationalist but which were in fact primarily black."

3, Indeed, the nonviolent Southern Christian Leadership Conference was labeled as a Black Nationalist "Hate Group."

4, Nor could anyone at the Bureau even define "New Left," except as "more or less an attitude."

5, Furthermore, the actual targets were chosen from a far broader group than the names of the programs would imply. The CPUSA program targeted not only Party members but also sponsors of the National Committee to Abolish the House Un-American Activities Committee and civil rights leaders allegedly under Communist influence or simply not "anti-Communist."

6, The Socialist Workers Party program included non-SWP sponsors of antiwar demonstrations which were cosponsored by the SWP or the Young Socialist Alliance, its youth group.

7, The Black Nationalist program targeted a range of organizations from the Panthers to SNCC to the peaceful Southern Christian Leadership Conference, and included most black student groups.

8, New Left targets ranged from the SDS to the Interuniversity Committee for Debate on Foreign Policy, from all of Antioch College ("vanguard of the New Left") to the New Mexico Free University 14 and other "alternate" schools, and from underground newspapers to students protesting university censorship of a student publication by carrying signs with four-letter words on them.

C. What Were the Purposes of COINTELPRO?

The breadth of targeting and lack of substantive content in the descriptive titles of the programs reflect the range of motivations for COINTELPRO activity: protecting national security, preventing violence, and maintaining the existing social and political order by "disrupting" and "neutralizing" groups and individuals perceived as threats.

1. Protecting National Security

The first COINTELPRO, against the CPUSA, was instituted to counter what the Bureau believed to be a threat to the national security. As the chief of the COINTELPRO unit explained it: "We were trying first to develop intelligence so we would know what they were doing [and] second, to contain the threat.... To stop the spread of communism, to stop the effectiveness of the Communist Party as a vehicle of Soviet intelligence, propaganda and agitation." Had the Bureau stopped there, perhaps the term "counterintelligence" would have been an accurate label for the program. The expansion of the CPUSA program to non-Communists, however, and the addition of subsequent programs, make it clear that other purposes were also at work.

2. Preventing Violence

One of these purposes was the prevention of violence. Every Bureau witness deposed stated that the purpose of the particular program or programs with which he was associated was to deter violent acts by the target groups, although the witnesses differed in their assessment of how successful the programs were in achieving that goal. The preventive function was not, however, intended to be a product of specific proposals directed at specific criminal acts. Rather, the programs were aimed at groups which the Bureau believed to be violent or to have the potential for violence.

The programs were to prevent violence by deterring membership in the target groups, even if neither the particular member nor the group was violent at the time. As the supervisor of the Black Nationalist COINTELPRO put it, "Obviously you are going to prevent violence or a greater amount of violence if you have smaller groups." (Black Nationalist supervisor deposition, 10/17/75, p. 24.) The COINTELPRO unit chief agreed: "We also made an effort to deter or counteract the propaganda ... and to deter recruitment where we could. This was done with the view that if we could curb the organization, we could curb the action or the violence within the organization." In short, the programs were to prevent violence indirectly, rather than directly, by preventing possibly violent citizens from joining or continuing to associate with possibly violent groups. The prevention of violence, is clearly not, in itself, an improper purpose; preventing violence is the ultimate goal of most law enforcement. Prosecution and sentencing are intended to deter future criminal behavior, not only of the subject but also of others who might break the law. In that sense, law enforcement legitimately attempts the indirect prevention of possible violence and, if the methods used are proper, raises no constitutional issues. When the government goes beyond traditional law enforcement methods, however, and attacks group membership and advocacy, it treads on ground forbidden to it by the Constitution. In Brandenberg v. Ohio, 395 U.S. 444 (1969), the Supreme Court held that the government is not permitted to "forbid or proscribe advocacy of the use of force or law violation except where such advocacy is directed toward inciting or producing imminent lawless action and is likely to incite or produce such action." In the absence of such clear and present danger, the government cannot act against speech nor, presumably, against association.

3. Maintaining the Existing Social and Political Order

Protecting national security and preventing violence are the purposes advanced by the Bureau for COINTELPRO. There is another purpose for COINTELPRO which is not explicit but which offers the only explanation for those actions which had no conceivable rational relationship to either national security or violent activity. The unexpressed major premise of much of COINTELPRO is that the Bureau has a role in maintaining the existing social order, and that its efforts should be aimed toward combating those who threaten that order. The "New Left" COINTELPRO presents the most striking example of this attitude. As discussed earlier, the Bureau did not define the term "New Left," and the range of targets went far beyond alleged "subversives" or "extremists." Thus, for example, two student participants in a "free speech" demonstration were targeted because they defended the use of the classic four-letter-word. Significantly, they were made COINTELPRO subjects even though the demonstration "does not appear to be inspired by the New Left" because it "shows obvious disregard for decency and established morality." In another case, reprints of a newspaper article entitled "Rabbi in Vietnam Says Withdrawal Not the Answer" were mailed to members of the Vietnam Day Committee "to convince [them] of the correctness of the U.S. foreign policy in Vietnam." Still another document weighs against the "liberal press and the bleeding hearts and the forces on the left" which were "taking advantage of the situation in Chicago surrounding the Democratic National

Convention to attack the police and organized law enforcement agencies." Upholding decency and established morality, defending the correctness of U.S. foreign policy, and attacking those who thought the Chicago police used undue force have no apparent connection with the expressed goals of protecting national security and preventing violence. These documents, among others examined, compel the conclusion that Federal law enforcement officers looked upon themselves as guardians of the status quo. The attitude should not be a surprise; the difficulty lies in the choice of weapons.

D. What Techniques Were Used?

1. The Techniques of Wartime

Under the COINTELPRO programs, the arsenal of techniques used against foreign espionage agents was transferred to domestic enemies. As William C. Sullivan, former Assistant to the Director, put it, "This is a rough, tough, dirty business, and dangerous. It was dangerous at times. No holds were barred.... We have used [these techniques] against Soviet agents. They have used [them] against us. . . . [The same methods were] brought home against any organization against which we were targeted. We did not differentiate. This is a rough, tough business." Mr. Sullivan's description -- rough, tough, and dirty -- is accurate. In the course of COINTELPRO's fifteen-year history, a number of individual actions may have violated specific criminal statutes; a number of individual actions involved risk of serious bodily injury or death to the targets (at least four assaults were reported as "results" ; and a number of actions, while not illegal or dangerous, can only be described as "abhorrent in a free Society." On the other hand, many of the actions were more silly than repellent. The Bureau approved 2,370 separate counterintelligence actions. Their techniques ranged from anonymously mailing reprints of newspaper and magazine articles (sometimes Bureau-authored or planted) to group members or supporters to convince them of the error of their ways, to mailing anonymous letters to a member's spouse accusing the target of infidelity ; from using informants to raise controversial issues at meetings in order to cause dissent, to the "snitch jacket" (falsely labeling a group member as an informant) and encouraging street warfare between violent groups; from contacting members of a "legitimate group to expose the alleged subversive background of a fellow member to contacting an employer to get a target fired; from attempting to arrange for reporters to interview targets with planted questions, to trying to stop targets from speaking at all; from notifying state and local authorities of a target's criminal law violations, to using the IRS to audit a professor, not just to collect any taxes owing, but to distract him from his political activities.

2. Techniques Carrying A Serious Risk of Physical, Emotional, or Economic Damage.

The Bureau recognized that some techniques were more likely than others to cause serious physical, emotional, or economic damage to the targets. Any proposed use of those techniques was scrutinized carefully by headquarters supervisory personnel, in an attempt to balance the "greater good" to be achieved by the proposal against the known or risked harm to the target. If the "good" was sufficient, the proposal was approved. For instance, in discussing anonymous letters to spouses, the agent who supervised the New Left COINTELPRO stated: "[Before recommending approval] I would want to know what you want to get out of this, who are these people. If it's somebody, and say they did split up, what would accrue from it as far as disrupting the New Left is concerned? Say they broke up, what then.... [The question would be] is it worth it?" Similarly, with regard to the "snitch jacket" technique -- falsely labeling a group member as a police informant -- the chief of the Racial Intelligence Section stated: "You have to be able to make decisions and I am sure that labeling somebody as an informant, that you'd want to make certain that it served a good purpose before you did it and not do it haphazardly. . . . It is a serious thing. . . . As far as I am aware, in the black extremist area, by using that technique, no one was killed. I am sure of that." Moore was asked whether the fact that no one was killed was the result of "luck or planning." He answered: "Oh, it just happened that way, I am sure."

It is thus clear that, as Sullivan said, "No holds were barred, although some holds were weighed more carefully than others. When the willingness to use techniques which were concededly dangerous or harmful to the targets is combined with the range of purposes and criteria by which these targets were chosen, the result is neither "within bounds" nor "justified" in a free society.

E. Legal Restrictions Were Ignored

What happened to turn a law enforcement agency into a law violator? Why do those involved still believe their actions were not only defensible, but right?

The answers to these questions are found in a combination of factors: the availability of information showing the targets' vulnerability gathered through the unrestrained collection of domestic intelligence; the belief both within and without the Bureau that it could handle any problem; and frustration with the apparent inability of traditional law enforcement methods to solve the problems presented.

There is no doubt that Congress and the public looked to the Bureau for protection against domestic and foreign threats. As the COINTELPRO unit chief stated:

At this time [the mid-1950s] there was a general philosophy too, the general attitude of the public at this time was you did not have to worry about Communism because the FBI would take care of it. Leave it to the FBI.

I hardly know an agent who would ever go to a social affair or something, if he were introduced as FBI, the comment would be, "we feel very good because we know you are handling the threat." We were handling the threat with what directives and statutes were available. There did not seem to be any strong interest of anybody to give us stronger or better defined statutes.

Not only was no one interested in giving the Bureau better statutes (nor, for that matter, did the Bureau request them), but the Supreme Court drastically narrowed the scope of the statutes available. The Bureau personnel involved trace the institution of the first formal counterintelligence program to the Supreme Court reversal of the Smith Act convictions. The unit chief testified: "The Supreme Court rulings had rendered the Smith Act technically unenforceable.... It made it ineffective to prosecute Communist Party members, made it impossible to prosecute Communist Party members at the time." This belief in the failure of law enforcement produced the subsequent COINTELPROs as well. The unit chief continued: "The other COINTELPRO programs were opened as the threat arose in areas of extremism and subversion and there were not adequate statutes to proceed against the organization or to prevent their activities." Every Bureau witness deposed agreed that his particular COINTELPRO was the result of tremendous pressure on the Bureau to do something about a perceived threat, coupled with the inability of law enforcement techniques to cope with the situation, either because there were no pertinent federal statutes, or because local law enforcement efforts were stymied by indifference or the refusal of those in charge to call the police.

Outside pressure and law enforcement frustration do not, of course, fully explain COINTELPRO. Perhaps, after all, the best explanation was proffered by George C. Moore, the Racial Intelligence Section chief:

The FBI's counterintelligence program came up because there was a point -- if you have anything in the FBI, you have an action-oriented group of people who see something happening and want to do something to take its place.

F. Command and Control

1. 1956-71

While that "action-oriented group of people" was proceeding with fifteen years of COINTELPRO activities, where were those responsible for the supervision and control of the Bureau? Part of the answer lies in the definition of "covert action"-- clandestine activities. No one outside the Bureau was supposed to know that COINTELPRO existed. Even within the Bureau, the programs were handled on a "need-to-know" basis.

Nevertheless, the Bureau has supplied the Committee with documents which support its contention that various Attorneys General, advisors to Presidents, members of the House Appropriations Subcommittee, and, in 1958, the Cabinet were at least put on notice of the existence of the CPUSA and White Hate COINTELPROs. The Bureau cannot support its claim that anyone outside the FBI was informed of the existence of the Socialist Workers Party, Black Nationalist, or New Left COINTELPROs, and even those letters or briefings which referred (usually indirectly) to the CPUSA and White Hate

COINTELPROs failed to mention the use of techniques which risked physical, emotional, or economic damage to their targets. In any event, there is no record that any of these officials asked to know more, and none of them appears to have expressed disapproval based on the information they were given.

As the history of the Domestic Intelligence Division shows, the absence of disapproval has been interpreted by the Bureau as sufficient authorization to continue an activity (and occasionally, even express disapproval has not sufficed to stop a practice). Perhaps, however, the crux of the "command and control" problem lies in the testimony by one former Attorney General that he was too busy to know what the Bureau was doing, and by another that, as a matter of political reality, he could not have stopped it anyway.

2. Post-1971

Whether the Attorney General can control the Bureau is still an open question. The Peterson Committee, which was formed within the Justice Department to investigate COINTELPRO at Attorney General Saxbe's request, worked only with Bureau-prepared summaries of the COINTELPRO files. Further, the fact that the Department of Justice must work with the Bureau on a day-to-day basis may influence the Department's judgment on Bureau activities.

G. Termination

If COINTELPRO had been a short-lived aberration, the thorny problems of motivation, techniques, and control presented might be safely relegated to history. However, COINTELPRO existed for years on an "ad hoc" basis before the formal programs were instituted, and more significantly, COINTELPRO-type activities may continue today under the rubric of "investigation."

1. The Grey Area Between Counterintelligence and Investigation

The word "counterintelligence" had no fixed meaning even before the programs were terminated. The Bureau witnesses agreed that there is a large grey area between "counterintelligence" and "aggressive investigation," and that, headquarters supervisors sometimes had difficulty in deciding which caption should go on certain proposals.

Aggressive investigation continues, and may be even more disruptive than covert action. An anonymous letter (COINTELPRO) can be ignored as the work of a crank; an overt approach by the Bureau ("investigation") is not so easily dismissed. The line between information collection and harassment can be extremely thin.

2. Is COINTELPRO Continuing?

COINTELPRO-type activities which are clearly not within the "grey area" between COINTELPRO and investigation have continued on at least three occasions. Although all COINTELPROs were officially terminated "for security reasons" on April 27, 1971, the documents discontinuing the program provided:

In exceptional circumstances where it is considered counterintelligence action is warranted, recommendations should be submitted to the Bureau under the individual case caption to which it pertains. These recommendations will be considered on an individual basis.

The Committee requested that the Bureau provide it with a list of any "COINTELPRO-type" actions Since April 28,1971. The Bureau first advised the Committee that a review failed to develop any information indicating post termination COINTELPRO activity. Subsequently, the Bureau located and furnished to the Committee two instances of COINTELPRO-type operations. The Committee has discovered a third instance; four months after COINTELPRO was terminated, information on an attorney's political background was furnished to friendly newspaper sources under the so-called "Mass Media Program," intended to discredit both the attorney and his client.

The Committee has not been able to determine with any greater precision the extent to which COINTELPRO may be continuing. Any proposals to initiate COINTELPRO-type action would be filed under the individual case caption. The Bureau has over 500,000 case files, and each one would have to be searched. In this context, it should be noted that a Bureau search of all field office COINTELPRO files revealed the existence of five operations in addition to those known to the Petersen committee. A search of all investigative files might be similarly productive.

3. The Future of COINTELPRO

Attitudes within and without the Bureau demonstrate a continued belief by some that covert action against American citizens is permissible if the need for it is strong enough. When the Petersen Committee report on COINTELPRO was released, Director Kelley responded, "For the FBI to have done less under the circumstances would have been an abdication of its responsibilities to the American people." He also restated his "feeling that the FBI's counterintelligence programs had an impact on the crises of the time and, therefore, that they helped to bring about a favorable change in this country." In his testimony before the Select Committee, Director Kelley continued to defend COINTELPRO, albeit with some reservations:

What I said then, in 1974, and what I believe today, is that the FBI employees involved in these programs did what they felt was expected of them by the President, the Attorney General, the Congress, and the people of the United States. . . .

Our concern over whatever abuses occurred in the Counterintelligence Programs, and there were some substantial ones, should not obscure the underlying purpose of those programs.

We must recognize that situations have occurred in the past and will arise in the future where the Government may well be expected to depart from its traditional role, in the FBI's case, as an investigative and intelligence-gathering agency, and take affirmative steps which are needed to meet an imminent threat to human life or property.

Nor is the Director alone in his belief that faced with sufficient threat, covert disruption is justified. The Department of Justice promulgated tentative guidelines for the Bureau which would have permitted the Attorney General to authorize "preventive action" where there is a substantial possibility that violence will occur and "prosecution is impracticable." Although those guidelines have now been dropped, the principle has not been rejected.

The American people need to be assured that never again will an agency of the government be permitted to conduct a secret war against those citizens it considers threats to the established order. Only a combination of legislative prohibition and Departmental control can guarantee that COINTELPRO will not happen again...

Source: Final Report of the Select Committee to Study Governmental Operations with Respect to Intelligence Activities of the United States Senate, 94th Congress, 2nd Session, 1976.

Masked Racism: Reflections on the Prison Industrial Complex

Imprisonment has become the response of first resort to far too many of the social problems that burden people who are ensconced in poverty. These problems often are veiled by being conveniently grouped together under the category "crime" and by the automatic attribution of criminal behavior to people of color. Homelessness, unemployment, drug addiction, mental illness, and illiteracy are only a few of the problems that disappear from public view when the human beings contending with them are relegated to cages.

Prisons thus perform a feat of magic. Or rather the people who continually vote in new prison bonds and tacitly assent to a proliferating network of prisons and jails have been tricked into believing in the magic of imprisonment. But prisons do not disappear problems, they disappear human beings. And the practice of disappearing vast numbers of people from poor, immigrant, and racially marginalized communities has literally become big business.

The seeming effortlessness of magic always conceals an enormous amount of behind-the-scenes work. When prisons disappear human beings in order to convey the illusion of solving social problems, penal infrastructures must be created to accommodate a rapidly swelling population of caged people. Goods and services must be provided to keep imprisoned populations alive. Sometimes these populations must be kept busy and at other times -- particularly in repressive super-maximum prisons and in INS detention centers -- they must be deprived of virtually all-meaningful activity. Vast numbers of handcuffed and shackled people are moved across state borders as they are transferred from one state or federal prison to another.

All this work, which used to be the primary province of government, is now also performed by private corporations, whose links to government in the field of what is euphemistically called "corrections" resonate dangerously with the military industrial complex. The dividends that accrue from investment in the punishment industry, like those that accrue from investment in weapons production, only amount to social destruction. Taking into account the structural similarities and profitability of business-government linkages in the realms of military production and public punishment, the expanding penal system can now be characterized as a "prison industrial complex."

The Color of Imprisonment

Almost two million people are currently locked up in the immense network of U.S. prisons and jails. More than 70 percent of the imprisoned population are people of color. It is rarely acknowledged that the fastest growing group of prisoners are black women and that Native American prisoners are the largest group per capita. Approximately five million people -- including those on probation and parole -- are directly under the surveillance of the criminal justice system.

To deliver up bodies destined for profitable punishment, the political economy of prisons relies on racialized assumptions of criminality -- such as images of black welfare mothers reproducing criminal children -- and on racist practices in arrest, conviction, and sentencing patterns. Colored bodies constitute the main human raw material in this vast experiment to disappear the major social problems of our time. Once the aura of magic is stripped away from the imprisonment solution, what is revealed is racism, class bias, and the parasitic seduction of capitalist profit. The prison industrial system materially and morally impoverishes its inhabitants and devours the social wealth needed to address the very problems that have led to spiraling numbers of prisoners.

As prisons take up more and more space on the social landscape, other government programs that have previously sought to respond to social needs -- such as Temporary Assistance to Needy Families -- are being squeezed out of existence. The deterioration of public education, including prioritizing discipline and security over learning in public schools located in poor communities, is directly related to the prison "solution."

Profiting from Prisoners
As prisons proliferate in U.S. society, private capital has become enmeshed in the punishment industry. And precisely because of their profit potential, prisons are becoming increasingly important to the U.S. economy. If the notion of punishment as a source of potentially stupendous profits is disturbing by itself, then the strategic dependence on racist structures and ideologies to render mass punishment palatable and profitable is even more troubling.

Prison privatization is the most obvious instance of capital's current movement toward the prison industry. While government-run prisons are often in gross violation of international human rights standards, private prisons are even less accountable. In March of this year, the Corrections Corporation of America (CCA), the largest U.S. private prison company, claimed 54,944 beds in 68 facilities under contract or development in the U.S., Puerto Rico, the United Kingdom, and Australia. Following the global trend of subjecting more women to public punishment, CCA recently opened a women's prison outside Melbourne. The company recently identified California as its "new frontier."

Wackenhut Corrections Corporation (WCC), the second largest U.S. prison company, claimed contracts and awards to manage 46 facilities in North America, U.K., and Australia. It boasts a total of 30,424 beds as well as contracts for prisoner health care services, transportation, and security.

Currently, the stocks of both CCA and WCC are doing extremely well. Between 1996 and 1997, CCA's revenues increased by 58 percent, from $293 million to $462 million. Its net profit grew from $30.9 million to $53.9 million. WCC raised its revenues from $138 million in 1996 to $210 million in 1997. Unlike public correctional facilities, the vast profits of these private facilities rely on the employment of non-union labor.

The Prison Industrial Complex
But private prison companies are only the most visible component of the increasing corporatization of punishment. Government contracts to build prisons have bolstered the construction industry. The architectural community has identified prison design as a major new niche. Technology developed for the military by companies like Westinghouse is being marketed for use in law enforcement and punishment.

Moreover, corporations that appear to be far removed from the business of punishment are intimately involved in the expansion of the prison industrial complex. Prison construction bonds are one of the many sources of profitable investment for leading financiers such as Merrill Lynch. MCI charges prisoners and their families outrageous prices for the precious telephone calls which are often the only contact prisoners have with the free world.

Many corporations whose products we consume on a daily basis have learned that prison labor power can be as profitable as third world labor power exploited by

U.S.-based global corporations. Both relegate formerly unionized workers to joblessness and many even wind up in prison. Some of the companies that use prison labor are IBM, Motorola, Compaq, Texas Instruments, Honeywell, Microsoft, and Boeing. But it is not only the hi-tech industries that reap the profits of prison labor. Nordstrom department stores sell jeans that are marketed as "Prison Blues," as well as t-shirts and jackets made in Oregon prisons. The advertising slogan for these clothes is "made on the inside to be worn on the outside." Maryland prisoners inspect glass bottles and jars used by Revlon and Pierre Cardin, and schools throughout the world buy graduation caps and gowns made by South Carolina prisoners.

"For private business," write Eve Goldberg and Linda Evans (a political prisoner inside the Federal Correctional Institution at Dublin, California) "prison labor is like a pot of gold. No strikes. No union organizing. No health benefits, unemployment insurance, or workers' compensation to pay. No language barriers, as in foreign countries. New leviathan prisons are being built on thousands of eerie acres of factories inside the walls. Prisoners do data entry for Chevron, make telephone reservations for TWA, raise hogs, shovel manure, make circuit boards, limousines, waterbeds, and lingerie for Victoria's Secret -- all at a fraction of the cost of 'free labor.'"

Devouring the Social Wealth
Although prison labor -- which ultimately is compensated at a rate far below the minimum wage -- is hugely profitable for the private companies that use it, the penal system as a whole does not produce wealth. It devours the social wealth that could be used to subsidize housing for the homeless, to ameliorate public

education for poor and racially marginalized communities, to open free drug rehabilitation programs for people who wish to kick their habits, to create a national health care system, to expand programs to combat HIV, to eradicate domestic abuse -- and, in the process, to create well-paying jobs for the unemployed.

By segregating people labeled as criminals, prison simultaneously fortifies and conceals the structural racism of the U.S. economy, Claims of low unemployment rates -- even in black communities -- make sense only if one assumes that the vast numbers of people in prison have really disappeared and thus have no legitimate claims to jobs. The numbers of black and Latino men currently incarcerated amount to two percent of the male labor force. According to criminologist David Downes, "treating incarceration as a type of hidden unemployment may raise the jobless rate for men by about one-third, to 8 percent. The effect on the black labor force is greater still, raising the [black] male unemployment rate from 11 percent to 19 percent."

Hidden Agenda
Mass incarceration is not a solution to unemployment, nor is it a solution to the vast array of social problems that are hidden away in a rapidly growing network of prisons and jails. However, the great majority of people have been tricked into believing in the efficacy of imprisonment, even though the historical record clearly demonstrates that prisons do not work. Racism has undermined our ability to create a popular critical discourse to contest the ideological trickery that posits imprisonment as key to public safety. The focus of state policy is rapidly shifting from social welfare to social control.

Black, Latino, Native American, and many Asian youth are portrayed as the purveyors of violence, traffickers of drugs, and as envious of commodities that they have no right to possess. Young black and Latina women are represented as sexually promiscuous and as indiscriminately propagating babies and poverty. Criminality and deviance are racialized. Surveillance is thus focused on communities of color, immigrants, the unemployed, the undereducated, the homeless, and in general on those who have a diminishing claim to social resources. Their claim to social resources continues to diminish in large part because law enforcement and penal measures increasingly devour these resources. The prison industrial complex has thus created a vicious cycle of punishment which only further impoverishes those whose impoverishment is supposedly "solved" by imprisonment.

Therefore, as the emphasis of government policy shifts from social welfare to crime control, racism sinks more deeply into the economic and ideological structures of U.S. society. Meanwhile, conservative crusaders against affirmative action and bilingual education proclaim the end of racism, while their opponents suggest that racism's remnants can be dispelled through dialogue and conversation. But conversations about "race relations" will hardly dismantle a prison industrial complex that thrives on and nourishes the racism hidden within the deep structures of our society.

The emergence of a U.S. prison industrial complex within a context of cascading conservatism marks a new historical moment, whose dangers are unprecedented. But so are its opportunities. Considering the impressive number of grassroots projects that continue to resist the expansion of the punishment industry, it ought to be possible to bring these efforts together to create radical and nationally visible movements that can legitimize anti-capitalist critiques of the prison industrial complex. It ought to be possible to build movements in defense of prisoners' human rights and movements that persuasively argue that what we need is not new prisons, but new health care, housing, education, drug programs, jobs, and education. To safeguard a democratic future, it is possible and necessary to weave together the many and increasing strands of resistance to the prison industrial complex into a powerful movement for social transformation.

Source: Davis, Angela Y. "Masked Racism: Reflections on the Prison Industrial Complex". Color Lines magazine. Oakland, CA: Applied Research Center. Vol. 1, Number 2, Fall 1998.

AMERICAN SOCIAL INSTUTIONS - INFORMAL

KEY CONCEPTS

Informal social institutions have less rigidity than those which are formal. The nature of social relationships in a family, for example, varies dramatically within a culture or society, as well as through time. The "average" American model of a family is far more limited in number now than it was a century ago. How and why the change? Although there are coercive elements ("stick and carrot" - or punishment and reward), informal institutions tend to be far more voluntary than formal institutions. There are rarely any written rules dictating behavior within informal social institutions, however, this does not mean that rules do not exist. The challenge is to examine where those rules originate, how they are communicated, why they are followed, and to what effect on the individual.

Thanksgiving

Soon they will be together again, all the people who travel between their own lives and each other's. The package tour of the season will lure them this week to the family table. By Thursday, feast day, family day, Thanksgiving day, Americans who value individualism like no other people will collect around a million tables in a ritual of belonging.

They will assemble their families the way they assemble dinner: each one bearing a personality as different as cranberry sauce and pumpkin pie. For one dinner they will cook for each other, fuss for each other, feed each other and argue with each other. They will nod at their common heritage, the craziness and caring of other generations. They will measure their common legacy. ..the children.

All these complex cells, these men and women, old and young, with different dreams and disappointments will give homage again to the group they are a part of and apart from: their family. Families and individuals. The "we" and the "I." As good Americans we all travel between these two ideals. We take value trips from the great American notion of individualism to the great American vision of family. We wear out our tires driving back and forth, using speed to shorten the distance between these two principles.

There has always been some pavement between a person and a family. From the first moment we recognize that we are separate we begin to wrestle with aloneness and togetherness. Here and now these conflicts are especially acute. We are, after all, raised in families...to be individuals. This double message follows us through life. We are taught about the freedom of the "I" and the safety of the "we. " The loneliness of the "I" and the intrusiveness of the "we." The selfishness of the "I" and the burdens of the "we."

We are taught what Andre Malraux said: "Without a family, man, alone in the world, trembles with the cold." And taught what he said another day: "The denial of the supreme importance of the mind's development accounts for many revolts against the family." In theory, the world rewards "the supreme importance" of the individual, the ego. We think alone, inside our heads. We write music and literature with an enlarged sense of self. We are graded and paid, hired and fired, on our own merit. The rank individualism is both exciting and cruel. Here is where the fittest survive.

The family, on the other hand, at its best, works very differently. We don't have to achieve to be accepted by our families. We just have to be. Our membership is not based on credentials but on birth. As Malraux put it, " A friend loves you for your intelligence, a mistress for your charm, but your family's love is unreasoning: You were born into it and of its flesh and blood."

The family is formed not for the survival of the fittest but for the weakest. It is not an economical unit, it is an emotional one. This is not the place where people ruthlessly compete with each other but where they work for each other. Its business is taking care, and when it works, it is not callous but kind.

There are fewer heroes, fewer stars in family life. While the world may glorify the self, the family asks us, at one time or another, to submerge it. While the world may abandon us, the family promises, at one time or another, to protect us. So we commute daily, weekly, yearly between one world and another, Between a life as a family member that can be nurturing or smothering. Between life as an individual that can free us or flatten us. We vacillate between two separate sets of demands and possibilities.

The people who will gather around this table Thursday live in both of these worlds, a part of and apart from each other. With any luck the territory they travel from one to another can be a fertile one, rich with care and space. It can be a place where the "I" and the "we" interact. On this day at least, they will bring to each other something both special and something to be shared: these separate selves.

Source: Goodman, Ellen. "Thanksgiving". Copyright 1993, The Boston Globe Company.

Our Country: It's Possible Future and It's Present Crisis

Again, another marked characteristic of the Anglo-Saxon is what may be called an instinct or genius for colonizing. His unequaled energy, his indomitable perseverance, and his personal independence, made him a pioneer. He excels all others in pushing his way into new countries. It was those in whom this tendency was strongest that came to America, and this inherited tendency has been further developed by the westward sweep of successive generations across the continent. So noticeable has this characteristic become that English visitors remark it. Charles Dickens once said that the typical American would hesitate to enter heaven unless assured that he could go farther west.

What is the significance of such facts? These tendencies enfold the future; they are the mighty alphabet with which God writes his prophecies. May we not, by a careful laying together of the letters, spell out something of his meaning? It seems to me that God, with infinite wisdom and skill, is training the Anglo-

Saxon race for an hour sure to come in the world's future. Heretofore there has always been in the history of the world a comparatively unoccupied land westward, into which the crowded countries of the East have poured their surplus populations. But the widening waves of migration, which millenniums ago rolled east and west from the valley of the Euphrates, meet to-day on our Pacific coast. There are no more new worlds. The unoccupied arable lands of the earth are limited, and will soon be taken. The time is coming when the pressure of population on the means of subsistence will be felt here as it is now felt in Europe and Asia. Then will the world enter upon a new stage of its history-the final competition of races, for which the Anglo-Saxon is being schooled. Long before the thousand millions are here, the mighty centrifugal tendency, inherent in this stock and strengthened in the United States, will assert itself. Then this race of unequaled energy, with all the majesty of numbers and the might of wealth behind it-the representative, let us hope, of the largest liberty, the purest Christianity, the highest civilization-having developed peculiarly aggressive traits calculated to impress its institutions upon mankind, will spread itself over the earth. If I read not amiss, this powerful race will move down upon Mexico, down upon Central and South America, out upon the islands of the sea, over upon Africa and beyond. And can any one doubt that the results of this competition of races will be the "survival of the fittest?" "Any people," says Dr. Bushnell, "that is physiologically advanced in culture, though it be only in a degree beyond another which is mingled with it on strictly equal terms, is sure to live down and finally live out its inferior. Nothing can save the inferior race but a ready and pliant assimilation. Whether the feebler and more abject races are going to be regenerated and raised up, is already, very much of a question. What if it

should be God's plan to people the world with better and finer material?"
Source: Strong, Josiah. <u>Our Country: It's Possible Future and It's Present Crisis</u>. 1885.

The Significance of the Frontier in American History

In a recent bulletin of the Superintendent of the Census for 1890 appear these significant words: "Up to and including 1880 the country had a frontier of settlement, but at present the unsettled area has been so broken into by isolated bodies of settlement that there can hardly be said to be a frontier line. In the discussion of its extent, its westward movement, etc., it can not, therefore, any longer have a place in the census reports." This brief official statement marks the closing of a great historic movement. Up to our own day American history has been in a large degree the history of the colonization of the Great West. The existence of an area of free land, its continuous recession, and the advance of American settlement westward, explain American development.

Behind institutions, behind constitutional forms and modifications, lie the vital forces that call these organs into life and shape them to meet changing conditions. The peculiarity of American institutions is, the fact that they have been compelled to adapt themselves to the changes of an expanding people--to the changes involved in crossing a continent, in winning a wilderness, and in developing at each area of this progress out of the primitive economic and political conditions of the frontier into the complexity of city life. Said Calhoun in 1817, "We are great, and rapidly--I was about to say fearfully--growing!", 2 So saying, he touched the distinguishing feature of American life. All peoples show development; the germ theory of politics has been sufficiently emphasized. In the case of most nations, however, the development has occurred in a limited area; and if the nation has expanded, it has met other growing peoples whom it has conquered. But in the case of the United States we have a different phenomenon. Limiting our attention to the Atlantic coast, we have the familiar phenomenon of the evolution of institutions in a limited area, such as the rise of representative government; into complex organs; the progress from primitive industrial society, without division of labor, up to manufacturing civilization. But we have in addition to this a recurrence of the process of evolution in each western area reached in the process of expansion. Thus American development has exhibited not merely advance along a single line, but a return to primitive conditions on a continually advancing frontier line, and a new development for that area. American social development has been continually beginning over again on the frontier. This perennial rebirth, this fluidity of American life, this expansion westward with its new opportunities, its continuous touch with the simplicity of primitive society, furnish the forces dominating American character. The true point of view in the history of this nation is not the Atlantic coast, it is the Great West. Even the slavery struggle, which is made so exclusive an object of attention by writers like Professor von Holst, occupies its important place in American history because of its relation to westward expansion.

In this advance, the frontier is the outer edge of the wave-- the meeting point between savagery and civilization. Much has been written about the frontier from the point of view of border warfare and the chase, but as a field for the serious study of the economist and the historian it has been neglected.

The American frontier is sharply distinguished from the European frontier--a fortified boundary line running through dense populations. The most significant thing about the American frontier is, that it lies at the hither edge of free land. In the census reports it is treated as the margin of that settlement which has a density of two or more to the square mile. The term is an elastic one, and for our purposes does not need sharp definition. We shall consider the whole frontier belt including the Indian country and the outer margin of the "settled area " of the census reports. This paper will make no attempt to treat the subject exhaustively; its aim is simply to call attention to the frontier as a fertile field for investigation, and to suggest some of the problems which arise in connection with it.

In the settlement of America we have to observe how European life entered the continent, and how America modified and developed that life and reacted on Europe. Our early history is the study of European germs developing in an American environment. Too exclusive attention has been paid by institutional students to the Germanic origins, too little to the American factors. The frontier is the line of most rapid and effective Americanization. The wilderness masters the colonist. It finds him a European in dress, industries, tools, modes of travel, and thought. It takes him from the railroad car and puts him in the birch canoe. It strips off the garments of civilization and arrays him in the hunting shirt and the moccasin. It puts him in the log cabin of the Cherokee and Iroquois and runs an Indian palisade around him. Before long he has gone to planting Indian corn and plowing with a sharp stick, he shouts the war cry and takes the scalp in orthodox Indian fashion. In short, at the frontier the environment is at first too strong for the man. He must accept the conditions which it furnishes, or perish, and so he fits himself into the Indian clearings and follows the Indian trails. Little by little he transforms the wilderness, but the outcome is not the old Europe, not simply the development of Germanic germs, any more than the first phenomenon was a case of reversion to the Germanic mark. The fact is, that here is a new product that is American. At first, the frontier was the Atlantic coast. It was the frontier of Europe in a very real sense. Moving westward, the frontier became more and more American. As successive terminal moraines result from successive glaciations, so each frontier leaves its traces behind it, and when it becomes a settled area the region still partakes of the frontier characteristics. Thus the advance of the frontier has meant a steady movement away from the influence of Europe, a steady growth of independence on American lines. And to study this advance, the men who grew up under these conditions, and the political, economic, and social results of it, is to study the really American part of our history...

Growth of Democracy
But the most important effect of the frontier has been in the promotion of democracy here and in Europe. As has been indicated, the frontier is productive of individualism. Complex society is precipitated by the wilderness into a kind of primitive organization based on the family. The tendency is anti-social. It produces antipathy to control, and particularly to any direct control. The tax-gatherer is viewed as a representative of oppression. Prof. Osgood, in an able article,46 has pointed out that the frontier conditions prevalent in the colonies are important factors in the explanation of the American Revolution, where individual liberty was sometimes confused with absence of all effective government. The same conditions aid in explaining the

difficulty of instituting a strong government in the period of the confederacy. The frontier individualism has from the beginning promoted democracy. The frontier States that came into the Union in the first quarter of a century of its existence came in with democratic suffrage provisions, and had reactive effects of the highest importance upon the older States whose peoples were being attracted there. An extension of the franchise became essential. It was western New York that forced an extension of suffrage in the constitutional convention of that State in 1821; and it was western Virginia that compelled the tide-water region to put a more liberal suffrage provision in the constitution framed in 1830, and to give to the frontier region a more nearly proportionate representation with the tide-water aristocracy. The rise of democracy as an effective force in the nation came in with western preponderance under Jackson and William Henry Harrison, and it meant the triumph of the frontier-- with all of its good and with all of its evil elements.47 An interesting illustration of the tone of frontier democracy in 1830 comes from the same debates in the Virginia convention already referred to. A representative from western Virginia declared:

But, sir, it is not the increase of population in the West which this gentleman ought to fear. It is the energy which the mountain breeze and western habits impart to those emigrants. They are regenerated, politically I mean, sir. They soon become working politicians, and the difference, sir, between a talking and a working politician is immense. The Old Dominion has long been celebrated for producing great orators; the ablest metaphysicians in policy; men that can split hairs in all abstruse questions of political economy. But at home, or when they return from Congress, they have negroes to fan them asleep. But a Pennsylvania, a New York, an Ohio, or a western Virginia statesman, though far inferior in logic, metaphysics, and rhetoric to an old Virginia statesman, has this advantage, that when he returns home he takes off his coat and takes hold of the plow. This gives him bone and muscle, sir, and preserves his republican principles pure and uncontaminated.

So long as free land exists, the opportunity for a competency exists, and economic power secures political power. But the democracy born of free land, strong in selfishness and individualism, intolerant of administrative experience and education, and pressing individual liberty beyond its proper bounds, has its dangers as well as its benefits. Individualism in America has allowed a laxity in regard to governmental affairs which has rendered possible the spoils system and all the manifest evils that follow from the lack of a highly developed civic spirit. In this connection may be noted also the influence of frontier conditions in permitting lax business honor, inflated paper currency and wild-cat banking. The colonial and revolutionary frontier was the region whence emanated many of the worst forms of an evil currency.48 The West in the War of 1812 repeated the phenomenon on the frontier of that day, while the speculation and wild-cat banking of the period of the crisis of 1837 occurred on the new frontier belt of the next tier of States. Thus each one of the periods of lax financial integrity coincides with periods when a new set of frontier communities had arisen, and coincides in area with these successive frontiers for the most part. The recent Populist agitation is a case in point. Many a State that now declines any connection with the tenets of the Populists, itself adhered to such ideas in an earlier stage of the development of the State. A primitive society can hardly be expected to show the intelligent appreciation of the complexity of business interests in a developed society. The continual recurrence of these

areas of paper-money agitation is another evidence that the frontier can be isolated and studied as a factor in American history of the highest importance.
Source: Turner, Frederick Jackson. The Significance of the Frontier in American History. (1893).

Self-Reliance

I read the other day some verses written by an eminent painter which were original and not conventional. The soul always hears an admonition in such lines, let the subject be what it may. The sentiment they instill is of more value than any thought they may contain. To believe your own thought, to believe that what is true for you in your private heart is true for all men, - that is genius. Speak your latent conviction, and it shall be the universal sense; for the inmost in due time becomes the outmost,-- and our first thought is rendered back to us by the trumpets of the Last Judgment. Familiar as the voice of the mind is to each, the highest merit we ascribe to Moses, Plato, and Milton is, that they set at naught books and traditions, and spoke not what men but what they thought. A man should learn to detect and watch that gleam of light which flashes across his mind from within, more than the lustre of the firmament of bards and sages. Yet he dismisses without notice his thought, because it is his. In every work of genius we recognize our own rejected thoughts: they come back to us with a certain alienated majesty. Great works of art have no more affecting lesson for us than this. They teach us to abide by our spontaneous impression with good-humored inflexibility then most when the whole cry of voices is on the other side. Else, to-morrow a stranger will say with masterly good sense precisely what we have thought and felt all the time, and we shall be forced to take with shame our own opinion from another.

There is a time in every man's education when he arrives at the conviction that envy is ignorance; that imitation is suicide; that he must take himself for better, for worse, as his portion; that though the wide universe is full of good, no kernel of nourishing corn can come to him but through his toil bestowed on that plot of ground which is given to him to till. The power which resides in him is new in nature, and none but he knows what that is which he can do, nor does he know until he has tried. Not for nothing one face, one character, one fact, makes much impression on him, and another none. This sculpture in the memory is not without pre-established harmony. The eye was placed where one ray should fall, that it might testify of that particular ray. We but half express ourselves, and are ashamed of that divine idea which each of us represents. It may be safely trusted as proportionate and of good issues, so it be faithfully imparted, but God will not have his work made manifest by cowards. A man is relieved and gay when he has put his heart into his work and done his best; but what he has said or done otherwise, shall give him no peace. It is a deliverance which does not deliver. In the attempt his genius deserts him; no muse befriends; no invention, no hope.

Trust thyself: every heart vibrates to that iron string. Accept the place the divine providence has found for you, the society of your contemporaries, the connection of events. Great men have always done so, and confided themselves childlike to the genius of their age, betraying their perception that the absolutely trustworthy was seated at their heart, working through their hands, predominating in all their being. And we are now men, and must accept in the highest mind the same transcendent destiny; and not minors and invalids in a protected corner, not cowards fleeing before a revolution, but guides, redeemers, and benefactors, obeying the Almighty effort, and advancing on Chaos and the Dark...

These are the voices which we hear in solitude, but they grow faint and inaudible as we enter into the world. Society everywhere is in conspiracy against the manhood of every one of its members. Society is a joint-stock company, in which the members agree, for the better securing of his bread to each shareholder, to surrender the liberty and culture of the eater. The virtue in most request is conformity. Self-reliance is its aversion. It loves not realities and creators, but names and customs.

Whoso would be a man must be a nonconformist. He who would gather immortal palms must not be hindered by the name of goodness, but must explore if it be goodness. Nothing is at last sacred but the integrity of your own mind. Absolve you to yourself, and you shall have the suffrage of the world. I remember an answer which when quite young I was prompted to make to a valued adviser, who was wont to importune me with the dear old doctrines of the church. On my saying, What have I to do with the sacredness of traditions, if I live wholly from within? my friend suggested, - "But these impulses may be from below, not from above." I replied, "They do not seem to me to be such; but if I am the Devil's child, I will live then from the Devil." No law can be sacred to me but that of my nature. Good and bad are but names very readily transferable to that or this; the only right is what is after my constitution, the only wrong what is against it. A man is to carry himself in the presence of all opposition, as if every thing were titular and ephemeral but he. I am ashamed to think how easily we capitulate to badges and names, to large societies and dead institutions. Every decent and well-spoken individual affects and sways me more than is right. I ought to go upright and vital, and speak the rude truth in all ways...

What I must do is all that concerns me, not what the people think. This rule, equally arduous in actual and in intellectual life, may serve for the whole distinction between greatness and meanness. It is the harder, because you will always find those who think they know what is your duty better than you know it. It is easy in the world to live after the world's opinion; it is easy in solitude to live after our own; but the great man is he who in the midst of the crowd keeps with perfect sweetness the independence of solitude.

The objection to conforming to usages that have become dead to you is, that it scatters your force. It loses your time and blurs the impression of your character. If you maintain a dead church, contribute to a dead Bible-society, vote with a great party either for the government or against it, spread your table like base housekeepers, - under all these screens I have difficulty to detect the precise man you are. And, of course, so much force is withdrawn from your proper life. But do your work, and I shall know you. Do your work, and you shall reinforce yourself. A man must consider what a blindman's-buff is this game of conformity. If I know your sect, I anticipate your argument. I hear a preacher announce for his text and topic the expediency of one of the institutions of his church. Do I not know beforehand that not possibly can he say a new and spontaneous word? Do I not know that, with all this ostentation of examining the grounds of the institution, he will do no such thing? Do I not know that he is pledged to himself not to look but at one side, - the permitted side, not as a man, but as a parish minister? He is a retained attorney, and these airs of the bench are the emptiest affectation. Well, most men have bound their eyes with one or another handkerchief, and attached themselves to some one of these communities of opinion. This conformity makes them not false in a few particulars, authors of a few lies, but false in all particulars. Their every truth is not quite true. Their two is not the real two, their four not the real four; so that every word they say chagrins us, and we know not where to begin to set them right. Meantime nature is not slow to equip us in the prison-uniform of the party to which we adhere. We come to wear one cut of face and figure, and acquire by degrees the gentlest asinine expression. There is a mortifying experience in particular, which does not fail to wreak itself also in the general history; I mean "the foolish face of praise," the forced smile which we put on in company where we do not feel at ease in answer to conversation which does not interest us. The muscles, not spontaneously moved, but moved by a low usurping willfulness, grow tight about the outline of the face with the most disagreeable sensation.

For nonconformity the world whips you with its displeasure. And therefore a man must know how to estimate a sour face. The by-standers look askance on him in the public street or in the friend's parlour. If this aversation had its origin in contempt and resistance like his own, he might well go home with a sad countenance; but the sour faces of the multitude, like their sweet faces, have no deep cause, but are put on and off as the wind blows and a newspaper directs. Yet is the discontent of the multitude more formidable than that of the senate and the college. It is easy enough for a firm man who knows the world to brook the rage of the cultivated classes. Their rage is decorous and prudent, for they are timid as being very vulnerable themselves. But when to their feminine rage the indignation of the people is added, when the ignorant and the poor are aroused, when the unintelligent brute force that lies at the bottom of society is made to growl and mow, it needs the habit of magnanimity and religion to treat it godlike as a trifle of no concernment.

The other terror that scares us from self-trust is our consistency; a reverence for our past act or word, because the eyes of others have no other data for computing our orbit than our past acts, and we are loath to disappoint them.

But why should you keep your head over your shoulder? Why drag about this corpse of your memory, lest you contradict somewhat you have stated in this or that public place? Suppose you should contradict yourself; what then? It seems to be a rule of wisdom never to rely on your memory alone, scarcely even in acts of pure memory, but to bring the past for judgment into the thousand-eyed present, and live ever in a new day. In your metaphysics you have denied personality to the Deity: yet when the devout motions of the soul come, yield to them heart and life, though they should clothe God with shape and color. Leave your theory, as Joseph his coat in the hand of the harlot, and flee.

A foolish consistency is the hobgoblin of little minds, adored by little statesmen and philosophers and divines. With consistency a great soul has simply nothing to do. He may as well concern himself with his shadow on the wall. Speak what you think now in hard words, and to-morrow speak what to-morrow thinks in hard words again, though it contradict every thing you said to-day. - 'Ah, so you shall be sure to be misunderstood.' - Is it so bad, then, to be misunderstood? Pythagoras was misunderstood, and Socrates, and Jesus, and Luther, and Copernicus, and Galileo, and Newton, and every pure and wise spirit that ever took flesh. To be great is to be misunderstood...

Source: Emerson, Ralph, Waldo. "Self-Reliance." Emerson's Complete Works. Cambridge, Massachusetts: The riverside Press. 1883-1893.

Unguarded Gates

WIDE open and unguarded stand our gates,

Named of the four winds, North, South, East, and West;

Portals that lead to an enchanted land

Of cities, forests, fields of living gold,

Vast prairies, lordly summits touched with snow,   5

Majestic rivers sweeping proudly past

The Arab's date-palm and the Norseman's pine-

A realm wherein are fruits of every zone,

Airs of all climes, for, lo! throughout the year

The red rose blossoms somewhere-a rich land,   10

A later Eden planted in the wilds,

With not an inch of earth within its bound

But if a slave's foot press it sets him free.

Here, it is written, Toil shall have its wage,

And Honor honor, and the humblest man   15

Stand level with the highest in the law.

Of such a land have men in dungeons dreamed,

And with the vision brightening in their eyes

Gone smiling to the fagot and the sword.

Wide open and unguarded stand our gates,   20

And through them presses a wild motley throng-

Men from the Volga and the Tartar steppes,

Featureless figures of the Hoang-Ho,

Malayan, Scythian, Teuton, Kelt, and Slav,

Flying the Old World's poverty and scorn;   25

These bringing with them unknown gods and rites,-

Those, tiger passions, here to stretch their claws.

In street and alley what strange tongues are loud,

Accents of menace alien to our air,

Voices that once the Tower of Babel knew!   30

O Liberty, white Goddess! is it well

To leave the gates unguarded? On thy breast

Fold Sorrow's children, soothe the hurts of fate,

Lift the down-trodden, but with hand of steel

Stay those who to thy sacred portals come   35

To waste the gifts of freedom. Have a care

Lest from thy brow the clustered stars be torn

And trampled in the dust. For so of old

The thronging Goth and Vandal trampled Rome,

And where the temples of the Cæsars stood   40

The lean wolf unmolested made her lair.

Source: Aldrich, Thomas Bailey. <u>The Poems of Thomas Bailey Aldrich</u>. 1907.

The New Colossus

Not like the brazen giant of Greek fame,
With conquering limbs astride from land to land;
Here at our sea-washed, sunset gates shall stand
A mighty woman with a torch, whose flame
Is the imprisoned lightning, and her name Mother of
Exiles.
From her beacon-hand
Glows world-wide welcome; her mild eyes command
The air-bridged harbor that twin cities frame.
"Keep, ancient lands, your storied pomp!" cries she
With silent lips. "Give me your tired, your poor,
Your huddled masses yearning to breathe free,
The wretched refuse of your teeming shore.
Send these, the homeless, tempest-tost to me,
I lift my lamp beside the golden door!"

Source: Lazarus, Emma. "The New Colossus." From <u>American Women Poets of the Nineteenth Century</u>, Cheryl Walker, ed. Rutgers State University Press. 1992.

Gathering Storm: America's Militia Threat
Morris Dees and James Corcoran

Introduction:
Louis Beam minced no words.

"I warn you calmly, coldly, and without reservation that over the next ten years you will come to hate government more than anything in your life," Beam, a spokesman for the Aryan Nations, told his audience of 160 white men. They ranged from white supremacists to pro-gun extremists, meeting at an invitation-only gathering two months after FBI sharpshooters killed Randy Weaver's wife and son on Ruby Ridge in Idaho. They called themselves patriots.

"The federal government in north Idaho has demonstrated brutally, horribly, and with great terror how it will enforce its claim that we are religious fanatics and enemies of the state," added Beam, his voice rising with each word. "We must, in one voice, cry out that we will not tolerate their stinking, murdering, lying, corrupt government.

"Men, in the name of our Father, we are called upon to make a decision, a decision that you will make in the quietness of your heart, in the still places of the night," Beam continued. "as you lie on your bed and you look up at the ceiling tonight, you must answer the question: Will it be liberty or will it be death?

"as for me," he concluded in the words of Patrick Henry to thunderous applause, "give me liberty or give me death."

At this gathering, now known as the Rocky Mountain Rendezvous, held on October 23-25, 1992, at a YMCA in Estes Park, Colorado, plans were laid for a citizens' militia movement like none this country has known. It is a movement that already has led to the most destructive act of domestic terrorism in our nation's history. Unless checked, it could lead to widespread devastation or ruin.

"We bear the torch of light, of justice, of liberty, and we will be heard," Beam shouted over the cheers of his audience. "We will not yield this country to the forces of darkness, oppression. and tyranny."

His face pockmarked, his hair slicked down, and speaking in a manner that evoked images of Adolf Hitler, Beam continued, "So if you believe in the truth, if you believe in justice, then join with us. We are marching to the beat of the same drum. The beat of that drum, like those heard at Valley Forge and at Gettysburg, has called good men everywhere to action."

I first met Louis Beam in a Texas federal court in 11981 when I forced him to stop harassing Vietnamese fishermen in Galveston Bay and to disband his 2,500-member paramilitary army. He later made the FBIs Ten Most Wanted list after being indicted, along with twelve other avowed racists, for seditious conspiracy against the United States. After his acquittal by an all-white Arkansas jury, Beam marched from the Fort Smith courthouse and saluted the Confederate memorial in the town square. "To hell with the federal government," he shouted to his supporters.

When I took Beam to court, his appeals to white supremacy and violence were the central tenets of his message. "Enough of this backing up and retreating," Louis Beam told the members of his Texas Emergency Reserve militia in 1981. "Enough of this lip service and no action. It's time to begin to train. It is time to begin to reclaim this country for white people. Now I want you to understand that they're not going to give it back to us. If you want it, you're gonna have to get it the way the founding fathers got it—Blood! Blood! Blood! The founding fathers shed their blood to give you this country, and if you want to hold on to it, you're gonna have to shed some of yours.

"Never let any race but the white race rule this country."

That racist message limited his popular appeal. Similar messages from others met with similarly limited success. Few people rallied to the likes of the Posse Comitatus, The Order, or the Aryan Nations when, during the farm crisis of the 1980s, they tried to bring embittered farmers into the fold by telling them that a Communist-Jewish-federal government conspiracy was responsible for destroying the family farm and that the only way they could protect their homes, families, and way of life was to join with the radical right in a battle for survival.

Few people rallied to the white supremacists when they echoed a similar theme to gain converts among blue-collar workers in the Northeast suffering from the decline f the steel industry. And few people rallied to them when they repeated variations on that theme during conflicts between whites and Native Americans over fishing rights in Wisconsin and between environmentalists and loggers over the spotted owl in the Northwest.

Their antigovernment theme resonated with some individuals during the 1980s, but their strident racist and anti-Semitic rhetoric kept Beam and the others at the fringes of the debate.

Nonetheless, the leader of the neo-Nazi National Alliance, William Pierce, who was never an optimist about the prospects for a white revolution, made a jarring prediction: "The win is shifting. The 1990s are going to be different."

Today is different. Beam and his militia followers are repackaging their message. They downplay racism and focus on people's fear and anger. The fear of, and anger at a government that overregulates, overtaxes, and, at times, murders its citizens. The fear of, and anger at, a government that is insensitive, uncaring, and callous to the needs of its people. The fear of, and anger at, a government that takes away a person's right to bear arms so that the country is vulnerable to domination by a New World Order.

Tens of thousands of people are hearing the message and thousands are joining their movement, man unaware that Beam and his fellow travelers are helping to set the agenda.

They are just the type of people racists and neo-Nazi leaders have long been after. They are mainly white and middle class. Most hold jobs, own homes, wear their hair short, don't use drugs, and, for one reason or another, they hate our government.

It is that virulent hatred of the federal government that is driving the militia movement, while at the same time masking its insidious racist underpinnings.

The racist message is never far from the surface. Timothy McVeigh condemned the federal government to anyone who would listen prior to the bombing of the Alfred P. Murrah Federal Building in Oklahoma City. His bible was The Turner Diaries, a fictional story of an Aryan revolt that begins with the bombing of a federal building and ends with the mass annihilation of Jews and blacks.

Hatred for the federal government is not just being preached by professional racists. Americans get a daily dose of antigovernment venom from radio talk shows, respectable lobbying organizations, and even members of Congress that competes in viciousness, mean-spiritedness, and hatefulness with anything said or written by members of the extremist movement. It has helped to create a climate and culture of hate, a climate and culture in which invective and irresponsible rhetoric is routinely use to demonize an opponent, legitimize insensitive stereotypes, and promote prejudice.

This point is not missed by the ideological thinkers behind this frightening movement. William Pierce, the author of 5 The Turner Diaries, pointed out to his followers in 1994 that "most people aren't joiners, but millions of white Americans who five years ago felt so cowed by the government and [the Jewish-] controlled media that they were afraid to agree with us are becoming fed up, and their exasperation is giving them courage."

Hatred and distrust of government are running so deep that many militia members believe that federal agents exploded the Oklahoma City bomb and murdered innocent children to discredit the militia movement and to facilitate passage of an antiterrorist crime bill. They want to reclaim their America with bullets and blood, not ballots and bluster. Ammunition stockpiles are brimming full as militia groups across the country prepare for a war "to protect citizens from their government." John Trochmann, founder of the militia of Montana, said, "We don't want bloodshed. We want to use the ballot box and the jury box. We don't want to go to the cartridge box. But we will if we have to."

I have had an all-too-close relationship with the type of fanatics who are seeking to exploit the militia movement. Because of my work against them, they have tried to kill me. In 1983, they burned the office where I work. In 1984, they came on my property to shoot me. In 1986, they plotted to blow me up with a military rocket. In 1995, they tried to build a bomb like the one that destroyed the Oklahoma City federal building to level my office. Twelve have been imprisoned for these crimes. Four await trial.

Since 1979, my associate and I at the Klanwatch Project of the Southern Poverty Law Center have been monitoring organized racists and far-right extremists through an intensive intelligence operation. Our investigative staff gathers its information from public sources, recorded speeches and publications of the leaders and groups we monitor law enforcement sources, court depositions, Internet postings, informers, and, in some cases, carefully conducted undercover operations. Our data, computerized and cross-referenced, now contain 12,094 photographs and videos and 65,891 entries on individuals and events. We share much of this information with more than six thousand law enforcement sources through our quarterly Intelligence Report. Prosecutors have used information our intelligence staff has gathered to help convict more than twenty white supremacists.

In October 1994, I wrote Attorney General Janet Reno to alert her to the danger posed by the growing number of radical militia groups. I had learned that some of the country's most notorious racists and neo-Nazis were infiltrating the leadership of the so-called citizen militias.

They are men who believe that we are in the middle of a "titanic struggle" between white Aryans, God's chosen people, and Jews, the children of Satan.

Their blueprint for winning the struggle is found in The Turner Diaries, the story of a race war that leads to the downfall of our government.

I told the attorney general that this "mixture of armed groups and those who hate is a recipe for disaster."

Six months later, 169 people lay dead. Whether the federal government, with its vast resources, could have done something to prevent the bombing if they had taken my warning seriously is something I can't claim to know.

But I do know the Oklahoma City tragedy was not an isolated event. Similar fanatics with close ties and fueled by the same missionary zeal are at work.

In June 1995, an open letter to me was published in Resistance, a widely circulated newsletter of an extremist group. It began"

Dear Morris:

Our future is Oklahoma City. I have a deep and abiding faith in the ultimate depravity of mankind. There will be no brotherhood, Morris, only racial hatred and contempt and fear and loathing and rage until one side or the other in this titanic struggle has perished completely. Count on it, my friend. There is a cruel, cold time coming.

We can make your liberal New World order pay for every inch of America in violence and pain and anguish until the ground is sodden with the blood and the tears of my dying race; until the land and the skies of North America are so poisoned with the emissions of the White man's death struggle that you and your kind cannot breathe.

America is at a very serious crossroads. We are deeply divided along racial, political, economic, and class lines. Fear, anger, and paranoia prevail tall too often.

The militia warriors fear the most and hate the most.

The have killed before. And they will kill again.

Rocky Mountain Rendezvous

They began arriving at Estes Park on Thursday, October 22, 1992. They came separately, and in pairs and threesomes. They came in cars, pickup trucks, and vans. Some flew in for the event that would come to be known as the Rocky Mountain Rendezvous.

It was a true cross-section of the far0right movement.

There was Louis Beam, of course, who came down from Idaho. So did Richard Butler, the founder of the Aryan Nations, and Tom Stetson, the leader of the Concerned Citizens of Idaho, the American Christian Patriots, and the Sovereign Citizens of America Network.

Red Beckman, longtime tax protester and leader of the so-called fully informed jury movement, came from Montana, as did Jubilee writer Chris Temple. The Jubilee's publisher, Paul Hall, was there from California, and Larry Pratt, founder of Gun Owners of America, came in from Virginia. Identity leader Charles Weisman of Minnesota was there. So, too, was Earl Jones, head of the Christian Crusade for Truth, who came up from New Mexico. Christian Identity minister James Bruggeman arrived from North Carolina, as did attorney Kirk Lyons, who had boasted that the number one priority of his CAUSE Foundation, an organization that offers legal support to extremist organizations, was to "sue the federal government back to the Stone Age."(CAUSE stands for Canada, Australia, United States, South Africa, and Europe—everywhere that "kindred" white people are found.)

Identity adherents Doug Evers of Wisconsin, John Nelson of Colorado, and Doug Pue of Arizona, also came. As did Beam's colleague John Trochmann and Trochmann's nephew Randy, who drove in from Montana.

The meeting was really extraordinary. It managed to bring together various factions of the hard extremist right into a kind of tacit agreement.

That fact was not lost on those who attended the Rendezvous....

At the conclusion of the conclave, it was clear those in attendance were feeling good about themselves and the movement's future.

"The world today sees a ragtag band that they would mock. Their laughter does not bother me," concluded Peters. "[T]hey may chide us and they may think they have the power in their riches, in their accumulated media. [But] may me leave this assembly knowing who has the greater power."

Pastor Charles Weisman of Minnesota, who chaired the Divine Ways and Means Committee, proclaimed in a similar vein, "[We] are in the process of growing into a Christian civil body politic. We're at an immature state right now, but we're in that process, growing into it... taking dominion once again. [W]hen the body is mature enough, we will be ready to punish all disobedience."

At Estes Park, the movement changed from a disparate, fragmented group of pesky—and at times dangerous—gadflies to serious, armed political challenge to the state itself.

During that weekend in the Rockies, a network of militant antigovernment zealots was created. Alliances were formed from diverse factions: Identity, Posse Comitatus, the Klan, Aryan Nations, reconstructionists and other fundamentalist Christians, neo-Nazis, tax resisters, Second Amendment advocates, and antiabortion extremists.

The Rocky Mountain Rendezvous that was held in tranquil Estes Park, Colorado, was a watershed for the racist right. Whether they knew that at the time doesn't matter. They know it now.

Source: Dees, Morris with James Corcoran. Gathering Storm: America's Militia Threat. New York: HarperCollins Publishers, Inc. 1996.

Stupid Is As Stupid Does!
Robert Lambert, Jr.

My life changed forever on July 9, 1989. The clouds had been gathering for more than two years. My monsoon season started on that day. The rain was to continue for another two years.

The 9th was a Sunday. I worked from 6 a.m. until 1 p.m. that day. I managed a store in Sacramento, California for Bi County Pools. My chores were in the country, finishing Saturday's pool route. After almost ten years of doing this same route, the task had progressed from merely routine, to mindlessly mundane. Twenty minutes, or so, at each pool, and twenty minutes driving to the next. I always, I mean always, drank a beer, or two, or three, while on the route. July 9th was a short day, probably a two 16oz. Old English day.

I arrived home around one thirty, after my usual stop for an after work half pint of Jack Daniels. I was a drunk, but I was not intoxicated when everything came down. I know about denial. I understand the principle, and I have practiced that fine art, but in this instance, I can only say that I wish to God I could use the crutch of incapacitation to explain what happened. I can't, for in my alcoholic existence, was doing nothing more than getting normal. I may have been more careless, had for some strange reason, alcohol been denied me that day. I have thought this out. I don't believe I am in a state of denial, in regards to my mind set, on that fateful day. Just the facts ma'am.

Steve was prone on the sofa. He had stayed out all night discoing. I used to give him the business about always striking out with the chicks. I was very close to Steve, I loved him like the brother that I never had. The feeling was mutual, he was my roommate, Steve didn't drink, in fact, he used to bitch about my drinking habits. He had been up all night, we had both been on a two week coke run. Steve was seven years my junior.

The young man was sniveling on the sofa, not asleep, but moaning and whining about how tired he was. I went to bed early that Saturday night, I knew I had to work the next day. I sat in a recliner next to the sofa relaxing with a cocktail in hand, giving Steve a hard time about being a big pussy. This went on for a few hours. I finished the J.D. and started drinking a couple God awful Coors someone had left in the refrigerator. I was not drunk! Considering my lifestyle, this was a mild relaxing Sunday afternoon.

Around 4 p.m. I got a little restless, and not wanting to waste what turned out to be my only half day off, I got the bright idea for us to take the 22's to the orchard, and shoot around some. I could see from the beginning, it was going to take some doing to get the little puke on his feet and out the door. I am a salesman, I was a practicing salesman at the time. I started in on lazy Steven.

Steve has an I.Q. of 140, he is the most arrogant, stubborn individual I have ever had the pleasure to know. He started to play the "I don't have to" game, just to spite me. I talked him into doing some of my coke, (real tough) that got him sitting up, a joint helped his disposition also. I brought my weapon into the living room, and began to clean it. Steve produced his rifle also. I figured we would be busting caps within the hour.

The semi-automatic Remington Nylon 66 I owned has it's magazine in the stock. The rifle holds fourteen rounds, loaded through an opening in the butt of the weapon. It is a neat little rifle, but it takes time to load individual rounds. I solved that problem by developing my own speed loads. One McDonalds milkshake straw holds seven 22 long rifle rounds. You removed the tape from the end of the straw, and dump those suckers into the magazine, in two shakes the magazine is fully loaded.

California Fish and Game regulations state that it is legal to transport a weapon to the field with the magazine loaded, as long as your intent is to hunt, and there is not a round in the chamber. The place we were going has numerous jack rabbit critters scampering around the area. On occasion we would get shots off from the road, while still in the truck. I loaded the magazine because of this possibility and also to give me two extra straws for speed loads. Loading the magazine was the mistake of my life!

By this time it was going on 5 p.m. I had cleaned and oiled the weapon, snapping the bolt back several times to work in the lubricant. The rifle was (naturally) unloaded during the cleaning and oiling procedure. To the best of my recollection, I loaded the magazine, put the safety on, and set the rifle aside. We were within minutes of moving out. Then came the knock at the door.

It was Joey, good old speed freak Joey, Steve's friend, not mine. Joey's arrival gave Steve the perfect excuse to start the "I don't have to" game all over again. We were almost out the door, this new development ticked me off a little. I invited Joey to come with us, but he declined, and plopped himself down in front of the T.V. Days later, Joey was to tell me, he had been watching "the bloodiest war movie I have ever seen" when it all came down.

After a few minutes of fruitless cajoling, I told Steve I was going with or without him. I picked up the weapon, bracing the butt of the rifle on my hip. I stood in front of him. He was sitting up on the sofa with his hands interlocked behind his head. I was turned profile to Steve, the weapon braced on my hip with the barrel pointed upward.

"Come on scum, we were almost out the door!" I said (or something to that effect).

Steve looked up at me, hands behind his head, he did not say anything, he just gave me his, "I'll go when I am good and ready, so, how do you like me now?" kind of smile. I lowered the barrel, leveled the weapon on his chest, and pulled the trigger.

I did not hear the report, my senses registered only on the muzzle flash. Talk about the surprise of one's life! I experienced an immediate cold sensation in the pit of my stomach, then the thought processes began. Why was there a round in the chamber? Why wasn't the safety on? Oh my God!

Steve's hands came down, the smile left his face, and he looked up at me.

"You fool, you shot me!"

The inflection of his voice was more indignant than angry. Steve's eyes began to roll up, he gasped for breath.

"Oh God! Steve, I'm sorry!"

I knelt down and lifted his T-shirt. I saw a small hole in his chest between his fifth and sixth ribs, no blood, only a small black hole. Steve began to panic, he was trying to get up. I held him down, and told him not to move, that he would be alright! I was highly excited and upset thirty seconds into the incident, but I did not panic. Joey was now standing behind me. I told him to make sure Steve didn't move, and I would go call an ambulance.

I was renting a two bedroom house, pretty nice place, but no phone. I sprinted around the corner to Marvin the landlord's house. I burst through the front door and grabbed the phone, there by shattering he and his wife's quiet Sunday afternoon. 911 is a great idea, I don't know if I could have dialed more than three numbers.

Marvin was a funny old bird, ex-Marine, he served in China during World War II. I was highly excited, I believed Steve to be dying. I wasn't very far off the mark. Marvin and Louise stared at me.

"Marvin! I shot Steve!" I shouted. "I need help, come over and help me!"

My plea was met by Marvin's blank stare. Louise snapped him out of it by saying,

Marvin! Get over there now!"

Any dialogue included in this narrative is pretty much paraphrased, and falls into the best of my recollection category. Except for the verbal exchange between Steve and I immediately following the shooting, I am not able to recall verbatim all the words spoken.

Marysville hospital is only six blocks away from my house, Thank God! Marvin and I went back to the house. I ran, Marvin walked. Steve was struggling for breath, his head turning from side to side. He was extremely frightened. I will always remember the look in his eyes. Joey stepped aside. I took Steve's hand, I kept telling him not to move and how sorry I was, that he would be all right. The police arrived before the paramedics.

When I heard the siren I gave Steve back to Joey, and went outside to move my dog from the front porch to the backyard. Marvin was on the porch, he had come in the house, surveyed the situation, done absolutely nothing, and gone back outside. I don't know what I had expected Marvin to do. I wanted someone to help me. To make Steve better. To make it all go away. Retrospect is a tricky concept, I was overdosing on reality at the time.

I was descending the porch steps with my dog as the officer parked in front of the house. I noticed as he exited the squad car, that he was using the vehicle to shield his body. I then realized the officer didn't know the circumstances pertaining to the shooting. I told the 911 operator that I had shot my friend, but I am not sure that I had included the adjective "accidental" in describing my supreme indiscretion. Obviously the officer had received only a "Shots Fired" call. Marvin knew the officer by name and set him straight, (that was Marvin's one positive contribution to my nightmare). The officer came out from behind his squad car. I explained the situation. I told him where to find Steve, then I put the dog in the back yard.

When I came back into the house the officer was standing in the middle of the living room looking at Steve. I felt that once an authority figure was on the scene things would be under control, first aid would be administered, a bandage, a blanket to ward off shock, a tourniquet, something. No such luck, the police do not administer first aid, that is not their primary responsibility, nor their forte.

I was highly excited, but still lucid. I knelt in front of Steve and held his hand. Joey drifted off into a corner, trying to blend into the furnishings. He had gotten out of jail only two days earlier.

Steve was looking bad. All the color had drained from his face. I knew he was going into shock, (If he wasn't already there). Steve was breathing hard and still trying to move!

"You're going to be OK buddy, just please don't move!" I said.

I looked over my shoulder and shouted.

"Officer!"

No response, a detached gaze.

"Officer! Help him!"

The cop's expression never changed. He stepped forward, bent over, and put his hand on Steve's cheek. He reminded me of a parent checking his child for a fever.

"You'll be all right son," he said calmly.

He then stood up, stepped back and resumed his post in the center of the room. Upon reflection, I realize his action was motivated by the look in my eyes, and the inflection in my voice. He made his one humanitarian gesture for my benefit, not Steve's. The officer may have felt that Steve was going to die anyway. A fair assumption at that point in the proceedings.

The paramedics arrived complete with black bags, computerized monitor, and a collapsible gurney. Although I took some comfort in the fact that the medical professions were finally on the scene, I can not say I felt at all assured of Steve's survival. I, too, was going into shock. The paramedic's presence removed the one distraction that had held my mind in check. I had nothing to do now. They would take charge of Steve. I moved as far away from where they treated Steve as I could. I turned my back on the scene and looked out the living room window. That is when the hyperventilation started. I began repeating, "Oh my God! Oh my God!" over and over again between convulsive gulps of air.

As the paramedics worked on Steve, the worst part of my unreal ordeal started. Steve was moaning quite loudly as the medics were strapping him on the gurney. God, how that sound hurt me! I really did love that guy. He had done so much for me, and I had done this to him. I knew too well how badly Steve had been hit. "I've killed him!" That one thought was forming into a certainty inside my confused brain.

There were now three policemen on the premises, the interrogation began.

"Did you two have an argument?" one cop asked.

"No sir, I love that guy!"

Hyperventilating.

"Was this the weapon?" queried another officer.

He was holding Steve's Rugar. It was modified to resemble an assault rifle. Thirty round banana clip, and folding stock.

"No sir, here it is." I said.

I retrieved my Nylon 66 from the floor beside the sofa.

"Be careful, the safety is off and there is still a round in the chamber."

As I presented the (murder?) weapon, my warning struck me as absurdly ironic. Why had I not considered these two fundamental aspects of firearm safety before I killed my best friend?

"I didn't know there was a round in the chamber! I didn't know there was a round in the chamber!" I said, as if by repetition of that disclaimer I might somehow vindicate myself.

"That is how these things happen, Robert." The tone of the officer was similar to that of a coach admonishing a team member for an error in ball handling.

"How much have you had to drink?" asked the same officer.

"Bingo! This is it!" I thought.

"A couple of beers, sir."

I was still hyperventilating. But I delivered the fallacy with conviction, S.O.P.

"Step over here please. Watch my finger without moving your head please."

He moved his first digit back and forth before my eyes. The other officers watched from directly behind each of the tester's shoulders. Six eyes scrutinized my two. The first and only three man drunk test that I have ever experienced. Judgment was swift. I was proclaimed sober after that one test. I am certain I would not have passed a breath test. I figure my eyes were so dilated from the effects of shock and cocaine, that the test was not an accurate assessment of my overall sobriety that day.

However, (to even this day) I do not believe my consumption of alcohol to have been excessive, and therefore, not a major contributing factor in my incredible carelessness. As I stated previously, I may have behaved even more carelessly had alcohol been denied me that day. Such was the status of my alcohol existence. I believe that the frat-house party atmosphere Steve and I were living in, contributed most to the tragedy. We played with guns.

Steve was wheeled out, still moaning. There was an I.V. in his arm, the computerized monitor lay across his thighs. The cloths the paramedics cut off Steve, and the refuse of various medical paraphernalia lay scattered about the floor. Steve's blood stained the inside arm of the sofa.

"What is this shit?" I thought. "Take me away, punish me! I just stupidly killed my best friend! They're taking him away to be buried! Look!"

I was not aware, until Steve was taken away, that the round had passed through his body. The officers informed me of that gruesome fact. We began a search for the bullet. The task of examining the area of the sofa where Steve had been seated was a distraction, it calmed me somewhat. The mood and bearing of the officers was overwhelmingly casual. It was not until some days later that I realized those professionals were trained to defuse panicky situations in this manner. It was as if I had just downed a buck, and my hunting buddies and I were examining the entrance and exit wounds on the carcass. The search was casual. We did not find the offending projectile.

The bullet struck Steve between the fifth and sixth ribs, on the left side of the chest, ricocheted off one of those ribs, on the lateral track across his torso, and exited through his right side. In the process of exiting, the round destroyed Steve's gall bladder, punctured some intestines, grazed a lung, and damaged his liver.

The distance from muzzle to impact was approximately twelve inches. I was told by one officer, that had the round entered two inches lower; Steve would have been defecating into a colostomy bag for the rest of his life. Two inches higher, and there would be no need to worry about Steve's defecation habits, he would have been dead. I came that close to killing Steve! Thank God, the .22 long rifle round was not a hollow point!

With Steve evacuated. The officers were finishing their investigation. The three huddled for a conference. With nothing to occupy me, I returned to the window. I looked out the window, turning my back on the scene of the crime. "Oh my God Oh my God!" I was hyperventilating again in earnest and beginning to feel faint. I glanced over my shoulder at their conference. One of them caught sight of my face.

"Are you going to be all right, Robert?"

Silly question.

"I don't know." I said. "Can you get me a chaplain?"

I have always been one to handle immediate stressful situations rather well. I have never panicked in my life. Even when informed of my father's death; I was able to channel my emotions toward concern for the other people affected by the consequences of that tragedy. Now, it was impossible to arrange my thoughts; emotion and shock overrode any cohesive logic. I wanted to be taken away and punished for my sin. The fact that I had very likely killed my best friend was a reality my overloaded mind could neither accept or comprehend.

The police were prepared to leave, the officer who asked if I was all right informed me one of them would stay and talk to me. I knew then I was not to be charged; I was not going with them. The officer that stayed was a part time minister, his kindness was not an official act.

He asked me to step out on the porch. I then experienced an attack of extreme hyperventilation. He ordered me to breath, my inhalations slowed somewhat.

"What are you thinking about?" he asked.

"My work," I said. "I have to tell the store owners what happened, Steve is my repairman, I manage a store in Sacramento for Bi County Pools." Steve and I worked together, partners, more than manager and employee.

It was strange the way my mind was working. The officer was trying to make me think. To talk me out of the numbness of shock. He asked me the owner's name, then he asked me to spell their last names. It took about three tries for each name. He offered to take me to the hospital to check on Steve's condition. I declined, stating I wished to wait and ride over with my employers. The officer told me that after I got back from the hospital, the chaplain would stop by. We agreed on between eight and nine o'clock. The chaplain never showed.

As he descended the porch steps to leave, he asked if there was anything else he could do for me.

As I looked into his blue cop eyes, I asked, "Officer, is my friend going to die?"

"I've seen a lot of gun shot wounds like that one, son, your buddy will be OK."

I knew, (though the tone of his voiced, and the look in his eyes, did not give him away), he was lying through his teeth. I loved him for that lie.

That night was the loneliest I have ever spent.

I wrote a long letter to my ex-girlfriend, the letter began: "I have just done the worst thing of my life."

I drank, a mere half pint, when a quart might have been the appropriate prescription,

I did go to the hospital with the owners, Steve was in surgery, (naturally). The tale of what took place after the officer-minister and I talked, I'll save for another day,

I estimate the time of impact at about 5:30 Sunday afternoon. I called the hospital at 11:30 that evening, Steve was still in surgery; that fact did not help me sleep; but he was still alive. I went to work in the morning unaware of Steve's status. It was 10:30 Monday morning before I was informed Steve T. Warren would live.

August 1994

Although close to seven years have now gone past since my supreme indiscretion, I still physically flinch when I recall that muzzle flash. It took me five years to acknowledge the anniversary date of the shooting. It would be the end of July or even early August before the passing of July 9th would occur to me. This story was (in part) a product of my recognition of the fifth year anniversary; on the actual anniversary date.

Older now, and (hopefully) somewhat wiser, I realize my drinking did play the major role in contributing to my insanity that day. I now understand that I was living a daily insanity back then, due to my alcoholism. I am no longer in denial about being in denial.

Perhaps time does in fact heal all wounds, but mine has not callused over yet. I am delighted however, that my wound is no longer raw and bleeding. I believe the writing of this chronicle was a giant leave toward personal healing. Life truly is for learning. As one very insightful individual once said, "The antidote to ignorance is experience."

The Battle over the Brady Bill and the Future of Gun Control Advocacy

Copyright © 1995 Fordham University School of Law & Richard M. Aborn

I. Introduction

The United States of America has earned the ignoble distinction of being considered the most violent country in the world. All too often the major dailies chronicle killings that take place in war torn regions of the world. Those dailies do not report, however, that fifteen children lose their lives to gunfire each and every day in the United States. [1] Among all age groups, approximately 103 persons are killed each day by gunfire. [2] The violence is now so widespread that we have almost become numb to the numbers and the statistics.

On a per capita basis, United States citizens kill each other with firearms at a rate of 14.8 per hundred thousand. [3] Among American males aged 15 - 24, the firearm death rate is much higher, skyrocketing to an astonishing 50.9 per hundred thousand. [4] In fact, firearm homicide is now the leading cause of death for African-American males between the ages of 15 and 34, [5] as well as the second leading cause of death for all persons between the ages of [begin pg. 418] 10 and 34.

[6] If current trends continue, firearms will cause more deaths than automobiles by the year 2003. [7]

Additionally, handguns are the principal instrumentality responsible for the increase in homicides in the country. From 1987 to 1992, murders committed with all weapons other than handguns actually declined by 7%, while murders with handguns rose 52%. [8] In addition to the 15,377 murders that occurred, nearly 1 million Americans had the horrifying experience of being the victim of a violent gun crime in 1992; this number is almost 50% higher than the average for the previous five years. [9] In comparison, the rate of violent crime committed with other weapons has steadily declined. [10]

Despite this phenomenon, which is by no means recent, the purchase of a handgun was a relatively simple endeavor until late 1993. Prior to that date, nothing in the federal law prevented an individual from obtaining a gun simply by filling out a form which stated that the potential purchaser was not a felon, ever dishonorably discharged from a branch of the armed services, under indictment, or a fugitive. A purchaser would then be permitted to purchase as many handguns as he or she wished -- prior to and without any verification of this information whatsoever. [11]

Congress finally limited handgun purchases on November 30, 1993, when President Clinton signed the Brady Handgun Violence Prevention Act (the Brady Bill) [12] into law. [13] This law requires that up to five business days pass between the time an individual seeks [begin pg. 419] to buy a handgun and the time that the purchase transpires. During those five days, local law enforcement officials must conduct a "reasonable background check" of the applicant. [14] Given the ever-escalating state of handgun violence in this country, one would think that the Brady Bill, a reasonable and mild step toward the control of such violence, would have very quickly passed through Congress and been signed into law. This sequence of events, however, did not occur. Although the measure was immensely popular in the polls, an arduous political struggle ensued before Congress finally passed it.

The battle over the Brady Bill was a long and torturous struggle from its introduction in 1987, to its final passage on November 24, 1993. During that period, the Brady Bill became one of the most contested issues in the country, dividing gun control supporters and opponents with a vehemence generally reserved for the most contentious social issues. The debate that surrounded the Bill provided the country with the opportunity to discuss numerous issues related to gun control, such as the need for a background check of a would-be handgun purchaser, bans on semi-automatic assault weapons and Saturday Night Specials, and the licensing and registration of handguns.

The debate also irrefutably framed the issue as a political one. Gun control opponents were far better organized and financed than gun control advocates. As a result, the opponents convinced many members of Congress that, although those opposed to gun control represented a minority view, they were a zealous single issue constituency that posed a political threat to any member who might support gun control laws. [begin pg. 420]

In light of the above, this Essay reviews the current state of gun control in this country. Part II chronicles the long legislative history of the Brady Law, including the lessons that gun control advocates learned from that struggle. Part III examines the regulatory changes that the Clinton Administration has instituted in order to broaden gun control beyond the Brady Law. Part IV summarizes gun control legislation that has been introduced since the passage of the Brady Law. Finally, Part V concludes with a proposal for future gun control advocacy.

II. The History of the Brady Bill

A. The 100th, 101st & 102d Congresses

Two Ohio Democrats, Representative Edward F. Feighan and Senator Howard M. Metzenbaum, introduced the Brady Bill for the first time in the 100th Congress on February 4, 1987. [15] As originally structured, the Bill required a seven-day waiting period between the time a person applies for a handgun and the time the sale may be consummated. [16] In June of the following year, the House Judiciary Committee passed the Bill on a voice vote as an amendment to the Omnibus Drug Initiative Act. [17] In its first floor vote on September 15, 1988, however, the Brady Bill failed in the House by a vote of 228 -182. [18]

Representative Feighan and Senator Metzenbaum reintroduced the Brady measure in the 101st Congress, on January 4, 1989. [19] The 1989 version of the Bill provided that the mandatory waiting period would cease once a nationwide instant felon identification system becomes operational. [20] On July 24, 1990, the House Judiciary Committee again approved the Bill, [21] but it never reached the floor for a vote by the full House.

In an effort to get the Bill to the floor of the House for a vote, supporters attempted to attach it to an omnibus anti-crime bill that was certain to receive a floor vote. This strategy failed, however, when Speaker of the House Thomas Foley implied that the legislation was too controversial to bring to the floor. The Speaker was criticized for this action, which was perceived by some to be a favor to gun control opponents, notably the National Rifle Association (the NRA). The Brady Bill again died when the 101st Congress adjourned.

Buoyed by the growing support for the Brady Bill among the general public, Representative Feighan and Senator Metzenbaum reintroduced the Bill in the 102d Congress. [22] Once again, the Bill moved successfully through the House Judiciary Committee, [23] and finally, on May 8, 1991, the House of Representatives passed the Brady Bill by a vote of 239 -186. [24] In less than three years, the Brady Bill had picked up an additional forty-two votes. Obviously, support for the gun control movement was growing, and the country was demanding a Congressional response. This growing support, however, did not deter those opposed to handgun control. The anti-control proponents not only rallied supporters, but also used effective lobbying to capitalize on Congressional procedural rules. The gun lobby clearly understood that the fight for the Brady Bill was anything but over.

The Bill that was passed by the House in 1991 required a seven-day waiting period before a purchaser could take possession of a handgun. [25] During that period, local law enforcement officials would have the opportunity to conduct a background check to ensure that federal or state law would not bar that individual from purchasing a gun. [26]

In the Senate, the Brady Bill was considered as part of an omnibus anti-crime bill (the Crime Bill) that had been introduced by Democrat Senator Joseph Biden of Delaware on June 6, 1991. [27] Concerned that it no longer had the votes to defeat the Bill, the NRA tried to block its consideration. When this effort began to fail, the NRA offered to cease its opposition in exchange for weakening the Bill. Unsuccessful at this strategy as well, the NRA tried a last-ditch effort to stop the Bill's passage. In the early morning hours of June 28, 1991, Senator Ted Stevens, a Republican from Alaska, offered a substitute amendment to the Crime Bill called the Stevens amendment to replace the Brady Bill with an "instant [begin pg. 422] check" bill. [28] The fatal flaw in the instant check bill was that there was no technology available to conduct the background check instantaneously. The instant check bill would have completely gutted the Brady Bill by eliminating the waiting period, thereby depriving law enforcement officials of the time necessary to conduct a background check of the purchaser. Fortunately, this amendment failed by a critical 54 - 44 vote. [29]

The vote on the Stevens amendment, which occurred in the very early morning hours of the June 28, 1992, was followed that afternoon by an announcement by Senators Robert Dole of Kansas, an opponent of the Bill, and Howard Metzenbaum of Ohio, the Bill's sponsor; they had reached a compromise. [30] This compromise changed the waiting period from seven days to five "working days" and then provided that the waiting period would no longer apply once an accurate instant background check system becomes feasible. [31] This measure, which was substantially different from the version of the Brady Bill approved by the House, was passed by the Senate 67-32. [32] The Bill was referred to a House-Senate Conference Committee to reconcile the differences in the two versions of the Bill. [33]

In its final Conference Report, the Conference Committee agreed to accept the version of the measure that was passed by the Senate. Once the Committee issued the Report, it was put once again to the House and the Senate for approval. Although obtaining this approval is normally a perfunctory process, nothing in the process of the passage of the Brady Bill had been perfunctory -- including ratification of the Conference Report. While the House of Representatives approved the Conference Report on November 26, 1991, [34] the

Senate did not vote on final passage of the Report, because it could not muster sufficient votes to end the debate on the Report.

Under the Senate Rules, which are designed to encourage debate, the Senate may not vote on a bill or amendment until 60% of the body agrees to end the debate. [35] This gives a minority of senators the power to block consideration of a measure by invoking what has come to be known as a "gentlemen's filibuster." [36] Lest one has visions of weary-eyed senators speaking in a continuous dialogue through the day and night, a "gentlemen's filibuster" permits the Senate to consider any other matter while the "filibuster" continues. [37] Sixty senators must agree to end the debate in order to "invoke cloture" and end the filibuster. [38]

A sixty-vote threshold is required to put contested legislation to a final vote, even though the vote on the vast majority of legislation that comes before the Senate requires only a simple majority. Stated another way, it takes nine more votes to end debate than are required to pass a bill. This ability to filibuster has often been used by a minority to thwart the will of the majority. [39]

The first attempt in the Senate to invoke cloture on the Crime Bill Conference Report occurred on November 27, 1991. [40] Because of partisan bickering and the inclusion of the Brady handgun control language in the Crime Bill, supporters were able to garner only 49 votes out of the required 60, and thus the motion to end the debate failed. [41] The crime issue remained stalemated until March of the following year. When the filibuster persisted in March, 1992, [42] it appeared that the approaching presidential election [43] and the inclusion of the Brady language made it very unlikely that the Crime Bill, including the Brady Bill, would become law. Some unusual action would be necessary to pass the

Bill before the 102d Congress adjourned in the fall and before the presidential election.

One of the principal obstacles to the passage of the Brady Bill was that opponents continually linked it to some form of comprehensive crime legislation, in order to use purported opposition to the underlying bill as a subterfuge to vote against the Brady Bill. [44] Additionally, it became apparent that comprehensive gun control legislation might be easier to pass if gun control assumed an independent identity as a political issue. According to the polls, this approach was feasible. Therefore, in order to prompt a vote on the Brady Bill and to force the presidential candidates to take a position on it, Handgun Control, Inc. mounted an effort to split the Brady Bill from the Crime Bill.

On September 1, 1992, Handgun Control launched a national campaign called "Free the Brady Bill." Conducting simultaneous press conferences in thirteen states, Brady Bill supporters urged Congress to separate the Brady Bill from the Crime Bill and vote on it immediately. Then-candidate Clinton immediately endorsed over our efforts. President Bush remained silent.

Although the "Free the Brady Bill" campaign received enormous attention throughout September, 1992, and lasted until the 102d Congress adjourned in early October, ultimately the campaign to pass the Brady Bill failed. Nonetheless, the campaign succeeded in defining gun control as a key issue in the 1992 presidential election. Most importantly, when Bill Clinton was elected President, the gun control movement had a supportive occupant in the White House for the first time in history. This would [begin pg. 425] lead to significant progress, both legislatively and from a regulatory standpoint, in the coming two years.

B. The 103d Congress: The Effect of the Clinton Election

When the 103d Congress convened, a record number of sponsors reintroduced the Brady Bill into Congress. This time the House sponsor was Congressman Charles Schumer, a Democrat from New York, and Senator Howard Metzenbaum once again introduced the Bill in the Senate. [45] A week earlier in his State of the Union Address, President Clinton had declared to rousing applause: "If you'll pass the Brady Bill, I'll sure sign it." [46] For the first time, a sitting President had stated that he was willing to sign such a bill. In addition, in the 103d Congress, unlike in previous Congresses, the Brady Bill would finally stand on its own, unencumbered by any crime legislation.

On October 29, 1993, the House Judiciary Subcommittee on Crime and Criminal Justice met to consider Representative Schumer's proposed bill. [47] The Subcommittee adopted an amendment to clarify that the instant check system would be based on the Interstate Identification Index, [48] unless the Attorney General determined that another system would be preferable. [49] The Subcommittee then favorably reported the Bill out of committee by a vote of 10 -3. [50] On November 4, 1993, the full Judiciary Committee of the House passed the Bill. In the process, it also adopted an amendment to it permitting persons who had been denied the opportunity to purchase a firearm on account of an error in criminal history records to sue the appropriate government agency to force it to correct the records. [51] Although this amendment was adopted, several other amendments were defeated both by voice vote and roll call vote. [52] The Committee then favorably reported out the Bill by a roll call vote of 23 - 12. [53]

On November 10, 1993, the full House debated and voted on the Brady Bill. Bill McCollum, a Republican Representative from Florida, offered an amendment that would preempt all state and local waiting periods and licensing laws. This amendment was defeated, 175 - 257. [54] Another amendment, offered by Representative George Gekas of Pennsylvania, required that the waiting period sunset in five years -- whether or not the instant check system was operational. This sunset provision was adopted, 236 - 198, [55] and the Brady Bill, as amended, passed the House, 238 -189. [56]

After intense negotiations, the Senate agreed to vote on a compromise Brady Bill on November 19, 1993. That Bill included language similar to the two amendments to the House bill: preemption of all state and local waiting periods and licensing laws, and sunset of the waiting period in five years whether or not the national instant check system was operational. [57] The agreement allowed two separate votes to delete the sunset and preemption provisions from the Bill. The amendment to delete the sunset language was offered by Senator Howard Metzenbaum, and it failed, 43 -56. [58] The amendment to delete the preemption language was sponsored by Senator George Mitchell, and it passed, 54 - 45. [59] Two attempts to obtain cloture later that day both failed, 57- 42 and 57- 42. [60] After another day of negotiations between Majority Leader George Mitchell and Minority Leader Robert Dole, the Senate finally voted on the amended Brady Bill, and on November 20, 1993, the Brady Bill passed the Senate by a vote of 63 -36. [61]

The House-Senate Conference Committee agreed on final language on Monday, November 22, 1993. The House Rules Committee scheduled a final vote on the Conference Report for later that day. That evening, the

House passed the Brady Bill Conference Report, by a vote of 238 -188. [62] The Senate still needed to confirm the Conference Report; unfortunately, even this seemingly ministerial act was delayed in a final, desperate effort on the part of NRA backers to defeat the Brady Bill.

Senator Dole refused to allow the Senate to act on the Conference Report. Once again, the gun control opposition mounted a filibuster that stymied the Senate. Thanksgiving was approaching, and, as was tradition, the Senate was going to adjourn the week prior to Thanksgiving until after the first of the new year. Brady opponents viewed this as an opportunity to delay final consideration of the legislation in the hope that during the month-long break, the pressure to pass the Bill would abate.

Both the Democratic leadership in the Senate and the Clinton White House, however, were confident that they had secured a sufficient number of votes to pass the Bill, and refused to comply with this strategy. With Senator Dole blocking consideration of the Bill, Senate Majority Leader Mitchell announced that the Senate would reconvene after the Thanksgiving weekend, and continue its consideration of the Brady Bill. Two days of intense negotiations followed, under extreme pressure. The notion that the entire Senate would have to return to Washington after Thanksgiving and stay until the Brady issue was resolved was not terribly inviting. Additionally, and far more importantly, there was a tremendous outburst of anger from Americans across the country. Supporters of the legislation could not believe that, despite the passage of the Brady Bill and the compromises reached, Senator Dole would continue to delay final passage of the Conference Report. The pressure proved to be too much, and Senator Dole relented. Finally, on November 24, 1993, the Senate voted on the Conference Report and passed the Brady Bill by unanimous consent. [63]

In a very emotional ceremony in the East Room of the White House on November 30, 1993, President Clinton signed the Brady Bill into law. [64] The law took effect on February 28, 1994, and its effects were felt immediately.

In its report, The Brady Law: The First 100 Days, the Bureau of Alcohol, Tobacco and Firearms reported that the Brady Law prevented approximately 5% of all attempted handgun purchases because the purchaser was a felon or otherwise prohibited from buying a firearm. [65] Based on this rate and the fact that over two million handguns are sold every year, background checks will likely prevent more than 100,000 criminals from purchasing handguns at retail outlets each year. Clearly, this is not an insignificant number. Additionally, it is impossible to determine the number of criminals who have been dissuaded from attempting to purchase a handgun because they feared a background check.

With the Brady Law, the nation established an affirmative gun control measure for the first time in thirty years. As a result, the nation would stop distributing our society's most deadly consumer product, the handgun, without even verifying whether the would-be purchaser had a criminal record. Through this legislation, the United States had clearly crossed a threshold. Gun control supporters had shown that they could defeat the much vaunted NRA, and the President was now openly challenging the nation to confront the epidemic of gun violence engulfing the entire country. No one was arguing, however, nor had anyone argued, that the Brady Bill alone would be sufficient to end gun violence. While the next great legislative fight would focus on the issue of banning semi-automatic assault weapons, [66] other gun control efforts were also underway on the regulatory front.

III. Regulatory Changes to Gun Control

In May, 1993, the Center to Prevent Handgun Violence, the research, legal advocacy and education affiliate of Handgun Control, submitted a memorandum to the Clinton Administration outlining a number of regulatory steps that could be taken by the Bureau of Alcohol, Tobacco and Firearms to reduce gun violence pursuant to the Bureau's broad regulatory authority. [67] Two of these proposals were put into effect by Presidential Directive on August 11, 1993, in a White House ceremony. The first Directive extended the ban on the importation of semi-automatic assault rifles, which had been signed by President Bush in March, 1989, to include semi-automatic pistols, such as the UZI. [68] The second Presidential Directive required that applications for federal licenses to sell guns be accompanied by a fingerprint check and a photo identification. [69]

Secretary of the Treasury Lloyd Bentsen put into effect on March 1, 1994, a third proposal of the Center to Prevent Handgun Violence. On that date, Bentsen announced that the Department of the Treasury had reclassified combat shotguns, such as the Street-sweeper, [70] Striker-12 and USAS-12, [71] as "destructive devices" under the National Firearms Act, thereby restricting future sales of those weapons. [72]

Finally, on May 27, 1994, President Clinton stopped the importation of Chinese-made guns [73] that had been modified slightly in order to avoid the assault weapon import ban, which had permitted the importation of non-sporting long guns.

The Center to Prevent Handgun Violence proposed a number of other regulations in its memorandum to the Administration that still need to be enacted in order to further diminish the illegal supply of guns. These proposals include, first, implementation of regulations to require gun dealers to meet certain minimum security standards to deter theft. Such a standard could be as simple as locking guns in a vault at night, thus reducing the increasing number of thefts of guns from gun stores.

Second, the Center's memorandum proposed requiring handgun purchasers to present proof of current residency at the time of application to buy a handgun. The necessity of this measure is demonstrated by the fact that Colin Ferguson, the alleged shooter in the Long Island Railroad case, [74] was able to purchase a gun over-the-counter in California. Even though he was a New York resident, he was able to get a California driver's license without showing any proof of residency. He then used the license to purchase the gun that was allegedly used in the shooting. Had he been required to present proof of current residency, he arguably would not have been able to do so, and thus may not have been able to secure that weapon.

Third, the Center's memorandum proposed requiring gun dealers to submit aggregate sales information with a license renewal application. This information would prove that they are actually engaged in the legitimate business of selling firearms as opposed to either stockpiling guns or supplying firearms to the illegal market.

Finally, the Center recommended suspending the licenses of dealers convicted of felonies, pending appeal of their conviction.

While these regulations would reduce the illegal traffic in firearms measurably, gun control advocates should not rely solely on executive action to reach their ultimate goal of comprehensive federal legislation. Advocates must capitalize on the shift in public support toward gun control and use that surge of public opinion to their advantage in the legislative arena.

IV. Politics of the Movement and Recommendations for Future Legislation

The polling data on gun control clearly shows that Americans overwhelmingly support the passage of additional gun control measures. A CNN/USA Today/Gallup poll on December 17, 1993, showed that 81% of the American people support gun registration, [75] and 69% support a limit of one gun purchase per month per person. [76] That same poll also showed that 89% of the American people support mandatory safety training for handgun purchasers. [77] Another poll, conducted by LH Research, Inc. on April 1, 1993, showed that 82% of the American people support the registration of handgun sales, [78] and 67% support one-gun-per-month laws. [79]

On the other hand, one indicator in the gun control area for which public support has decreased is the support for a complete ban on handguns. This support has declined from 43% in 1991 to 39% in 1993. [80] Moreover, there is anecdotal evidence that more and more Americans are buying guns. [81]

Combining this data supports the conclusion that the American people: i) want more gun control; ii) understand that it will not interfere with a law-abiding citizen's ability to acquire a handgun; iii) do not think that it is necessary to ban all handguns; and iv) do not believe that supporting controls over distribution inevitably leads to an outright ban.

Given the amount of gun violence in America and the clear lack of an effective body of federal law regulating the distribution of handguns, as well as the strong support in the polls for gun control, one would think that it would be easy to pass gun control legislation.

But, as we have seen from the difficult journey of the Brady Bill through Congress, [82] this is hardly the case. Gun control advocates make a serious mistake when they rely on the strength of polls to persuade legislators to vote affirmatively for gun control measures. Politicians are not motivated by support for a particular issue in the polls, unless the polls overwhelmingly show that the topic is of "single issue" importance to the voters. There are few such topics, and certainly gun control has never been one. [83] Gun control supporters must understand that the effort to reduce gun violence in this nation is at its core a political struggle. As such, the effort requires nationwide mobilization and a highly concerted effort with the sole goal being effective political action. The opposition has long understood that the key to political power is organization. Gun control advocates must not be so proud that they fail to learn from their adversaries. [84]

It is the responsibility of gun control advocates to state clearly the goals of the movement. Such a policy statement must lay out both legislative and non-legislative goals, and clarify their position on banning all guns. The prospect of a total ban on firearms is the greatest concern for reasonable gun owners, and is the area where the movement is most frequently, and most effectively attacked. This attack is effective not because of the persuasiveness of the other side, but because it is virtually impossible to prove that proponents of gun control do not support a total ban.

A principal problem that has retarded the development of an effective national gun control policy has been the insistence that gun control legislation move forward incrementally. [85] At this pace, it will be well into the next century before the nation has a comprehensive gun control policy. Therefore, it is the intention of Handgun Control, Inc. to change the debate. We intend to reject the incrementalism of the past and adopt a comprehensive approach.

Handgun Control has made its legislative goals quite clear. These goals are contained in legislation that was introduced in the 103d Congress as the Gun Violence Prevention Act of 1994, [86] which has since become widely known as "Brady II." This bill is designed to confront the complexity of the problem honestly and to construct an effective national body of law that will give the country a measurable means of reducing gun violence.

Any national gun control policy must aim to reduce illegal traffic in guns. Approximately 27% of guns used in crime enter the market from over-the-counter sales. Additionally, another 9% are stolen in burglaries every year. [87] Studies and anecdotal information supplied by law enforcement agencies show that gun traffickers most often go to jurisdictions with very weak or nonexistent gun control laws. [88] They then purchase handguns in bulk, using either straw purchasers or phony identification, and transport the weapons and ammunition to jurisdictions with very strict gun control laws. Nothing in current federal law prevents this. There is no federal requirement that a handgun purchaser be licensed, that the sale be registered, that a limit be placed on the number of handguns or rounds of handgun ammunition that can be purchased at any one time, or that there be any restriction on the resale of the handguns by the purchaser to another private individual or individuals.

The Brady II Bill addresses this trafficking problem by establishing a system of state-based licensing and registration throughout the nation. This system would prohibit anyone from selling a handgun to an individual who does not possess a valid state handgun license, and would require that the sale be registered prior to its consummation. [89] The Bill proposes the establishment of federally mandated minimum standards for the issuance of the state license. Under Brady II, the license would not be issued unless:

a) the licensee is at least 21 years of age;

b) the licensee has presented a valid government issued identification card, such as a driver's license or social security card, and proof of current residency within the jurisdiction, such as a utility bill, lease or telephone bill;

c) the licensee has passed a background check based on a fingerprint; and

d) the licensee has passed a safety training course. The license would be valid for a two-year period, and a licensee would be required to report the theft or loss of a handgun to local law enforcement.

The Brady II Bill would also adapt legislation that was passed by the State of Virginia in 1993 for nationwide application. By 1992, Virginia had become the number one source state of guns used in crime in the northeast. In New York City alone, over 40% of the guns used in crime in 1991 had originated in Virginia. [90] In response, then-Governor of Virginia, Douglas Wilder, proposed that the state prohibit the purchase of more than one handgun in a thirty-day period. This proposal, aimed solely at illegal gun trafficking, was opposed adamantly by the gun lobby. This legislative fight garnered national attention, and ultimately it passed. [91] Unfortunately, however, adjacent states continue to permit multiple purchases, and traffickers have simply taken their deadly business elsewhere.

The licensing plan outlined in the Brady II Bill, which is significantly less onerous than obtaining a driver's license or registering a car, will help ensure that an individual seeking to purchase a handgun is doing so for legitimate purposes. The plan will reduce the ability to use aliases supported by false identification and, additionally, will make it significantly more difficult to use a "straw man" to purchase a gun. These goals will be achieved by instituting substantial requirements that must be complied with prior to the completion of the sale.

The registration element will provide both a "paper trail" for investigatory purposes and a deterrent to gun traffickers. Once registration is required, traffickers will be aware that law enforcement will learn the ownership history of a handgun. Thus, the largely correct sense that traffickers now have that law enforcement does not have a viable way of identifying them will be greatly diminished. In order to prevent traffickers from stockpiling guns, a special license would be required for anyone other than a dealer to possess more than twenty firearms or one thousand rounds of ammunition at any one time.

The Brady II Bill would prohibit persons who have been indicted or convicted of attempting to use physical force against another from possessing a handgun. [92] Additionally, anyone under the age of twenty-one would be prohibited from possessing a handgun except under certain circumstances. [93] The Bill also contains a number of reforms for the federal licensing system of weapons sellers. [94] These reforms are designed to ensure that federal license recipients engage in legitimate retail sales and do not supply guns to illegal markets.

The proposed legislation would also help prevent the horrific and often tragic problem of children finding their parents' handguns. The Bill would make it illegal to leave a loaded firearm, or unloaded firearm with ammunition, where a juvenile under the age of sixteen is likely to gain access to it. [95] Thirteen states now provide a penal sanction for anyone who leaves a handgun accessible to a child if the child causes injury with that handgun.

The Brady II Bill also proposes the elimination of another category of guns -- Saturday Night Specials. [96] Like semi-automatic assault weapons, Saturday Night Specials are used criminally at an alarming rate and have no legitimate social utility. Semi-automatic assault weapons have now been banned [97] and, under Brady II, Saturday Night Specials would be banned as well. This is the only remaining category of guns that Handgun Control believes should be banned.

Finally, the Bill examines the design and construction of handguns in an effort to reduce the number of unintentional discharges. The Bill requires that all firearms manufactured one year after the Bill is enacted must contain a device or devices to prevent a child under seven from discharging a weapon. Furthermore, if the weapon is a semi-automatic, the safety device must prevent discharge of the weapon once the magazine has been removed.

Additional studies are also evaluating technology that would prevent anyone other than the owner from firing a gun. The technology ranges from a simple mechanical device, i.e., a combination lock built into the handle of the gun, to computer chips that require the shooter to wear an encoded ring that corresponds to the firing mechanism in the handgun.

This technology, if feasible, would do three things. First, it would drastically reduce the number of individuals who improperly use someone else's weapon. Second, it would greatly reduce the value of stealing a gun in a home burglary. Like the car radio that cannot be used in any car other than the one for which it was designed, such guns would have no utility whatsoever in the illegal market. Given that a significant number of guns are stolen in burglaries, [98] such technology would have an impact on trafficking. Third, this technology would make it more difficult to sell guns on the illegal market because the coding device or lock combination would have to accompany each sale down the line of distribution. Should such technology prove technically feasible, Congress should consider mandating its incorporation into the manufacture of guns. Ample precedent exists for Congress to do so. [99]

As stated earlier this combination of legislative interventions would reduce the amount of gun violence that plagues this nation. How quickly gun control advocates will be able to move this legislation through Congress will depend largely on how much support is mobilized. The current leadership of the Republican party in Congress has not been terribly hospitable to gun control measures in the past. Whether it will be in the future will be a function of the amount of political pressure that can be brought to bear. That of course, will be the responsibility of gun control advocates across the country.

V. The Second Amendment

The Second Amendment is perhaps one of the most widely misconstrued -- and therefore misunderstood -- amendments to the Constitution. No federal court has ever used the Second Amendment to overturn a gun control law. [100] In fact, courts have consistently ruled that there is no constitutional right to own a gun for private purposes unrelated to the organized state militia. [101]

Gun control opponents have long argued that the amendment bars gun control laws. In fact, they often couch their inflammatory rhetoric with calls to "protect the constitutional right to own any gun." They have even claimed that the Constitution protects the right of all Americans to own machine guns. [102]

The Second Amendment, a compromise between the anti-federalists and federalists, was designed to preserve the ability of individual states to maintain state militias. This is clear not only from the cases that have reviewed the issue, [103] but from the language of the amendment itself. The amendment states that, "[a] well regulated Militia, being necessary to the security of a free State, the right of the people to keep and bear Arms, shall not be infringed." [104]

It is long past time for lawyers and others to speak about the true meaning of the amendment. In an interview with Charlayne Hunter-Gault on The MacNeil/Lehrer Newshour on December 16, 1991, former United States Chief Justice Warren Burger stated that the Second Amendment "has been the subject of one of the greatest pieces of fraud, I repeat the word 'fraud' on the American public by special interest groups that I have ever seen in my lifetime." [105] He continued, "they (the NRA) have mislead the American people." [106] The gun control debate is difficult enough without entering false issues into it. [107]

VI. Conclusion

No matter how effective a legislative scheme is, legislation alone will not eradicate the deeply rooted culture of gun violence that exists in this country. Accordingly, Handgun Control divides its efforts between legislative and non-legislative efforts.

In this regard, the Center to Prevent Handgun Violence carries out the non- legislative interventions of Handgun Control. These efforts include working with elementary, secondary and high schools to promote a gun violence reduction curriculum; litigating on behalf of gun victims; defending gun control legislation in the courts; working with the entertainment industry concerning the [begin pg. 439] messages in popular entertainment about gun violence; and working with the public health profession both to research the causes of and the most effective solutions to gun violence, and to disseminate the message that guns do not make us safer.

It is our belief that only through such a comprehensive, multifaceted approach, can America hope to reduce the gun violence that affects us all.

* Richard M. Aborn has been involved with the gun violence issue since 1979. From 1979 -1984 he served in the Manhattan District Attorney's Office, where he investigated and prosecuted homicide and large scale gun distribution cases. Upon leaving the government, Mr. Aborn began serving as a volunteer for Handgun Control, Inc., and in 1988 was elected to the Board of Trustees of Handgun Control by the organization's national membership. He was elected president of Handgun Control in June of 1992. The author wishes to thank the staffs of Handgun Control, Inc., and the Center to Prevent Handgun Violence for their assistance in the preparation of this Essay, especially the help of Robin Terry.

Source: Aborn, Richard. "The Battle Over the Brady Bill and the Future of Gun Control Advocacy." Fordham Urban Law Journal. Vol. 22. 1995: 417.

Why Nothing Works

At the beginning of this book, we set out to see if America's cultural crisis was understandable as a response to the growth of bureaucracy and oligopoly, and to changes in the nature of work, and in the composition of the labor force. How useful has this idea been for explaining why there is so much that is new and strange in America today? Has it been able to show the interconnectedness of changes that seem to be unrelated? Let us go back to the beginning and sum up the main arguments.

The principal point of departure was that since the end of World War II, the United States has become a beaucratized and oligopolized country, oriented more to people-processing and information-processing that to the production of goods. What was once a decentralized manufacturing society has become a centralized service and information-processing society. And equally important, what was once a society where women stayed home to work has become a society where women leave home to work.

Why did America's decentralized, individualistic, free-enterprise, goods-producing economy turn into a centralized, regulated, bureaucratized service-and-information-producing economy? Processes operating in both the private sector and in the government have to be considered. Let me review those in the private sector first. Through mergers and acquisitions, a handful of giant companies gained ascendancy in manufacturing, trade, commerce, transport, farming, mining, and energy production. In a sense this had to happen. It was a development inherent in the practice of free enterprise. Some corporations were bound to succeed more than others; some were bound to swallow, and others to be swallowed by their competitors. Some would go out of business; others would grow to giant size. To say that this process was "inherent" is not to say that it was inevitable. The United States instituted anti-monopoly laws. Yet the consequences of oligopoly are very similar to the consequences of monopoly. For example, take prices. With only a handful of giant corporations dominating a given industry, prices tend to be set by the cost of production rather than demand and supply in the marketplace. This allows for the growth of layers of redundant and inefficient administrators, office workers, promotional specialists, and sales help. It also encourages the toleration of inefficiencies and redundancies in union contracts which impede the substitution of machines for labor and which force up wage rates faster than productivity.

Turning to the government sector, one can readily understand why oligopoly and bureaucracy were fostered by the continuous enlargement of government agencies at the federal, state, and local levels. Again, one can argue that this development was a highly predictable (but not inevitable) consequence of having a capitalist economy with its cycle of booms and busts. After 1932 there was little choice but to seek to modify the effects of the business cycle by manipulating taxes, interest rates, money supply, enlarging the civil service, subsidizing jobs, and by doling out various kinds of welfare payments and subsidies to individuals and corporations. That is why the U.S. government set off on the road to becoming the largest employer in the United States and the second largest multinational conglomerate in the world (second only to the Soviet Union).

The reason for the turn from goods production to service-and-information production is far less obvious than the reason for the growth of corporate oligopoly and big government. It was a matter of needs and opportunities. In the name of efficiency, goods production became automated, concentrated, unionized. Hence the labor market could no longer grow by adding goods-producing jobs.

Yet something had to be done to accommodate the increasing numbers of people who were looking for work. Not that the whole expansion of service-and-information jobs was planned as a national make-work scheme. But the closing down of job opportunities in goods-production meant that an enormous labor force was becoming available for white- and pink-collar enterprises which had not yet been automated or unionized. The relative cheapness of the nonunionized white- and pink-collar workers encouraged private businesses to expand their investment in information-processing and the production of services. At the same time, wasn't the increase in government employees a less provocative expedient for coping with the unemployment problem than putting twenty million extra people on the dole?

Now we are on the way toward understanding the epidemic of shoddy goods, catastrophic disservices, and shrinking dollars. After three decades of the most astonishing labor-saving technological advances in the history of the human species, everything became more expansive. Why? Because at the same time that factory automation was saving labor and raising productivity, something else was wasting labor and lowering productivity on an even grander scale. It seems to me that this something else was none other than the rise of public and private bureaucratic oligopolies and the shift from a predominantly blue-collar to a predominantly pink- and white-collar labor force. People who work in and for bureaucracies whether at white-collar, pink-collar, or blue-collar jobs, become inflexible, bored, and alienated. They may turn out more products, information, or services per unit-time but the quality of what they produce suffers. And so let us face up to an unpleasant truth: by lowering quality, industrial bureaucracy can waste labor as fast as industrial machinery can save it.

Bureaucracy and oligopoly can be even more costly when it comes to producing services and information rather than goods. Bureaucracies and oligopolies(government or private) do not stop at wasting labor; they actively produce disservices and misinformation which may range from inconveniences to life-shattering ordeals for customers or clients. From a holistic perspective, therefore, the main cause of inflation has been the deteriorating quality of goods and services produced by inefficient bureaucracies and oligopolies. Several intermediary causes help to round out this picture. For example, economists emphasize the ever-increasing burden of debt being shouldered by government, businesses and consumers. Debt is inflationary since borrowing money from a bank is equivalent to putting more money in circulation(the banks back only a small proportion of what they lend with liquid assets_. The more dollars in circulation, the less each dollar can buy unless there is an equivalent increase in the value of marketable goods and services. It is true that in quantity the amount of goods and services did increase, but this was canceled out by the qualitative decline of these same goods and services. Hence the real value of goods and services did not increase as fast as the money supply.

What prompted the rise in debt? I suggest that it was none other than the decreasing efficiency of this oligopolized and bureaucratized economy. Government went into debt to finance its huge bureaucratic expansion, because real taxable income was not growing as fast as government expenditures. Private corporations went into debt for a similar reason: they were not efficient enough to expand their production out of the income generated from sales.

To make matters worse, as the dollar shrank, long-term loans became hard to find. Interest rates rose, creating acute cash-flow problems which the corporations met by quality-destroying expedients such as planned obsolescence and the debauchery of brand names.

Many economists have also pointed to the inflationary effects of the price-administering powers of the corporate oligopolies. The weakening of price competition buffered the oligopolies from the normal free-market effects of business depressions and rising unemployment rates. By their ability to set prices to cover costs regardless of falling demand, the oligopolies helped to create the unprecedented problem known as stagflation. But government had a hand in this also. After all, whether for humanitarian or selfish political reason, it was the government that refused to let the Great Depression return during which inefficient oligopolies would either have had to lower prices or go out of business.

The depletion of natural resources, especially of fossil fuels, has also had an inflationary impact. Yet productivity gains associated with automation and other technological advances were more than sufficient to cancel out the rising cost of fuel had these technological advances themselves not been canceled out or held back by bureaucratic bungling, inefficiency, and waste. One might even say that had it not been for the oligopoly structure of the petroleum corporations, alternative and cheaper sources of energy would have been developed long before the depletion of domestic oil reserves reached crisis proportions.

Now we have some idea why inflation and shoddy goods and catastrophic disservices went hand in hand with the switch to a predominantly service-and-information-oriented economy. The next step is to show that these same developments provided the conditions responsible for wrenching women out of the home and into the job market. I think it happened this way:

Married women needed to find jobs because the male breadwinner's take-home pay did not increase fast enough after 1960 to feed, clothe, house, transport, and educate the children of the baby boom. Although officially the inflation rate was insignificant until after 1965, the era of planned obsolescence and catastrophic disservices had already begun well before then.

But one must explain not only why women wanted jobs but why the jobs wanted women. The jobs wanted women because they were low-paying nonunionized people-processing and word-processing jobs. Not only did women have the literacy and other educational credentials for office jobs, retail sales, teaching, nursing, and other white- and pink-collar services, but they were initially willing to accept part-time and temporary work and less pay than breadwinner males with comparable credentials.

While this shift was taking place, no one realized that it would act as an interface between great changes occurring in the political and economic spheres and equally great changes that were about to occur in the family and sexual spheres. As prices zoomed and quality problems became more severe, women found themselves locked into the wage labor force. The entire marital and procreative complex surrounding housewifery and motherhood came into conflict with the physical and psychological demands placed upon women in their child-rearing and wage-earning roles. In conformity with the "feminine mystique" women were supposed to accept a subordinate position both in the home and at their jobs. This made some sense as long as the breadwinner male brought home the bread; but as the cost of rearing children zoomed upwards, the wife-mother's second income became essential for couples with middle-class aspirations. The sentimental veneer—the "mystique"—covering up the exploitation inherent in the traditional sex roles began to peel off. The entire edifices of the marital and procreative imperative with its Victorian double standards and its patriarchal prudery began to crumble. Down came the fertility and first-time marriage rates. Up went the divorce rate, consensual liaisons, delayed marriages, childless and one-child families, and a whole new antiprocreationist and libertine sexual consciousness.

With a substantial majority of younger men and women committed to the proposition that sex is primarily for pleasure rather than for procreation, tolerance of and experiment with pornography, nonheterosexual, and nongenital relationships were bound to increase. It is no mystery therefore why homosexuals with their effective nonprocreative sex-for-joy relationships were embo9ldened to come out of the closet.

Of course powerful defenders of the old marital and procreative standards still remain. But even as the anti-abortion and anti-homosexual forces struggle with their adversaries, their own life-styles reflect the underlying shift toward more libertine sexual standards. The video evangelists (unlike the old-style fundamentalists-, for example, are strongly committed to the proposition that sex-for-joy is a sacrament and that it is the Christian wife's duty to be attractive by wearing makeup and sexy lingerie. Noteworthy also is the isolation of the issue of abortion from that of contraception. With the fertility rate among Catholic right-to-life enthusiasts indistinguishable from that of pro-abortionists, it is difficult to interpret the right-to-life movement in the United States as being essentially pro-natal. Anti-abortion legislation would only inhibit the abortion rate among the poor, largely black women on welfare; one might conclude therefore that the real target of the right-to-life movement is the right of inner-city blacks to enjoy sex at government expense.

There are other aspects of America's cultural crisis for which the shift in women's status has played a crucial role. Some of these, specifically race relations, crime, and the decay of the inner cities, appear at first to be unrelated. Yet to ignore the connections is to bury one's head in the sand. Women are of course not responsible for the fact that information- and people-processing jobs increased while goods-producing jobs decreased. Nor were they responsible for the inflation that drove them into the job market. But one cannot ignore the devastating significance of this change for the inner-city black community. Black males have not been able to find work either in the shrinking job markets in agriculture, mining, and manufacture, nor in the people-processing and information-processing fields, where better-educated literate white women have had a strong competitive advantage over them. Bad as the plight of white employed females might be, the plight of the unemployment caused by automation has fallen upon inner-city men. Whites have shown little comprehension of why this has been the case and even less sympathy. Rather than pay the bill for a genuine system of relief and welfare, the white majority has sanctioned the growth of an insane system which rewards mothers of "fatherless" children with bonuses, while the fathers of such children are given neither welfare nor jobs and turn to crime as an alternative career. To repeat, my point here is not that white women are the cause of the structural unemployment of black males, but that the rhetoric of women's liberation has done much to obscure the interconnectedness of America's problems and the futility of trying to solve them separately by pressing for the short-run benefits of one special interest group, no matter how just its cause.

Finally, what is the explanation for the surge of interest in shamanism, exorcism, witchcraft, extraterrestrial beings, and expansionist cults and churches? There cannot be much doubt that the new religious consciousness reflects the bewilderment and insecurity engendered by rapid cultural change. But how shall we interpret the specific content of this "Awakening"? Does it signal the end of America's quest for earthly dominion, a retreat from consumerism and materialism, and the triumph of spiritual over practical needs? Or are we witnessing a desperate end-of-the-line attempt to achieve earthly dominion and material well-being by magical and supernatural means? The second hypothesis seems to me to be much closer to the truth. If one studies the actual worldly involvements of the human-potential movement, the video-evangelist movement, and even that of the communitarian cults, there is very little evidence of an unalloyed commitment to spiritual transcendence, Why is this distinction important? Because in the first instance one sees a benign spiritualized America escaping from its material problems into mystical union with God; while in the second instance, one sees a dangerously frustrated America becoming increasingly receptive to charismatic, messianic, and fanatical solutions to its material problems.

America is in deep trouble; but let no one suppose that our plight cannot get a whole lot worse. Our standard of living—even with due consideration of its quality problems—is still among the highest on earth. And compared with most of the state-level societies that have ever existed, the degree of personal security and freedom enjoyed by the average U.S. citizen—except for the inner cities—is extraordinary. Can we find a way to defend, improve, and broaden the base of material welfare without giving up the cherished personal liberties which are America's splendid heritage?

The reader was warned not to expect a detailed set of prescriptions for restoring the American dream. In writing this book, I have proceeded on the premise that people cannot rationally offer a solution to a problem unless they understand its cause. It seems to me that if we act on the basis of sterile political formula, irrational impulses, or unsound knowledge, we are likely to make matters worse rather than better. The question of what or who is to blame for things falling apart, for catastrophic disservices, for stagflation, crime, and the rest haunts Americans of all political persuasions. Yet up to now there has been little public discussion of the root causes of these problems. Sad to say, by using technical jargon, and by pursuing isolated studies of interest only to specialists, the social sciences have been a source of confusion rather than of enlightenment as far as the vast majority of people is concerned.

Although I insist that it is important to achieve an objective and holistic understanding of U.S. social life prior to and independent of political action, the reader has a right to know what policy implications I draw from this work. One clear implication is that Americans are unlikely to acquiesce to cuts in their standard of living in the name of spiritual salvation. While it would be convenient to both Republicans and Democrats if America really were on the verge of renouncing the quest for material progress in favor of a life of "voluntary simplicity," or of born-again other-worldly austerity, I have found no evidence to support such a view. Hence, there is little prospect that administrations which fail to reverse the downward trend in living standards will survive the wrath of the electorate.

The current interest in abandoning the quest for universal material affluence reminds me of the pessimism which attended the birth of the industrial era. So strong was this view that at the beginning of the nineteenth century, economics came to be known as the "dismal science." Economists of the period held that there was no way to solve the problem of poverty. Drawing their inspiration from the work of Thomas Malthus, they gloomily predicted that if wages went up, population would increase, more people would enter the job market and wages would fall back down to poverty levels. Today a new breed of dismal scientists has come into existence. These new prophets of gloom no longer say that poverty is inevitable. But they insist that the American dream of universal prosperity will never come true. We must not permit ourselves to surrender to this vision of the future without a struggle.

The new dismal science was born toward the end of the 1960s amid dire warnings by ecologists about "limits to growth," global heat death from the burning of fossil fuels, and exhaustion of nonrenewable resources. These warnings have inspired a far-ranging philosophical and theological critique of the whole idea of material progress. According to social critic Jeremy Rifkin for example, there is no scientific basis for the belief in progress since the law of evolution is negated by the law of entropy. The entropy law states that energy flows from higher to lower levels and thereby guarantees the ultimate running down of the universe. Rifkin maintains that recognition of entropy as the supreme physical law demands that Americans abandon their dream of material affluence based on dominion over nature and dedicate themselves instead to conserving nature and getting rid of their possessions. Does your car give you trouble? The entropy ethic offers a simple solution: "If you don't own an automobile, you don't need to worry about steel-belted radials, gas lines, traffic tie-ups, and car thieves," writes Rifkin.

I would find the new dismal science more acceptable if it could be shown that the changes in U.S. culture discussed in previous chapters have been caused by ecological limits to growth. But where is the evidence that depletions account for a significant part of inflation, unemployment, terror in the streets, and the outpouring of shoddy goods and catastrophic disservices in America today? All of these problems had already reached excruciating levels by 1970 at the very height of the era of the cheapest energy supply the world had ever known. Moreover, the depletion of U.S. domestic oil reserves was not a natural disaster. It was a people-made disaster, foreseen and predicted (if not premeditated) and entirely evitable had alternate sources of energy been developed during the period when the United States was foolishly becoming dependent on importing oil from one of the most remote and politically unstable regions on earth.

The central fallacy of the new dismal science is that it interprets the present crisis in the light of a future crisis. Perhaps depletions of natural resources will indeed drag us down into an entropic death. But why impose a distant morbid possibility on a present that is still pregnant with life and hope? George Gilder, a staunch believer in the ability of unfettered capitalism to solve America's problems, suggests that the current infatuation with the idea of entropy as a substitute for the idea of progress may be more symptomatic of psychological rather than ecological stress:

At a time when radically important new technologies are being spawned on every hand, leading experts imagine that we are entering a technological climacteric, a period of diminishing scientific returns. Such views are suitable for analysis not in the universities (where they often prevail) but on the couch.

While I find myself in substantial agreement with Gilder's arguments against no-growth pessimists, I cannot accept his standard right-wing Republican belief that America's problems will be solved simply by giving U.S. corporations a free hand to do business as they please. Is it realistic to expect that the deregulation of the private sector will cure the ills of hyperindustrialization? Left to their own devices, what will prevent the conglomerates from becoming even more oligopolized and bureaucratized than they already are? What will prevent them from producing more shoddy goods and catastrophic disservices, more chronic unemployment and poverty, and more broken families and terror in the streets?

Believers in unfettered capitalism profess to be concerned about improving the well-being of the poor, but it quickly becomes apparent that they are far more concerned about protecting the well-being of the rich. While the new dismal scientists want to solve the problem of poverty by abolishing everyone's material desires, the unfettered capitalists want to solve it by convincing the poor that they have only themselves to blame for not being rich. In his book, Wealth and Poverty, which has acquired something of the status of a holy scripture in unfettered capitalist circles, Gilder writes: "The first principle is that in order to move up, the poor must not only work, they must work harder than the classes above them." Hard-nosed capitalist-roader and woolly-brained entropy freak meet each other on common ground here, each proposing to change society by offering people less rather than more for helping to solve America's cultural crisis. What Gilder fails to acknowledge is that people who can't find jobs can scarcely be expected to work harder than the "classes above them"—unless he intends to exhort such people to work harder at muggings and other disagreeable alternatives to welfare.

The ethic of unfettered capitalism, in other words, is no more likely to provide a satisfactory solution to the current crisis than the ethic of entropy. In the light of the contribution of private oligopoly and bureaucracy to America's malaise, what sense does it make to attack only government oligopoly and bureaucracy? To restore quality in goods and services we must reverse the trend toward economic concentration and the mindless division of labor in both public and private spheres of endeavor. If we act to remove al restraints on the conglomerates, they will simply expand their production of shoddy goods and catastrophic disservices, and continue to inflate prices to cover up their inefficiencies. Furthermore, there is not even a remote chance that by granting the conglomerates a freer hand they will create enough jobs in the private sector to break the cycle of unemployment-crime-welfare in the inner cities. In fact, there is a very high probability that the demand for labor in the private sector will not be sufficient to avoid a steady increase in "normal" unemployment. The immense effort now being launched to complete the automation of goods-production by robotizing assembly lines, in conjunction with the equally great effort to substitute microchip computers for clerks, typists, receptionists, and sales help, virtually guarantees that there will be more unemployment in the future.

It is true that similar dire predictions about the effect of labor-saving devices were made during the 1950s and yet the economy managed to find employment for thirty-five million new workers. But as we now realize, almost all of these new jobs were in the information-processing and people-processing fields which temporarily escaped the main thrust of technological progress. Looking back over the past two hundred years we can see that the sequence of industrial development has moved inexorably from agriculture to manufacture and mining; and from manufacturing and mining to people- and information-processing. As productivity rose in agriculture, agricultural employment fell and the surplus labor was drawn off into manufacturing and mining; then as productivity in manufacturing and mining rose, surplus labor was drawn off into the production of information and services. What next?

With micro-chip computerization of information-and-service jobs the fastest growth industry in the United States, who can doubt that the same process is abut to be repeated in the service-and-information fields? But with one difference: There is no conceivable realm of profitable employment whose expansion can make up for even modest productivity gains among the nation's sixty million service-and-information workers.

Before long, therefore, America will have to resolve the contradiction between saving labor and making jobs—between making people more productive and putting them out of work. Because of this structural contradiction, a policy of slashing taxes, shrinking the government bureaucracy, reducing welfare and deregulating the private sector cannot long endure. Pursuit of this policy may prevent a runaway inflation but it will add millions of middle-class white-collar workers—especially women—to the tanks of the jobless, and thereby further erode the standards of consumption of a substantial portion of the American people.

Since the major parties are well aware of the danger of run-away inflation on the one hand and of Great Depression un-employment on the other, both will want to follow middle-of-the-road strategies. Neither will admit that it has no plan for restoring the American dream of prosperity with freedom and justice for all.

While muddling through from one election to another, each will concentrate on placating the demands of the most strident special-interest groups and single-issue constituencies in the hope that the rest of the people will not notice that the country is sinking into a pit of unknown depth.

How long will this period of creeping stagflation and covert subversion of the American dream last? The answer may depend o n how long the burden of austerity is willing to see used against inner-city riots and crime. A lot depends also on the course o f the arms race and on the ability of the incumbent parties to postpone their day of reckoning with the electorate by making austerity for the many, and socialism for the rich, a matter of patriotic duty.

Since the politics of muddling, temporizing, and prevaricating will not prevent a further rise in structural unemployment nor put an end to inflation, movements responsive to concrete and immediate solutions are bound to gain strength. Wage and price controls, federal subsidies to endangered corporations, and massive make-work programs may prove to be irresistible with the next swing of the political pendulum. One has merely to project world-wide trends toward centralized, bureaucratized industrial states to realize that other solutions are far less probable.

But what would this American super-state look like? In the "best case" scenario, America's great democratic heritage would prevail and civil liberties would not necessarily be destroyed. Perhaps the burden of austerity would be distributed more evenly, and the public transport system and the inner cities would be rebuilt b giant federal work and welfare program, and perhaps violent street crimes would diminish. But is there not already sufficient evidence from the Soviet bloc and the Western welfare states that the penalties of bureaucracy and oligopoly would grow worse? If an America that is only half bureaucratized and oligopolized is already a cornucopia of shoddy goods, catastrophic disservices, and soul-deadening alienation, what reasons do we have to believe that this situation will improve when the country is totally bureaucratized and oligopolized? None that I know of.

Moreover the assumption that democratic institutions and civil liberties will flourish under a super government may not hold up. If the movement to create a totally bureaucratized and oligopolized economy takes place in an atmosphere of urban rioting, heightened international tensions, and military buildup, a grimmer scenario may unfold. As in George Orwell's morbid vision of 1984, there is a significant chance that the endangered political species known as Western democracy will be come extinct, victim of a totalitarian takeover (from the right or the left-they would by then be hard to tell apart).

And finally, to move to the worst case, can we discount the possibility of a suicidal "white night" nuclear crusade led by born-again Christian ayatollahs hellbent on reasserting U.S. global military and economic hegemony? The nuclear stalemate rests entirely on the assumption that neither side wants to see the world annihilated. While the majority of born-again Christians certainly accepts this covenant with the future, can we ignore the fact that the idea of a military-messianic apocalypse lies at the very bas of the Judeo-Christian tradition?

Must we then give up the American dream? Is there no way to avoid the known penalties of bureaucracy and oligopoly? Yes, there is a way. And that is to reverse the centralizing trend of industrialization. Resolution of America's cultural crisis could conceivable take the form of encouraging the development of small-scale private enterprises, manned by hard-driving, efficient, profit-sharing work teams producing enough of a surplus to pay for first-class educational and community services as well as for the compassionate care of the sick and the elderly. But is this a realistic proposal in view of the fact that no industrial society has yet managed to reverse the centralizing trend? My own personal feeling on this matter is that knowledge of the unwanted and detested features of the centralizing scenarios rationally compels us to consider the alternative of radical decentralization.

First of all, it is self-defeating to regard America's future as predetermined by the experiences of other nations. The heritage of private initiative, pragmatic know-how, mechanical ingenuity, and grass roots town-hall democracy probably still runs stronger and deeper in the United States than anywhere else.

Moreover, while decentralization goes against the grain of modern history, it need not go against the grain of human nature. Until recently, decentralization presented itself as a form of voluntary austerity, conjuring up images of iron pumps in muddy farmyards, and rooms lit by candlelight. But the technology of solar and other decentralized forms of energy production is rapidly advancing toward the point where small communities may be able to achieve relatively high per capita cash incomes from a variety of profit-making enterprises, in addition to enjoying the amenities of clean air and water, personal safety, and humane interpersonal relationships. The hope is that the decentralized configuration would spread not as a cult of poverty, nor as an otherworldly gospel of wealth, but as a down-to-earth practical means of achieving higher-quality goods and services and rising instead of falling consumption standards through elimination or bureaucracy and oligopoly and the unfettering of individual initiative.

All this will take time. I see no way of creating a decentralized society by means of a revolution aimed at dismembering America's public and private oligopolies. The existing organizations are too entrenched and powerful to be broken up all at once. Rather, decentralization will come about, if at all, as a result of a series of strategic decisions which can slowly tip the balance against the thralldom of hyper-industrialization. For example, very little progress can be made toward decentralization without scaling down America's military-industrial complex, and very little progress can be made in that direction unless some way can be found to lower international tensions and halt the arms race. Much also depends on stimulating the development of the right kind of solar and other forms of decentralized energy production, and of appropriate energy-efficient machinery to be used in small manufacturing plants and in the home. Equally important will be the development of legal barriers against takeovers of new energy technologies and decentralized industries by multinational conglomerates, and the passage of legislation favorable to small businesses and community-based cooperatives. Thus the creation of an affluent egalitarian, decentralized society may be a long way off, but decisions that open and shut doors for radically different kinds of futures will have to be made in the months and years immediately ahead.

Given the enormous power and formidable inertia of the hyper-industrial oligopolies and bureaucracies, there is only a slim chance of achieving a future more in accord with the vision of freedom and affluence on which past generations of Americans were nourished. Nonetheless, this chance is sufficient to support a rational hope of reversing the trends that have led to

America's present malaise. The will to resist and to try for something better is an important component in the struggle against oligopoly and bureaucracy. Of course, to desire something strongly enough to fight for it does not guarantee success. But it changes the odds. The renewal of the American dream may be improbable, but it will become finally impossible only when the last dreamer gives up trying to make it come true.

Source: Harris, Marvin. Why Nothing Works. New York: Simon & Schuster, Inc. 1981.

AMERICAN CULTURES - RACE and ETHNICITY

KEY CONCEPTS

Culture is a universe of diversity. As per Einstein, all things cultural are relative. Like the Heisenberg Principle of Uncertainty, it is impossible to measure both the position of a culture and its momentum at the same time. The convenient current categories of culture are artificial constructs that bridge the gap between the assumptions of society and the ultimate cultural realities of the individual. There is a tremendous range of variation within any of the following cultural groups, and far more similarities between cultural groups than is evident on the surface. It is in the experiences of these ethnic groups and their interactions with the formal and informal social institutions already described that we see the institutionalization of race and the social meanings of racism. There are five basic cultural complexes identified by social institutions as races: Native Americans, European Americans, African Americans, Asian Americans, and Latino Americans. Historically, they have been color-coded: red, white, black, yellow, and brown.

NATIVE AMERICA / INDIGENOUS AMERICANS

Tecumseh's Speech to Governor William Henry Harrison at Vincennes, August 1810.

It is true I am a Shawnee. My forefathers were warriors. Their son is a warrior. From them I take only my existence; from my tribe I take nothing. I am the maker of my own fortune; and oh! that I could make that of my red people, and of my country, as great as the conceptions of my mind, when I think of the Spirit that rules the universe. I would not then come to Governor Harrison to ask him to tear the treaty and to obliterate the landmark; but I would say to him: "Sir, you have liberty to return to your own country."

The being within, communing with past ages, tells me that once, nor until lately, there was no white man on this continent; that it then all belonged to red men, children of the same parents, placed on it by the Great Spirit that made them, to keep it, to traverse it, to enjoy its productions, and to fill it with the same race, once a happy race, since made miserable by the white people who are never contented but always encroaching. The way, and the only way, to check and to stop this evil, is for all the red men to unite in claiming a common and equal right in the land, as it was at first, and should be yet; for it never was divided, but belongs to all for the use of each. For no part has a right to sell, even to each other, much less to strangers--those who want all, and will not do with less.

The white people have no right to take the land from the Indians, because they had it first; it is theirs. They may sell, but all must join. Any sale not made by all is not valid. The late sale is bad. It was made by a part only. Part do not know how to sell. It requires all to make a bargain for all. All red men have equal rights to the unoccupied land. The right of occupancy is as good in one place as in another. There cannot be tow occupations in the same place. The first excludes all others. It is not so in hunting or traveling; for there the same ground will serve many, as they may follow each other all day; but the camp is stationary, and that is occupancy. It belongs to the first who sits down on his blanket or skins which he has thrown upon the ground; and till he leaves it no other has a right.

Source: Drake, Samuel G. <u>Biography and History of the Indians of North America.</u> Boston: O.L.Perkin, 1834.

Crossing the San Joaquin Valley

During the first three years we were on Sycamore Creek, the Indians furnished most of our food. At first we used to hunt and fish a great deal, but we gradually quit it because they used to keep game hanging in the large oak tree in front of the house, and also left their acorn bread at the back door. Most of the time we would never see them do this as they would bring the things while we were gone, or at night while we were asleep. We appreciated this a great deal, as it was a long, hard trip to Stockton after supplies, and we also had very little cash to spend. Several years later I learned from the Indians that they kept us in meat in order to keep us from firing our guns and scaring the game. Of course, we were always good to the Indians and gave them green corn and wheat, but we never in any way came near repaying them for what they did for us…

On the south bank of Kings River, about opposite the mouth of Sycamore Creek, there was an Indian rancheria. There was also another about a mile or two upstream from the first one. These were the people we knew best, and we soon came to know them well, and to trust them completely.

We made a very great distinction between the mountain Indians, or Monaches, and the valley Indians [Yokuts] .Our neighbors at the rancherias belonged to the valley group. Then we later knew the Indians about the north shore of Tulare Lake as lake Indians. I later learned that they belonged to the Tache tribe. Of course, the Telumnes and Wukchumnes around Visalia were valley Indians also, but I did not know them until later and knew very little about them even then.

The valley Indians would not mix with the mountain Indians. They did not talk the same dialect and considered themselves very much better than the Monaches. I knew both tribes quite well, and I believe the valley Indians were justified in their belief. When members of the two groups would meet on a trail they would ignore each other. Some trading was carried on between the two groups, but I am sure it was done by a few members of each group who made a business of it and traveled back and forth between the groups.

On Sycamore Creek we were at about the upstream limits of the valley Indians and the downstream limits of the Monaches. Our territory was really used in common by both groups. They both seemed to travel over it at will, but I believe it was used more by the valley group than by the Monaches.

We soon found that we could not trust the Monaches, and came to consider them as treacherous. Whether they behaved that way toward us because we were friendly with the valley people or not, I do not know. But our neighbors at the rancheria said that the Monaches were thieves and murderers. It is possible that we would have found them all right had we gone directly to them in the first place and not associated with the valley tribes. But it has been my experience that it made no difference how honest Indians may have been within their own tribe, they always considered it their duty to the tribe to do all the damage they could to an enemy, about as the white nations do today...

As I recollect, and I have not been back there for more than seventy years, Sycamore Creek ran between high hills and had only very small patches of level land along it. On these patches my daddy used to raise grain and corn and other crops. This made the work very much scattered, and we had to travel several miles to care for the crops farthest upstream. There were many pools of water in Sycamore Creek, and in them we caught trout and speared a fish we called a steelhead...

Sometimes an Indian would come to the edge of the clearing at the back of the house and stand there for hours, looking in the back door and just watching what was going on. We were a whole lot more of a curiosity to them than they were to us, and when we were sure it was one of the valley Indians we paid no attention to him, as we knew that he was just curious to see how we did things. Of course, he would go back to the rancheria and, as I heard them do later when I was living with them. talk for hours to the rest of the Indians about what he had seen. But we never felt safe when the Monaches did that, as they were generally spying out something that they could come back and steal.

Speaking of curiosity reminds me how, when we first came to Kings River, the Indians used to go around after we had planted corn or potatoes and dig up the hills. They did not mean to do any damage, and I believe that in many instances where the white settlers had trouble with the Indians it all started because the Indians were just curious to know what in the world the white settlers were doing and not because they wanted to, or even knew, they were doing any damage...

One of the Indians made me a present of a fine sinew-backed bow of juniper, and a half dozen arrows. This was really as nice a bow as they could get and was painted in pretty colors. It was about three and one-half feet long, and was made like they made their hunting bows, wide and flat and recurved at the ends, but pinched in or narrowed at the grip. It had been made by one of the Monaches and traded to the people who lived near us.

The Monaches did a lot of fighting and knew how to make good bows. The string was made of sinew and secured at one end by wrapping about the end of the bow. At the other end was a loop which would be slipped up into a nock. The string could be shortened by twisting, or by adjusting at the end opposite the nock.

The valley Indians could not make good bows, as they did not know how to make the waterproof glue with which to fasten the sinew to the back. They really had little use for a bow except for hunting, as they did no fighting among themselves. And there were so many of them that the mountain Indians very seldom bothered them. Then, too, most of their game was caught with snares and traps. They made a crude sort of bow of elderwood without backing and without recurving at the ends. This they used when they could not get the Monache bows.

Shortly after we settled on Kings River my mother died. It was a terrible blow to all of us and we never realized what she meant to us out there in the wilderness until she was gone. My daddy was gone a great deal of the time, running stock in the valley, and in the mountains. John was riding part of the time for my daddy and part of the time for other settlers who had come to Kings

River soon after we had. Ben was old enough to go with either of them, or to look out for himself. But I was younger, and was quite a problem after mother died.

The Indians at the rancheria had always taken an interest in me and I had spent a great deal of time there before my mother died. She was always willing for me to go across the river with them, and I am sure she felt that I was perfectly safe with them...

While I was at the rancheria I came and went as I pleased. No one of the women claimed me. I was looked after by several of them. They treated me better than they did their own children and probably made a pretty badly spoiled boy of me. I was given the best of everything. They dressed me just as they did their own children while I was small. When I grew older I wore more clothing, generally a breechcloth like the older Indians.

Source: Mayfield, Thomas Jefferson. "Crossing the San Joaquin Valley". Indian Summer. Berkeley, CA: Heyday Books & the California Historical Society. 1993.

The Destruction of California Indians -Correspondences

Sir: I have the honor to enclose herewith a communication of the Ron R. N. Wood, Judge of the Court of Sessions of Contra Costa County Cal, in relation to the compensation which ought to be allowed to Maj. Wm. McDaniel for conducting certain prosecutions in that state for the offence of kidnapping Indians and selling them into servitude. It was agreed between Maj. McDaniel and myself at the time he was employed in that service, that he should receive for his services in bringing to trial, persons guilty of this offence, one hundred dollars per month and such fee for conducting the prosecutions as should be approved by the Commissioner of Indian Affairs. It was deemed by me absolutely imperative upon the Department to take such decisive steps as would speedily put an end to this infamous practice. The traffic was conducted by Mexicans desperate in their character and difficult to arrest. They reside at remote points in the vicinity of the Indians, and were strongly banded together by the prospects of gain in this inhuman trade. Their character for desperation, recklessness and revenge being so well known, there was but few men who were willing to risk their lives in prosecuting them.

It would have been utterly useless to depend for one moment on the district attorney of each county to conduct these prosecutions. Being liable to the midnight assaults of these desperadoes, they shrank from the duty of executing the laws and there was no alternative but to employ counselor fail entirely in the object of suppressing this crime.

It is proper to say that the practice had been carried to an extraordinary extent. I have undoubted evidence that hundreds of Indians have been stolen and carried into the settlements and sold; in some instances entire tribes were taken en masse, driven to a convenient point, and such as were suitable for servants, selected from among them, generally the children and young women, while the old men and the infirm were left to starve or make their way back to their mountain homes, as best they could.

In many other cases it has come to my knowledge that the fathers and mothers have been brutally killed when they refused assistance to the taking away of their children. One instance of this kind came under my own observation.

I recommended that in the cases alluded to by Judge Wood, as they had been tried twice in Solano county where the jury failed to agree on account of Mexican influence on them by change of venue and Judge Wood. That Maj. McDaniel be allowed a fee of five hundred dollars and one hundred dollars each for other causes tried by him in Nappa and other counties, not to exceed in all, the sum of eight hundred dollars.

Very Respectfully,
Thos. J. Henley
Supt Ind. Affairs, Cal.

Sir

Your favor making inquiries of me relative to the professional services rendered by Wm McDaniel as attorney in certain causes wherein the U. S. were prosecutors of various persons for kidnapping Indians in California. In reply it affords me pleasure to state that Mr. M.D. appeared before the Court of Sessions of Contra Costa County, of which I was presiding judge and successfully prosecuted to conviction several persons who violated the laws of u. S. and of California in kidnapping Indians, that those causes were tried before me on a change of venue, and that Mr. M.D.'s services were well worth five hundred Dollars, that those prosecutions were the immediate and direct means by which the kidnapping of Indians in that section of California was broken up, and that Mr. M.D. is not only entitled to fair compensation but the thanks of all good citizens. I am pleased to add from actual knowledge that his efforts were held in high estimation by the people. The sum I indicate for professional services is but of a minimum amount and should be paid him at once.

Respectfully,

R. N. WOOD

A San Francisco Newspaper Article:

Horrible Massacre of 200 Indians in Humboldt County
By the steamer Columbia, which arrived this forenoon from the North, we have tidings of a terrible butchery, by a band of white murderers, of the Indians around Humboldt Bay. Mr. Lord, the express messenger of Wells, Fargo & Co., favors us with the following statement of the massacre:

Between three and four o'clock on Sunday morning last, (26 February,) an attack was made by a party of white men, upon Indians at several villages around Humboldt Bay. At Indian Island, opposite the town of Eureka, and distant but a few hundred yards, more than 40 Indians were killed, three-fourths of the number being women and children. On the beach, south of the entrance to the bay, forty or fifty Indians were also killed. Report says all that were there-every one-was killed. It is also reported, and is no doubt true, that a simultaneous attack was made upon the villages on Eel river. From what was known in Eureka not less than two hundred Indians-men, women and children-were killed on this Sabbath morning.

It is believed that the farmers and graziers of Eel river county, who have suffered from Indian depredations, during the past year, were the men who performed the deed. The cause assigned is, that the coast Indians furnished arms and ammunition to those in the mountains, and gave them asylum, when hard pressed by the volunteers. They have been seen to take large quantities of beef from the mountains to their houses nearer the settlements. Most of the people at Eureka and vicinity were bitter in their denunciation of this wholesale butchery.

TO THE EDITOR OF THE BULLETIN: I learn from Mr. Van Ness, Sheriff of Humboldt county, who arrived in

San Francisco this forenoon, passenger on the steamer Columbia that the massacre which took place on Humboldt Bay, last Sunday morning, was committed by a body of men, some 40 in number, from Eel river. They rode through to the south end of the bay in the night, hitched their horses, took Capt. Buhne's boat, crossed to the south shore, and killed all the Indians they found. They then proceeded up the Bay to Indian Island, and commenced an indiscriminate slaughter of men, women and children, and left before daylight. They gave as their reason, that the Indians of the Bay and the mountains are leagued together, and are constantly killing their cattle. When pursued, those in the mountains leave that region and go down to the coast. Parties of Indians, from ten to twenty, had been seen during the past week going to the Bay. Those men from Eel river, becoming exasperated, followed the Indians, and determined to clean out every thing that wore a red skin. Sheriff Van Ness thinks that the number of Indians (including men, women and children} who have been thus slaughtered amounts, probably to about eighty.

This is but the commencement of an Indian war in that section of the country. An intelligent Indian to\d the people of Eureka, that the white men had killed his wives and children, and he had nothing more to live for; and he was going to the mountains with what few of his tribe were left, to fight against the whites.

Letter, From Raines to Asst. Adjt. General

Assistant Adjutant General Fort Humboldt March 10, 1860.

I have just been to Indian Island, the home of a band of friendly Indians between Eureka and Uniontown, where I beheld a scene of atrocity and horror unparalleled not only in our own Country, but even in history, for it was done by men self acting and without necessity, color of law, or authority-the murder of little innocent babes and women, from the breast to maturity, barbarously and I can't say brutally-for it is worse-perpetrated by men who act in defiance of and probably in revenge upon the Governor of the State for not sending them arms and having them mustered in as a Volunteer Company for the murder of Indians by wholesale, goaded also by Legislative acts of inquiry into such matters. At any rate such is the opinion of the better class of community as related to me this Sunday morning. I was informed by these men, Volunteers, calling themselves such, from Eel River, had employed the earlier part of the day in murdering all the women and children of the above Island and I repaired to the place, but the villians-some S in number had gone-and midst the bitter grief of parents and fathers-many of whom had returned-I beheld a spectacle of horror, of unexampled description-babes, with brains oozing out of their skulls, cut and hacked with axes, and squaws exhibiting the most frightful wounds in death which imagination can paint-and this done. ...without cause, otherwise, as far as I can learn, as I have not heard of any of them losing life or cattle by the Indians. Certainly not these Indians, for they lived on an Island and nobody accuses them.

[Major Raines then describes the murdered Indians, as he found them in each lodge, the number killed being as follows: 1st lodge-2 women, 3 children; 2nd lodge-I man, S women, 2 children; 3rd lodge-2 women; 4th lodge-3 women, S children; 4th lodge-4 women, 1 child; 6th lodge, 1 woman. In addition to these Major Raines says that 18 women and an unknown number of children had been carried away by the Indians for burial before his arrival.]

(In another letter to the Assistant Adjutant General, March 10, 1860, Major Raines says " About 188 Indians, mostly women and children have been murdered,, Viz., 55 at Indian Island; 58 at South Beach; 40 on South Fork Eel River and 35 at Prairie.}

Major G.J. Raines

Newspaper Article, San Francisco, 1860:

The Recent Massacre of Indians at Humboldt Bay

Fort Humboldt, Cal. , May 22, 1860

To the Editor of the San Francisco Bulletin-Sir: Attempts having been vilely made, again and again, to palm off upon the military, and mainly upon myself, the cause of the blackest crimes perpetuated on this Bay which have ever disgraced the history of mankind, by false and contemptible lies, incriminating along with me even revered gentlemen; and as some of these lies have found themselves in the columns of your newspaper, please favor me by publishing the inclosed, (a copy of which has been forwarded to Sheriff Van Nest,) in order to "disabuse the public:"
I would premise by stating that instructions similar in substance have been given to each officer on the same service, and also that up to this date I can find no excuse whatever for the horrid massacre on this Bay and the removal of Indians thereof from the county, whom I have considered as safeguards to the citizens of this vicinity and their property, by acting as spies upon the mountain tribes, to destroy small numbers and betray larger ones who might come for spoilation or murder.

Very respectfully, your obed't serv't.,
G. J. Raines
Major U.S.A. Comd't Post.

Source: Heizer, Robert F., ed. The Destruction Of California Indians. Lincoln, NA: the University of Nebraska Press & Bison Books. 1993.

The Ghost Dance and Wounded Knee

Turning Hawk, Pine Ridge (Mr. Cook, interpreter). When we heard that these people were coming toward our agency we also heard this. These people were coming toward Pine Ridge agency, and when they were almost on the agency they were met by the soldiers and surrounded and finally taken to the Wounded Knee creek, and there at a given time their guns were demanded. When they had delivered them up, the men were separated from their families, from the tipis, and taken to a certain spot. When the guns were thus taken and the men thus separated, there was a crazy man, a young man of very bad influence and in fact a nobody, among that bunch of Indians fired his gun, and of course the firing of a gun must have been the breaking of a military rule of some sort, because immediately the soldiers returned fire and indiscriminate killing followed.

Spotted Horse: This man shot an officer in the army; the first shot killed this officer. I was a voluntary scout at that encounter and I saw exactly what was done, and that was what I noticed; that the first shot killed an officer. As soon as this shot was fired the Indians immediately began drawing their knives, and they were exhorted from all sides to desist, but this was not obeyed. Consequently the firing began immediately on the part of the soldiers.

Turning Hawk: All the men who were in a bunch were killed right there, and those who escaped that first fire got into the ravine, and as they went along up the ravine for a long distance they were pursued on both sides by the soldiers and shot down, as the dead bodies showed afterwards. The women were standing off at a different place form where the men were stationed, and when the firing began, those of the men who escaped the first onslaught went in one direction up the ravine, and then the women, who were bunched together at another place, went entirely in a different direction through an open field, and the women fared the same fate as the men who went up the deep ravine.

American Horse: The men were separated, as has already been said, from the women, and they were surrounded by the soldiers. Then came next the village of the Indians and that was entirely surrounded by the soldiers also. When the firing began, of course the people who were standing immediately around the young man who fired the first shot were killed right together, and then they turned their guns, Hotchkiss guns, etc., upon the women who were in the lodges standing there under a flag of truce, and of course as soon as they were fired upon they fled, the men fleeing in one direction and the women running in two different directions. So that there were three general directions in which they took flight.
There was a woman with an infant in her arms who was killed as she almost touched the flag of truce, and the women and children of course were strewn all along the circular village until they were dispatched. Right near the flag of truce a mother was shot down with her infant; the child not knowing that its mother was dead was still nursing, and that especially was a very sad sight. The

women as they were fleeing with their babes were killed together, shot right through, and the women who were very heavy with child were also killed. All the Indians fled in these three directions, and after most all of them had been killed a cry was made that all those who were not killed wounded should come forth and they would be safe. Little boys who were not wounded came out of their places of refuge, and as soon as they came in sight a number of soldiers surrounded them and butchered them there.

Of course we all feel very sad about this affair. I stood very loyal to the government all through those troublesome days, and believing so much in the government and being so loyal to it, my disappointment was very strong, and I have come to Washington with a very great blame on my heart. Of course it would have been all right if only the men were killed; we would feel almost grateful for it. But the fact of the killing of the women, and more especially the killing of the young boys and girls who are to go to make up the future strength of the Indian people, is the saddest part of the whole affair and we feel it very sorely.

Source: The Report of the Commissioner of Indian Affairs for 1891, volume 1, Washington, February 11, 1891, pages 179-181.

Makhpiyaluta (Red Cloud), 1891

"Everybody seems to think that the belief in the coming of the Messiah has caused all the trouble. This is a mistake. I will tell you the cause.

When we first made treaties with the Government...the Government promised us all the means necessary to make our living out of our land, and to instruct us how to do it, and abundant food to support us until we could take care of ourselves. We looked forward with hope to the time when we could be as independent as the whites, and have a voice in the Government.

The officers of the army could have helped us better than any others, but we were not left to them. An Indian Department was made, with a large number of agents and other officials drawing large salaries, and these men were supposed to teach us the ways of the whites. Then came the beginning of trouble. These men took care of themselves but not of us. It was made very hard to deal with the Government except through them.... We did not get the means to work our land.... Our rations began to be reduced....

Remember that even our little ponies were taken away under the promise that they would be replaced by oxen and large horses, and that it was long before we saw any, and then we got very few.... Great efforts were made to break up our customs, but nothing was done to introduce the customs of the whites. Everything was done to break the power of the real chiefs, who really wished their people to improve, and little men, so-called chiefs, were made to act as disturbers and agitators. Spotted Tail wanted the ways of the whites, and a cowardly assassin was found to remove him....

Rations were further reduced, and we were starving....The people were desperate from starvation-- they had no hope. They did not think of fighting. What good would it do? They might die like men, but what would all the women and children do? Some say they saw the son of God. All did not see Him. I did not see Him.... We doubted it, because we saw neither Him nor His works....

We were faint with hunger and maddened by despair. We held our dying children, and felt their little bodies tremble as their souls went out and left only a dead weight in our hands.... There was no hope on earth, and God seemed to have forgotten us. Some one had again been speaking of the Son of God, and said He had come. The people did not know; they did not care. They snatched at the hope. They screamed like crazy to Him for mercy. They caught at the promises they heard He had made.

The white men were frightened, and called for soldiers.... We heard that soldiers were coming. We did not fear. We hoped that we could tell them our troubles and get help. A white man said the soldiers meant to kill us. We did not believe it, but some were frightened and ran away to the Bad Lands. The soldiers came. They said: "Don't be afraid; we come to make peace, and not war." It was true. They brought us food, and did not threaten us."

Source: W. Fletcher Johnson, Life of Sitting Bull and History of the Indian War (Philadelphia, 1891), 460-67.

Indian Self Determination

I propose a new goal for our Indian programs: A goal that ends the old debate about "termination" of Indian programs and stresses self-determination; a goal that erases old attitudes of paternalism and promotes partnership self-help. Our goal must be:

A standard of living for the Indians equal to that of the country as a whole.

Freedom of Choice: An opportunity to remain in their homelands, if they choose, without surrendering their dignity; an opportunity to move to the towns and cities of America, if they choose, equipped with the skills to live in equality and dignity.

Full participation in the life of modern America, with a full share of economic opportunity and social justice.

I propose, in short, a policy of maximum choice for the American Indian: a policy expressed in programs of self-help, self-development, self-determination.
Source: Public Papers of the Presidents of the United States: Lyndon B. Johnson, 1968-69, Vol. I, 336-37.

EUROPEAN AMERICANS

White Privilege: Unpacking the Invisible Knapsack

I was taught to see racism only in individual acts of meanness, not in invisible systems conferring dominance on my group.

Through work to bring materials from women's studies into the rest of the curriculum, I have often noticed men's unwillingness to grant that they are over-privileged, even though they may grant that women are disadvantaged. They may say they will work to improve women's status, in the society, the university, or the curriculum, but they can't or won't support the idea of lessening men's. Denials that amount to taboos surround the subject of advantages that men gain from women's disadvantages. These denials protect male privilege from being fully acknowledged, lessened, or ended.
Thinking through unacknowledged male privilege as a phenomenon, I realized that, since hierarchies in our society are interlocking, there are most likely a phenomenon of while privilege that was similarly denied and protected. As a white person, I realized I had been taught about racism as something that puts others at a disadvantage, but had been taught not to see on of its corollary aspects, white privilege, which puts me at an advantage.

I think whites are carefully taught not to recognize white privilege, as males are taught not to recognize male privilege. So I have begun in an untutored way to ask what it is like to have white privilege. I have come to see white privilege as an invisible package of unearned assets that I can count on cashing in each day, but about which I was "meant" to remain oblivious. White privilege is like an invisible weightless knapsack of special provisions, maps, passports, codebooks, visas, clothes, tools, and blank checks.

Describing white privilege makes one newly accountable. As we in Women's Studies work to reveal male privilege and ask men to give up some of their power, so one who writes about having white privilege must ask, "Having described it, what will I do to lessen or end it?"

After I realized the extent to which men work from a base of unacknowledged privilege, I understood that much of their oppressiveness was unconscious. Then I remembered the frequent charges from women of color that white women whom they encounter are oppressive. I began to understand why we are justly seen as oppressive, even when we don't see ourselves that way. I began to count the ways in which I enjoy unearned skin privilege and have been conditioned into oblivion about its existence.

My schooling gave me no training in seeing myself as an oppressor, as an unfairly advantaged person, or as a participant in a damaged culture. I was taught to see myself as an individual whose moral state depended on her individual moral will. My schooling followed the pattern my colleague Elizabeth Minnich has pointed out: whites are taught to think of their lives as morally neutral, normative, and average, and also ideal, so that when we work to benefit others, this is seen as work which will allow "them" to be more like "us".

I decided to try to work on myself at least by identifying some of the daily effects of white privilege in my life. I have chosen those conditions which I think in my case attach somewhat more to skin color privilege than to class, religion, ethnic status, or geographical location, though of course all these other factors are intricately intertwined. As far as I can see, my African American coworkers, friends and acquaintances with whom I come into daily or frequent contact in this particular time, place, and line of work cannot count on most of these conditions.

I usually think of privilege as being a favored state, whether earned or conferred by birth or luck. Yet some of the conditions I have described here work to systematically over-empower certain groups. Such privilege simply confers dominance because of one's race or sex.

1. I can if I wish arrange to be in the company of people of my race most of the time.

2. If I should need to move, I can be pretty sure renting or purchasing housing in an area which I can afford and in which I would want to live.

3. I can be pretty sure that my neighbors in such a location will be neutral or pleasant to me.

4. I can go shopping alone most of the time, pretty well assured that I will not be followed or harassed.

5. I can turn on the television or open to the front page of the paper and see people of my race widely represented.

6. When I am told about our national heritage or about "civilization," I am shown that people of my color made it what it is.

7. I can be sure that my children will be given curricular materials that testify to the existence of their race.

8. If I want to, I can be pretty sure of finding a publisher for this piece on white privilege.

9. I can go into a music shop and count on finding the music of my race represented, into a supermarket and find the staple foods which fit with my cultural traditions, into a hairdresser's shop and find someone who can cut my hair.

10. Whether I use checks, credit cards, or cash, I can count on my skin color not to work against the appearance of financial reliability.

11. I can arrange to protect my children most of the time from people who might not like them.

12. I can swear, or dress in second hand clothes, or not answer letters, without having people attribute these choices to the bad morals, the poverty, or the illiteracy of my race.

13. I can speak in public to a powerful male group without putting my race on trial.

14. I can do well in a challenging situation without being called a credit to my race.

15. I am never asked to speak for all the people of my racial group.

16. I can remain oblivious of the language and customs of persons of color who constitute the world's majority without feeling in my culture any penalty for such oblivion.

17. I can criticize our government and talk about how much I fear its policies and behavior without being seen as a cultural outsider.

18. I can be pretty sure that if I ask to talk to "the person in charge," I will be facing a person of my race.

19. If a traffic cop pulls me over or if the IRS audits my tax return, I can be sure I haven't been singled out because of my race.

20. I can easily buy posters, postcards, picture books, greeting cards, dolls, toys, and children's magazines featuring people of my race.

21. I can go home from most meetings of organizations I belong to feeling somewhat tied in, rather than isolated, out-of-place, out numbered, unheard, held at a distance, or feared.

22. I can take a job with an affirmative action employer without having coworkers on the job suspect that I got it because of race.

23. I can choose public accommodation without fearing that people of my race cannot get in or will be mistreated in the places I have chosen.

24. I can be sure that if I need legal or medical help, my race will not work against me.

25. If my day, week, or year is going badly, I need not ask of each negative episode or situation whether it has racial overtones.

26. I can choose blemish cover or bandages in flesh color and have them more or less match my skin.

I repeatedly forgot each of the realizations on this list until I wrote it down. For me white privilege has turned out to be an elusive and fugitive subject. The pressure to avoid it is great, for in facing it I must give up the myth of meritocracy. If these things are true, this is not such a free country; one's life is not what one makes it; many doors open for certain people through no virtues of their own.

In unpacking this invisible knapsack of white privilege, I have listed conditions of daily experience which I once took for granted. Nor did I think of any of these prerequisites as bad for the holder. I now think that we need a more finely differentiated taxonomy of privilege, for some of these varieties are only what one would want for everyone in a just society, and others give license to be ignorant.

I see a pattern running through the matrix of white privilege, a pattern of assumptions which were passed on to me as a white person. There was one main piece of cultural turf; it was my own turf, and I was among those who could control the turf. My skin color was an asset for any move I was educated to want to make. I could think of myself as belonging in major ways, and of making social systems work for me. I could freely disparage, fear, neglect, or be oblivious to anything outside of the dominant cultural forms. Being of the main culture, I could also criticize it fairly freely.

In proportion as my racial group was being made confident, comfortable, and oblivious, other groups were likely being made unconfident, uncomfortable, and alienated. Whiteness protected me from many kinds of hostility, distress, and violence, which I was being subtly trained to visit in turn upon people of color. For this reason, the word "privilege" now seems to me misleading. We want, then, to distinguish between earned strength and unearned power conferred systematically. Power from unearned privilege can look like strength when it is in fact permission to escape or to dominate. But not all of the privileges on my list are inevitably damaging. Some, like the expectation that neighbors will be decent to you, or that your race will not count against you in court, should be the norm in a just society. Others, like the privilege to ignore less powerful people, distort the humanity of the holders as well as the ignored groups.

We might at least start by distinguishing between positive advantages which we can work to spread, and negative types of advantages which unless rejected will always reinforce our present hierarchies. For example, the feeling that one belongs within the human circle, as Native Americans say, should not be seen as privilege for a few. Ideally it is an unearned entitlement. At present, since only a few have it, it is an unearned advantage for them. This paper results from a process of coming to see that some of the power which I originally saw as attendant on being a human being in the U.S. consisted in unearned advantage and conferred dominance.

I have met very few men who are truly distressed about systemic, unearned male advantage and conferred dominance. And so one question for me and others like me is whether we will be like them, or whether we will get truly distressed, even outraged, about unearned race advantage and conferred dominance and if so, what we will do to lessen them. In any case, we need to do more work in identifying how they actually affect our daily lives. Many, perhaps most, of our white students in the U.S. think that racism doesn't affect them because they are not people of color; they do not see "whiteness" as a racial identity. In addition, since race and sex are not the only advantaging systems at work, we need similarly to examine the daily experience of having age advantage, or ethnic advantage, or physical ability, or advantage related to nationality, religion, or sexual orientation.

Difficulties and dangers surrounding the task of finding parallels are many. Since racism, sexism, and heterosexism are not the same, the advantaging associated with them should not be seen as the same. In addition, it is hard to disentangle aspects of unearned advantage which rest more on social class, economic class, race, religion, sex and ethnic identity than on other factors. Still, all of the oppressions are interlocking, as the Combahee River Collective Statement of 1977 continues to remind us eloquently. One factor seems clear about all of the interlocking oppressions. They take both active forms which we can see and embedded forms which as a member of the dominant group one is taught not to see. In my class and place, I did not see myself as a racist because I was taught to recognize racism only in individual acts of meanness by members of my group, never in invisible systems conferring unsought racial dominance on my group from birth.

Disapproving of the systems won't be enough to change them. I was taught to think that racism could end if white individuals changed their attitudes. But a white skin in the United States opens many doors for whites whether or not we approve of the way dominance has been conferred on us. Individual acts can palliate, but cannot end, these problems.

To redesign social systems we need first to acknowledge their colossal unseen dimensions. The silences and denials surrounding privilege are the key political tool here. They keep the thinking about equality or equity incomplete, protecting unearned advantage and conferred dominance by making these taboo subjects. Most talk by whites about equal opportunity seems to be now to be about equal opportunity to try to get into a position of dominance while denying that systems of dominance exist.

It seems to me that obliviousness about white advantage, like obliviousness about male advantage, is kept strongly inculturated in the United States so as to maintain the myth of meritocracy, the myth that democratic choice is equally available to all. Keeping most people unaware that freedom of confident action is there for just a small number of people props up those in power, and serves to keep power in the hands of the same groups that have most of it already.

Though systemic change takes many decades, there are pressing questions for me and I imagine for some others like me if we raise our daily consciousness on the perquisites of being light skinned. What will we do with such knowledge? As we know from watching men, it is an open question whether we will choose to use unearned advantage to weaken hidden systems of advantage, and whether we will use any of our arbitrarily awarded power to try to reconstruct power systems on a broader base.

Source: McIntosh, Peggy. "White Privilege: Unpacking the Invisible Knapsack". From Working Paper 189. "White Privilege and Male Privilege: A Personal Account of Coming To See Correspondences Through Work In Women's Studies" (1988), Wellesley College Center for Research on Women, Wellesley MA 02181.

The Ghettos

The place was important too. Settlement in America had snipped the continuity of the immigrants' work and ideas, of their religious life. It would also impose a new relationship to the world of space about them. In the Old Country setting, the physical scene had been integral with the existence of the men in it. Changes would have explosive repercussions.

In the United States, the newcomers pushed their roots into many different soils. Along the city's unyielding asphalt streets, beside the rutted roads of mill or mining towns, amidst the exciting prairie acres, they established the homes of the New World. But wherever the immigrants went, there was one common experience they shared: nowhere could they transplant the European village. Whatever the variations among environments in America, none was familiar. The pressure of that strangeness exerted a deep influence upon the character of resettlement, upon the usual forms of behavior, and upon the modes of communal action that emerged as the immigrants became Americans.

The old conditions of living could not survive in the new conditions of space. Ways long taken for ranted in the village adjusted slowly and painfully to density of population in the cities, to disorder in the towns, and o distance on the farms. That adjustment was the means of creating the new communities within which these people would live.

Although the great mass of immigrants spent out their days in the great cities, there was always an unorganized quality to settlement in such places that left a permanent impress upon every fresh arrival. Chance was so large an element in the course of migration, it left little room for planning. The place of landing was less often the outcome of an intention held at the outset of the journey than of a blind drift along the routes of trade or of a sudden halt due to the accidents of the voyage. Consequently the earliest concentrations of the foreign-born were in the chain of Atlantic seaports: Boston, Philadelphia, Baltimore, New Orleans, and most of all New York, the unrivaled mart of Europe's commerce with America. For the same reasons, later concentrations appeared at the inland termini, the points of exchange between rail and river or lake traffic— Cleveland, Chicago, Cincinnati, Pittsburgh, an St. Louis.

In all such places the newcomers pitched themselves in the midst of communities that were already growing rapidly and that were therefore already crowded. Between 1840 and 1870, for instance, the population of New York City mounted by fully 50 per cent every ten years, for every two people at the start of a decade, there were three at its end (In all, the 312,000 residents of 1840 had become 3,437,000 in 1900.) Chicago's rise was even more precipitate; the 4000 inhabitants there in 1840 numbered 1,700,000 in 1900. Every ten-year interval saw two people struggling for the space formerly occupied by one.

These largest cities were representative of the rest. The natural increase through the excess of births over deaths, with the additional increase through the shift of native-born population from rural to urban areas, and with the further increase through oversea immigration, all contributed to the enormous growth of American municipalities. To house all the new city dwellers was a problem of staggering proportions. Facilities simply did not keep pace with the demand.

To house the immigrants was more difficult still. For these people had not the mobility to choose where they should live or the means to choose how. Existing on the tenuous income supplied by unskilled labor, they could not buy homes; nor could they lay out much in payment of rent. Their first thought in finding accommodations was that the cost be as little as possible. The result was they got as little as possible.

The willingness to accept a minimum of comfort and convenience did not, however, mean that such quarters would always be available. Under the first impact of immigration, the unprepared cities had not ready the housing immigrants could afford. The newcomers were driven to accept hand-me-downs, vacated places that could be converted to their service at a profit.

The immigrants find their first homes in quarters the old occupants no longer desire. As business grows, the commercial center of each city begins to blight the neighboring residential districts. The well-to-do are no longer willing to live in close proximity to the bustle of warehouses and offices; yet that same proximity sets a high value on real estate. To spend money on the repair or upkeep of houses in such areas is only wasteful; for they will soon be torn down to make way for commercial buildings. The simplest, most profitable use is to divide the old mansions into tiny lodgings. The rent on each unit will be low; but the aggregate of those sums will, without substantial investment or risk, return larger dividends than any other present use of the property.

Such accommodations have additional attractions for the immigrants. They are close to the familiar region of the docks and they are within walking distance of the places where labor is hired; precious carfare will be saved by living here. In every American city some such district of first settlement receives the newcomers.

Not that much is done to welcome them. The carpenters hammer shut connecting doors and build rude partitions up across the halls' middle-class homes thus become laborers'—only not one to a family, but shared among many. What's more, behind the original structures are grassy yards where children once had run about at play. There is to be no room for games now. Sheds and shanties, hurriedly thrown up, provide living space; and if a stable is there, so much the better: that too can be turned to account. In 1850 already in New York some seven thousand households are finding shelter in such rear buildings. By this time too ingenuity has uncovered still other resources: fifteen hundred cellars also do service as homes.

If these conversions are effected without much regard for the convenience of the ultimate occupants, they nevertheless have substantial advantages. The carpenter aims to do the job as expeditiously as possible; he has not the time to contrive the most thorough use of space; and waste square feet leave luxurious corners. There are limits to the potentialities for crowding in such quarters.

There were no such limits when enterprising contractors set to work devising edifices more suitable for the reception of these residents. As the population continued to grow, and the demand with it, perspicacious owners of real estate saw profit in the demolition of the old houses and the construction, between narrow alleys, of compact barracks that made complete use of every inch of earth.

Where once had been Mayor Delavall's orchard, Cherry Street in New York ran its few blocks to the East River shipyards. At Number 36, in 1853, stood Gotham Court, one of the better barracks buildings. Five stories in height, it stretched back one hundred and fifty feet from the street, between two tight alleys (one nine, the other seven feet wide). Onto the more spacious alley opened twelve doors through each of which passed the ten families that lived within, two to each floor in identical two-room apartments (one room, 9 x 14; one bedroom, 9 x 6). Here without interior plumbing or heat were the homes of five hundred people. Ten years later, there were some improvements: for the service of the community, a row of privies in the basement, flushed occasionally by Croton water. But by then there were more than eight hundred dwellers in the structure, which indeed continued in use till the very end of the century.

That these conditions were not then reckoned outlandish was shown in the model workmen's home put up by philanthropic New Yorkers at Elizabeth and Mott Street. Each suite in this six-story structure had three rooms; but the rooms were smaller (4 x 11, 8 x7, and 8 x 7). There were gas lights in the halls; but the water closets were in sheds in the alleys. And well over half the rooms had no windows at all.

At the middle of the nineteenth century, these developments were still chaotic, dependent upon the fancy of the individual builder. But the pressure of rising demand and the pattern of property holding gradually shaped a common form for the tenement house. The older barracks still left waste space in alleys, halls, and stair well; and they did not conform to the uniform city real-estate plot. Attached to its neighbors on either side, it left vacant only a strip, perhaps ten feet deep, in the rear. On a floor space of approximately twenty by ninety feet, it was possible, within this pattern, to get four four-room apartments.

The feat was accomplished by narrowing the building at its middle so that it took on the shape of a dumbbell. The indentation was only two-and-a-half feet wide and varied in length from five to fifty feet; but, added to the similar indentations of the adjoining houses, it created on each side an airshaft five feet wide. In each apartment three of the rooms could present their windows to the shaft, draw from it air and light as well; only one chamber in each suite need face upon the street or rear yard. The stairs, halls and common water closets were cramped into the narrow center of the building so that almost the whole of its surface was available for living quarters.

These structures were at least six stories in height, sometimes eight. At the most moderate reckoning, twenty-four to thirty-two families could be housed on this tiny space, or more realistically, anywhere from one hundred and fifty to two hundred human beings. It was not a long block that held ten such tenements on either side of the street, not an unusual block that was home for some four thousand people.

There were drastic social consequences to living under these dense conditions. The immigrants had left villages which counted their populations in scores. In the Old World a man's whole circle of acquaintances had not taken in as many individuals as lived along a single street here. By a tortuous course of adjustments, the newcomers worked out new modes of living in response to their environment. But the cost of those adjustments was paid out of the human energies of the residents and through the physical deterioration of the districts in which they lived.

The tenement flourished most extensively in New York, the greatest point of immigrant concentration. But it was also known in Boston and in the other Atlantic ports. In the interior cities it was less common; there land values were not so rigid and commercial installations not such barriers to the centrifugal spread of population. From the barrack like buildings of the area of first settlement, the immigrants could move out to smaller units where at least the problems of density were less oppressive. Little two-story cottages that held six families were characteristic of places like Buffalo. Elsewhere were wooden three- or four-floor structures that contained a dozen households. Even single homes were to be found, dilapidated shanties or jerry-built boxes low in rent. Yet internally these accommodations were not superior to those of the tenement. In one form or another, the available housing gave the districts to which the immigrants went the character of slums.

Well, they were not ones to choose, who had lived in the thatched peasant huts of home. Nor was it unbearably offensive to reside in the least pleasant parts of the city, in Chicago over against the slaughterhouses, in Boston hemmed in by the docks and markets of the North End, in New York against the murky river traffic of the East Side. Such disadvantages they could survive. The hardship came in more subtle adjustments demanded of them.

Certainly the flats were small and overcrowded. In no room of the dumbbell tenement could you pace off more than eleven feet; and the reforming architects of 1900 still thought of chambers no larger than those of Gotham Court. In addition, the apartments shrank still further when shared by more than one family or when they sheltered lodgers, as did more than half those in New York at the end of the century. But that was not the worst of it.

Here is a woman. In the Old Country she had lived much of her life, done most of her work, outdoors. In America, the flat confines her. She divides up her domain by calico sheets hung on ropes, tries to make a place for her people and possessions. But there is no place and she has not room to turn about. It is true, everything is in poor repair, the rain comes through the ceilings, the wind blows dirt through the cracks in the wall. But she does not even know how to go about restoring order, establishing cleanliness. She breaks her back to exterminate the proliferating vermin. What does she get? A dozen lice behind the collar.

The very simplest tasks become complex and disorganizing. Every day there is a family to feed. Assume she knows how to shop, and can manage the unfamiliar coal stove or gas range. But what does one do with rubbish who has never known the meaning of waste? It is not really so important to walk down the long flight of narrow stairs each time there are some scraps to be disposed of. The windows offer and easier alternative. After all, the obnoxious wooden garbage boxes that adorn the littered fronts of the houses expose their contents unashamed through split sides and, rarely emptied, themselves become the nests of boldly foraging rodents.

The filthy streets are seldom cleaned; the municipality is not particularly solicitous of these, the poorest quarters of the city. The alleys are altogether passed b and the larger thoroughfares receive only occasionally the services of the scavenger. The inaccessible alleys and rear yards are never touched and, to be sure, are redolent of the fact. In the hot summer months the stench of rotting things will mark these places and the stained snow of winter will not conceal what lies beneath. Here and there an unwitting newcomer tries the disastrous experiment of keeping a goat, adds thereby to the distinctive flavor of his neighborhood.

It was the same in every other encounter with the new life. Conveniences not missed in the villages became sore necessities in the city; although often the immigrants did not know their lack till dear experience taught them. Of what value were sunlight and fresh air on the farm? But how measure their worth for those who lived in the three hundred and fifty thousand dark interior rooms of New York in 1900!

There was the rude matter of what Americans called sanitation. Some of the earliest buildings had had no privies at all; the residents had been expected to accommodate themselves elsewhere as best they could. Tenements from mid-century onward had generally water closets in the yards and alleys, no great comfort to the occupants of the fifth and sixth floors. The newest structures had two toilets to each floor; but these were open to the custom of all comers, charged to the care of none, and left to the neglect of all. If in winter the pipes froze in unheated hallways and the clogged contents overflowed, weeks would go by before some dilatory repairman set matters right. Months thereafter a telling odor hung along the narrow hallways.

What of it? The filth was inescapable. In these districts where the need was greatest, the sewage systems were primitive and ineffectual. Open drains were long common; in Boston one such, for years, tumbled down the slope of Jacob's Ladder in the South Cove; and in Chicago the jocosely named Bubbly Creek wended its noisome way aboveground until well into the twentieth century.

With the water supply there had always been trouble at home too: poor wells, shallow, and inconveniently situated. The inconvenience here was not unexpected. Still it was a burden to carry full tubs and jugs from the taps in the alley up the steep stairs. Not till late was the city water directly connected with the toilets; it was later still to reach the kitchen sink; and bathrooms had not yet put in an appearance in these quarters. Then, too, the consequences were more painful: city dirt was harder to scrub away, and there was no nearby creek. It could well be, as they came to say, that a man got a good bath only twice in his life: from midwife and undertaker.

All might yet be tolerable were not the confining dimensions of the flat so oppressive. The available space simply would not yield to all the demands made upon it. Where were the children to play if the fields were gone? Where were things to be stored or clothes to be hung? Beds or bedding consumed the bedroom; there was only one living room, and sink and stove left little free of that. The man in the evening, come home from work, found not a niche for rest; the tiny intervals of leisure were wasted for want of a place to spend them. Privacy now was more often sought for than in the Old Country where every person and every thing had its accustomed spot. Yet privacy now was difficult to achieve; there was no simple way of dividing space too mall to share. Under pressure of the want, the constricted beings bowed to a sense of strain.

Disorganization affects particularly the life of the home. In these tiny rooms that now are all they call their home, many traditional activities wither and disappear. Not here will the friends be welcomed, festivals commemorated, children taught, and the family unite to share n the warmth of its security. Emptied of the meaning of these occurrences and often crowded with strange lodgers, home is just the feeding and sleeping place. All else moves to the outside.

The street becomes the great artery of life for the people of these districts. Sometimes, the boys and girls play in the back in the narrow yards, looking up at the lines of drying clothes that spiderweb the sky above them. More often the crowded street itself is the more attractive playground. They run in games through the moving traffic, find fun in the appearance of some hopeful street musician, or regard with dejected envy the wares of the itinerant vendors of seasonal delicacies, the sweet shaved ice of summer, the steaming potatoes and chestnuts of fall and winter.

The adults too drift out, sit on the steps, flow over onto the sidewalks. The women bring their work outdoors, the men at evening hang about, now and then talk. They begin to be neighborly, learn to be sensitive to each other. That is the good of it.

There is also the bad. The street in its strangeness is the evidence of the old home's disintegration. Why, the very aspect is forbidding: the dear sun never shines brightly, the still air between the high buildings is so saturated with stench it would take a dragon to hold out. These are all signs of the harshness of the physical environment, of the difficulties of living in these quarters, of the disintegration here of old ways. Those children in earnest play at the corner—who controls them, to what discipline are they subject? They do not do the things that children ought. No one does the things he ought. The place prevents it.

Almost resignedly, the immigrants witnessed in themselves a deterioration. All relationships became less binding, all behavior more dependent on individual whim. The result was a marked personal decline and a noticeable wavering of standards.

Some of the reactions to the new conditions of living were immediate, direct, and overt. The low level of health and the high incidence of disease were certain products of overcrowding. Residents of the tenements did not need the spotted maps of later students to tell them where tuberculosis hit, a terror of an illness that spread from victim to victim in the stifling rooms. If the cholera came, or smallpox, or diphtheria—and all did in their time—it was impossible to limit their decimating course. Little else by now remained communal; but contagion and infection these people could not help but share with each other.

The mortality rate was an indication of their helplessness against disease. The immigrants were men and women in the prime of life, yet they died more rapidly than the generality of Americans. Everywhere their life expectancy was lower; and. as might be anticipated, it was particularly infants who suffered. In one Chicago precinct at the end of the nineteenth century, three babies of every five born died before they reached their first birthday.

§ § §

There were other means of release, temporary of duration and therefore more subject to control. It was thus possible, for a time, to dissolve in alcohol the lease soluble of problems. After a day's effort to hammer happiness out of the unyielding American environment it was good, now and then, to go not to the narrow realities of home but to the convivial places where the glass played the main part. The setting could take a variety of forms: basement shops, combination kitchen-and-bars, little cafes, the Irish grocery of 1850, the German Bierstube of 1870, the Italian speakeasy of 1900 to which prohibition would later bring another clientele. But the end was the same, a temporary relaxation of tension. And the end was so clear that some could achieve it alone, in the fastness of their own rooms, with the solitary company of a bottle.

There were immigrants who came to America with the inclination to drunkenness already well established. In Ireland, whisky went farther than bread as a relief from hunger; in Norway, eighteen quarts of alcohol were consumed for every person in the country each year; and elsewhere through Europe the habit of imbibing was well known. There were other newcomers who learned to know the consolations of a dram in the course of the crossing. A bit of grog was the regular prescription for seasickness; if it effected no cure, it dulled the misery.

It was that relief a man needed as much as the eyes in his head. Sometimes he drank away without thought what he had bathed in sweat to earn but he gained in return an interval free of recollection or anticipation. In the good company, as his burdens lightened, he discovered in himself altogether unexpected but exhilarating powers, acquired daring and self-confidence beyond any sober hope. Well, and sometimes it would lead to a brawl, and the falling clubs of policemen, and the cold awakening of a cell; or, if not that, simply to the next day's throbbing reckoning of costs: what things the money might have bought! but there was none to point the finger of blame; and the temptation came again and again. Not a few succumbed in every group of immigrants, though more in some groups than in others.

There was still another way of entering immediately into a realm of hope that shone in bright contrast to the visible dreariness about them. In that realm the evil dame, Chance, was transfigured into a luminous goddess; no longer as in real life did she strike down the lowly, but elevated them. Chance, here, ceased to deal out disaster; instead, conjured up the most heartwarming dreams.

Sometimes the men gambled among themselves, drew cards or lots for little stakes. There was a finger game Italians played, and among eastern Europeans a liking for pinochle. But these were sociable as much as gambling occasions, and had unpleasant disadvantages. The sum of little fortunes around the table hardly made a total worth the winning. One man's gain was another's loss; the joy of one, another's sorrow. Chance had not free rein; skill was as well involved, and the strain of calculation. Most of all, there was not the solitude in which the mind could drift away from time and place and rock itself in the comfort of hope.

Much preferable was some form of the lottery: the stakes were small, the rewards enormous; one might wind, but none lost much; and chance was absolute. Lottery took many guises from the informal picks and chances of bar and shop to the highly organized enterprises city-wide in extension. Beneath was the attractiveness of an identical dream.

He can sit with a card, one of scores, in a club or saloon, check the squares, wait the call. Over and over and over again the little cage spins and no one knows when the little cage stops and a little ball hops and the number comes forth for the fortunate man. There's no telling—who knows? This may be when. The word's on his lips; let but chance give the sign and he win rise, keno, lotto, bingo, and all will be his.

She buys the slip from a policy man, who may be the corner grocer, the mailman, or anyone who in a daily round encounters a constant circle of people. Her number costs what she can spare, a dime, a nickel, just a penny. She chooses by what signs chance may give, a dream, an omen, a sudden intuition, and all day carries hope in her apron.

Did they really think to win who could not afford to lose? Yes, in a way they did, although they knew what odds were against them. But why not they? They would grant you that thousands lost for one who won b, but could they surrender that one hope too? His hand that holds the card is soft and white, a hand that signs checks and gestures commands, the hand of a man who will drive to the comfort of a decent home. Her slip rests in the pocket of a gown, a gown that rustles leisurely as she walks with shining children up the steps. Indeed they have so often spent the money, and had the pleasure of dreaming it, it hardly mattered that they lost. At the price they paid, such dreams were cheap enough.

§ § §

Without a doubt they wished also to escape from the physical environment itself. As the years went by they got to know that the city held also pleasant tree-shaded streets where yards and little gardens set the houses off from each other. To these green spaces the most daring hearts aspired.

After 1850, cheaper rapid-transit systems brought the suburbs closer to the heart of the city. On the street railway the trolley took the horse's place and was joined by subway and elevated lines. Through these channels, the laboring masses spilled out from the district of first settlement to the surrounding regions. Naturally, this was a selective process; those who had a modicum of well-being, who could afford the higher rents and transportation charges, moved most freely. The poorest were immobilized by their poverty.

Those who went gained by going, but not by any means all they hoped for. Somehow, what they touched turned to dross. The fine house they saw in their mind's vision across the bridge or over the ferry turned out in actuality to have been converted into narrow flats for several families. In the empty spaces, little cottages rose; and long rows of two- and three-story attached buildings shut off the sight of the trees. The trouble was, so many moved that these newer places began to repeat the experience of the area of first settlement.

Never mind, for a time at least it was better. There was room to keep a goat, a few chickens; the men could sit at ease in their own front rooms facing the friendly street, while the women visited through the sociable low windows. This was a home to which attachments could grow, a place where deviations were less likely to appear.

And if in time the pressure of mounting population brought here too the tenement, and the spreading slum engulfed this first refuge, then those who could launched upon a second remove. Then a third. Till at last the city was a patchwork of separated districts, the outlines of which were shaped by the transit facilities, by the quality of available housing, and by the prior occupancy of various groups of immigrants. Always in this winnowing process the poorest were left in the older sections; the ability to move outward went with prosperity. Unfortunately it was the outer regions that were the thinnest settled. Least capable of organizing their lives to the new environment, the great mass long clustered at the center.

On the farms, space was too ample, not too little. Emptiness, not overcrowding, was the disorganizing element; and for those whose habits of life were developed in the peasant village, the emptiness of the prairie farm was in its own way as troublesome as the crowding of the city slum.

Here they called them neighbors who lived two or three miles off. Here one could stand on the highest rise of land and see nowhere but in the one farmstead any sign of man's tenancy. Such distances were too great to permit easy adjustment by the newcomers.

The peculiar characteristics of the prairie where the distances were greatest tested the immigrants to the utmost. In the midst of the open places they came by wagon and confronted the problem of shelter. They would live in what they could themselves build, for there was no community to help them; and certainly nothing was ready, awaiting their arrival. If they were fortunate, they found a nearby wood where the stove could rest and they could camp while the men chopped the logs for the cabin.

The cabin, no doubt, had its defects as a residence. it was small, perhaps twelve by fourteen feet in all; and above and below and about was mud, for the floor was as they found it and the spaces in the roof and walls were chinked with clay to keep the weather out.

But the people who settled into such quarters had only to compare situations with those who found no wood nearby, to count their own blessings. The cost of bringing timber in was at first prohibitive. If there were none on the spot, home would be of another material. Some would burrow dugouts into the slopes, return unknowingly to the life of the caves. Many cut the sunbaked surface of the earth, piled the sod in a double wall with dirt between, and in these huts spent a long period of trial.

Often years went by before such farmers advanced to the dignity of a frame house, with separate plastered rooms. There were first a barn and all the appurtenances of agriculture to be acquired. Meanwhile they got on in narrow quarters, felt the wind of winter through the cracks, heard the sides settle in the spring thaw, saw surprised snakes or gophers penetrate the floor.

Under such circumstances, there was an additional depth to their helplessness. No trees shielded them against the blast of winds. They were parched in the dry heat and they perished in the merciless blizzards. Hail and drought came and the clouds of grasshoppers that ate up their crops. On a limited monotonous diet the immigrants sickened, from the sudden shifts in climate the ague got them, from the prevalence of dirt, the itch. No doctors were near and home remedies or self-prescribed cures from bottles put a sad but decisive end to their misery. Alone in these distances they could expect no help.

That was the worst of it. The isolation which all immigrants sensed to some degree, on the farm was absolute; and not only on the prairie but everywhere. In the older Midwestern states, where the newcomers were not the first to settle, they found homes built and clearings made at their arrival; and soil and climate were not so hostile. Still, even there, they were detached, cut off from the company of other men. Each family was thrown in upon itself; every day the same faces round the same table and never the sight of outsiders. To have no familiar of one's own age and sex was a hard deprivation.

They would think sometimes of the friendly village ways, of the common tasks lightened for being done in common; they would remember the cheering inn, and the road on which some reassuring known figure could always be seen. At such times, alone in the distance, helpless in their isolation, a vague and disturbing melancholia fell over them. It was easier for them when they added acres and when stocked barns and heavy wagonloads gave a sense of substance and achievement to their lives. Still, even then would come regrets for the disorganization wrought in their existence by the place. Insanity appeared among some; others sought solace in alcohol and most continued to work, under strain, eager for relief.

They would probably have said that it was the mill town made the least demand upon them. This was not so large as a single city ward and here space was not at a premium; yet neither was there here the complete isolation of the farm. The immigrants' round of activities here fell into a unit the size of which they could comprehend.

What pressure there was came from the situation of such communities. Often a single company or at most a single industry supplied the employment for all the residents. Any man who came to work in the mine or factory was altogether dependent upon the sole hirer. He was not free to choose among jobs or to argue long about terms; he could only acquiesce or leave. In that sense, it was a condition of his membership in this community that he cut himself off from the world outside the town.

Confined within the immediate locality, the laborers discovered that there was plenty of space, but not plenty of housing. Despite the low density of population, the available quarters were so restricted there was serious overcrowding. As the workers arrived they found at first only the farm or village buildings, quickly converted to their use. The single men were likely to live in makeshift boarding-houses; those with families in cup-up portions of the old houses. Shortly either the company or individual investors threw up additional facilities. Into the surrounding farm land, narrow alleys were pushed, lined with three-story frame tenements or with tiny two-room cottages. The company which controlled all was hardly interested in increasing the supply of housing to an unprofitable excess over demand; nor was it anxious to go to the expense of providing gas, water, and sewerage. The results matched those of the city slums.

Still, the open fields were not far off, and there was not the same total lack of space. The disorganizing effects of the environment were therefore probably less harsh, the deviations less pronounced. What strain there was, was the product of confinement in the town and of constricted housing.

To some degree, these factory town immigrants, like those who went to the cities and those who settled on farms, found the physical conditions of life in America hostile. Nowhere could they recapture the terms of village life; everywhere a difficult adjustment began with the disorganization of the individual, now grown uncertain as to his own proper role. Reorganization would involve first the creation of new means of social action within which the man alone could locate himself.

From the physical as from the religious experience with the New World, the immigrants had gained a deep consciousness of their separateness. It seemed sometimes as if there were only one street in the world, and only a single house on it, and nothing more—only walls and very few people, so that I am in American and I do not even know whether it is America. This street was apart as if a ghetto wall defined it. On other streets were other men, deeply different because they had not the burden of this adjustment to bear. This street and those did not run into each other; nor this farm into those. If the immigrants were to achieve the adjustment to their new environment, it had to be within the confines of the ghettos in the environment created.

Source: Handlin, Oscar. "The Ghettos." Excerpted from chapter 6 in The Uprooted: The Epic Story of the Great Migrations That Made the American People. Little, Brown, & Company. 1951.

Plunkitt of Tammany Hall

Everybody is talkin' these days about Tammany men growin' rich on graft, but nobody thinks of drawin' the distinction between honest graft and dishonest graft. There's all the difference in the world between the two. Yes, many of our men have grown rich in politics. I have myself. I've made a big fortune out of the game, and I'm gettin' richer every day, but I've not gone in for dishonest graft-blackmailin' gamblers, saloonkeepers, disorderly people, etc.-and neither has any of the men who have made big fortunes in politics.

There's an honest graft, and I'm an example of how it works. I might sum up the whole thing by sayin': "I seen my opportunities and I took 'em." Just let me explain by examples. My party's in power in the city, and it's goin' to undertake a lot of public improvements. Well, I'm tipped off, say, that they're going to lay out a new park at a certain place.

I see my opportunity and I take it. I go to that place and I buy up all the land I can in the neighborhood. Then the board of this or that makes its plan public, and there is a rush to get my land, which nobody cared particular for before.

Ain't it perfectly honest to charge a good price and make a profit on my investment and foresight? Of course, it is. Well, that's honest graft. Or supposin' it's a new bridge they're goin' to build. I get tipped off and I buy as much property as I can that has to be taken for approaches. I sell at my own price later on and drop some more money in the bank.

Wouldn't you? It's just like lookin' ahead in Wall Street or in the coffee or cotton market. It's honest graft, and I'm lookin' for it every day in the year. I will tell you frankly that I've got a good lot of it, too.

I'll tell you of one case. They were goin' to fix up a big park, no matter where. I got on to it, and went lookin' about for land in that neighborhood.

I could get nothin' at a bargain but a big piece of swamp, but I took it fast enough and held on to it. What turned out was just what I counted on. They couldn't make the park complete without Plunkitt's swamp, and they had to pay a good price for it. Anything dishonest in that?

Up in the watershed I made some money, too. I bought up several bits of land there some years ago and made a pretty good guess that they would be bought up for water purposes later by the city.

Somehow, I always guessed about right, and shouldn't I enjoy the profit of my foresight? It was rather amusin' when the condemnation commissioners came along and found piece after piece of the land in the name of George Plunkitt of the Fifteenth Assembly District, New York City. They wondered how I knew just what to buy. The answer is-I seen my opportunity and I took it. I haven't confined myself to land; anything that pays is in my line.

For instance, the city is repavin' a street and has several hundred thousand old granite blocks to sell. I am on hand to buy, and I know just what they are worth.

How? Never mind that. I had a sort of monopoly of this business for a while, but once a newspaper tried to do me. It got some outside men to come over from Brooklyn and New Jersey to bid against me.

Was I done? Not much. I went to each of the men and said: "How many of these 250,000 stones do you want?" One said 20,000, and another wanted 15,000, and other wanted 10,000. I said: "All right, let me bid for the lot, and I'll give each of you all you want for nothin'." They agreed, of course. Then the auctioneer yelled:

"How much am I bid for these 250,000 fine pavin'
stones?"
"Two dollars and fifty cents," says I.
"Two dollars and fifty cents" screamed the auctioneer.
"Oh, that's a joke Give me a real bid."
He found the bid was real enough. My rivals stood
silent. I got the lot for $2.50 and gave them their share.
That's how the attempt to do Plunkitt ended, and that's
how all such attempts end.
I've told you how I got rich by honest graft. Now, let me
tell you that most politicians who are accused of robbin'
the city get rich the same way.
They didn't steal a dollar from the city treasury. They
just seen their opportunities and took them. That is why,
when a reform administration comes in and spends a
half million dollars in tryin' to find the public robberies
they talked about in the campaign, they don't find them.
The books are always all right. The money in the city
treasury is all right. Everything is all right. All they can
show is that the Tammany heads of departments looked
after their friends, within the law, and gave them what
opportunities they could to make honest graft. Now, let
me tell you that's never goin' to hurt Tammany with the
people. Every good man looks after his friends, and any
man who doesn't isn't likely to be popular. If I have a
good thing to hand out in private life, I give it to a friend.
Why shouldn't I do the same in public life?
Another kind of honest graft. Tammany has raised a
good many salaries. There was an awful howl by the
reformers, but don't you know that Tammany gains ten
votes for every one it lost by salary raisin'?
The Wall Street banker thinks it shameful to raise a
department clerk's salary from $1500 to $1800 a year,
but every man who draws a salary himself says: "That's
all right. I wish it was me." And he feels very much like

votin' the Tammany ticket on election day, just out of sympathy.

Tammany was beat in 1901 because the people were deceived into believin' that it worked dishonest graft. They didn't draw a distinction between dishonest and honest graft, but they saw that some Tammany men grew rich, and supposed they had been robbin' the city treasury or levyin' blackmail on disorderly houses, or workin' in with the gamblers and lawbreakers.

As a matter of policy, if nothing else, why should the Tammany leaders go into such dirty business, when there is so much honest graft lyin' around when they are in power? Did you ever consider that?

Now, in conclusion, I want to say that I don't own a dishonest dollar. If my worst enemy was given the job of writin' my epitaph when I'm gone, he couldn't do more than write:

"George W. Plunkitt. He Seen His Opportunities, and He Took 'Em."

Source: Riordan, William. <u>Plunkitt of Tammany Hall</u>. E.P. Dutton. 1905.

On The Subway

The boy and I face each other.
His feet are huge, in black sneakers
laced with white in a complex pattern like a
a set of intentional scars. We are stuck on
opposite sides of the car, a couple of
molecules stuck in a rod of light
rapidly moving through darkness. He has the
casual cold look of a mugger,
alert under hooded lids. He is wearing
red, like the inside of the body
exposed. I am wearing dark fur, the
whole skin of an animal taken and

used. I look at his raw face,
he looks at my fur coat, and I didn't
know if I am in his power-
he could take my coat so easily, my
briefcase, my life-
of if he is in my power, the way I am
living off his life, eating the steak
he does not eat, as if I am taking
the food from his mouth. And he is black
and I am white, and without meaning or
trying to I must profit from his darkness,
the way he absorbs the murderous beams of the
nation's heart, as black cotton
absorbs the heat of the sun and holds it. There is
no way to know how easy this
white skin makes my life, this
life he could take so easily and
break across his knee like a stick the way
his own back is being broken, the
rob of his soul that at birth was dark and
fluid and rich as the heart of a seedling
ready to thrust up into any available light.
Source: Olds, Sharon. <u>The Gold Cell</u>. Alfred A. Knopf, Inc. 1987.

A Black Man Ponders His Power To Alter Public Space

My first victim was a woman - white, well dressed, probably in her early twenties. I came upon her late one evening on a deserted street in Hyde Park, a relatively affluent neighborhood in an otherwise mean, impoverished section of Chicago. As I swung onto the avenue behind her, there seemed to be a discreet, un-inflammatory distance between us. Not so. She cast back a worried glance. To her, the youngish black man-a broad six feet two inches with a beard and billowing hair, both hands shoved into the pockets of a bulky military jacket-seemed menacingly close. After a few more quick glimpses, she picked up her pace and was soon running in earnest. Within seconds she disappeared into a cross street.

That was more than a decade ago. I was twenty-two years old, a graduate student newly arrived at the University of Chicago. It was in the echo of that terrified woman's footfalls that I first began to know the unwieldy inheritance I'd come into-the ability to alter public space in ugly ways. It was clear that she thought herself the quarry of a mugger, a rapist, or worse. Suffering a bout of insomnia, however, I was stalking sleep, not defenseless wayfarers. As a softy who is scarcely able to take a knife to a raw chicken - let alone hold it to a person's throat - I was surprised, embarrassed, and dismayed all at once. Her flight made me feel like an accomplice in tyranny. It also made it clear that I was indistinguishable from the muggers who occasionally seeped into the area from the surrounding ghetto. That first encounter, and those that followed, signified that a vast, unnerving gulf lay between nighttime pedestrians - particularly women - and me. And I soon gathered that being perceived as dangerous is a hazard in itself. I only needed to turn a corner into a dicey situation, or crowd some frightened, armed person in a foyer somewhere, or make an errant move after being pulled over by a policeman. Where fear and weapons meet - and they often do in urban America - there is always the possibility of death.

In that first year, my first away from my hometown, I was to become thoroughly familiar with the language of fear. At dark, shadowy intersections in Chicago, I could cross in front of a car stopped at a traffic light and elicit the thunk, thunk, thunk, thunk of the driver - black, white, male, or female-hammering down the door locks. On less traveled streets after dark, I grew accustomed to but never comfortable with people who crossed to the other side of the street rather than pass me. Then there were the standard unpleasantries with police, doormen, bouncers, cabdrivers, and others whose business is to screen out troublesome individuals before there is any nastiness.

I moved to New York nearly two years ago and I have remained an avid night walker. In central Manhattan, the near-constant crowd cover minimizes tense one-on-one street encounters. Elsewhere - visiting friends in SoHo,1 where sidewalks are narrow and tightly spaced buildings shut out the sky - things can get very taut indeed.

Black men have a firm place in New York mugging literature. Norman Podhoretz2 in his famed (or infamous) 1963 essay, "My Negro Problem - And Ours," recalls growing up in terror of black males; they "were tougher than we were, more ruthless," he writes-and as an adult on the Upper West Side of Manhattan, he continues, he cannot constrain his nervousness when he meets black men on certain streets. Similarly, a decade later, the essayist and novelist Edward Hoagland extols a New York where once "Negro bitterness bore down mainly on other Negroes." Where some see mere panhandlers, Hoagland sees" a mugger who is clearly screwing up his nerve to do more than just ask for money." But Hoagland has "the New Yorker's quick-hunch posture for broken-field maneuvering," and the bad guy swerves away.

I often witness that "hunch posture," from women after dark on the warren-like streets of Brooklyn where I live. They seem to set their faces on neutral and, with their purse straps strung across their chests bandolier style, they forge ahead as though bracing themselves against being tackled. I understand, of course, that the danger they perceive is not a hallucination. Women are particularly vulnerable to street violence, and young black males are drastically over-represented among the perpetrators of that violence. Yet these truths are no solace against the kind of alienation that comes of being ever the suspect, against being set apart, a fearsome entity with whom pedestrians avoid making eye contact.

It is not altogether clear to me how I reached the ripe old age of twenty-two without being conscious of the lethality nighttime pedestrians attributed to me. Perhaps it was because in Chester, Pennsylvania, the small, angry industrial town where I came of age in the 1960s, I was scarcely noticeable against a backdrop of gang warfare, street knifings, and murders. I grew up one of the good boys, had perhaps a half-dozen fistfights. In retrospect, my shyness of combat has clear sources.

Many things go into the making of a young thug. One of those things is the consummation of the male romance with the power to intimidate. An infant discovers that random flailings send the baby bottle flying out of the crib and crashing to the floor. Delighted, the joyful babe repeats those motions again and again, seeking to duplicate the feat. Just so, I recall the points at which some of my boyhood friends were finally seduced by the perception of themselves as tough guys. When a mark cowered and surrendered his money without resistance, myth and reality merged - and paid off. It is, after all, only manly to embrace the power to frighten and intimidate. We, as men, are not supposed to give an inch of our lane on the highway; we are to seize the fighter's edge in work and in play and even in love; we are to be valiant in the face of hostile forces.

Unfortunately, poor and powerless young men seem to take all this nonsense literally. As a boy, I saw countless tough guys locked away; I have since buried several, too. They were babies, really-a teenage cousin, a brother of twenty-two, a childhood friend in his mid-twenties - all gone down in episodes of bravado played out in the streets. I came to doubt the virtues of intimidation early on. I chose, perhaps even unconsciously, to remain a shadow-timid, but a survivor. The fearsomeness mistakenly attributed to me in public places often has a perilous flavor. The most frightening of these confusions occurred in the late 1970s and early 1980s when I worked as a journalist in Chicago. One day, rushing into the office of a magazine I was writing for with a deadline story in hand, I was mistaken for a burglar. The office manager called security and, with an ad hoc posse, pursued me through the labyrinthine halls, nearly to my editor's door. I had no way of proving who I was. I could only move briskly toward the company of someone who knew me.

Another time I was on assignment for a local paper and killing time before an interview. I entered a jewelry store on the city's affluent Near North Side. The proprietor excused herself and returned with an enormous red Doberman pinscher straining at the end of a leash. She stood, the dog extended toward me, silent to my questions, her eyes bulging nearly out of her head. I took a cursory look around, nodded, and bade her good night. Relatively speaking, however, I never fared as badly as another black male journalist. He went to nearby Waukegan, Illinois, a couple of summers ago to work on a story about a murderer who was born there. Mistaking the reporter for the killer, police hauled him from his car at gunpoint and but for his press credentials would probably have tried to book him. Such episodes are not uncommon. Black men trade tales like this all the time.

In "My Negro Problem-And Ours," Podhoretz writes that the hatred he feels for blacks makes itself known to him through a variety of avenues - one being his discomfort with that "special brand of paranoid touchiness" to which he says blacks are prone. No doubt he is speaking here of black men. In time, I learned to smother the rage I felt at so often being taken for a criminal. Not to do so would surely have led to madness - via that special "paranoid touchiness" that so annoyed Podhoretz at the time he wrote the essay.

I began to take precautions to make myself less threatening. I move about with care, particularly late in the evening. I give a wide berth to nervous people on subway platforms during the wee hours, particularly when I have exchanged business clothes for jeans. If I happen to be entering a building behind some people who appear skittish, I may walk by, letting them clear the lobby before I return, so as not to seem to be following them. I have been calm and extremely congenial on those rare occasions when I've been pulled over by the police.

And on late-evening constitutionals along streets less traveled by, I employ what has proved to be an excellent tension-reducing measure: I whistle melodies from Beethoven and Vivaldi and the more popular classical composers. Even steely New Yorkers hunching toward nighttime destinations seem to relax, and occasionally they even join in the tune. Virtually everybody seems to sense that a mugger wouldn't be warbling bright, sunny selections from Vivaldi's Four Seasons. It is my equivalent of the cowbell that hikers wear when they know they are in bear country.

Source: Staples, Brent. "Just Walk On By: A Black Man Ponders His Power To Alter Public Space",Ms. Magazine, Sept. 1986.

AFRICAN AMERICANS

An African Captive on a Slave Ship in 1789

I now saw myself deprived of all chance of returning to my native country or even the least glimpse of hope of gaining the shore, which I now considered as friendly; and I even wished for my former slavery in preference to my present situation, which was filled with horrors of every kind, still heightened by my ignorance of what I was to undergo. I was not long suffered to indulge my grief; I was soon put down under the decks, and there I received such a salutation in my nostrils as I had never experienced in my life: so that with the loathsomeness of the stench and crying together, I became so sick and low that I was not able to eat, nor had I the least desire to taste anything. I now wished for the last friend, death, to relieve me; but soon, to my grief, two of the white men offered me eatables, and on my refusing to eat, one of them held me fast by the hands and laid me across I think the windlass, and tied my feet while the other flogged me severely. I had never experienced anything of this kind before, and although, not being used to the water, I naturally feared that element the first time I saw it, yet nevertheless could I have got over the nettings I would have jumped over the side, but I could not; and besides, the crew used to watch us very closely who were not chained down to the decks, lest we should leap into the water: and I have seen some of these poor African prisoners most severely cut for attempting to do so, and hourly whipped for not eating. This indeed was often the case with myself. In a little time after, amongst the poor chained men I found some of my own nation, which in a small degree gave ease to my mind. I inquired of these what was to be done with us; they gave me to understand we were to be carried to these white people's country to work for them. I then was a little revived, and thought if it were no worse than working, my situation was not so desperate: but still I feared I should be put to death, the white people looked and acted, as I thought, in so savage a manner; for I had never seen among my people such instances of brutal cruelty, and this not only shown towards us blacks but also to some of the whites themselves. One white man in particular I saw, when we were permitted to be on deck, flogged so unmercifully with a large rope near the foremast that he died in consequence of it; and they tossed him over the side as they would have done a brute. This made me fear these people the more, and I expected nothing less than to be treated in the same manner. . . .

The stench of the hold while we were on the coast was so intolerably loathsome that it was dangerous to remain there for any time, and some of us had been permitted to stay on the deck for the fresh air; but now that the whole ship's cargo were confined together it became absolutely pestilential. The closeness of the place and the heat of the climate, added to the number in the ship, which was so crowded that each had scarcely room to turn himself, almost suffocated us. This produced copious perspirations, so that the air soon became unfit for respiration from a variety of loathsome smells, and brought on a sickness among the slaves, of which many died, thus falling victims to the improvident avarice, as I may call it, of their purchasers. This wretched situation was again aggravated by the galling of the chains, now become insupportable and the filth of the necessary tubs, into which the children often fell and were almost suffocated. The shrieks of the women and the groans of the dying rendered the whole a scene of horror almost inconceivable. Happily perhaps for myself I was soon reduced so low here that it was thought necessary to keep me almost always on deck, and from my extreme youth I was not put in fetters. In this situation I expected every hour to share the fate of my companions, some of whom were almost daily brought upon deck at the point of death, which I began to hope would soon put an end to my miseries. Often did I think many of the inhabitants of the deep much more happy than myself. I envied them the freedom they enjoyed, and as often wished I could change my condition for theirs. Every circumstance I met with served only to render my state more painful, and heighten my apprehensions and my opinion of the cruelty of the whites. One day they had taken a number of fishes, and when they had killed and satisfied themselves with as many as they thought fit, to our astonishment who were on the deck, rather than give any of them to us to eat as we expected, they tossed the remaining fish into the sea again, although we begged and prayed for some as well as we could, but in vain; and some of my countrymen, being pressed by hunger, took an opportunity when they thought no one saw them of trying to get a little privately; but they were discovered, and the attempt procured them some very severe floggings. One day, when we had a smooth sea and moderate wind, two of my wearied countrymen who were chained together (I was near them at the time), preferring death to such a life of misery, somehow made through the nettings and jumped into the sea: immediately another quite dejected fellow, who on account of his illness was suffered to be out of irons, also followed their example; and I believe many more would very soon have done the same if they had not been prevented by the ship's crew, who were instantly alarmed. Those of us that were the most active were in a moment put down under the deck, and there was such a noise and confusion amongst the people of the ship as I never heard before, to stop her and get the boat out to go after the slaves. However two of the wretches were drowned, but they got the other and afterwards flogged him unmercifully for thus attempting to prefer death to slavery. In this manner we continued to undergo more hardships than I can now relate, hardships which are inseparable from this accursed trade.

Source: Equiano, Olaudah. <u>The Interesting Narrative of the Life of Olaudah Equiano or Gustavus Vasa, The African</u>. New York: n.p., 1791.

Incidents in the Life of a Slave Girl

During the first years of my service in Dr. Flint's family, I was accustomed to share some indulgences with the children of my mistress. Though this seemed to me no more than right, I was grateful for it, and tried to merit the kindness by the faithful discharge of my duties. But I now entered on my fifteenth year—a sad epoch in the life of a slave girl. My master began to whisper foul words in my ear. Young as I was, I could not remain ignorant of their import. I tried to treat them with indifference or contempt. The master's age, my extreme youth, and the fear that his conduct would be reported to my grandmother, made him bear this treatment for many months. He was a crafty man, and resorted to many means to accomplish his purposes. Sometimes he had stormy, terrific ways that made his victims tremble; sometimes he assumed a gentleness that he thought must surely subdue. Of the two, I preferred his stormy moods, although they left me trembling. He tried his utmost to corrupt the pure principles my grandmother had instilled. He peopled my young mind with unclean images, such as only a vile monster could think of. I turned from him with disgust and hatred. But he was my master. I was compelled to live under the same roof with him—where I saw a man forty years my senior daily violating the most sacred commandments of nature. He told me I was his property; that I must be subject to his will in all things. My soul revolted against the mean tyranny. But where could I turn for protection? No matter whether the slave girl be as black as ebony or as fair as her mistress. In either case, there is no shadow of law to protect her from insult, from violence, or even from death; all these are inflicted by fiends who bear the shape of men. The mistress, who ought to protect the helpless victim, has no other feelings towards her but those of jealousy and rage. The degradation, the wrongs, the vices, that grow out of slavery, are more than I can describe. They are greater than you would willingly believe. Surely, if you credited one half the truths that are told you concerning the helpless millions suffering in this cruel bondage, you at the north would not help to tighten the yoke. You surely would refuse to do for the master, on your own soil, the mean and cruel work which trained bloodhounds and the lowest class of whites do for him at the south.

Every where the years bring to all enough of sin and sorrow; but in slavery the very dawn of life is darkened by these shadows. Even the little child, who is accustomed to wait on her mistress and her children, will learn, before she is twelve years old, why it is that her mistress hates such and such a one among the slaves. Perhaps the child's own mother is among those hated ones. She listens to violent outbreaks of jealous passion, and cannot help understanding what is the cause. She will become prematurely knowing in evil things. Soon she will learn to tremble when she hears her master's footfall. She will be compelled to realize that she is no longer a child. If God has bestowed beauty upon her, it will prove her greatest curse. That which commands admiration in the white woman only hastens the degradation of the female slave. I know that some are too much brutalized by slavery to feel the humiliation of their position; but many slaves feel it most acutely, and shrink from the memory of it. I cannot tell how much I suffered in the presence of these wrongs, nor how I am still pained by the retrospect. My master met me at every turn, reminding me that I belonged to him, and swearing by heaven and earth that he would compel me to submit to him. If I went out for a breath of fresh air, after a day of unwearied toil, his footsteps dogged me. If I knelt by my mother's grave, his dark shadow fell on me even there. The light heart which nature had given me became heavy with sad forebodings. The other slaves in my master's house noticed the change. Many of them pitied me; but none dared to ask the cause. They had no need to inquire. They knew too well the guilty practices under that roof; and they were aware that to speak of them was an offence that never went unpunished.

I longed for some one to confide in. I would have given the world to have laid my head on my grandmother's faithful bosom, and told her all my troubles. But Dr. Flint swore he would kill me, if I was not as silent as the grave. Then, although my grandmother was all in all to me, I feared her as well as loved her. I had been accustomed to look up to her with a respect bordering upon awe. I was very young, and felt shamefaced about telling her such impure things, especially as I knew her to be very strict on such subjects. Moreover, she was a woman of a high spirit. She was usually very quiet in her demeanor; but if her indignation was once roused, it was not very easily quelled. I had been told that she once chased a white gentleman with a loaded pistol, because he insulted one of her daughters. I dreaded the consequences of a violent outbreak; and both pride and fear kept me silent. But though I did not confide in my grandmother, and even evaded her vigilant watchfulness and inquiry, her presence in the neighborhood was some protection to me. Though she had been a slave, Dr. Flint was afraid of her. He dreaded her scorching rebukes. Moreover, she was known and patronized by many people; and he did not wish to have his villainy made public. It was lucky for me that I did not live on a distant plantation, but in a town not so large that the inhabitants were ignorant of each other's affairs. Bad as are the laws and customs in a slaveholding community, the doctor, as a professional man, deemed it prudent to keep up some outward show of decency.

O, what days and nights of fear and sorrow that man caused me! Reader, it is not to awaken sympathy for myself that I am telling you truthfully what I suffered in slavery. I do it to kindle a flame of compassion in your hearts for my sisters who are still in bondage, suffering as I once suffered.

I once saw two beautiful children playing together. One was a fair white child; the other was her slave, and also her sister. When I saw them embracing each other, and heard their joyous laughter, I turned sadly away from the lovely sight. I foresaw the inevitable blight that would fall on the little slave's heart. I knew how soon her laughter would be changed to sighs. The fair child grew up to be a still fairer woman. From childhood to womanhood her pathway was blooming with flowers, and overarched by a sunny sky. Scarcely one day of her life had been clouded when the sun rose on her happy bridal morning.

How had those years dealt with her slave sister, the little playmate of her childhood? She, also, was very beautiful; but the flowers and sunshine of love were not for her. She drank the cup of sin, and shame, and misery, whereof her persecuted race are compelled to drink.

In view of these things, why are ye silent, ye free men and women of the north? Why do your tongues falter in maintenance of the right? Would that I had more ability! But my heart is so full, and my pen is so weak! There are noble men and women who plead for us, striving to help those who cannot help themselves. God bless them! God give them strength and courage to go on! God bless those, everywhere, who are laboring to advance the cause of humanity!

Source: Jacobs, Harriet. Incidents in the Life of a Slave Girl. Boston. 1861.

What to a Slave is the Fourth of July?
By Frederick Douglas

Fellow-citizens, pardon me, allow me to ask, why am I called upon to speak here today? What have I, or those I represent, to do with your national independence? Are the great principles of political freedom and of natural justice, embodied in that Declaration of Independence, extended to us? and am I, therefore, called upon to bring our humble offering to the national altar, and to confess the benefits and express devout gratitude for the blessings resulting from your independence to us? Would to God, both for your sakes and ours, that an affirmative answer could be truthfully returned to these questions! Then would my task be light, and my burden easy and delightful. For who is there so cold, that a nation's sympathy could not warm him? Who so obdurate and dead to the claims of gratitude, that would not thankfully acknowledge such priceless benefits?

Who so stolid and selfish, that would not give his voice to swell the hallelujahs of a nation's jubilee, when the chains of servitude had been torn from his limbs? I am not that man. In a case like that, the dumb might eloquently speak, and the "lame man leap as an hart."

But, such is not the state of the case. I say it with a sad sense of the disparity between us. I am not included within the pale of this glorious anniversary! Your high independence only reveals the immeasurable distance between us. The blessings in which you, this day, rejoice, are not enjoyed in common. The rich inheritance of justice, liberty, prosperity and independence, bequeathed by your fathers, is shared by you, not by me. The sunlight that brought life and healing to you, has brought stripes and death to me. This Fourth [of] July is yours, not mine. You may rejoice, I must mourn. To drag a man in fetters into the grand illuminated temple of liberty, and call upon him to join you in joyous anthems, were inhuman mockery and sacrilegious irony. Do you mean, citizens, to mock me, by asking me to speak to-day? If so, there is a parallel to your conduct. And let me warn you that it is dangerous to copy the example of a nation whose crimes, lowering up to heaven, were thrown down by the breath of the Almighty, burying that nation in irrecoverable ruin! I can to-day take up the plaintive lament of a peeled and woe-smitten people!

"By the rivers of Babylon, there we sat down. Yea! we wept when we remembered Zion. We hanged our harps upon the willows in the midst thereof. For there, they that carried us away captive, required of us a song; and they who wasted us required of us mirth, saying, Sing us one of the songs of Zion. How can we sing the Lord's song in a strange land? If I forget thee, O Jerusalem, let my right hand forget her cunning. If I do not remember thee, let my tongue cleave to the roof of my mouth."

Fellow-citizens; above your national, tumultuous joy, I hear the mournful wail of millions! whose chains, heavy and grievous yesterday, are, to-day, rendered more intolerable by the jubilee shouts that reach them. If I do forget, if I do not faithfully remember those bleeding children of sorrow this day, "may my right hand forget her cunning, and may my tongue cleave to the roof of my mouth!" To forget them, to pass lightly over their wrongs, and to chime in with the popular theme, would be treason most scandalous and shocking, and would make me a reproach before God and the world. My subject, then fellow-citizens, is AMERICAN SLAVERY. I shall see, this day, and its popular characteristics, from the slave's point of view. Standing, there, identified with the American bondman, making his wrongs mine, I do not hesitate to declare, with all my soul, that the character and conduct of this nation never looked blacker to me than on this 4th of July! Whether we turn to the declarations of the past, or to the professions of the present, the conduct of the nation seems equally hideous and revolting. America is false to the past, false to the present, and solemnly binds herself to be false to the future. Standing with God and the crushed and bleeding slave on this occasion, I will, in the name of humanity which is outraged, in the name of liberty which is fettered, in the name of the constitution and the Bible, which are disregarded and trampled upon, dare to call in question and to denounce, with all the emphasis I can command, everything that serves to perpetuate slavery-the great sin and shame of America! "I will not equivocate; I will not excuse;" I will use the severest language I can command; and yet not one word shall escape me that any man, whose judgment is not blinded by prejudice, or who is not at heart a slaveholder, shall not confess to be right and just.

But I fancy I hear some one of my audience say, it is just in this circumstance that you and your brother abolitionists fail to make a favorable impression on the public mind. Would you argue more, and denounce less, would you persuade more, and rebuke less, your cause would be much more likely to succeed. But, I submit, where all is plain there is nothing to be argued. What point in the anti-slavery creed would you have me argue? On what branch of the subject do the people of this country need light? Must I undertake to prove that the slave is a man? That point is conceded already. Nobody doubts it. The slaveholders themselves acknowledge it in the enactment of laws for their government. They acknowledge it when they punish disobedience on the part of the slave. There are seventy-two crimes in the State of Virginia, which, if committed by a black man, (no matter how ignorant he be), subject him to the punishment of death; while only two of the same crimes will subject a white man to the like punishment. What is this but the acknowledgement that the slave is a moral, intellectual and responsible being? The manhood of the slave is conceded. It is admitted in the fact that Southern statute books are covered with enactments forbidding, under severe fines and penalties, the teaching of the slave to read or to write. When you can point to any such laws, in reference to the beasts of the field, then I may consent to argue the manhood of the slave. When the dogs in your streets, when the fowls of the air, when the cattle on your hills, when the fish of the sea, and the reptiles that crawl, shall be unable to distinguish the slave from a brute, their will I argue with you that the slave is a man!

For the present, it is enough to affirm the equal manhood of the negro race. Is it not astonishing that, while we are plowing, planting and reaping, using all kinds of mechanical tools, erecting houses, constructing bridges, building ships, working in metals of brass, iron, copper, silver and gold; that, while we are reading, writing and ciphering, acting as clerks, merchants and secretaries, having among us lawyers, doctors, ministers, poets, authors, editors, orators and teachers; that, while we are engaged in all manner of enterprises common to other men, digging gold in California, capturing the whale in the Pacific, feeding sheep and cattle on the hill-side, living, moving, acting, thinking, planning, living in families as husbands, wives and children, and, above all, confessing and worshipping the Christian's God, and looking hopefully for life and immortality beyond the grave, we are called upon to prove that we are men!

Would you have me argue that man is entitled to liberty? that he is the rightful owner of his own body? You have already declared it. Must I argue the wrongfulness of slavery? Is that a question for Republicans? Is it to be settled by the rules of logic and argumentation, as a matter beset with great difficulty, involving a doubtful application of the principle of justice, hard to be understood? How should I look to-day, in the presence of Americans, dividing, and subdividing a discourse, to show that men have a natural right to freedom? speaking of it relatively, and positively, negatively, and affirmatively. To do so, would be to make myself ridiculous, and to offer an insult to your understanding. There is not a man beneath the canopy of heaven, that does not know that slavery is wrong for him.

What, am I to argue that it is wrong to make men brutes, to rob them of their liberty, to work them without wages, to keep them ignorant of their relations to their fellow men, to beat them with sticks, to flay their flesh with the lash, to load their limbs with irons, to hunt them with dogs, to sell them at auction, to sunder their families, to knock out their teeth, to burn their flesh, to starve them into obedience and submission to their masters? Must I argue that a system thus marked with blood, and stained with pollution, is wrong? No! I will not. I have better employments for my time and strength, than such arguments would imply.

What, then, remains to be argued? Is it that slavery is not divine; that God did not establish it; that our doctors of divinity are mistaken? There is blasphemy in the thought. That which is inhuman, cannot be divine! Who can reason on such a proposition? They that can, may; I cannot. The time for such argument is past.

At a time like this, scorching irony, not convincing argument, is needed. O! had I the ability, and could I reach the nation's ear, I would, to-day, pour out a fiery stream of biting ridicule, blasting reproach, withering sarcasm, and stern rebuke. For it is not light that is needed, but fire; it is not the gentle shower, but thunder. We need the storm, the whirlwind, and the earthquake. The feeling of the nation must be quickened; the conscience of the nation must be roused; the propriety of the nation must be startled; the hypocrisy of the nation must be exposed; and its crimes against God and man must be proclaimed and denounced.

What, to the American slave, is your 4th of July? I answer: a day that reveals to him, more than all other days in the year, the gross injustice and cruelty to which he is the constant victim. To him, your celebration is a sham; your boasted liberty, an unholy license; your national greatness, swelling vanity; your sounds of rejoicing are empty and heartless; your denunciations of tyrants, brass fronted impudence; your shouts of liberty and equality, hollow mockery; your prayers and hymns, your sermons and thanksgivings, with all your religious parade, and solemnity, are, to him, mere bombast, fraud, deception, impiety, and hypocrisy - a thin veil to cover up crimes which would disgrace a nation of savages. There is not a nation on the earth guilty of practices, more shocking and bloody, than are the people of these United States, at this very hour.

Go where you may, search where you will, roam through all the monarchies and despotisms of the old world, travel through South America, search out every abuse, and when you have found the last, lay your facts by the side of the everyday practices of this nation, and you will say with me, that, for revolting barbarity and shameless hypocrisy, America reigns without a rival.

Source: Douglass, Frederick. "What to a Slave is the Fourth of July?" Rochester, NY: Frederick Douglass. 1852.

Letter From A Birmingham Jail

You deplore the demonstrations taking place In Birmingham. But your statement, I am sorry to say, fails to express a similar concern for the conditions that brought about the demonstrations. I am sure that none of you would want to rest content with the superficial kind of social analysis that deals merely with effects and does not grapple with underlying causes. It is unfortunate that demonstrations are taking place in Birmingham, but it is even more unfortunate that the city's white power structure left the Negro community with no alternative.

In any nonviolent campaign there are four basic steps: collection of the facts to determine whether injustices exist; negotiation; self-purification; and direct action. We have gone through these steps in Birmingham. There can be no gainsaying the fact that racial injustice engulfs this community. Birmingham is probably the most thoroughly segregated city in the United States. Its ugly record of brutality is widely known. Negroes have experienced grossly unjust treatment in the courts. There have been more unsolved bombings of Negro homes and churches in Birmingham than in any other city in the nation. These are the hard, brutal facts of the case...

We know through painful experience that freedom is never voluntarily given by the oppressor; it must be demanded by the oppressed. Frankly, I have yet to engage in a direct-action campaign that was "well timed" in the view of those who have not suffered unduly from the disease of segregation. For years now I have heard the word "Wait!" It rings in the ear of every Negro with piercing familiarity. This "Wait" has almost always meant 'Never." We must come to see, with one of our distinguished jurists, that "justice too long delayed is justice denied."

We have waited for more than 340 years for our constitutional and God-given rights. The nations of Asia and Africa are moving with jet-like speed toward gaining political independence, but we stiff creep at horse-and-buggy pace toward gaining a cup of coffee at a lunch counter. Perhaps it is easy for those who have never felt the stinging dark of segregation to say, "Wait." But when you have seen vicious mobs lynch your mothers and fathers at will and drown your sisters and brothers at whim; when you have seen hate-filled policemen curse, kick and even kill your black brothers and sisters; when you see the vast majority of your twenty million Negro brothers smothering in an airtight cage of poverty in the midst of an affluent society; when you suddenly find your tongue twisted and your speech stammering as you seek to explain to your six-year-old daughter why she can't go to the public amusement park that has just been advertised on television, and see tears welling up in her eyes when she is told that Funtown is closed to colored children, and see ominous clouds of inferiority beginning to form in her little mental sky, and see her beginning to distort her personality by developing an unconscious bitterness toward white people; when you have to concoct an answer for a five-year-old son who is asking: "Daddy, why do white people treat colored people so mean?"; when you take a cross-county drive and find it necessary to sleep night after night in the uncomfortable corners of your automobile because no motel will accept you; when you are humiliated day in and day out by nagging signs reading "white" and "colored"; when your first name becomes "nigger," your middle name becomes "boy" (however old you are) and your last name becomes "John," and your wife and mother are never given the respected title "Mrs."; when you are harried by day and haunted by night by the fact that you are a Negro, living constantly at tiptoe stance, never quite knowing what to expect next, and are plagued with inner fears and outer resentments; when you no forever fighting a degenerating sense of "nobodiness" then you will understand why we find it difficult to wait. There comes a time when the cup of endurance runs over, and men are no longer willing to be plunged into the abyss of despair. I hope, sirs, you can understand our legitimate and unavoidable impatience.

You express a great deal of anxiety over our willingness to break laws. This is certainly a legitimate concern. Since we so diligently urge people to obey the Supreme Court's decision of 1954 outlawing segregation in the public schools, at first glance it may seem rather paradoxical for us consciously to break laws. One may won ask: "How can you advocate breaking some laws and obeying others?" The answer lies in the fact that there fire two types of laws: just and unjust. I would be the Brat to advocate obeying just laws. One has not only a legal but a moral responsibility to obey just laws. Conversely, one has a moral responsibility to disobey unjust laws. I would agree with St. Augustine that: "an unjust law is no law at all"

Now, what is the difference between the two? How does one determine whether a law is just or unjust? A just law is a man-made code that squares with the moral law or the law of God. An unjust law is a code that is out of harmony with the moral law. To put it in the terms of St. Thomas Aquinas: An unjust law is a human law that is not rooted in eternal law and natural law. Any law that uplifts human personality is just. Any law that degrades human personality is unjust. All segregation statutes are unjust because segregation distort the soul and damages the personality. It gives the segregator a false sense of superiority and the segregated a false sense of inferiority. Segregation, to use the terminology of the Jewish philosopher Martin Buber, substitutes an "I-it" relationship for an "I-thou" relationship and ends up relegating persons to the status of things. Hence segregation is not only politically, economically and sociologically unsound, it is morally wrong and awful. Paul Tillich said that sin is separation. Is not segregation an existential expression 'of man's tragic separation, his awful estrangement, his terrible sinfulness? Thus it is that I can urge men to obey the 1954 decision of the Supreme Court, for it is morally right; and I can urge them to disobey segregation ordinances, for they are morally wrong...

Let me give another explanation. A law is unjust if it is inflicted on a minority that, as a result of being denied the right to vote, had no part in enacting or devising the law. Who can say that the legislature of Alabama which set up that state's segregation laws was democratically elected? Throughout Alabama all sorts of devious methods are used to prevent Negroes from becoming registered voters, and there are some counties in which, even though Negroes constitute a majority of the population, not a single Negro is registered. Can any law enacted under such circumstances be considered democratically structured?...

We should never forget that everything Adolf Hitler did in Germany was "legal" and everything the Hungarian freedom fighters did in Hungary was "illegal." It was "illegal" to aid and comfort a Jew in Hitler's Germany. Even so, I am sure that, had I lived in Germany at the time, I would have aided and comforted my Jewish brothers. If today I lived in a Communist country where certain principles dear to the Christian faith are suppressed, I would openly advocate disobeying that country's antireligious laws...

I must make two honest confessions to you, my Christian and Jewish brothers. First, I must confess that over the past few years I have been gravely disappointed with the white moderate. I have almost reached the regrettable conclusion that the Negro's great stumbling block in his stride toward freedom is not the White Citizen's Counciler or the Ku Klux Klanner, but the white moderate, who is more devoted to "order" than to justice; who prefers a negative peace which is the absence of tension to a positive peace which is the presence of justice; who constantly says: "I agree with you in the goal you seek, but I cannot agree with your methods of direct action"; who paternalistically believes he can set the timetable for another man's freedom; who lives by a mythical concept of time and who constantly advises the Negro to wait for a "more convenient season." Shallow understanding from people of good will is more frustrating than absolute misunderstanding from people of ill will. Lukewarm acceptance is much more bewildering than outright rejection...

You speak of our activity in Birmingham as extreme. At first I was rather disappointed that fellow clergymen would see my nonviolent efforts as those of an extremist. I began thinking about the fact that stand in the middle of two opposing forces in the Negro community. One is a force of complacency, made up in part of Negroes who, as a result of long years of oppression, are so drained of self-respect and a sense of "somebodiness" that they have adjusted to segregation; and in part of a few middle class Negroes who, because of a degree of academic and economic security and because in some ways they profit by segregation, have become insensitive to the problems of the masses. The other force is one of bitterness and hatred, and it comes perilously close to advocating violence. It is expressed in the various black nationalist groups that are springing up across the nation, the largest and best-known being Elijah Muhammad's Muslim movement. Nourished by the Negro's frustration over the continued existence of racial discrimination, this movement is made up of people who have lost faith in America, who have absolutely repudiated Christianity, and who have concluded that the white man is an incorrigible "devil."

I have tried to stand between these two forces, saying that we need emulate neither the "do-nothingism" of the complacent nor the hatred and despair of the black nationalist. For there is the more excellent way of love and nonviolent protest. I am grateful to God that, through the influence of the Negro church, the way of nonviolence became an integral part of our struggle.

If this philosophy had not emerged, by now many streets of the South would, I am convinced, be flowing with blood. And I am further convinced that if our white brothers dismiss as "rabble-rousers" and "outside agitators" those of us who employ nonviolent direct action, and if they refuse to support our nonviolent efforts, millions of Negroes will, out of frustration and despair, seek solace and security in black-nationalist ideologies a development that would inevitably lead to a frightening racial nightmare.

Oppressed people cannot remain oppressed forever. The yearning for freedom eventually manifests itself, and that is what has happened to the American Negro. Something within has reminded him of his birthright of freedom, and something without has reminded him that it can be gained...

But though I was initially disappointed at being categorized as an extremist, as I continued to think about the matter I gradually gained a measure of satisfaction from the label. Was not Jesus an extremist for love: "Love your enemies, bless them that curse you, do good to them that hate you, and pray for them which despitefully use you, and persecute you." Was not Amos an extremist for justice: "Let justice roll down like waters and righteousness like an ever-flowing stream." Was not Paul an extremist for the Christian gospel: "I bear in my body the marks of the Lord Jesus." Was not Martin Luther an extremist: "Here I stand; I cannot do otherwise, so help me God." And John Bunyan: "I will stay in jail to the end of my days before I make a butchery of my conscience." And Abraham Lincoln: "This nation cannot survive half slave and half free." And Thomas Jefferson: "We hold these truths to be self-evident, that an men are created equal ..." So the question is not whether we will be extremists, but what kind of extremists we will be. Be we extremists for hate or for love? Will we be extremist for the preservation of injustice or for the extension of justice? In that dramatic scene on Calvary's hill three men were crucified. We must never forget that all three were crucified for the same crime---the crime of extremism. Two were extremists for immorality, and thus fell below their environment. The other, Jeans Christ, was an extremist for love, truth and goodness, and thereby rose above his environment. Perhaps the South, the nation and the world are in dire need of creative extremists...

One day the South will recognize its real heroes. They will be the James Merediths, with the noble sense of purpose that enables them to face Jeering, and hostile mobs, and with the agonizing loneliness that characterizes the life of the pioneer. They will be old, oppressed, battered Negro women, symbolized in a seventy-two-year-old woman in Montgomery, Alabama, who rose up with a sense of dignity and with her people decided not to ride segregated buses, and who responded with ungrammatical profundity to one who inquired about her weariness: "My fleets is tired, but my soul is at rest." They will be the young high school and college students, the young ministers of the gospel and a host of their elders, courageously and nonviolently sitting in at lunch counters and willingly going to jail for conscience' sake. One day the South will know that when these disinherited children of God sat down at lunch counters, they were in reality standing up for what is best in the American dream and for the most sacred values in our Judaeo-Christian heritage, thereby bringing our nation back to those great wells of democracy which were dug deep by the founding fathers in their formulation of the Constitution and the Declaration of Independence...

Source: King, Jr., Martin Luther. Why We Wait. Copyright Coretta Scott King, 1991.

Malcolm X on Black Nationalism

"I'm still a Muslim but I'm also a nationalist, meaning that my political philosophy is black nationalism, my economic philosophy is black nationalism, my social philosophy is black nationalism. And when I say that this philosophy is black nationalism, to me this means that the political philosophy of black nationalism is that which is designed to encourage our people, the black people, to gain complete control over the politics and the politicians of our own community.

Our economic philosophy is that we should gain economic control over the economy of our own community, the businesses and the other things which create employment so that we can provide jobs for our own people instead of having to picket and boycott and beg someone else for a job.

And, in short, our social philosophy means that we feel that it is time to get together among our own kind and eliminate the evils that are destroying the moral fiber of our society, like drug addiction, drunkenness, adultery that leads to an abundance of bastard children, welfare problems. We believe that we should lift the level or the standard of our own society to a higher level wherein we will be satisfied and then not inclined toward pushing ourselves into other societies where we are not wanted."

Source: X, Malcolm. "Malcolm X Speech. 1964" excerpted from "The Black Revolution." From Two Speeches by Malcolm X. Pathfinder Press & Betty Shabazz. 1969 & 1990.

Mommy, What Does "Nigger" Mean?

Language is the subject. It is the written form with which I've managed to keep the wolf away from the door and, in diaries, to keep my sanity. In spite of this, I consider the written word inferior to the spoken, and much of the frustration experienced by novelists is the awareness that whatever we manage to capture in even the most transcendent passages falls far short of the richness of life. Dialogue achieves its power in the dynamics of a fleeting moment of sight, sound, smell, and touch.

I'm not going to enter the debate here about whether it is language that shapes reality or vice versa. That battle is doomed to be waged whenever we seek intermittent reprieve from the chicken and egg dispute. I will simply take the position that the spoken word, like the written word, amounts to a nonsensical arrangement of sounds or letters without a consensus that assigns "meaning." And building from the meanings of what we hear, we order reality. Words themselves are innocuous; it is the consensus that gives them true power.

I remember the first time I heard the word nigger. In my third-grade class, our math tests were being passed down the rows, and as I handed the papers to a little boy in back of me, I remarked that once again he had received a much lower mark than I did. He snatched his test from me and spit out that word. Had he called me a nymphomaniac or a necrophiliac, I couldn't have been more puzzled. I didn't know what a nigger was, but I knew that whatever it meant, it was something he shouldn't have called me. This was verified when I raised my hand, and in a loud voice repeated what he had said and watched the teacher scold him for using a "bad" word. I was later to go home and ask the inevitable question that every black parent must face-- "Mommy, what does nigger mean?"

And what exactly did it mean? Thinking back, I realize that this could not have been the first time the word was used in my presence. I was part of a large extended family that had migrated from the rural South after World War II and formed a close-knit network that gravitated around my PAGE 306 maternal grandparents. Their ground-floor apartment in one of the buildings they owned in Harlem was a weekend mecca for my immediate family, along with countless aunts, uncles, and cousins who brought along assorted friends. It was a bustling and open house with assorted neighbors and tenants popping in and out to exchange bits of gossip, pick up an old quarrel, or referee the ongoing checkers game in which my grandmother cheated shamelessly. They were all there to let down their hair and put up their feet after a week of labor in the factories, laundries, and shipyards of New York.

Amid the clamor, which could reach deafening proportions--two or three conversations going on simultaneously, punctuated by the sound of a baby's crying somewhere in the back rooms or out on the street--there was still a rigid set of rules about what was said and how. Older children were sent out of the living room when it was time to get into the juicy details about "you-know-who" up on the third floor who had gone and gotten herself "p-r-e-g-n-a-n-t!" But my parents, knowing that I could spell well beyond my years, always demanded that I follow the others out to play. Beyond sexual misconduct and death, everything else was considered harmless for our young ears. And so among the anecdotes of the triumphs and disappointments in the various workings of their lives, the word nigger was used in my presence, but it was set within contexts and inflections that caused it to register in my mind as something else.

In the singular, the word was always applied to a man who had distinguished himself in some situation that brought their approval for his strength, intelligence, or drive:

"Did Johnny really do that?"

"I'm telling you, that nigger pulled in $6,000 of overtime last year. Said he got enough for a down payment on a house."

When used with a possessive adjective by a woman--"my nigger"--it became a term of endearment for her husband or boyfriend. But it could be more than just a term applied to a man. In their mouths it became the pure essence of manhood--a disembodied force that channeled their past history of struggle and present survival against the odds into a victorious statement of being: "Yeah, that old foreman found out quick enough--you don't mess with a nigger."

In the plural, it became a description of some group within the community that had overstepped the bounds of decency as my family defined it. Parents who neglected their children, a drunken couple who fought in public, people who simply refused to look for work, those with excessively dirty mouths or unkempt households were all "trifling niggers." This particular circle could forgive hard times, unemployment, the occasional bout of depression--they had gone through all of that themselves--but the unforgivable sin was a lack of self-respect.

A woman could never be a "nigger" in the singular, with its connotations of confirming worth. The noun girl was its closest equivalent in that sense, but only when used in direct address and regardless of the gender doing the addressing. Girl was a token of respect for a woman. The one-syllable word was drawn out to sound like three in recognition of the extra ounce of wit, nerve, or daring that the woman had shown in the situation under discussion.

"G-i-r-l, stop. You mean you said that to his face?"

But if the word was used in a third-person reference or shortened so that it almost snapped out of the mouth, it always involved some element of communal disapproval. And age became an important factor in these exchanges. It was only between individuals of the same generation, or from any older person to a younger (but never the other way around), that girl would be considered a compliment.

I don't agree with the argument that use of the word nigger at this social stratum of the black community was an internalization of racism. The dynamics were the exact opposite: the people in my grandmother's living room took a word that whites used to signify worthlessness or degradation and rendered it impotent. Gathering there together, they transformed nigger to signify the varied and complex human beings they knew themselves to be. If the word was to disappear totally from the mouths of even the most liberal of white society, no one in that room was naive enough to believe it would disappear from white minds. Meeting the word head-on, they proved it had absolutely nothing to do with the way they were determined to live their lives.

So there must have been dozens of times that nigger was spoken in front of me before I reached the third grade. But I didn't "hear" it until it was said by a small pair of lips that had already learned it could be a way to humiliate me. That was the word I went home and asked my mother about. And since she knew that I had to grow up in America, she took me in her lap and explained.

Source: Naylor, Gloria. "Mommy, What Does "Nigger" Mean?" New York Times Magazine, 1986.

ASIAN AMERICANS

An Asian American Timeline
1600s
Chinese and Filipinos reach Mexico on ships of the Manila galleon.
1830s
Chinese "sugar masters" working in Hawaii. Chinese sailors and peddlers in New York.
1835
U.S. and China sign first treaty.
1848
Gold discovered in California. Chinese begin to arrive.
1850
California imposes Foreign Miner's Tax and enforces it mainly against Chinese miners, who often had to pay more than once.
1852
First group of 195 Chinese contract laborers land in Hawaii. Over 20,000 Chinese enter California. Chinese first appear in court in California. Missionary Willian Speer opens Presbyterian mission for Chinese in San Francisco.
1854
Chinese in Hawaii establish a funeral society, their first community association in the islands. People v. Hall rules that Chinese can't give testimony in court. U.S. and Japan sign first treaty.
1857
San Francisco opens a school for Chinese children (changed to an evening school two years later). Missionary Augustus Loomis arrives to serve the Chinese in San Francisco.
1858
California passes a law to bar entry of Chinese and "Mongolians."

1860
Japan sends a diplomatic mission to U.S.
1862
Six Chinese district associations in San Francisco form loose federation. California imposes a "police tax" of $2.50 a month on every Chinese.
1865
Central Pacific Railroad Co. recruits Chinese workers for the transcontinental railroad.
1867
Two thousand Chinese railroad workers strike for a week.
1868
U.S. and China sign Burlingame - Seward Treaty recognizing rights of their citizens to emigrate. Eugene Van Reed illegally ships 149 Japanese laborers to Hawaii. Sam Damon opens Sunday school for Chinese in Hawaii.
1869
Completion of first transcontinental railroad. J.H. Schnell takes several dozen Japanese to California to establish the Wakamatsu Tea and Silk Colony. Chinese Christian evangelist S.P. Aheong starts preaching in Hawaii.
1870
California passes a law against the importation of Chinese, Japanese, and "Mongolian" women for prostitution. Chinese railroad workers in Texas sue company for failing to pay wages.
1872
California's Civil Procedure Code drops law barring Chinese court testimony.
1875
Page Law bars entry of Chinese, Japanese, and "Mongolian" prostitutes, felons, and contract laborers.
1877

Anti-Chinese violence in Chico, California. Japanese Christians set up the Gospel Soceity in San Francisco, the first immigrant association formed by the Japanese.
1878
In re Ah Yup rules Chinese not eligible for naturalized citizenship.
1879
California's second constitution prevents municipalities and corporations from employing Chinese. California state legislature passes law requiring all incorporated towns and cities to remove Chinese outside of city limits, but U.S. circuit court declares the law unconstitutional.
1880
U.S. and China sign treaty giving the U.S. the right to limit but "not absolutely prohibit" Chinese immigration. Section 69 of California's Civil Code prohibits issuing of licenses for marriages between whites and "Mongolians, Negroes, mulattoes and persons of mixed blood."
1881
Hawaiian King Kalakaua visits Japan during his world tour. Sit Moon becomes pastor of the first Chinese Christian church in Hawaii.
1882
Chinese Exclusion Law suspends immigration of laborers for ten years. Chinese community leaders form Chinese Consolidated Benevolent Association (CCBA or Chinese Six Companies) in San Francisco. U.S. and Korea sign first treaty.
1883
Chinese in New York establish CCBA.
1884
Joseph and Mary Tape sue San Francisco school board to enroll their daughter Mamie in a public school. Chinese Six Companies sets up Chinese language school in San Francisco. United Chinese Society

established in Honolulu. CCBA established in Vancouver. 1882 Chinese Exclusion Law amended to require a certificate as the only permissible evidence for reentry.

1885

San Francisco builds new segregated "Oriental School." Anti-Chinese violence at Rock Springs, Wyoming Territory. First group of Japanese contract laborers arrives in Hawaii under the Irwin Convention.

1886

Residents of Tacoma, Seattle, and many places in the American West forcibly expel the Chinese. End of Chinese immigration to Hawaii. Chinese laundrymen win case in Yick Wo v. Hopkins, which declares that a law with unequal impact on different groups is discriminatory.

1888

Scott Act renders 20,000 Chinese reentry certificates null and void.

1889

First Nishi Hongwanji priest from Japan arrives in Hawaii. Chae Chan Ping v. U.S. upholds constitutionality of Chinese exclusion laws.

1892

Geary Law renews exclusion of Chinese laborers for another ten years and requires all Chinese to register. Fong Yue Ting v. U.S. upholds constitutionality of Geary Law.

1893

Japanese in San Francisco form first trade association, the Japanese Shoemakers' League. Attempts are made to expel Chinese from towns in southern California.

1894

Sun Yat-sen founds the Xingzhonghui in Honolulu. U.S. circuit court in Massachusetts declares in In re Saito that Japanese are ineligible for naturalization. Japanese immigration to Hawaii under Irwin Convention ends and emigration companies take over.

1895

Lem Moon Sing v. U.S. rules that district courts can no longer review Chinese habeas corpus petitions for landing in the U.S.

1896

Shinsei Kaneko, a Japanese Californian, is naturalized. Bubonic plague scare in Honolulu - Chinatown burned.

1897

Nishi Hongwanji includes Hawaii as a mission field.

1898

Wong Kim Ark v. U.S. decides that Chinese born in the U.S. can't be stripped of their citizenship. Japanese in San Francisco set up Young Men's Buddhist Association. U.S. annexes Hawaii and the Philippines.

1899

Chinese reformers Kang Youwei and Liang Qichao tour North America to recruit members for the Baohuanghui. First Nishi Hongwanji priests arrive in California and set up North American Buddhist Mission.

1990

Japanese Hawaiian plantation workers begin going to the mainland after the Organic Act ended contract labor. Bubonic plague scare in San Francisco - Chinatown cordoned and quarantined.

1902

Chinese exclusion extended for another ten years. Immigration officials and the police raid Boston's Chinatown and, without search warrants, arrest almost 250 Chinese who allegedly had no registration certificates on their persons.

1903

First group of Korean workers arrives in Hawaii. 1500 Japanese and Mexican sugar beet workers strike in Oxnard, California. Koreans in Hawaii form Korean

Evangelical Society. Filipino students (pensionados) arrive in the U.S. for higher education.

1904

Chinese exclusion made indefinite and applicable to U.S. insular possessions. Japanese plantation workers engage in first organized strike in Hawaii. Punjabi Sikhs begin to enter British Columbia.

1905

Chinese in the U.S. and Hawaii support boycott of American products in China. Koreans establish Korean Episcopal Church in Hawaii and Korean Methodist Church in California. San Francisco School Board attempts to segregate Japanese schoolchildren. Korean emigration ends. Koreans in San Francisco form Mutual Assistance Society. Asiatic Exclusion League formed in San Francisco. Section 60 of California's Civil Code amended to forbid marriage between whites and "Mongolians."

1906

Anti-Asian riot in Vancouver. Japanese nurserymen form California Flower Growers' Association. Koreans establish Korean Presbyterian Church in Los Angeles. Japanese scientists studying the aftermath of the San Francisco earthquake are stoned.

1907

Japan and the U.S. reach "Gentlemen's Agreement" whereby Japan stops issuing passports to laborers desiring to emigrate to the U.S. President Theodore Roosevelt signs Executive Order 589 prohibiting Japanese with passports for Hawaii, Mexico, or Canada to re-emigrate to the U.S. Koreans form United Korean Society in Hawaii. First group of Filipino laborers arrives in Hawaii. Asian Indians are driven out of Bellingham, Washington.

1908

Japanese form Japanese Association of America. Canada curbs Asian Indian immigrants by denying entry to immigrants who haven't come by "continuous journey" from their homelands (there is no direct shipping between Indian and Canadian ports). Asian Indians are driven out of Live Oak, California.

1909

Koreans form Korean Nationalist Association. 7000 Japanese plantation workers strike major plantations on Oahu for four months.

1910

Administrative measures used to restrict influx of Asian Indians into California.

1911

Pablo Manlapit forms Filipino Higher Wages Association in Hawaii. Japanese form Japanese Association of Oregon in Portland.

1912

Sikhs build gurdwara in Stockton and establish Khalsa Diwan. Japanese in California hold statewide conference on Nisei education.

1913

California passes alien land law prohibiting "aliens ineligible to citizenship" from buying land or leasing it for longer than three years. Sikhs in Washington and Oregon establish Hindustani Association. Asian Indians in California found the revolutionary Ghadar Party and start publishing a newspaper. Pablo Manlapit forms Filipino Unemployed Association in Hawaii. Japanese form Northwest Japanese Association of America in Seattle. Korean farm workers are driven out of Hemet, California.

1914

Aspiring Asian Indian immigrants who had chartered a ship to come to Canada by continuous journey are denied landing in Vancouver.

1915

Japanese form Central Japanese Association of Southern California and the Japanese Chamber of Commerce.

1917

Arizona passes an Alien Land Law. 1917 Immigration Law defines a geographic "barred zone" (including India) from which no immigrants can come. Syngman Rhee founds the Korean Christian Church in Hawaii.

1918

Servicemen of Asian ancestry who had served in World War I receive right of naturalization. Asian Indians form the Hindustani Welfare Reform Association in the Imperial and Coachella valleys in southern California.

1919

Japanese form Federation of Japanese Labor in Hawaii.

1920

10,000 Japanese and Filipino plantation workers go on strike. Japan stops issuing passports to picture brides due to anti-Japanese sentiments. Initiative in California ballot plugs up loopholes in the 1913 alien land law.

1921

Japanese farm workers driven out of Turlock, California. Filipinos establish a branch of the Caballeros Dimas Alang in San Francisco and a branch of the Legionarios del Trabajo in Honolulu. Washington and Louisiana pass alien land laws.

1922

Takao Ozawa v. U.S. declares Japanese not eligible for naturalized citizenship. New Mexico passes an alien land law. Cable Act declares that any American female citizen who marries "an alien ineligible to citizenship" would lose her citizenship.

1923

U.S. v. Bhagat Singh Thind declares Asian Indians not eligible for naturalized citizenship. Idaho, Montana, and

Oregon pass alien land laws. Terrace v. Thompson upholds constitutionality of Washington's alien land law. Porterfield v. Webb upholds constitutionality of California's alien land law. Webb v. O'Brien rules that sharecropping is illegal because it is a ruse that allows Japanese to possess and use land. Frick v. Webb forbids aliens "ineligible to citizenship" from owning stocks in corporations formed for farming.

1924

Immigration Act denies entry to virtually all Asians. 1600 Filipino plantation workers strike for eight months in Hawaii.

1925

Warring tongs in North America's Chinatowns declare truce. Hilario Moncado founds Filipino Federation of America.

1928

Filipino farm workers are driven out of Yakima Valley, Washington. Filipinos in Los Angeles form Filipino American Christian Fellowship.

1930

Anti-Filipino riot in Watsonville, California.

1931

Amendment to Cable Act declares that no American-born woman who loses her citizenship (by marrying an alien ineligible to citizenship) can be denied the right of naturalization at a later date.

1934

Tydings - McDuffie Act spells out procedure for eventual Philippine independence and reduces Filipino immigration to 50 persons a year. Filipino lettuce pickers in the Slinas Valley, California, go on strike.

1936

American Federation of Labor grants charter to a Filipino - Mexican union of fieldworkers.

1937

Last ethnic strike in Hawaii.
1938
150 Chinese women garment workers strike for three months against the National Dollar Stores (owned by a Chinese).
1940
AFL charters the Filipino Federated Agricultural Laborers Association.
1941
After declaring war on Japan, 2000 Japanese community leaders along Pacific Coast states and Hawaii are rounded up and interned in Department of Justice camps.
1942
President Franklin D. Roosevelt signs Executive Order 9066 authorizing the secretary of war to delegate a military commander to designate military areas "from which any and all persons may be excluded" - primarily enforced against Japanese. Congress passes Public Law 503 to impose penal sanctions on anyone disobeying orders to carry out Executive Order 9066. Protests at Poston and Manzanar relocation centers.
1943
Protest at Topaz Relocation Center. Registration crisis leads to Tule Lake Relocation Center's designation as a segregation center. Hawaiian Nisei in the 100th Battalion sent to Africa. Congress repeals all Chinese exclusion laws, grants right of naturalization and a small immigration quota to Chinese.
1944
Tule Lake placed under martial law. Draft reinstated for Nisei. Draft resistance at Heart Mountain Relocation Center. 442nd Regimental Combat Team gains fame. Exclusion orders revoked.
1946

Luce - Celler bill grants right of naturalization and small immigration quotas to Asian Indians and Filipinos. Wing F. Ong becomes first Asian American to be elected to state office in the Arizona House of Representatives.
1947
Amendment to 1945 War Brides Act allows Chinese American veterans to bring brides into the U.S.
1949
5000 highly educated Chinese in the U.S. granted refugee status after China institutes a Communist government.
1952
One clause of the McCarran - Walter Act grants the right of naturalization and a small immigration quota to Japanese.
1956
California repeals its alien land laws. Dalip Singh from the Imperial Valley, California, is elected to Congress.
1962
Daniel K. Inouye becomes U.S. senator and Spark Matsunaga becomes U.S. congressman from Hawaii.
1964
Patsy Takemoto Mink becomes first Asian American woman to serve in Congress as representative from Hawaii.
1965
Immigration Law abolishes "national origins" as basis for allocating immigration quotas to various countries - Asian countries now on equal footing.
1968
Students on strike at San Francisco State University to demand establishment of ethnic studies programs.
1969
Students at the University of California, Berkeley, go on strike for establishment of ethnic studies programs.
1974

March Fong Eu elected California's secretary of state. Lau v. Nichols rules that school districts with children who speak little English must provide them with bilingual education.

1975

More than 130,000 refugees enter the U.S. from Vietnam, Kampuchea, and Laos as Communist governments are established there.

1976

President Gerald Ford rescinds Executive Order 9066.

1978

National convention of the Japanese American Citizens League adopts resolution calling for redress and reparations for the internment of Japanese Americans. Massive exodus of "boat people" from Vietnam.

1979

Resumption of diplomatic relations between the People's Republic of China and the United States of America reunites members of long-separated Chinese American families.

1980

The Socialist Republic of Vietnam and the United Nations High Commissioner for Refugees set up an Orderly Departure Program to enable Vietnamese to emigrate legally.

1981

Commission on Wartime Relocation and Internment of Civilians (set up by Congress) holds hearings across the country and concludes the internment was a "grave injustice" and that Executive Order 9066 resulted from "race prejudice, war hysteria and a failure of political leadership."

1982

Vincent Chin, a Chinese American draftsman, is clubbed to death with a baseball bat by two Euro-American men.

1983
Fred Korematsu, Min Yasui, and Gordon Hirabayashi file petitions to overturn their World War II convictions for violating the curfew and evacuation orders.
1986
Immigration Reform and Control Act imposes civil and criminal penalties on employers who knowingly hire undocumented aliens.
1987
The U.S. House of Representatives votes 243 to 141 to make an official apology to Japanese Americans and to pay each surviving internee $20,000 in reparations.
1988
The U.S. Senate votes 69% to 27 to support redress for Japanese Americans. American Homecoming Act allows children in Vietnam born of American fathers to emigrate to the U.S.
1989
President George Bush signs into law an entitlement program to pay each surviving Japanese American internee $20,000. U.S. reaches agreement with Vietnam to allow political prisoners to emigrate to the U.S.

Asian Americans: An Interpretive History

According to [U.S. Census] figures, Chinese and Japanese Americans had outpaced whites even in terms of median family income by 1970. Japanese American median Family income was almost $3,000 higher, and Chinese American $1,000 higher than the U.S. median family income. But the federal government's study failed to place these figures alongside other relevant information, such as the fact that 60 percent of the Japanese American and Chinese American families (compared to only 51 percent among the U.S. population as a whole), more than one person worked, which helps to account for their higher family income. If per capita income, rather than family income, had been used as the measure, then the public would have learned that Chinese Americans (thought not Japanese Americans) were making considerably less than the national average. Moreover, if Hispanic groups, which earned much lower than other whites, had been removed from the aggregate white figures, then Asian Americans would not have outranked whites.

Social scientists who analyzed the 1970 census data reached various conclusions depending on whether they used statistics for the nation as a whole or for states with particularly high Asian concentrations, whether they separated the American-born from the foreign-born, and whether they distinguished between males and females. Studies based on national data, such as those by Barry Chiswick and by Charles Hirschman and Morrison Wong, invariably showed that American-born Chinese and Japanese men had a higher income than white men, but as Robert Jiobu, Amado Cabezas, and David Moulton have documented, such was not the case in California, where 58 percent and 45 percent, respectively, of the Japanese and Chinese in the contiguous states resided in 1970. In that state, American-born Chinese and Japanese men indeed had significantly more years of school than non-Hispanic whites, but their median incomes were no higher than that of the latter, because their returns to education - that is, the additional income derived from increased years of schooling - were lower than those for whites. According to Robert Jiobu's 1976 study of American-born men in California in 1970, for each additional year of education, whites earned $522 more, compared to $438 for Japanese, $320 for Chinese, $340 for Mexican

Americans, and $284 for blacks. Thus, the Asian-white parity in income was made possible mainly by the Asian American's higher level of education.

Other criticisms have been raised against the model minority thesis, mainly by researchers associated with the Asian American community organization, ASIAN, Inc., in San Francisco. First, more than half of the Asian/Pacific American population in the United States lives in only five metropolitan areas - Honolulu, San Francisco, Los Angeles, Chicago, and New York - and of these, more than nine-tenths are found in urban centers. These cities are not only high-income areas but also high-cost-of-living-areas. Thus, while Asian Americans (and others) living there may earn more, they also have to spend more.

Second, in areas with the highest density of Asian Americans, the percentage of Asian Americans in low-status, low-income occupations - that is, service workers, laborers, farm laborers, and private household workers - is considerably higher than among whites. In 1970, for example, fully 25 percent of all gainfully employed Chinese men in the United States were cooks, waiters, busboys, dishwashers, and janitors. Such a figure gives an impression of Asian American economic well-being that is quite different from based on consideration of median income alone.

Third, a detailed study of the San Francisco-Oakland Standard Metropolitan Statistical Area (SMSA) showed that Asian Americans were unevenly distributed in the economy. Professionals clustered in accounting, dentistry, nursing, health technology, and engineering and were underrepresented in law, teaching, administration, social services, and the higher levels of the medical professions. Managers were more likely to be self-employed than employees of large firms. Salespersons were retail clerks but seldom brokers or insurance agents. Clerical workers were mostly file clerks, typists, or office machine operators, and not secretaries or receptionists. Few Asian Americans held jobs in the heavy-machine, electrical, paper, chemical, or construction industries. Most female operatives were garment workers. In short, Asian Americans were concentrated in occupations that did not pay as well as other jobs in the same industries.

Fourth, the low unemployment rate of Asian Americans-another measure often used to depict their economic success - merely camouflages high underemployment. Wary of being of welfare, many Asian American workers apparently would rather hold low-paid, part-time, or seasonal jobs than receive public assistance.

Fifth, the high labor force participation rate of Asian American women in both 1970 and 1980 - supposedly a sign of their ready acceptance by employers - is in reality a reflection of the fact that more Asian American women are compelled to work because the male members of their families earn such low wages. It is true that working Asian American women earn a higher median income than do white working women, but they also have superior educational qualifications and live in localities with higher wages. Furthermore, compared to white women, a larger percentage of them work full time, which helps to drive their median income upward. But despite their high educational level, they receive lower returns their education than do white women, while the disparity between their returns and those of white men is even greater. In other words, they are not receiving earnings that are commensurate with their years of schooling. Sixth, with regard to the educational attainment of Asian Americans, the sizable influx of highly educated professionals after 1965 has inflated the average years of schooling completed. Critics of the model minority stereotype point out that the most important consideration should not be educational level, but returns to education, which more clearly reveal the existence of discrimination. For Asian Americans, even in 1980, these returns were still not on par with those received by white men.

The entry of professionals has had another effect. Since some of them have not been able to find professional jobs, they have bought small businesses, thereby increasing the number of "managers" in the Asian American -- particularly the Korean American - population. However, many of them operate only small mom-and-pop stores with no paid employees and very low gross earnings. Unlike journalists who tout Korean entrepreneurship as a sign of success, scholars who have examined the situation argue that the kind of business Korean immigrants engage in is, in fact, a disguised form of cheap labor: owners of small businesses run a high risk of failure and work long hours. Many of them could not stay afloat were it not for the unpaid labor they extract from their spouses, children, and other relatives. Nonetheless, small business currently is an important channel of upward mobility open to nonwhite immigrants who face obstacles in obtaining well-paying and secure jobs.

Finally, other groups of Asian Americans do not share the improved economic standing achieved by Japanese and Chinese Americans. In 1970 in the San Francisco-Oakland SMSA, according to Amado Cabezas and his associates, Filipinos (lumping together foreign- and American-born) earned only 58 percent of what white men earned, while Filipinas earned only 38 percent. The respective figures in the Los Angeles-Long Beach SMSA were 62 percent and 47 percent. In 1980, in the San Francisco-Oakland SMSA American-born Filipino men made 64 percent of what American-born white males made, while American-born Filipinas made 45 percent. In the Los Angeles-Long Beach SMSA, the comparable figures were 72 percent and 48 percent. Foreign-born men fared about the same as their American-born peers, while the foreign-born women did slightly better than their American- born sisters. A larger proportion of American-born Filipinos hold working-class jobs than do Chinese and Japanese Americans. They also seem to receive no discernible returns to schooling.

Source: Chan, Sucheng. Asian Americans: An Interpretive History. New York: Twayne Publishers, an imprint of Macmillan Publishing Company. 1991.

The Chinese Exclusion Act of 1882

Chapter 126. An act to execute certain treaty stipulations relating to Chinese.

Preamble. Whereas, in the opinion of the Government of the United States the coming of Chinese laborers to this country endangers the good order of certain localities within the territory thereof:

Therefore, Be it enacted by the Senate and House of Representatives of the United States of America in Congress assembled, That from and after the expiration of ninety days next after the passage of this act, and until the expiration of ten years next after the passage of this act, the coming of Chinese laborers to the United States be, and the same is hereby, suspended; and during such suspension it shall not be lawful for any Chinese laborer to come, or, having so come after the expiration of said ninety days, to remain within the United States.

SEC. 2. That the master of any vessel who shall knowingly bring within the United States on such vessel, and land or permit to be landed, and Chinese laborer, from any foreign port of place, shall be deemed guilty of a misdemeanor, and on conviction thereof shall be punished by a fine of not more than five hundred dollars for each and every such Chinese laborer so brought, and may be also imprisoned for a term not exceeding one year.

SEC. 3. That the two foregoing sections shall not apply to Chinese laborers who were in the United States on the seventeenth day of November, eighteen hundred and eighty, or who shall have come into the same before the expiration of ninety days next after the passage of this act, and who shall produce to such master before going on board such vessel, and shall produce to the collector of the port in the United States at which such vessel shall arrive, the evidence hereinafter in this act required of his being one of the laborers in this section mentioned; nor shall the two foregoing sections apply to the case of any master whose vessel, being bound to a port not within the United States by reason of being in distress or in stress of weather, or touching at any port of the United States on its voyage to any foreign port of place: Provided, That all Chinese laborers brought on such vessel shall depart with the vessel on leaving port.

SEC. 4. That for the purpose of properly indentifying Chinese laborers who were in the United States on the seventeenth day of November, eighteen hundred and eighty, or who shall have come into the same before the expiration of ninety days next after the passage of this act, and in order to furnish them with the proper evidence of their right to go from and come to the United States of their free will and accord, as provided by the treaty between the United States and China dated November seventeenth, eighteen hundred and eighty, the collector of customs of the district from which any such Chinese laborer shall depart from the United States shall, in person or by deputy, go on board each vessel having on board any such Chinese laborer and cleared or about to sail from his district for a foreign port, and on such vessel make a list of all such Chinese laborers, which shall be entered in registry-books to be kept for that purpose, in which shall be stated the name, age, occupation, last place of residence, physical marks or peculiarities, and all facts necessary for the indentification of each of such Chinese laborers, which books shall be safely kept in the custom-house; and every such Chinese laborer so departing from the United States shall be entitled to, and shall receive, free of any charge or cost upon application therefor, from the collector or his deputy, at the time such list is taken, a certificate, signed by the collector or his deputy and attested by his seal of office, in such form as the Secretary of the Treasury shall prescribe, which certificate shall contain a statement of the name, age, occupation, last place of residence, personal description, and fact of identification of the Chinese laborer to whom the certificate is issued, corresponding with the said list and registry in all particulars. In case any Chinese laborer after having received such certificate shall leave such vessel before her departure he shall deliver his certificate to the master of the vessel, and if such Chinese laborer shall fail to return to such vessel before her departure from port the certificate shall be delivered by the master to the collector of customs for cancellation. The certificate herein provided for shall entitle the Chinese laborer to whom the same is issued to return to and re-enter the United States upon producing and delivering the same to the collector of customs of the district at which such Chinese laborer shall seek to re-enter; and upon delivery of such certificate by such Chinese laborer to the collector of customs at the time of re-entry in the United States, said collector shall cause the same to be filed in the custom house and duly canceled.

SEC. 5. That any Chinese laborer mentioned in section four of this act being in the United States, and desiring to depart from the United States by land, shall have the right to demand and receive, free of charge or cost, a certificate of indentification similar to that provided for in section four of this act to be issued to such Chinese laborers as may desire to leave the United States by water; and it is hereby made the duty of the collector of customs of the district next adjoining the foreign country to which said Chinese laborer desires to go to issue such certificate, free of charge or cost, upon application by such Chinese laborer, and to enter the same upon registry-books to be kept by him for the purpose, as provided for in section four of this act.

SEC. 6. That in order to the faithful execution of articles one and two of the treaty in this act before mentioned, every Chinese person other than a laborer who may be entitled by said treaty and this act to come within the United States, and who shall be about to come to the United States, shall be identified as so entitled by the Chinese Government in each case, such identity to be evidenced by a certificate issued under the authority of said government, which certificate shall be in the English language or (if not in the English language) accompanied by a translation into English, stating such right to come, and which certificate shall state the name, title, or official rank, if any, the age, height, and all physical peculiarities, former and present occupation or profession, and place of residence in China of the person to whom the certificate is issued and that such person is entitled conformably to the treaty in this act mentioned to come within the United States. Such certificate shall be prima-facie evidence of the fact set forth therein, and shall be produced to the collector of customs, or his deputy, of the port in the district in the United States at which the person named therein shall arrive.

SEC. 7. That any person who shall knowingly and falsely alter or substitute any name for the name written in such certificate or forge any such certificate, or knowingly utter any forged or fraudulent certificate, or falsely personate any person named in any such certificate, shall be deemed guilty of a misdemeanor; and upon conviction thereof shall be fined in a sum not exceeding one thousand dollars, an imprisoned in a penitentiary for a term of not more than five years.

SEC. 8. That the master of any vessel arriving in the United States from any foreign port or place shall, at the same time he delivers a manifest of the cargo, and if there be no cargo, then at the time of making a report of the entry of vessel pursuant to the law, in addition to the other matter required to be reported, and before landing, or permitting to land, any Chinese passengers, deliver and report to the collector of customs of the district in which such vessels shall have arrived a separate list of all Chinese passengers taken on board his vessel at any foreign port or place, and all such passengers on board the vessel at that time. Such list shall show the names of such passengers (and if accredited officers of the Chinese Government traveling on the business of that government, or their servants, with a note of such facts), and the name and other particulars, as shown by their respective certificates; and such list shall be sworn to by the master in the manner required by law in relation to the manifest of the cargo. Any willful refusal or neglect of any such master to comply with the provisions of this section shall incur the same penalties and forfeiture as are provided for a refusal or neglect to report and deliver a manifest of cargo.

SEC. 9. That before any Chinese passengers are landed from any such vessel, the collector, or his deputy, shall proceed to examine such passengers, comparing the certificates with the list and with the passengers; and no passenger shall be allowed to land in the United States from such vessel in violation of law.

SEC. 10. That every vessel whose master shall knowingly violate any of the provisions of this act shall be deemed forfeited to the United States, and shall be liable to seizure and condemnation on any district of the United States into which such vessel may enter or in which she may be found.

SEC. 11. That any person who shall knowingly bring into or cause to be brought into the United States by land, or who shall knowingly aid or abet the same, or aid or abet the landing in the United States from any vessel of any Chinese person not lawfully entitled to enter the United States, shall be deemed guilty of a misdemeanor, and shall, on conviction thereof, be fined in a sum not exceeding one thousand dollars, and imprisoned for a term not exceeding one year.

SEC. 12. That no Chinese person shall be permitted to enter the United States by land without producing to the proper officer of customs the certificate in this act required of Chinese persons seeking to land from a vessel. And any Chinese person found unlawfully within the United States shall be caused to be removed therefrom to the country from whence he came, by direction of the United States, after being brought before some justice, judge, or commissioner of a court of the United States and found to be one not lawfully entitled to be or remain in the United States.

SEC. 13. That this act shall not apply to diplomatic and other officers of the Chinese Government traveling upon the business of that government, whose credentials shall be taken as equivalent to the certificate in this act mentioned, and shall exempt them and their body and household servants from the provisions of this act as to other Chinese persons.

SEC. 14. That hereafter no State court or court of the United States shall admit Chinese to citizenship; and all laws in conflict with this act are hereby repealed.

SEC. 15. That the words "Chinese laborers", whenever used in this act, shall be construed to mean both skilled and unskilled laborers and Chinese employed in mining.
Source: The United States Congress. Forty-Seventh Congress. Session I. 1882 Approved, May 6, 1882.

Chinese Miners Describe the Rock Springs Massacre

We, the undersigned, have been in Rock Springs, Wyoming Territory, for periods ranging from one to fifteen years, for the purpose of working on the railroads and in the coal mines.
Up to the time of the recent troubles we had worked along with the white men, and had not had the least ill feeling against them. The officers of the companies employing us treated us and the white man kindly, placing both races on the same footing and paying the same wages.
Several times we had been approached by the white men and requested to join them in asking the

companies for an increase in the wages of all, both Chinese and white men. We inquired of them what we should do if the companies refused to grant an increase. They answered that if the companies would not increase our wages we should all strike, then the companies would be obliged to increase our wages. To this we dissented, wherefore we excited their animosity against us.

During the past two years there has been in existence in "Whitemen's Town," Rock Springs, an organization composed of white miners, whose object was to bring about the expulsion of all Chinese from the Territory. To them or to their object we have paid no attention. About the month of August of this year notices were posted up, all the way from Evanston to Rock Springs, demanding the expulsion of the Chinese, & c. On the evening of September I, 1885, the bell of the building in which said organization meets rang for a meeting. It was rumored on that night that threats had been made against the Chinese.

On the morning of September 2, a little past seven o'clock, more than ten white men, some in ordinary dress and others in mining suits, ran into Coal Pit No. 6, loudly declaring that the Chinese should not be permitted to work there. The Chinese present reasoned with them in a few words, but were attacked with murderous weapons, and three of their number wounded. The white foreman of the coal pit, hearing of the disturbance, ordered all to stop work for the time being.

After the work had stopped, all the white men in and near Coal Pit No. 6 began to assemble by the dozen. They carried firearms, and marched to Rock Springs by way of the railroad from Coal Pit No. 6, and crossing the railroad bridge, went directly to "Whitemen's Town." All this took place before 10:00 A.M. We now heard the bell ringing for a meeting at the white men's organization building. Not long after, all the white men came out of that building, most of them assembling in the barrooms, the crowds meanwhile growing larger and larger.

About two o'clock in the afternoon a mob, divided into two gangs, came toward "Chinatown," one gang coming by way of the plank bridge, and the other by way of the railroad bridge. The gang coming by way of the railroad bridge was the larger, and was subdivided into many squads, some of which did not cross the bridge, but remained standing on the side opposite to "Chinatown"; others that had already crossed the bridge stood on the right and left at the end of it. Several squads marched up the hill behind Coal Pit No. 3.

One squad remained at Coal Shed No. 3 and another at the pump house. The squad that remained at the pump house fired the first shot, and the squad that stood at Coal Shed No. 3 immediately followed their example and fired. The Chinese by name of Lor Sun Kit was the first person shot, and fell to the ground. At that time the Chinese began to realize that the mob were bent on killing. The Chinese, though greatly alarmed, did not yet begin to flee.

Soon after, the mob on the hill behind Coal Pit No. 3 came down from the hill, and joining the different squads of the mob, fired their weapons and pressed on to Chinatown.

The gang that were at the plank bridge also divided into several squads, pressing near and surrounding "Chinatown." One squad of them guarded the plank bridge in order to cut off the retreat of the Chinese.

Not long after, it was everywhere reported that a Chinese named Leo Dye Bah, who lived in the western part of "Chinatown," was killed by a bullet, and that another named Yip Ah Marn, resident in the eastern end of the town, was likewise killed. The Chinese now, to save their lives, fled in confusion in every direction, some going up the hill behind Coal Pit No. 3, others along the foot of the hill where Coal Pit No. 4 is; some from the eastern end of the town fled across Bitter Creek to the opposite hill, and others from the western end by the foot of the hill on the right of Coal Pit No. 5. The mob were now coming in the three directions, namely, the east and west sides of the town and from the wagon road.

Whenever the mob met a Chinese they stopped him and, pointing a weapon at him, asked him if he had any revolver, and then approaching him they searched his person, robbing him of his watch or any gold or silver that he might have about him, before letting him go. Some of the rioters would let a Chinese go after depriving him of all his gold and silver, while another Chinese would be beaten with the butt ends of the weapons before being let go. Some of the rioters, when they could not stop a Chinese, would shoot him dead on the spot, and then search and rob him. Some would-overtake a Chinese, throw him down and search and rob him before they would let him go. Some of the rioters would not fire their weapons, but would only use the butt ends to beat the Chinese with. Some would not beat a Chinese, but rob him of whatever he had and let him go, yelling to him to go quickly. Some, who took no part either in beating or robbing the Chinese, stood by, shouting loudly and laughing and clapping their hands.

There was a gang of women that stood at the "Chinatown" end of the plank bridge and cheered; among the women, two of them each fired successive shots at the Chinese. This was done about a little past 3:00 P.M.

Most of the Chinese fled toward the eastern part of "Chinatown." Some of them ran across Bitter Creek, went up directly to the opposite hill, crossing the grassy plain. Some of them went along the foot of the hill where Coal Pit No. 4 stood, to cross the creek, and by a devious route reached the opposite hill. Some of them ran up to the hill of Coal Pit No. 3, and thence winding around the hills went to the opposite hill. A few of them fled to the foot of the hill where Coal Pit No. 5 stood, and ran across the creek, and thence by a winding course to the western end of the "Whitemen's Town." But very few did this.

The Chinese who were the first to flee mostly dispersed themselves at the back hills, on the opposite bank of the creek, and among the opposite hills. They were scattered far and near, high and low, in about one hundred places. Some were standing, or sitting, or lying hid on the grass, or stooping down on the low grounds. Every one of them was praying to Heaven or groaning with pain. They had been eyewitnesses to the shooting in "Chinatown," and had seen the whites, male and female, old and young, searching houses for money, household effects, or gold, which were carried across to "Whitemen's Town."

Some of the rioters went off toward the railroad of Coal Pit No. 6, others set fire to the Chinese houses. Between 4:00 P.M. and a little past 9:00 P.M. all the camp houses belonging to the coal company and the Chinese huts had been burned down completely, only one of the company's camp houses remaining. Several of the camp houses near Coal pit No. 6 were also burned, and the three Chinese huts there were also burned. All the Chinese houses burned numbered seventy-nine.

Some of the Chinese were killed at the bank of Bitter Creek, some near the railroad bridge, and some in "Chinatown." After having been killed, the dead bodies of some were carried to the burning buildings and thrown into the flames. Some of the Chinese who had hid themselves in the houses were killed and their bodies burned; some, who on account of sickness could not run, were burned alive in the houses. One Chinese was killed in "Whitemen's Town" in a laundry house, and his house demolished. The whole number of Chinese killed was twenty-eight and those wounded fifteen.

The money that the Chinese lost was that which in their hurry they were unable to take with them, and consequently were obliged to leave in their houses, or that which was taken from their persons. The goods, clothing, or household effects remaining in their houses were either plundered or burned.

When the Chinese fled to the different hills they intended to come back to "Chinatown" when the riot was over, to dispose of the dead bodies and to take care of the wounded. But to their disappointment, all the houses were burned to ashes, and there was then no place of shelter for them; they were obliged to run blindly from hill to hill. Taking the railroad as their guide, they walked toward the town of Green River, some of them reaching that place in the morning, others at noon, and others not until dark. There were some who did not reach it until the fourth of September. We felt very thankful to the railroad company for having telegraphed to the conductors of all its trains to pick up such of the Chinese as were to be met with along the line of the railroad and carry them to Evanston.

On the fifth of September all the Chinese that had fled assembled at Evanston; the native citizens there threatened day and night to burn and kill the Chinese. Fortunately, United States troops had been ordered to come and protect them, and quiet was restored. On the ninth of September the United States government instructed the troops to escort the Chinese back to Rock Springs. When they arrived there they saw only a burnt tract of ground to mark the sites of their former habitations. Some of the dead bodies had been buried by the company, while others, mangled and decomposed, were strewn on the ground and were being eaten by dogs and hogs. Some of the bodies were not found until they were dug out of the ruins of the buildings. Some had been burned beyond recognition. It was a sad and painful sight to see the son crying for the father, the brother for the brother, the uncle for the nephew, and friend for friend.

By this time most of the Chinese have abandoned the desire of resuming their mining work, but inasmuch as the riot has left them each with only the one or two torn articles of clothing they have on their persons, and as they have not a single cent in their pockets, it is a difficult matter for them to make any change in their location. Fortunately, the company promised to lend them clothing and provisions, and a number of wagons to sleep in. Although protected by government troops, their sleep is disturbed by frightful dreams, and they cannot obtain peaceful rest.

Some of the rioters who killed the Chinese and who set fire to the homes could be identified by the Chinese, and some not. Among them the two women heretofore mentioned, and who killed some Chinese, were specially recognized by many Chinese. Among the rioters who robbed and plundered were men, women, and children. Even the white woman who formerly taught English to the Chinese searched for and took handkerchiefs and other articles.

The Chinese know that the white men who worked in Coal Pit No. 1 did not join the mob, and most of them did not stop work, either. We heard that the coal company's officers had taken a list of the names of the rioters who were particularly brutal and murderous, which list numbered forty or fifty.

From a survey of all the circumstances, several causes may be assigned for the killing and wounding of so many Chinese and the destruction of so much property:

1. The Chinese had been for a long time employed at the same work as the white men. While they knew that the white men entertained ill feelings toward them, the Chinese did not take precautions to guard against this sudden outbreak, inasmuch as at no time in the past had there been any quarrel or fighting between the races.

2. On the second day of September 1885, in Coal Pit No. 6, the white men attacked the Chinese. That place being quite a distance from Rock Springs, very few Chinese were there. As we did not think that the trouble would extend to Rock Springs, we did not warn each other to prepare for flight.

3. Most of the Chinese living in Rock Springs worked during the daytime in the different coal mines, and consequently did not hear of the fight at Coal Pit No. 6, nor did they know of the armed mob that had assembled in "Whitemen's Town." When twelve o'clock came, everybody returned home from his place of work to lunch. As yet the mob had not come to attack the Chinese; a great number of the latter were returning to work without any apprehension of danger.

4. About two o'clock the mob suddenly made their appearance for the attack. The Chinese thought that they had only assembled to threaten, and that some of the company's officers would come to disperse them. Most of the Chinese, acting upon this view of the matter, did not gather up their money or clothing, and when the mob fired at them they fled precipitately. Those Chinese who were in the workshops, hearing of the riot, stopped work and fled in their working clothes, and' did not have time enough to go home to change their clothes or to

gather up their money. What they did leave at home was either plundered or burned.

5. None of the Chinese had firearms or any defensive weapons, nor was there any place that afforded an opportunity for the erection of a barricade that might impede the rioters in their attack. The Chinese were all like a herd of frightened deer that let the huntsmen surround and kill them.

6. All the Chinese had, on the first of September, bought from the company a month's supply of provision and the implements necessary for the mining of coal. This loss of property was therefore larger than it would be later in the month.

We never thought that the subjects of a nation entitled by treaty to the rights and privileges of the most favored nation could, in a country so highly civilized like this, so unexpectedly suffer the cruelty and wrong of being unjustly put to death, or of being wounded and left without the means of cure, or being abandoned to poverty, hunger, and cold, and without the means to betake themselves elsewhere.

To the great President of the United States, who, hearing of the riot, sent troops to protect our lives, we are most sincerely thankful.

In behalf of those killed or wounded, or of those deprived of their property, we pray that the examining commission will ask our minister to sympathize, and to endeavor to secure the punishment of the murderers, the relief of the wounded, and compensation for those despoiled of their property, so that the living and the relatives of the dead will be grateful, and never forget his kindness for generations.

Hereinabove we have made a brief recital of the facts of this riot, and pray your honor will take them into your kind consideration.

(Here follow the signatures of 559 Chinese laborers, resident at Rock Springs, Wyoming Territory.)

LIST OF KILLED

(Investigation made by Huang Sih Chuen, Chinese consul at New York, of the Chinese Examining Commission, of Chinese laborers killed at Rock Springs, Wyoming Territory, September 2, 1885.)

The said Huang Sih Chuen submitted the following report:

I examined the dead bodies of the following Chinese laborers killed at Rock Springs:

1. The dead body of Leo Sun Tsung, found in his own hut in the native settlement, was covered with many wounds. The left jawbone was broken, evidently by a bullet. The skin and bone of the right leg below the knee were injured. I also ascertained that the deceased was fifty-one years old, and had a mother, wife, and son living at home (in China).

2. The dead body of Leo Kow Boot was found between mines No. 3 and 4, at the foot of the mountain. The neck was shot through crosswise by a bullet, cutting the windpipe in two. I also ascertained that the deceased was twenty-four years old. His family connections have not yet been clearly made known.

3. The dead body of Yii See Yen was found near the creek. The left temple was shot by a bullet, and the skull broken. The age of the deceased was thirty-six years. He had a mother living at home (in China).

4. The dead body of Leo Dye Bah was found at the side of the bridge, near the creek, shot in the middle of the chest by a bullet, breaking the breastbone. I also ascertained that the deceased was 'fifty-six years old, and had a wife, son, and daughter at home.

5. The dead body of Choo Bah Quot was found in the hut adjoining Camp No. 34, together with the remains of Lor Han Lung. The front part of the body was not

injured, but the flesh on the back was completely gone, and the bones were scorched; the hair was also burned off. I also ascertained that the deceased was twenty-three years old, and had parents living at home.

The above five bodies were found more or less mutilated.

6. A portion of the dead body of Sia Bun Ning was found in a pile of ashes in the hut near the Chinese temple. It consisted of the head, neck, and shoulders. The two hands, together with the rest of the body below the chest, were completely burned off. I also ascertained that the deceased was thirty-seven years old, and had a mother, wife, son, and daughter living at home.

7. A portion of the dead body of Leo Lung Hong was found in a pile of ashes in a hut adjoining Camp No. 27. It consisted of the head, neck, and breast. The two hands, together with rest of body below the waist, were burned off completely. I also ascertained that deceased was forty-five years old, and had a wife and three sons living at home.

8. A portion of the dead body of Leo Chih Ming was found in a pile of ashes in the hut of the deceased near the temple where the remains of Liang Tsun Bong and Hsu Ah Cheong were found. It consisted of the head and chest. The hands, together with the rest of the body below the waist, were burned off completely. I also ascertained that deceased was forty-nine years old, and had a mother, wife, and son living at home; also another son working with him in the coal mines.

9. A portion of the dead body of Liang Tsun Bong was found in a pile of ashes in the hut near the temple where the deceased, together with Leo Chih Ming and Hsu Ah Cheong, had lived. It consisted of the head, shoulders, and hands. The rest of the body below the chest was burned off completely. The age of the deceased was

forty-two years. He had a wife and two sons living at home.

10. A portion of the dead body of Hsu Ah Cheong was found in a pile of ashes in the hut near the temple where the deceased, together with Leo Chih Ming and Liang Tsun Bong, had lived. It consisted of the skull bone, the upper and lower jawbones, and teeth. I also ascertained that the deceased was thirty-two years old, and had parents, wife, and son living at home.

11. A portion of the dead body of Lor Han Lung was found in the hut adjoining No. 34, where the remains of Choo Bah Quot was also found. It consisted of the sole and heel of the left foot. The rest of the body was completely burned. I also ascertained that the deceased was thirty-two years old, and had a mother, wife, son, and daughter, all living at home.

12. A portion of the dead body of Hoo Ah Nii was found in a pile of ashes in his own hut. It consisted of the right half of a head and the backbone. The rest of the body was completely burned. I also ascertained that the deceased was forty-three years old, and had a wife living at home.

13. A portion of the dead body of Leo Tse Wing was found in a pile of ashes in the hut adjoining Camp No. 14. It consisted of the bones of the lower half of the body, extending from hip to foot. The rest of the body was burned off completely. I also ascertained that the deceased was thirty-nine years old. His family connection has not yet been clearly made known.

The last-named eight dead bodies were found partly, destroyed by fire.

The following fifteen persons were killed: Leo Jew Foo, Leo Tim Kwong, Hung Qwan Chuen, Tom He Yew, Mar Tse Choy, Leo Lung Siang, Yip Ah Marn, Leo Lung Hon, Leo Lung Hor, Leo Ah Tsun, Leang Ding, Leo Hoy Yat, Yuen Chin Sing, Hsu Ah Tseng, and Chun Quan

Sing. Twelve fragments of bones, belonging to twelve of the above-named persons, were found in twelve different places in the Chinese settlement. No trace of the remaining three persons was found.

I also ascertained that the age of Leo Jew Foo was thirty-five years; he had a mother at home. Leo Tim Kwong was thirty-one years; family connection not known. Hung Quan Chuen was forty-two years; he had a father at home. Tom He Yew was thirty-four years; he had a mother, wife, and daughter at home.

Source: Memorial of Chinese Laborers, Resident at Rock Springs, Wyoming Territory, to the Chinese Consul at New York (1885). Reprinted in Cheng-Tsu Wu, ed., Chink! (New York: The World Publishing Company, 1972), 152–164.

Ordering Japanese Interment

Whereas, the successful prosecution of the war requires every possible protection against espionage and against sabotage to national-defense material, national-defense premises and national defense utilities as defined in Section 4, Act of April 20, 1918, 40 Stat. 533, as amended by the Act of November 30, 1940, 54 Stat. 1220. and the Act of August 21, 1941, 55 Stat. 655 (U.S.C.01 Title 50, Sec. 104):

Now therefore, by virtue of the authority vested in me as President of the United States, and Commander in Chief of the Army and Navy, I hereby authorize and direct the Secretary of War, and the Military Commanders whom he may from time to time designate, whenever he or any designated Commander deems such action to be necessary or desirable, to prescribe military areas in such places and of such extent as he or the appropriate Military Commander may determine, from which any or all persons may be excluded, and with respect to which, the right of any persons to enter, remain in, or leave shall be subject to whatever restriction the Secretary of War or the appropriate Military Commander may impose in his discretion.

The Secretary of War is hereby authorized to provide for residents of any such area who are excluded therefrom, such transportation, food, shelter, and other accommodations as may be necessary, in the judgment of the Secretary of War or the said Military Commander, and until other arrangements are made, to accomplish the purpose of this order. The designation of military areas in any region or locality shall supersede designations of prohibited and restricted areas by the Attorney General under the Proclamation of December 7 and 8, 1941, and shall supercede the responsibility and authority of the Attorney General under the said Proclamations in respect of such prohibited and restricted areas.

I hereby further authorize and direct the Secretary of War and the said Military Commanders to take such other steps as he or the appropriate Military Commander may deem advisable to enforce compliance with the restrictions applicable to each military area herein above authorized to be designated, including the use of Federal troops and other Federal Agencies, with authority to accept assistance of state and local agencies.

I hereby further authorize and direct all Executive Departments, independent establishments and other Federal Agencies, to assist the Secretary of War or the said Military Commanders in carrying out this Executive Order, including the furnishing of medical aid, hospitalization, food, clothing, transportation, use of land, shelter, and other supplies, equipment, utilities, facilities and services.

This order shall not be construed as modifying or limiting in any way the authority heretofore granted under Executive Order No. 8972, dated December 12, 1941, nor shall it be construed as limiting or modifying the duty and responsibility of the Federal Bureau of Investigation, with respect to the investigations of alleged acts of sabotage or the duty and responsibility of the Attorney General and the Department of Justice under the Proclamations of December 7 and 8, 1941, prescribing regulations for the conduct and control of alien enemies, except as such duty and responsibility is superseded by the designation of military areas hereunder.

Source: Roosevelt, Franklin D., Executive Order 9066, February 19, 1942. The White House.

Concentration Camps in the United States during World War II

Eight months after Pearl Harbor, on August 7, 1942, all the West Coast Japanese Americans had been rounded up, one way or another, and were either in Wartime Civil Control Administration (WCAA) Assembly Centers or War Relocation Authority (WRA) camps. By November 3 the transfer to WRA was complete; altogether 119,803 men, women, and children were confined behind barbed wire. Almost six thousand new American citizens would be born in the concentration camps and some eleven hundred were sent in from the Hawaiian Islands. The rest—112,704 people—were West Coast Japanese. Of these, almost two-thirds—64.9 percent—were American-born, most of them under 21 and 77.4 percent under 25. Their foreign-born parents presented a quite different demographic profile. More than half of them—57.2 percent—were over 50. The camps, then, were primarily places of confinement for the young and the old, and since young adults of the second generation were, in the main, the first to be released, the unnatural age distribution within these artificial communities became more and more disparate as time went by.

Life in these places was not generally brutal; there were no torture chambers, firing squads, or gas ovens waiting for the evacuated people. The American concentration camps should not be compared, in that sense, to Auschwitz or Vorkuta. They were, in fact, much more like a century-old American institution, the Indian reservation, that like the institutions that flourished in totalitarian Europe. They were, however, places if confinement ringed with barbed wire and armed sentries. Despite WRA propaganda about community control, there was an unbridgeable gap between the Caucasian custodians and their Oriental charges; even the mess halls were segregated by race. Although some of the staff, particularly those in the upper echelons of the WRA, disapproved of the racist policy that brought the camps into being, the majority of the camp personnel, recruited from the local labor force, shared the contempt of the general population for "Japs."...

Most of the existing literature about the camps stresses the cooperation and compliance of the inmates, thus perpetuating the basic line of both the WRA and the JACL. [Japanese American Citizens League]. Like most successful myths, this one contains elements of truth. There was little spectacular, violent resistance; no desperate attempts to escape; even sustained mass civil disobedience rarely occurred. But from the very beginning of their confinement, the evacuated people were in conflict, both with their keepers and with each other. These conflicts started even before the evacuation began, grew in the Assembly Centers, and were intensified in the concentration camps; their effects are still felt in the contemporary Japanese American community as the questioning and often angry members of the third, or Sansei, generation—many of whom began their lives behind barbed wire or in exile=-question the relative compliance of most of their parents a quarter century ago.

Although resignation rather than resistance was more the common response of the internees, resistance, both active and passive, did occur and was more frequent and significant than is generally realized.... The most effective early opposition to the JACL and its deliberate policy of collaboration came not from the older generation from the Kibei, American-born Japanese who had been sent back to Japan for education of employment. The older Issei generation seemed to feel powerless: they were, after all, enemy aliens, and treatment of them was generally in accord with the Geneva Convention. The partly Americanized Kibei, who were, whatever their loyalties, American citizens, led what might be called the "right-wing" opposition among the evacuee population. Some of them, and many Issei as well, were undoubtedly rooting for Imperial Japan. The bulk of the early active conflict within the internee population was between the Nisei and the Kibei, with the former blaming the latter for everything that went wrong....

Sometimes these "Kibei" attacks received great support from the camp populations; one of them led to the most serious outbreak of violence in the entire evacuation, the Manzanar riot of December 6, 1942. The previous evening Fred Tayama, a restaurant owner who had been a leading JACL official, was attacked by an unknown group and beaten seriously enough to require hospitalization. Although he could not positively identify his attackers, the WRA authorities arrested several Kibei [whose]... arrest sparked a mass demonstration led not by a Kibei but by Joe Kurihara, a Hawaiian Nisei who was the most effective anti WRA-JACL agitator in the camp. A veteran of the United States Army who had been wounded in World War I, Kurihara was understandably embittered by his imprisonment. . . .

After some fruitless discussions with the Manzanar management, another and more heated mass meeting was held about 6 p.m. . . . The WRA authorities. . . called in the military police, who pushed the crowd back from the jail but failed to disperse it. The troops then tear-gassed the crowd of several hundred, mostly teenagers and young men, which scattered in great confusion, but re-formed later. At this juncture the troops, apparently without orders, fired submachine guns, shotguns, and rifles into the unarmed crowd. Two young men were killed and ten other evacuees were treated for gunshot wounds, as was one soldier, apparently hit by a ricocheting army bullet. . . . Sixteen malcontents were sent to isolation camps in Moab, Utah, and Leupp, Arizona, and 65 of the most prominent JACL leaders were taken into protective custody at an abandoned Civilian Conservation Corps camp in the Mohave Desert. . . .

Four months later a trigger-happy military policeman at Topaz was responsible for another death. Camp regulations forbade any alien to approach an outer fence, and when an elderly and obviously harmless Issei man did so and allegedly failed to respond to a command of "Halt!" the sentry shot and killed him in broad daylight. A mass funeral was held and much indignation was expressed, but there was no significant prisoner violence at Topaz. At all the camps there were, at one time or another, protest demonstrations and "strikes" over this or that inequity, but other serious internal violence was avoided except for the crisis at Tule Lake in late 1954 and early 1944. . . .

These outbreaks of violence were obviously not characteristic of camp life, whose salient feature was probably boredom and mild discomfort. Normal family life was obviously impossible. . . . Not only semiprivate housing, but public feeding created problems for parents. . . . The children, particularly the teenagers, had a degree of freedom within the confines of the camp far greater than they would have known on the outside. Among the parents, the authority of the father was greatly reduced' not only did he have less control over his children, but he also often lost his traditional role as provider. If he was an alien, his citizen children were in a superior legal position to him. If his wife worked, she brought in the same meager wage as he did. . . .

. . . [T]he camps . . . were not static places . . . . [E]ven as the evacuation and relocation began, two significant groups of Japanese Americans were allowed to leave reception centers and relocation camps: the college students who left permanently and the farm workers who left temporarily. On October 1, 1942, new WRA "leave clearance procedures" went into effect which eventually enabled many of the Nisei to reenter civilian life. . . . During 1943 some 17,000 evacuees were allowed to leave and reenter civilian life. The great majority of these were Nisei between 18 and 30. The increasing shortage of skilled and semiskilled civilian labor undoubtedly facilitated their absorption into the economy with, all things considered, a minimum of friction. Chicago, in particular, became the favorite city for relocatees, with many others being attracted to Denver and Salt Lake City. The WRA helped by setting up local resettlement committees of volunteers from civic and religious groups in the receiving communities which cooperated with field offices set up by the WRA. . . .

The decision to allow "leaves" still left the question of loyalty unsettled in the minds of many within the WRA, and, when it became known outside the centers that some "Japs" were being turned loose, all kinds of protests were made. . . .

In the meantime, the United States Army had decided that it needed Japanese American manpower. . . . [T]he Army had decided to recruit an all-Nisei combat team of about 5000 men drawn from both the Hawaiian Islands and the Relocation Centers. Obviously, only "loyal" Japanese Americans would volunteer or be acceptable for such a unit, and the Army directed that the loyalty of the Nisei males of military age be determined by a questionnaire. . . .

The WRA quickly adapted the Army's proposal to its own purposes. Instead of administering the loyalty questionnaire to male Nisei over seventeen years of age, the agency decided to determine administratively the loyalty of all internees over seventeen, regardless of sex or nationality. National publicity was given to the decision. On January 28, 1943, War Secretary Stimson announced the decision to form an all-Nisei combat team. Three days later, President Roosevelt issued a public statement praising the decision. . . .

The resulting questionnaire was singularly inappropriate. First distributed on February 10, 1943, it was headed "Application for Leave Clearance." Many of the Issei, particularly the more elderly, had no desire to leave the camps, so the very title created confusion. The public announcement of the Japanese American combat team had already created all kinds of rumors in the camps, and, it must be remembered, the inmates had little reason to trust the United States government. But the most serious problems were created by questions 27 and 28 on the questionnaire, which had originally been intended for Nisei of military age.

No. 27. Are you willing to serve in the armed forces of the United States on combat duty, wherever ordered?

No. 28. Will you swear unqualified allegiance to the United States of America and faithfully defend the United States from any or all attack by foreign or domestic forces, and forswear any form of allegiance or obedience to the Japanese emperor, to any other foreign government, power or organization?

What aged Issei or women of any age were to make of question 27 is hard to say. But even worse was question 28. For the Issei, who were by law ineligible because of race to become United States citizens, it was asking them voluntarily to assume stateless status, and, in addition, a violation of the Geneva Convention governing the treatment of enemy aliens. Eventually, the question was rewritten for Issei to read:

No. 28. Will you swear to abide by the laws of the United States and to take no action which would in any way interfere with the war effort of the United States?

This, of course, was a more proper question which many Issei were able to answer affirmatively, but great confusion had already been caused. For the Nisei, both questions created problems. Some contended that question 28 was a trap and that to forswear allegiance to Japan was to confess that such allegiance had once existed. Many answered question 27 conditionally, saying things like: "Yes, if my rights as a citizen are restored," or "No, not unless the government recognized my right to live anywhere in the United States." Some simply answered "No—No" out of understandable resentment over their treatment and others refused to fill out the forms at all. On the other hand, the JACLers viewed the questionnaire and the opportunity to volunteer as a way to redeem their questioned loyalty. As a former University of California student who volunteered wrote to Monroe Deutsch, it was "a hard decision. . . . I know that this will be the only way that my family can resettle n Berkeley without prejudice and persecution."

Out of the nearly 78,000 inmates who were eligible to register almost 75,000 eventually filled out the questionnaires. Approximately 6700 of the registrants answered "No" to question 28, nearly 2000 qualified their answers in one way or another, and thus were set down in the government's books as "disloyal"; and a few hundred simply left the question blank. The overwhelming majority—more than 65,000— answered "Yes" to question 28. More than 1200 Nisei volunteered for combat and about two-thirds of them were eventually accepted for military service. . . .

Although originally designed as a method of getting volunteers for an Army program, the loyalty questionnaires were eventually used by the WRA as a basis for separating the "loyal" from the "disloyal" and shipping the latter to Tule Lake, which became a segregation center for "disloyals," with "loyal" inmates shipped out to other camps and segregants moved in. Apart from the spurious nature of the loyalty determination, other factors entered into the decision of individuals to go to Tule Lake or remain there. Family loyalties, the desire to remain where they were, and often sheer resentment and disillusionment were as significant as "loyalty" or "disloyalty." . . . Eventually, more than 18,000 Japanese Americans were segregated at Tule Lake; almost a third of these were family members of segregants rather than segregants themselves. Another third were "Old Tuleans," many of whom just simply did not want to move. . . .

Predictably, Tule Lake became a trouble spot and was turned over to the Army for a time and placed under martial law. Even there some inmates were accused by others of being "inu," and several serious beatings and one murder occurred. During the period of Army control one evacuee was shot and killed by a sentry, who, although exonerated by both civilian and military courts, seems to have overreacted. Within Tule Lake, a strong minority movement for what was called "resegregation" grew up. Its proponents, strongly pro-Japanese and desirous of returning to Japan, objected to the presence of a majority, who, despite their presumably "disloyal" status, had no such orientation or desire. Eventually more than a third of those at Tule Lake formally applied for repatriation to Japan after the war; of the 7222 persons who did so, almost 65 percent were American-born. . . .

. . . [L]ike the "no" answer on question 28, statements made about repatriation and citizenship renunciation were motivated by many factors. Chief, of course, was the fact that the incarcerated people were subject to all kinds of pressures, real and imaginary. . . . [T]he fear of being thrust back, virtually penniless, into a hostile, wartime atmosphere was frightening. Many, as we have seen, went to or stayed at Tule Lake because it seemed to offer a kind of refuge in an otherwise stormy world. . . .

But trouble and reluctance to leave were not confined to Tule Lake. Protests and resistance to resettlement characterized the history of the other nine camps even after the "disloyals" had been segregated. Hear Mountain, Wyoming, often classified as a "happy camp," is a good case in point. From the very beginning there had been conflict and organized resistance there. In October and November 1942, protests and demonstrations occurred over the erection of the standard barbed wire fence surrounding the camp, which had not yet been erected when the evacuees began to arrive in August. The fence and other guard facilities were denounced in a petition signed by half the adults in the camp as "devoid of all humanitarian principles . . . an insult to any free human being." The fence, of course, stayed, but other, more pragmatic protests continued. . . . One of the major inarticulated premises behind the segregation of "disloyals" at Tule Lake, an assumption shared by WRA administrators and "loyal" JACLers alike, was that with "troublemakers" removed, the camps would become more placid and that resistance and protest would all but cease. At Heart Mountain such was not the case; there was more tangible protest, and protest of greater consequence, after segregation than before. As it turned out, almost all the key leaders . . . remained at Heart Mountain after segregation because they had either answered "Yes— Yes" to the crucial questions or had so qualified their answers that they were not "eligible" for segregation.

One such leader was Kiyoshi Okamoto. . . . In November 1943 he formed what he called a "Fair Play Committee of One" and began to agitate and speak to his fellow prisoners about doing something to clarify the legal status of the incarcerated Nisei. . . . Soon he was running "open forums" in the camp, and he attracted a number of followers who eventually formed what they called the Fair Play Committee. . . .

Although it had considerable support, the Fair Play Committee would not have had much impact had not the Army changed the rules again. On January 20, 1944, War Secretary Stimson announced that because of the fine record of Nisei volunteers normal selective service procedures would again be applied to Japanese Americans, both inside and outside the camps. (Actually, the fact that there were not enough volunteers from the camps was equally a factor.) The WRA and the JACL had long urged such a step, and of course it had been an issue raised during the loyalty-registration crisis. The Sentinel [a newspaper published by the Japanese American internees in the Heart Mountain Relocation Camp], now under the editorship of Haruo Omura but still following the JACL line, hailed Stimson's announcement as "the most significant development in returning Japanese Americans to full civic status," but it soon had to admit that "to say that the War Department's announcement . . . brought joy to the hearts of all draft-age men would be misleading and inaccurate." Nevertheless the Sentinel urged Heart Mountaineers to avoid another "senseless" round of "endless questions" and "picayune issues."

By mid-February the Fair Play Committee members had allies outside the camp: Samuel Menin, a Denver attorney, was advising them about their legal rights, and James Omura, who had been one of the few Japanese Americans to take an anti-JACL line at the Tolan Committee hearings before the evacuation and was not resettle in Denver, opened the columns of the Denver Rocky Shimpo, of which he was English language editor, to the Fair Play Committee. In addition, with funds raised from at $2 membership fee, the Committee purchased a mimeograph machine and began to distribute its own bulletin within Heart Mountain. The Committee members were warned both by camp authorities and local selective service officials against counseling draft resistance. The evacuee dissidents contended that the were merely advising Nisei to get a clarification of their rights, and an FBI investigation in February could find no indictable behavior. . . .

As a counterweight to the Fair Play Committee, the evacuee community council, perhaps at the instigation of the WRA circulated a petition to President Roosevelt accepting the draft but mildly protesting other aspects of government policy. Opposed by the Fair Play Committee, the petition was viewed as a test of strength. Only slightly over a third of the adult inmates signed, much to the disappointment of the Heart Mountain administration. Shortly after the test of strength, the first tangible results of the Fair Play Committee's agitation appeared: in the first weeks of March twelve Nisei refused to board the bus to take their selective service physicals, and an increasing number of potential draftees were promising to do likewise.

At this juncture the Heart Mountain Sentinel launched a full-scale attack on the Committee, and the Rocky Shimpo retaliated with a blast at the camp paper. . . . Naturally the question of loyalty came up. The Sentinel suggested that the leading spirits, at least, of the Fair Play Committee had answered questions 27 and 28 untruthfully, thus implying that they should be sent to Tule Lake, while the Committee leadership insisted that the real disloyalty to American democracy and its traditions was the "patriotism equals submission" formula of the Sentinel and the JACL.

The Sentinel couched some of its arguments in pragmatic terms insisting that "fighting against issues that are beyond our control . . . is a waste of time and space." The real fallacy of the resisters' case was, according to the Sentinel:

The contention that a restriction of our right means a loss of those rights. We don't lose any rights unless the constitution itself is changed. . . . If the Supreme Court rules evacuation was constitutional, then we will not have been deprived of any rights.

Whatever the merits of the debate, many Heart Mountain draft eligibles were won to the militants' position. By the end of March 1944, 54 of the 315 evacuees ordered to report for physicals had failed to do so. Late that month the Fair Play Committee, broadening its attack, began to agitate for a general strike at Heart Mountain. Predictably, the WRA reacted. The project director was informed from Washington that a reexamination of the papers of Fair Play Committee leader Kiyoshi Okamoto had discovered evidence of disloyalty; he was quickly taken into custody and shipped off to Tule Lake. Okamoto's "transfer" angered his fellow protestants; Isamu Horino, also a Fair Play committee leader, in order to dramatize the lack of freedom, publicly announced his intention of leaving Heart Mountain and tried in broad daylight to walk out the main gate. Naturally, the military police stopped him, and, with this over evidence of "disloyalty," the administration soon shipped him off to Tule Lake. . . .

On April 1, 1944, Project Director Robertson wrote to WRA Director Dillon Myer, arguing that Omura's editorials in the Rocky Shimpo bordered on "sedition" and asked for an investigation of the newspaper, whose assets were administered by the Alien Property Custodian, its original owners having been Issei and thus enemy aliens. The following week, in what can hardly have been a coincidence, the

Sentinel attacked Omura as "the number one menace to the post-war assimilation of the Nisei," insisted that he was "responsible for wrecking the lives" of the draft evaders, and charged that he was "prostituting the privileges of freedom of the press to advocate an un-American stand." By the end of April federal officials had seized Omura's records and correspondence, and the Alien property Custodian fired him and his staff. The Heart Mountain resistance was all but dead; only if its exponents could be vindicated in the courts would it stay alive.

Before his transfer to Tule Lake, Okamoto had written to the American Civil Liberties Union asking for help in testing the constitutionality of drafting citizens who were behind barbed wire. In mid-April, American Civil Liberties Union Director Roger Baldwin, in a public letter, disassociated himself and his organization from the Fair Play Committee fight. The dissidents had, Baldwin admitted, "a strong moral case," but, he insisted, "no legal case at all." . . .

On May 10, 1944, a federal grand jury in Cheyenne indicted the draft resisters, whose number had grown to 63. They were tried the next month in the largest mass trial for draft resistance in our history. The defense, by attorney Menin, argued that the defendants violated the draft orders only to clarify their ambiguous draft status and that no felonious intent was involved. The court was not impressed. Federal District Judge T. Blake Kennedy found all 63 guilty and sentenced them to three years' imprisonment and, in a memorandum, questioned their loyalty: "If they are truly loyal American citizens they should . . . embrace the opportunity to discharge the duties [of citizenship] by offering themselves in the cause of our National Defense."

An appeal filed by their attorney, which also argued that the defendants had been deprived of liberty without due process of law, was rejected in March 1945 by the Tenth Circuit Court of Appeals in Denver, and the Supreme Court refused certiorari.

In the meantime, however, other charges were brought against the Heart Mountain resisters and one of their allies. The same federal grand jury that had indicted the draft resisters had also brought in an indictment against seven members of the Fair Play Committee's executive council . . . and editor James Omura for unlawful conspiracy to counsel, aid, and abet violations of the draft. The indictments were kept secret by federal authorities until after the initial conviction of the draft violators themselves. A few days after the first convictions, the Sentinel, perhaps in on the secret, argued that those who encouraged the draft resisters not to report "deserve penitentiary sentences even more than those convicted. On July 21, 1944, the indictments were made public and the eight defendants arrested.

The seven evacuee defendants were represented by Abraham Lincoln Wirin, a Southern California ACLU [American Civil Liberties Union] attorney whose views about the evacuation and other matters were often more libertarian than those of the national body; Omura was represented by a Denver attorney, Sidney Jacobs. Jacobs unsuccessfully tried to get a separate trial for Omura on the grounds that he had never seen the other defendants (he had corresponded with some of them) before they appeared in court together. Wirin, using an argument that probably would have been successful two decades later, tried to get the case dismissed on the grounds that evacuees were systematically excluded from jury duty. The government contended that the Fair Play Committee was a conspiracy against the selective service system in particular and the war effort in general. Editor Omura was found innocent, but all seven of the evacuees were found guilty and sentenced to terms of four and two years' imprisonment.

After the verdict, Nisei war hero Ben Kuroki, who had been a government witness, told the press:

These men are fascists in my estimation and no good to any country. They have torn down [what] all the rest of us have tried to do. I hope that these members of the Fair play Committee won't worm the opinion of America concerning all Japanese-Americans.

Attorney Wirin filed an appeal contending that there was insufficient evidence and that the judge's instructions to the jury were improper. More than a year later the Tenth Circuit Court of Appeals, in a 2—1 decision, upheld Wirin's second contention while rejecting the first, and the defendants were free. But even while this was going on, resistance to the draft was continuing at Heart Mountain, although on a reduced scale. Between the summer of 1944 and the closing of the camp in November 1945, 22 more men were indicted and convicted for draft resistance, bringing the total of such convictions at Heart Mountain to 85. To put draft resistance into numerical perspective, more than 700 Heart Mountain men did board the bus for their draft physicals, and 385 were inducted; of these 11 were killed and 52 wounded. Nor was the Heart Mountain case an isolated one; similar figures for both draft resistance and compliance can be tabulated for the other regular camps.

This account of the "loyal" Japanese American resistance—what I have called the "left opposition"—is highly significant. It calls into question the stereotype of the Japanese American victim of oppression during World War II who met his fate with stoic resignation and responded only with superpatriotism. This stereotype, like most, has some basis in reality. Many Japanese Americans, conforming to the JACL line, honestly felt that the only way the could ever win a place for themselves in America was by being better Americans than most. Whether or not this kind of passive submission is the proper way for free men to respond to injustice and racism, is, of course, a matter of opinion. But it is important to note that not all "loyal" Japanese Americans submitted; the resistance of the Heart Mountain Fair Play Committee and of other individuals and groups in the other camps, has been almost totally ignored and in some instances deliberately suppressed by chroniclers of the Japanese Americans. The JACL-WRA view has dominated the writing of the evacuation's postwar history, thereby nicely illustrating E. H. Carr's dictum that history is written by the winners. The authors of these works have in some cases been ignorant of the nature and scope of the "left opposition"; others, more knowledgeable, have either consciously underplayed it or suppressed it completely, hoping thereby, in their view at least, to manage and improve the image of an oppressed people. There are those, however, who will find more heroism in the resistance than in patient resignation.

Source: Daniels, Roger. Concentration Camps, North America: Japanese in the United States and Canada during World War II. Robert E Kreieger Pub. Co., Inc. 1981.

LATINO-AMERICANS

The Mission History

The object of the missions is to convert as many of the wild Indians as possible, and to train them up within the walls of the establishment in the exercise of a good life, and of some trade, so that they may in time be able to provide for themselves and become useful members of civilized society. As to the various methods employed for bringing proselytes to the mission, there are several reports, of which some are not very creditable to the institution: nevertheless, on the whole I am of [the] opinion that the priests are innocent, from a conviction that they are ignorant of the means employed by those who are under them.

Immediately the Indians are brought to the mission they are placed under the tuition of some of the most enlightened of their countrymen, who teach them to repeat in Spanish the Lord's Prayer and certain passages in the Romish litany; and also to cross themselves properly on entering the church. In a few days a willing Indian becomes proficient in these mysteries, and suffers himself to be baptized, and duly initiated into the church. If, however, as it not infrequently happens, any of the captured Indians show a repugnance to conversion, it is the practice to imprison them for a few days, and then to allow them to breathe a little fresh air in a walk around the mission, to observe the happy mode of life of their converted countrymen; after which they are again shut up, and thus continue to be incarcerated until they declare their readiness to renounce the religion of their forebears....

The Indians are so averse to confinement that they very soon become impressed with the manifest superior and more comfortable mode of life of those who are at liberty, and in a very few days declare their readiness to have the new religion explained to them. A person acquainted with the language of the parties, of which there are sometimes several dialects in the same mission, is then selected to train them, and having duly prepared them takes his pupils to the padre to be baptized, and to receive the sacrament. Having become Christians they are put to trades, or if they have good voices they are taught music, and form part of the choir of the church. Thus there are in almost every mission weavers, tanners, shoemakers, bricklayers, carpenters, blacksmiths, and other artificers. Others again are taught husbandry, to rear cattle and horses,; and some to cook for the mission; while the females card, clean, and spin wool, weave, and sew; and those who are married attend to their domestic concerns.

In requital of these benefits, the services of the Indians, for life, belong to the mission, and if any neophyte should repent of his apostasy from the religion of his ancestors and desert, an armed force is sent in pursuit of him, and drags him back to punishment apportioned to the degree of aggravation attached to his crime. It does not often happen that a voluntary convert succeeds in his attempt to escape, as the wild Indians have a great contempt and dislike for those who have entered the missions, and they will frequently not only refuse to re-admit them to their tribe, but will sometimes even discover their retreat to their pursuers. The animosity between the wild and converted Indians is of great importance to the missions, as it checks desertion, and is at the same time a powerful defense against the wild tribes, who consider their territory invaded, and have other just causes of complaint. The Indians, besides, from political motives, are, I fear, frequently encouraged in a contemptuous feeling toward their converted countrymen, by hearing them constantly held up to them in the degrading light of bestias! [beasts] and in hearing the Spaniards distinguished by the appellation of génte de razón....

The children and adults of both sexes, in all the missions, are carefully locked up every night in separate apartments, and the keys are delivered into the possession of the padre; and as, in the daytime, their occupations lead to distinct places, unless they form a matrimonial alliance, they enjoy very little of each other's society. It, however, sometimes happens that they endeavor to evade the vigilance of their keepers, and are locked up with the opposite sex; but severe corporal punishment, inflicted...with a whip...is sure to ensue if they are discovered.... It is greatly to be regretted that, with the influence these men have over their pupils,...the priests do not interest themselves a little more in the education of their converts, the first step to which would be in making themselves acquainted with the Indian language. Many of the Indians surpass their pastors in this respect, and can speak the Spanish language. They have besides, in general, a lamentable contempt for the intellect of these simple people, and think them incapable of improvement beyond a certain point. Notwithstanding this, the Indians are...clothed and fed; they have houses of their own...; their meals are given to them three times a day, and consist of thick gruel made of wheat, Indian corn, and sometimes acorns, to which at noon is generally added meat....

Having served ten years in the mission, an Indian may claim his liberty.... A piece of ground is then allotted for his support, but he is never wholly free from the establishment, as part of his earnings must still be given to them.... When these establishments were first founded, the Indians flocked to them in great numbers for the clothing with which the neophytes were supplied; but after they became acquainted with the nature of the institution, and felt themselves under restraint, many absconded. Even now, notwithstanding the difficulty of escaping, desertions are of frequent occurrence, owing probably, in some cases, to the fear of punishment--in others to the deserters having been originally inveigled into the missions by the converted Indians or the neophyte....

Source: Captain F. W. Beechey, Narratives of a Voyage to the Pacific and Bering's Strait (London, 1831), 3: 1-23.

Joaquin Murieta

He had been brought in contact with many of the natives of the United States during the war between that nation and his own, and had become favorably impressed with the American character, and thoroughly disgusted with the imbecility of his own countrymen; so much so that he often wished he had been born on the soil of freedom....

His meditations were suddenly cut short by the wild shouting and yelling of hundreds of miners in the streets, intermixed with cries of "hang 'em!" "hang 'em!" "string 'em up and try 'em afterwards!" "the infernal Mexican thieves!" Joaquín rushed out, and was just in time to see his brother and Flores hauled up by their necks to the limb of a tree. They had been accused of horse-stealing by the two Americans from San Francisco, who claimed the animals as their own, and had succeeded in exciting the fury of the crowd to such an extent that the doomed men were allowed no opportunity to justify themselves, and all their attempts to explain the matter and to prove that the horses were honestly obtained, were drowned by the fierce hooting and screaming of the mob....

The country was then full of lawless and desperate men, calling themselves Americans, who looked with hatred upon all Mexicans, and considered them as a conquered race, without rights or privileges, and only fitted for serfdom or slavery. The prejudice of color, the antipathy of races, which are always stronger and bitterer with the ignorant, they could not overcome, or would not, because it afforded them an excuse for their unmanly oppression. A band of these men, possessing the brute power to do as they pleased, went to Joaquín's cabin and ordered him to leave his claim, as they would not permit any of his kind to dig gold in that region. Upon his refusing to leave a place where he was amassing a fortune, they knocked him senseless with the butts of their pistols, and while he was in that condition, ravished and murdered his faithful bosom-friend, his wife.

The soul of Joaquín now became shadowed with despair and deadly passion; but still, although he thirsted for revenge, he... would not endanger his freedom and his life in attempting to destroy single-handed, the fiendish murderers of his wife and brother.... Then came a change, suddenly and heavily, and Joaquín was at once hurled into the deep and dark abyss of crime. He had gone a short distance from camp to see a friend by the name of Valenzuelo, and returned...with a horse which his friend had lent him. The animal, it was proved by certain individuals in town, had been stolen some time previously, and a great excitement was immediately raised. Joaquín found himself surrounded by a furious mob and charged with the theft. He informed them when and where he had borrowed the horse, and endeavored to convince them of Valenzuelo's honesty. They would hear no explanation, but tied him to a tree and disgraced him publicly with the lash. They then went to the residence of Valenzuelo and hung him without allowing him a moment to speak. Immediately there came a terrible change in Joaquín's character, suddenly and irrevocably. His soul swelled beyond its former boundaries, and the barriers of honor, rocked into atoms by the strong passion which shook his heart like an earthquake, crumbled and fell. Then it was that he resolved to live henceforth only for revenge, and that his path should be marked with blood....

It became generally known, in 1851, that an organized banditti was ranging the country, and that Joaquín was the leader. Travelers were stopped on the roads and invited to "stand and deliver"; men riding alone in wild and lonesome regions, were dragged from their saddles by means of the lasso, and murdered in the adjacent chaparral. Horses were stolen from the ranches, and depredations were being committed in all parts of the State, almost at the same time.

Source: John Rollin Ridge, *Life of Joaquín Murieta* (San Francisco: California Police Gazette, 1859).

School Segregation in California – The Mendez Case: a "Brown v Board" for Mexican Americans

That all children or persons of Mexican or Latin descent or extraction, though Citizens of the United States of America...have been and are now excluded from attending, using, enjoying and receiving the benefits of the education, health and recreation facilities of certain schools within their respective Districts and Systems....

In the Westminister, Garden Grove and El Modeno school districts the respective boards of trustees had taken official action, declaring that there be no segregation of pupils on a racial basis but that non-English-speaking children...be required to attend schools designated by the boards separate and apart from English-speaking pupils; that such group should attend such schools until they had acquired some proficiency in the English language.

The petitioners contend that such official action evinces a covert attempt by the school authorities in such school districts to produce an arbitrary discrimination against school children of Mexican extraction or descent and that such illegal result has been established in such school districts respectively....

The ultimate question for decision may be thus stated: Does such official action of defendant district school agencies and the usages and practices pursued by the respective school authorities as shown by the evidence operate to deny or deprive the so-called non-English-speaking school children of Mexican ancestry or descent within such school districts of the equal protection of the laws?...

We think they are....

We think the pattern of public education promulgated in the Constitution of California and effectuated by provisions of the Education Code of the State prohibits segregation of the pupils of Mexican ancestry in the elementary schools from the rest of the school children.

...The common segregation attitudes and practices of the school authorities in the defendant school districts in Orange County pertain solely to children of Mexican ancestry and parentage. They are singled out as a class for segregation. Not only is such method of public school administration contrary to the general requirements of the school laws of the State, but we think it indicates an official school policy that is antagonistic in principle to...the Education Code of the State....

We perceive in the laws relating to the public educational system in the State of California a clear purpose to avoid and forbid distinctions among pupils based upon race or ancestry except in specific situations not pertinent to this action. Distinctions of that kind have recently been declared by the highest judicial authority of the United States "by their very nature odious to a free people whose institutions are founded upon the doctrine of equality." They are said to be "utterly inconsistent with American traditions and ideals."...

The evidence clearly shows that Spanish-speaking children are retarded in learning English by lack of exposure to its use because of segregation, and that commingling of the entire student body instills and develops a common cultural attitude among the school children which is imperative for the perpetuation of American institutions and ideals. It is also established by the record that the methods of segregation prevalent in the defendant school districts foster antagonisms in the children and suggest inferiority among them where none exists....

Source: Civil Action No. 4292. District Court, San Diego, Calif., Central Division, Feb. 18, 1946. Federal Supplements, Vol 64, 1946, 544-51.

The World War II Zoot Suit Riots

There are approximately 250,000 persons of Mexican descent in Los Angeles County. Living conditions among the majority of these people are far below the general level of the community. Housing is inadequate; sanitation is bad and is made worse by congestion. Recreational facilities for children are very poor; and there is insufficient supervision of the playgrounds, swimming pools and other youth centers. Such conditions are breeding places for juvenile delinquency....

Mass arrests, dragnet raids, and other wholesale classifications of groups of people are based on false premises and tend merely to aggravate the situation.

Any American citizen suspected of crime is entitled to be treated as an individual, to be indicted as such, and to be tried, both at law and in the forum of public opinion, on his merits or errors, regardless of race, color, creed, or the kind of clothes he wears.

Group accusations foster race prejudice, the entire group accused want revenge and vindication. The public is led to believe that every person in the accused group is guilty of crime.

It is significant that most of the persons mistreated during the recent incidents in Los Angeles were either persons of Mexican descent or Negroes. In undertaking to deal with the cause of these outbreaks, the existence of race prejudice cannot be ignored....

On Monday evening, June seventh, thousands of Angelenos, in response to twelve hours' advance notice in the press, turned out for a mass lynching. Marching through the streets of downtown Los Angeles, a mob of several thousand soldiers, sailors, and civilians, proceeded to beat up every zoot-suiter they could find. Pushing its way into the important motion picture theaters, the mob ordered the management to turn on the house lights and then ranged up and down the aisles dragging Mexicans out of their seats. Street cars were halted while Mexicans, and some Filipinos and Negroes, were jerked out of their seats, pushed into the streets, and beaten with sadistic frenzy. If the victims wore zoot-suits, they were stripped of their clothing and left naked or half-naked on the streets, bleeding and bruised. Proceeding down Main Street from First to Twelfth, the mob stopped on the edge of the Negro district. Learning that the Negroes planned a warm reception for them, the mobsters turned back and marched through the Mexican cast side spreading panic and terror.

Throughout the night the Mexican communities were in the wildest possible turmoil. Scores of Mexican mothers were trying to locate their youngsters and several hundred Mexicans milled around each of the police substations and the Central Jail trying to get word of missing members of their families. Boys came into the police stations saying: "Charge me with vagrancy or anything, but don't send me out there!" pointing to the streets where other boys, as young as twelve and thirteen years of age, were being beaten and stripped of their clothes... not more than half of the victims were actually wearing zoot-suits. A Negro defense worker, wearing a defense-plant identification badge on his workclothes, was taken from a street car and one of his eyes was gouged out with a knife. Huge half-page photographs, showing Mexican boys stripped of their clothes, cowering on the pavement, often bleeding profusely, surrounded by jeering mobs of men and women, appeared in all the Los Angeles newspapers....

At midnight on June seventh, the military authorities decided that the local police were completely unable or unwilling to handle the situation, despite the fact that a thousand reserve officers had been called up. The entire downtown area of Los Angeles was then declared "out of bounds" for military personnel. This order immediately slowed down the pace of the rioting. The moment the Military Police and Shore Patrol went into action, the rioting quieted down.

Source: The Governor's Citizen's Committee Report on Los Angeles Riots, 1943.

Cesar Chavez
and The United Farm Workers Movement

Mr. Chavez: After 3 months of striking in 1979 we have come to the conclusion very little progress has been made in the last 40 years.

In the 1930's when the farm workers tried to organize a strike, they were looked upon and treated by the local power structures in the rural communities as un-American, as subversive, and as some sort of criminal element. We today are looked upon pretty much the same way.

Just as in the 1930s, when a strike occurred, they were called criminal whether they be in Salinas, Calexico, Monterey County, Imperial County, or in Delano and Bakersfield, Calif. When a union strikes, it becomes then not simply a labor-management dispute as you see in other cases, but in our experience it becomes then on one side the workers, on the other side agribusiness and all of the local institutions, political and social, organize then to break the strike--the police, the sheriffs, the courts, the schools, the boards of supervisors, city councils. Not only that, but the State or Federal agencies that reside within those rural areas, are also greatly influenced by this overwhelming political power. The agribusiness industry wields the political power and uses it to break our strikes and destroy the union.

They have two standards of conduct against Mexicans and against unions. As long as we, Mexican farm workers, keep our place and do our work we are tolerated, but if the Mexican worker joins a union, if he stands up for justice and if he dares to strike, then all the local institutions feel duty-bound to defend what they consider to be their ideal of the American way of life. These communities, then, do not know what to do with us and they don't know what to do without us....

For so many years we have been involved in agricultural strikes; organizing almost 30 years as a worker, as an organizer, and as president of the union--and for all these almost 30 years it is apparent that when the farm workers strike and their strike is successful, the employers go to Mexico and have unlimited, unrestricted use of illegal alien strikebreakers to break the strike. And, for over 30 years, the Immigration and Naturalization Service has looked the other way and assisted in the strikebreaking.

I do not remember one single instance in 30 years where the Immigration service has removed strikebreakers.... The employers use professional smugglers to recruit and transport human contraband across the Mexican border for the specific act of strikebreaking....

We have observed all these years the Immigration Service has a policy as it has been related to us, that they will not take sides in any agricultural labor dispute.... They have not taken sides means permitting the growers to have unrestricted use of illegal aliens as strikebreakers, and if that isn't taking sides, I don't know what taking sides means.

The growers have armed their foremen. They have looked to professional agencies to provide them unlimited numbers of armed guards recruited from the streets, young men who are not trained, many of them members of the Ku Klux Klan and the Nazi Party...who are given a gun and a club and a badge and a canister of tear gas and the authority and permission to go and beat our people up, frighten them, maim them, and try to break the strike by using this unchecked raw power against our people....

Source: Hearings Before the Committee on Labor and Human Resources, U.S. Senate, 96th Congress, 1st Session, 1997.

Youth Identity, and Power: The Chicano Movement

The dramatic emergence of the civil rights movement generated reform in education and politics. Although chiefly aimed at benefiting African Americans, the movement created a political atmosphere beneficial to Mexican American working- class youth, for it gave them more access to institutions of higher education. Their access to college was no longer limited to patronage by the YMCA and the Protestant and Catholic churches, as had been the case in the 1930s, nor was it limited to veterans with G.I. Bill benefits, as it had largely been in the 1940s. There were now hundreds of youth of Mexican descent attending college as a direct result of federal educational programs made possible by the civil rights movement and implemented especially during the Johnson administration.

The growing numbers of Mexican American students on college campuses did not come close to representing a significant proportion of the Mexican American population: Mexican American youth remained severely underrepresented. Neither did they produce a visible Mexican American student activism. But from those numbers came a few student activists who, between 1963 and 1967, participated in some activities and organizations of the civil rights movement. Some of them became active indirectly or directly as members of the Student Nonviolent Coordinating Committee [SNCC]. For example, Maria Varela became a key SNCC organizer in Alabama where she established an adult literacy project. By 1964, She, and many other Mexican Americans had gained valuable experience in the struggles for civil rights. Most had realized that the Black leadership of the movement had little concern for Mexican Americans. Finally, a trip to Cuba by students and Progressive Labor Party members Luis Valdez and Roberto Rubalcava produced a radical manifesto of Mexican American youth:

The Mexican in the United States has been... no less a victim of American imperialism than his impoverished brothers in Latin America. In the words of the Second Declaration of Havana, tell him of "misery, feudal exploitation, illiteracy, starvation wages," and he will tell you that you speak of Texas; tell him of "unemployment, the policy of repression against the workers, discrimination. ..oppression by the oligarchies," and he will tell you that you speak of California; tell him of US domination in Latin America, and he will tell you that he knows that Shark and what he devours, because he has lived in its very entrails. The history of the American Southwest provides a brutal panorama of nascent imperialism.

The manifesto represented a radical departure from the political thought of the Mexican-American Generation and a harsh critique of its political leadership.

Valdez returned from Cuba and after graduating from college joined the radical San Francisco Mime Troupe, where he continued to refine his critique of the assimilationist and accommodationist perspective of the Mexican-American Generation and worked to develop a new cultural identity and politics for Mexican Americans. Some of that thinking came to fruition when he joined the farmworkers' struggle in Delano, California in 1965 and founded the Teatro Campesino. Many of the ideas behind the conceptualization of the Chicano identity and the development of the Chicano Generation of the late 1960s emanated from the ideas of Luis Valdez and the cultural work of his Teatro Campesino. Key members of the Teatro were student activists he recruited from college campuses in Northern California. One of the most prominent of them was Ysidro Ramon Macias, an undergraduate activist at the University of California,

Berkeley. Macias became one of the Teatro's original playwrights; his influential play The Ultimate Pende., jada dramatized the rejection of the assimilationism of Mexican-American identity and the emergence of Chicano identity. ...

By 1966, student activists, though still relatively few in number, were seriously discussing the formation of distinct Mexican American student organizations on their campuses throughout the Southwest. By the fall of 1967 organizations had emerged on several college campuses in Los Angeles and on two campuses in Texas. At St. Mary's College in San Antonio, Texas it was named the Mexican American Youth Organization (MA YO). At the University of Texas at Austin it was called the Mexican American Student Organization (MASO), later changing its name to MA YO. In the Los Angeles area, chapters of the United Mexican American Students (UMAS) were formed at UCLA; California State College, Los Angeles; Loyola University; University of Southern California; California State College, Long Beach; and San Fernando State College. At East Los Angeles Community College, another group organized as the Mexican American Student Association (MASA).

At about the same time, the Student Initiative organization at San Jose State College in Northern California changed its name to the Mexican American Student Confederation (MASC). Chapters followed at Fresno State, Hayward State, and Sacramento State colleges. The following year, 1968, students formed a chapter of UMAS at the University of Colorado at Boulder, and a MASC chapter at the University of California, Berkeley. By 1969 UMAS chapters were emerging in other parts of the Southwest. The first UMAS chapter in the Midwest was organized at the

University of Notre Dame by Gilbert Cardenas, a first-year graduate student in sociology and former undergraduate member of UMAS in California.

Ideologically, most of these new student organizations had objectives similar to those of the Mexican Youth Conferences of the 1930s and the Mexican-American Movement of the 1940s. They emphasized the theme of "progress through education," and concentrated on activities related to recruitment of Mexican American students and helping them stay in college. The new student organizations worked with Mexican American professionals to raise scholarship funds for needy students, and sought their advice on matters relating to the education of Mexican Americans. Some of the student activists themselves attended college with help from scholarships made available by middle-class organizations like LULAC [League of United Latin American Citizens]. With few exceptions, the new student groups mirrored the political consciousness of the Mexican-American Generation of the 1930s and were committed to the development of a new generation of professionals who could playa leading role in the betterment of the Mexican American community within the context of middle- class politics.

These student organizations did not yet represent a student movement in political terms. But as they came into direct contact with community politics and learned more about the Chavez and Tijerina movements they came to represent a student movement in the making. By the end of 1967, the antiwar and Black Power movements had become other sources of growing militancy among some of the student leaders. The politics of the times were now characterized by mass protest, and the fact that the main protagonists in the unfolding drama were white and Black radical youth did not go unnoticed by the leadership of the Mexican

American student organizations. Some of them joined with SDS and the Black student unions in planning campus protests. ...

On the morning of3 March 1968, shouts of "Blow Out!" rang through the halls of Abraham Lincoln High School, a predominantly Mexican American school in East Los Angeles. Over a thousand students walked out of their classes, teacher Sal Castro among them. Waiting for them outside the school grounds were members of UMAS and various community activists. They distributed picket signs listing some of the thirty-six demands that had been developed by a community and student strike committee. The signs of protested racist school policies and teachers and called for freedom of speech, the hiring of Mexican American teachers and administrators, and classes on Mexican American history and culture. As might be expected, the signs that caught the attention of the mass media and the police were those reading "Chicano Power!"; "Viva La Raza!"; and "Viva La Revolucion!" By the afternoon of that day, several thousand more students had walked out of five other barrio high schools to join the strike. The strike brought the Los Angeles city school system, the largest in the nation, to a standstill and made news across the country; a Los Angeles Times reporter interpreted the strike as "The Birth of Brown Power." Over ten thousand students had participated by the time the Los Angeles "blow-outs" ended a week and a half later.
But the strike accomplished something much more important than shaking up school administrators or calling public attention to the educational problems of Mexican American youth. Although not one of its original objectives, the strike was the first major mass protest explicitly against racism undertaken by Mexican Americans in the history of the United States. As such, it

had a profound impact on the Mexican American community in Los Angeles and in other parts of the country, and it generated an increased political awareness along with visible efforts to mobilize the community. This was manifested in the revitalization of existing community political organizations and the emergence of new ones, with youth playing significant leadership roles.

Overnight, student activism reached levels of intensity never before witnessed. A few Mexican American student activists had participated in civil rights marches, anti-Vietnam War protests, and had walked the picket lines for the farmworker movement. But the high school strike of 1968 was the first time students of Mexican descent had marched en masse in their own demonstration against racism and for educational change. It was also the first time that they had played direct leadership roles in organizing a mass protest. The slogans of "Chicano Power!"; "Viva La Raza!"; and "Viva La Revolucion!" that rang throughout the strike reflected an increasing militancy and radicalism in the ranks of UMAS and other student organizations. The nature of these concerns and the momentum built up among Mexican American students-both in high school and on college campuses-broke the ideological bonds that characteristically keep student organizations, and students in general, from questioning authority and the status quo. Membership grew as those organizations and their leaders became protagonists in struggles for change in Mexican American communities. The strike moved student activism beyond the politics of accommodation and integration which had been shaped by the Mexican-American Generation and the community's middle-class leadership.

However, it was not student activists who conceived of the strike; the idea originated with Sal Castro, the teacher at Lincoln High School who had walked out with his students. ...[H]e had become disillusioned with the Democratic Party and with Mexican American middle-class leadership. ...[H]e had played a prominent role in the "Viva Kennedy" campaign in 1960, serving as the student coordinator of the Southern California campaign. He was a Korean War-era veteran attending college on the G.I. Bill at the time. Like other veterans, he played a role in MAPA and was a founder of the Association of Mexican American Educators. ...

But by 1964 Castro had come to the realization that the Democrats did not have the interests of Mexican Americans at heart and that corruption was inherent in the political system. A product of the barrio schools in East Los Angeles, Castro returned to the neighborhood as a teacher only to find that racism toward Mexican American youth remained virulent. Through the AMAE [Association of Mexican American Educators] organization he worked hard to make reforms within the school bureaucracy but was not able to accomplish much. Like other middle-class leaders, he saw that the civil rights movement ignored Mexican Americans and that they were low on the agenda of the War on Poverty and in education reform plans. But unlike most other middle-class leaders, Castro came to the conclusion that his people needed their own civil rights movement and that the only alternative in the face of a racist educational system was nonviolent protest against the schools. He therefore prepared to sacrifice his teaching career, if necessary, in the interest of educational change for Mexican American children. The strike made Castro one of the movement's leaders.

The strike of 1968 went beyond the objectives of Castro and others concerned only with improving education. It was the first loud cry for Chicano Power and self-determination, serving as the catalyst for the formation of the Chicano student movement as well as the larger Chicano Power Movement of which it became the most important sector. ...

After the strike the UMAS leadership urged the members to assume a more political role in both the community and on campus and to think in terms of being part of a student movement. In the first Mexican American student organization newsletter to be published and distributed throughout the Southwest, the UMAS chapter at California State College, Los Angeles, described its role:

UMAS is cognizant of the social, economic, and political ills of our Mexican people. The desire of UMAS is to play a vital role in the liberation of the Mexican American people from second class citizen- ship. To do this we see our role to stand united in the effort to affect social change for the betterment of our people. We believe the ills that beset our people are not products of our culture, but that said ills have been inflicted by the institutions which today comprise the establishment in the American society.

This first newsletter urged students to participate in the Poor People's March on Washington scheduled for later in the spring of 1968 and to join the Mexican American delegation to it being led by Reies Lopez Tijerina. It also called on students to support Sal Castro, who had been suspended by the Los Angeles Board of Education for his role in the strike and for his continued support for change in the schools. Finally, UMAS advocated an "internal and external" plan of action for the student movement:

[Recognizing] that the system cannot be changed overnight, we feel it is necessary that we work within the existing framework to the degree that it not impede our effectiveness. It is historically evident that working within the existing framework is not sufficient; therefore, our external approach will consist of exerting outside pressure on those institutions that directly affect the Mexican American community.

The term Chicano appeared often-mostly interchangeably with Mexican American-but UMAS advanced no particular ideology for the student movement at this point.

...UMAS continued to stress educational issues, involvement in the community to assist high school students and defend them from harassment by racist teachers, the need to establish tutorial programs, and efforts to increase enrollments of Mexican American college students. ...

In the weeks following the strike, the leadership of each UMAS chapter in the Los Angeles area formed a coordinating body called UMAS Central. The first newsletter of this group called on Chicanos to take pride in their Mexican identity and on students to see themselves as a political vanguard.
We have begun to recognize our role as an organizational agent through which Chicano students are able to recognize themselves as Mexicans and to take pride in it. We are the avant-garde of the young Mexican American liberation movement. We formulate a philosophy for our people and we provide the hope for the future of Mexicans of all generations. We recognize ourselves as a generation of doers as well as thinkers. ...We are resolved to perpetuate an atmosphere of respect and dignity for our people. ...We are the agents

of progress and unity. We demanded social justice for a people too long oppressed.

Militancy in the ranks of the developing student movement accelerated as a consequence of the response to the strike on the part of the power structure of the city of Los Angeles and the implementation of directives from the Federal Bureau of Investigation. On 4 March 1968, FBI Director J. Edgar Hoover issued a memo to local law enforcement officials across the country urging them to place top priority on political intelligence work to prevent the development of nationalist movements in minority communities. Hoover's chief goal was to undermine the Black Power Movement, but his directive was considered applicable to other similar movements...

On 2 June 1968, three months after the strike and two days before California's primary elections, thirteen young Mexican American political activists who had been identified as leaders of the emerging "Brown Power" movement were indicted by the Los Angeles County Grand Jury on conspiracy charges for their roles in organizing the strike. The indictments charged that the thirteen activists had conspired to "will- fully disturb the peace and quiet" of the city of Los Angeles and disrupt the educational process in its schools. They were characterized as members of communist "subversive organizations" or outside agitators intent on radicalizing Mexican American students. Each of the thirteen activists faced a total of sixty-six years in prison if found guilty.

None of the "LA Thirteen" were in fact communists or members of "subversive organizations." They included Sal Castro; Eliezer Risco, editor of a new community newspaper named La Raza; and Patricio Sanchez, a member of MAP A. The remaining ten were all student activists and key leaders of their respective organizations. ... Instead of preventing the rise of another "nationalist movement," the indictments of the LA Thirteen simply fueled the fire of an emerging radicalism among Mexican American students.

Several weeks later, Mexican American graduating seniors at San Jose State College and members of the audience walked out during commencement exercises. Approximately two hundred people were involved in the demonstration. They denounced the college for its lack of commitment to the surrounding Mexican American community, as shown by the low enrollment of Mexican American students on campus. The walkout was also a protest against the inadequate training of professionals such as teachers, social workers, and policemen, who, after graduating, would work in the Mexican American community with no understanding of the culture and needs of that community, or - most important - of how their own racism affected their dealings with Mexican Americans. ...

That walkout was the first protest activity undertaken by Mexican American students on a college campus. Five months later, in November 1968, Mexican American students became part of the strike at San Francisco State College, organized by the Third World Liberation Front (TWLF). It was marked by violent confrontations between students and the police, and many students were injured. The strike began over issues initially raised by Black students and lasted until March 1969. Although the students' demands mostly focused on the needs of Black students, one demand called for the creation of a Department of Raza Studies under the umbrella of a proposed School of Ethnic Studies. The TWLF also demanded open admission for all third world students. The San Francisco State strike was significant because it marked the first time that Mexican American and other third world student activists united to create a politically explosive "rainbow" coalition.

In October 1968, the Mexican American Student Confederation took over the office of Charles Hitch, president of the University of California system, to protest his refusal to discontinue the purchase of grapes while Chavez's farmworkers were on strike-part of a national campaign to boycott grapes in support of the UFW. The takeover of Hitch's office resulted in the arrest of eleven MASC members for trespassing and unlawful assembly. This was the first in a series of third world student confrontations with university authorities on the Berkeley campus, which eventually culminated in the formation of another Third World Liberation Front and student strike.

Patterning itself after the Third World Liberation Front at San Francisco State across the Bay, the TWLF at Berkeley organized its own student strike, which lasted from January through April 1969. It was the first major third world student confrontation within the University of California system, and one of the most violent to occur at any of the university's campuses: many students were arrested or became victims of police violence.

In contrast to the strike at San Francisco State, Mexican American students played a leading role in the organization of the Third World Liberation Front and. the strike on the UC Berkeley campus. The strike was aimed at exposing the university's lack of commitment to meeting the educational needs of third world people. Although there were many differences within the TWLF, the strike demands incorporated previous issues raised by both African American and Mexican American student activists. The TWLF demanded the creation of a Third World College with departments of Mexican American, Black [Native American,] and Asian-American studies. It also demanded sufficient resources for the proposed college to involve itself in minority communities and contribute effectively to their development. TWLF demanded that the new college be under the full control of its students, faculty, and representatives of the community; "self-determination" was to be its principle of governance. Other demands called for open admission for all third world people and poor working-class whites and the recruitment of third world faculty and staff.

There were other high school student strikes throughout the Southwest during 1969, patterned after the 1968 strike in Los Angeles. In Denver, Colorado and Crystal City, Texas, high school strikes also resulted in significant political developments beyond the immediate issues of educational change. In Denver, the strike contributed to the further development of the Crusade for justice and made Corky Gonzales a national leader of the emerging Chicano movement. In contrast to the relatively violence-free student strike in Los Angeles, the Denver demonstrations resulted in violent confrontations between police, students, and members of the Crusade for justice, and Corky Gonzales was himself arrested. After his release he praised the striking students for risking "revolutionary" actions to make history: "You kids don't realize you have made history. We just talk about revolution. But you act it by facing the shotguns, billies, gas, and mace. You are the real revolutionaries."

In Crystal City, a high school strike contributed directly to the founding of La Raza Unida Party, a second electoral revolt in that city that resulted in the party's takeover of city government and the school system, and the making of Jose Angel Gutierrez into another national leader of the Chicano Movement.

The movement was given further impetus by other events that took place in 1968, the year that was the turning point of the decade. The antiwar movement became a potent political force in national politics as mass protest against the war in Vietnam dramatically increased. ...It was also the year that Dr. Martin Luther King, Jr., led the Poor People's March on Washington, which included a contingent of Mexican Americans. Later in the year Dr. King and Senator Robert F. Kennedy were assassinated. Even more important, 1968 was also the year of international student uprisings from Paris and Berlin to Tokyo to Mexico City. From the ranks of these militant students came artists, poets and actors who collectively generated a cultural renaissance and whose work played a key role in creating the ideology of the Chicano movement. In Oakland, California, the first group of radical artists organized themselves as the Mexican American Liberation Art Front (MALAF). Elsewhere in the Bay Area, Jose and Malaquias Montoya, Esteban Villa, Rene Yafiez, Ralph Maradiaga and Rupert Garcia produced posters whose striking art reflected the movement's quest for identity and power. Other artists emerged in other parts of the nation, and by 1970 a distinct Chicano art movement was in full bloom, which, in addition to radical poster art included a Chicano mural art in the tradition of the Mexican revolutionary artists David Alfaro Sequieros, Jose Clemente Orozco, and Diego Rivera.

...Between 1968 and 1969, Mexican American student militancy intensified as more and more of them became convinced that they were part of an international revolution in the making.

The student strikes in the community and on the college campus, in conjunction, with the political upheavals of the late sixties, thus generated the framework for the

eventual transformation of student activist organizations into a full-blown student movement with clear social and political goals and an ethnic nationalist ideology that came to be known as cultural nationalism. ~
Source: Munoz, Jr., Carlos. Youth, Identity, Power: The Chicano Movement. Verso Publishers. 1989.

The Development of Chicana Feminist Discourse, 1970-1980

Between 1970 and 1980, a Chicana feminist movement developed in the United States that addressed the specific issues that affected Chicanas as women of color. The growth of the Chicana feminist movement can be traced in the speeches, essays, letters, and articles published in Chicano and Chicana newspapers, journals, newsletters, and other printed materials.

During the sixties, American society witnessed the development of the Chicano movement, a social movement characterized by a politics of protest. The Chicano movement focused on a wide range of issues: social justice, equality, educational reforms, and political and economic self-determination for Chicano communities in the United States. Various struggles evolved within this movement: the United Farmworkers unionization efforts; the New Mexico Land Grant movement; the Colorado-based Crusade for Justice; the Chicano student movement; and the Raza Unida Party.

Chicanas participated actively in each of these struggles. By the end of the sixties, Chicanas began to assess the rewards and limits of their participation. The 1970s witnessed the development of Chicana feminists whose activities, organizations, and writings can be analyzed in terms of a feminist movement by women of color in American society. Chicana feminists outlined a cluster of ideas that crystallized into an emergent

Chicana feminist debate. In the same way that Chicano males were reinterpreting the historical and contemporary experience of Chicanos in the United States, Chicanas began to investigate the forces shaping their own experiences as women of color. ...

Throughout the seventies and. ..eighties, Chicana feminists have been forced to respond to the criticism that cultural nationalism and feminism are irreconcilable. In the first issue of the newspaper, Hijas de Cuauhtemoc [Daughters of Cuauhtemoc}, Anna Nieto Gomez stated that a major issue facing Chicanas active in the Chicano movement was the need to organize to improve their status as women within the larger social movement. Francisca Flores, another leading Chicana feminist, stated:

[Chicanas] can no longer remain in a subservient role or as auxiliary forces in the [Chicano] movement. They must be included in the front line of communication, leadership and organizational responsibility. ...The issue of equality, freedom and self-determination of the Chicana-like the right of self-determination, equality, and liberation of the Mexican [Chicano] community--'-is not negotiable. Anyone opposing the right of women to organize into their own form of organization has no place in the leadership of the movement.

Supporting this position, Bernice Rincon argued that a Chicana feminist movement that sought equality and justice for Chicanas would strengthen the Chicano movement. Yet in the process, Chicana feminists challenged traditional gender roles because they limited their participation and acceptance within the Chicano movement.

Throughout the seventies, Chicana feminists viewed the struggle against sexism within the Chicano movement and the struggle against racism in the large society as integral parts of Chicana feminism. As Nieto Gomez said:

Chicana feminism is in various stages of development. However, in general, Chicana feminism is the recognition that women are oppressed as a group and are exploited as part of la Raza people. It is a direction to be responsible to identify and act upon the issues and needs of Chicana women. Chicana feminists are involved in understanding the nature of women's oppression.

Cultural nationalism represented a major ideological component of the Chicano movement. Its emphasis on Chicano cultural pride and cultural survival within an Anglo-dominated society gave significant political direction to the Chicano movement. One source of ideological disagreement between Chicana feminism and this cultural nationalist ideology was cultural survival. Many Chicana feminists believed that a focus on cultural survival did not acknowledge the need to alter male-female relations within Chicano communities. For example, Chicana feminists criticized the notion of the "ideal Chicana" that glorified Chicanas as strong, long-suffering women who had endured and kept Chicano culture and the family intact. To Chicana feminists, this concept represented an obstacle to the redefinition of gender roles. Nieto stated:

Some Chicanas are praised as they emulate the sanctified example set by [the Virgin] Mary. The woman par excellence is mother and wife. She is to love and support her husband and to nurture and teach her children. Thus, may she gain fulfillment as a woman. For a Chicana bent upon fulfillment of her personhood, this restricted perspective of her role as a woman is not only inadequate but crippling.

Chicana feminists were also skeptical about the cultural nationalist interpretation of machismo. Such an interpretation viewed machismo as an ideological tool used by the dominant Anglo society to justify the inequalities experienced by Chicanos. According to this interpretation, the relationship between Chicanos and the larger society was that of an internal colony dominated and exploited by the capitalist economy. Machismo, like other cultural traits, was blamed by Anglos for blocking Chicanos from succeeding in American society. In reality, the economic structure and colony-like exploitation were to blame.

Some Chicana feminists agreed with this analysis of machismo, claiming that a mutually reinforcing relationship existed between internal colonialism and the development of the myth of machismo. According to Sosa Riddell, machismo was a myth "propagated by subjugators and colonizers, which created damaging stereotypes of Mexican/Chicano males." As a type of social control imposed by the dominant society on Chicanos, the myth of machismo distorted gender relations within Chicano communities, creating stereotypes of Chicanas as passive and docile women. At this level in the feminist discourse, machismo was seen as an Anglo myth that kept both Chicanos and Chicanas in a subordinate status. As Nieto concluded:

Although the term "machismo" is correctly denounced by all because it stereotypes the Latin man. ..it does a great disservice to both men and women. Chicano and

Chicana alike must be free to seek their own individual fulfillment.

While some Chicana feminists criticized the myth of machismo used by the dominant society to legitimate racial inequality, others moved beyond this level of analysis to distinguish between the machismo that oppressed both men and women and the sexism in Chicano communities in general, and the Chicano movement in particular, that oppressed Chicana women. According to Vidal, the origins of a Chicana feminist consciousness were prompted by the sexist attitudes and behavior of Chicano males, which constituted a "serious obstacle to women anxious to playa role in the struggle for Chicana liberation."

Furthermore, many Chicana feminists disagreed with the cultural nationalist view that machismo could be a positive value within a Chicano cultural value system. They challenged the view that machismo was a source of masculine pride for Chicanos and therefore a defense mechanism against the dominant society's racism. Although Chicana feminists recognized that Chicanos faced discrimination from the dominant society, they adamantly disagreed with those who believed that machismo was a form of cultural resistance to such discrimination. Chicana feminists called for changes in the ideologies responsible for distorting relations between women and men. One such change was to modify the cultural nationalist position that viewed machismo as a source of cultural pride.

Chicana feminists called for a focus on the universal aspects of sexism that shape gender relations in both Anglo and Chicano culture. While they acknowledged the economic exploitation of all Chicanos, Chicana feminists outlined the double exploitation experienced by Chicanas. Sosa Riddell concluded: "It was when

Chicanas began to seek work outside of the family groups that sexism became a key factor of oppression along with racism." Francisca Flores summarized some of the consequences of sexism:

It is not surprising that more and more Chicanas are forced to go to work in order to supplement the family income. The children are farmed out to a relative to baby-sit with them, and since these women are employed in the lower income jobs, the extra pressure placed on them can become unbearable.

Thus, while the Chicano movement was addressing the issue of racial oppression facing all Chicanos, Chicana feminists argued that it lacked an analysis of sexism. Similarly, Black and Asian American women stressed the interconnectedness of race and gender oppression. Hooks analyzes racism and sexism in terms of their "intersecting, complementary nature." She also emphasizes that one struggle should not take priority over the other. White criticizes Black men whose nationalism limited discussions of Black women's experiences with sexist oppression. The writings of other Black feminists criticized a Black cultural nationalist ideology that overlooked
the consequences of sexist oppression. Many Asian American women were also critical of the Asian American movement whose focus on racism ignored the impact of sexism on the daily lives of women. The participation of Asian American women in various community struggles increased their encounters with sexism. As a result, some Asian American women developed a feminist consciousness and organized as women around feminist issues.
The systematic analysis by Chicana feminists of the impact of racism and sexism on Chicanas in American

society and, above all, within the Chicano movement was often misunderstood as a threat to the political unity of the Chicano movement. As Marta Cotera, a leading voice of Chicana feminism, pointed out:

The aggregate cultural values we [Chicanas] share can also work to our benefit if we choose to scrutinize our cultural traditions, isolate the positive attributes and interpret them for the benefit of women. It's unreal that Hispanas have been browbeaten for so long about our so-called conservative {meaning reactionary) culture. It's also unreal that we have let men interpret culture only as those practices and attitudes that determine who does the dishes around the house. We as women also have the right to interpret and define the philosophical and religious traditions beneficial to us within our culture, and which we have inherited as our tradition. To do this, we must become both conversant with our history and philosophical evolution, and analytical about the institutional and behavioral manifestations of the same.

Such Chicana feminists were attacked for developing a "divisive ideology"-a feminist ideology that was frequently viewed as a threat to the Chicano movement as a whole. As Chicana feminists examined their roles as women activists within the Chicano movement, an ideological split developed. One group active in the Chicano movement saw themselves as "loyalists" who believed that the Chicano movement did not have to deal with sexual inequities since Chicano men as well as Chicano women experienced racial oppression. According to Nieto Gomez, who was not a loyalist, their view was that if men oppress women, it is not the men's fault but rather that of the system.

Even if such a problem existed, and they did not believe that it did, the loyalists maintained that such a matter would best be resolved internally within the Chicano movement. They denounced the formation of a separate Chicana feminist movement on the grounds that it was a politically dangerous strategy, perhaps Anglo inspired. Such a movement would undermine the unity of the Chicano movement by raising an issue that was not seen as a central one. Loyalists viewed racism as the most important issue within the Chicano movement. Nieto Gomez quotes one such loyalist:

I am concerned with the direction that the Chicanas are taking in the movement. The words such as liberation, sexism, male chauvinism, etc., were prevalent. The terms mentioned above plus the theme of individualism is a concept of the Anglo society; terms prevalent in the Anglo women' s movement. Thefamilia has always been our strength in our culture. But it seems evident. ..that you [Chicana feminists] are not concerned with the familia. but are influenced by the Anglo woman's movement.

Chicana feminists were also accused of undermining the values associated with Chicano culture. Loyalists saw the Chicana feminist movement as an "anti-family, anti-cultural, anti-man and therefore an anti-Chicano movement." Feminism was, above all, believed to be an individualistic search for identity that detracted from the Chicano movement's "real" issues, such as racism. Nieto Gomez quotes a loyalist as stating:

And since when does a Chicana need identity? If you are a real Chicana then no one regardless of the degrees needs to tell you about it. The only ones who need identity are the vendidas. the falsas, and the opportunists.

The ideological conflicts between Chicana feminists and loyalists persisted throughout the seventies. Disagreements between these two groups became exacerbated during various Chicana conferences. At times, such confrontations served to increase Chicana feminist activity that challenged the loyalists' attacks, yet these attacks also served to suppress feminist activities. Chicana feminist lesbians experienced even stronger attacks from those who viewed feminism as a divisive ideology. In a political climate that already viewed feminist ideology with suspicion, lesbianism as a sexual lifestyle and political ideology came under even more attack. Clearly, a cultural nationalist ideology that perpetuated such stereotypical images of Chicanas as "good wives and good mothers" found it difficult to accept a Chicana feminist lesbian movement.

Cherrie Moraga' s writings during the 1970s reflect the struggles of Chicana feminist lesbians who, together with other Chicana feminists, were finding the sexism evident within the Chicano movement intolerable. Just as Chicana feminists analyzed their life circumstances as members of an ethnic minority and as women, Chicana feminist lesbians addressed themselves to the oppression they experienced as lesbians. As Moraga stated:

My lesbianism is the avenue through which I have learned the most about silence and oppression. ...In this country, lesbianism is a poverty-as is being brown, as is being a woman, as is being just plain poor. The danger lies in ranking the oppressions. The danger lies in failing to acknowledge the specificity of the oppression.

Chicana, Black, and Asian American feminists experienced similar cross-pressures of feminist-baiting and lesbian-baiting attacks. As they organized around feminist struggles, these women of color encountered criticism from both male and female cultural nationalists who often viewed feminism as little more than an "anti-male" ideology. Lesbianism was identified as an extreme derivation of feminism. A direct connection was frequently made that viewed feminism and lesbianism as synonymous. Feminists were labeled lesbians, and lesbians as feminists. Attacks against feminists-Chicanas, Blacks, and Asian Americans-derived from the existence of homophobia within each of these communities. As lesbian women of color published their writings, attacks against them increased.

Responses to such attacks varied within and between the feminist movements of women of color. Some groups tried one strategy and later adopted another. Some lesbians pursued a separatist strategy within their own racial and ethnic communities. Others attempted to form lesbian coalitions across racial and ethnic lines. Both strategies represented a response to the marginalization of lesbians produced by recurrent waves of homophobic sentiments in Chicano, Black, and Asian American communities. A third response consisted of working within the broader nationalist movements in these communities and the feminist movements within them in order to challenge their heterosexual biases and resultant homophobia. As early as 1974, the "Black Feminist Statement" written by a Boston-based feminist group-the Combahee River Collective-stated: "We struggle together with Black men against racism, while we also struggle with Black men against sexism." Similarly, Moraga challenged the white feminist movement to examine its racist tendencies; the Chicano movement, its sexist tendencies; and both, their homophobic tendencies. In this way, Moraga argued that such movements to end oppression would begin to respect diversity within their own ranks.

Chicana feminists as well as Chicana feminist lesbians continued to be labeled vendidas or "sellouts." Chicana loyalists continued to view Chicana feminism as associated, not only with melting into white society, but more seriously, with dividing the Chicano movement. Similarly, many Chicano males were convinced that Chicana feminism was a divisive ideology incompatible with Chicano cultural nationalism. Nieto Gomez said that "[with] respect to [the] Chicana feminist, their credibility is reduced when they are associated with [feminism] and white women." She added that, as a result, Chicana feminists often faced harassment and ostracism within the Chicano movement. Similarly, Cotera stated that Chicanas "are suspected of assimilating into the feminist ideology of an alien [white] culture that actively seeks our cultural domination."

Chicana feminists responded quickly and often vehemently to such charges. Flores answered these antifeminist attacks in an editorial in which she argued that birth control, abortion, and sex education were not merely "white issues." In response to the accusation that feminists were responsible for the "betrayal of [Chicano) culture and heritage," Flores said, "Our culture hell"-a phrase that became a dramatic slogan of the Chicana feminist movement.

Chicana feminists' defense throughout the 1970s against those claiming that a feminist movement was divisive for the Chicano movement was to reassess their roles within the Chicano movement and to call for an end to male domination. Their challenges of traditional gender roles represented a means to achieve equality. In order to increase the participation of and opportunities for women in the Chicano movement, feminists agreed that both Chicanos and Chicanas had to address the issue of gender inequality. Furthermore, Chicana feminists argued that the resistance that they encountered reflected the existence of sexism on the part of Chicano males and the antifeminist attitudes of the Chicana loyalists. Nieto Gomez, reviewing the experiences of Chicana feminists in the Chicano movement, concluded that Chicanas "involved in discussing and applying the women's question have been ostracized, isolated and ignored." She argued that "in organizations where cultural nationalism is extremely strong, Chicana feminists experience intense harassment and ostracism." ~

Source: Garcia, Alma M. Gender and Society, vol. 3, 1989.

GENDER IN AMERICA

KEY CONCEPTS

There are biological differences between the sexes - male, female, gay, and lesbian - should there be social differences? Is there such a thing as "feminist culture"? Why? To what degree is the existence of gender-based culture necessary? Consider the effects of the social constructions of gender on race and class. How are social benefits and punishments tied to gender performance? What internal and external pressures in American society perpetuate gender culture and genderism - the differential access to power, privilege, and identity?

Familiar Letters of Abigail Adams
To her husband John Adams

Abigail to John

. . . I long to hear that you have declared an independancy—and by the way in the new Code of Laws which I suppose it will be necessary for you to make I desire you would Remember the Ladies, and be more generous and favourable to them than your ancestors. Do not put such unlimited power into the hands of the Husbands. Remember all Men would be tyrants if they could. If perticuliar care and attention is not paid to the Laidies we are determined to foment a Rebelion, and will not hold ourselves bound by any Laws in which we have no voice, or Representation.

That your Sex are Naturally Tyrannical is a Truth so thoroughly established as to admit of no dispute, but such of you as wish to be happy willingly give up the harsh title of Master for the more tender and endearing one of Friend. Why then, not put it out of the power of the vicious and the Lawless to use us with cruelty and indignity with impunity. Men of Sense in all Ages abhor those customs which treat us only as the vassals of your Sex. Regard us then as Beings placed by providence under your protection and in immitation of the Supreem Being make use of that power only for our happiness.

John to Abigail

. . . As to your extraordinary Code of Laws, I cannot but laugh. We have been told that our Struggle has loosened the bands of Government every where. That Children and Apprentices were disobedient—that schools and Colleges were grown turbulent—that Indians slighted their Guardians and Negroes grew insolent to their Masters. But your Letter was the first Intimation that another Tribe more numerous and powerfull than all the rest were grown discontented.—

This is rather too coarse a Compliment but you are so saucy, I wont blot it out.

Depend upon it, We know better than to repeal our Masculine systems. Altho they are in full Force, you know they are little more than Theory. We dare not exert our Power in tis full Latitude. We are obliged to go fair, and softly, and in Practice you know We are the subjects. We have only the Name of Masters, and rather than give up this, which would compleatly subject Us to the Despotism of the Peticoat, I hope General Washington, and all our brave Heroes would fight. I am sure every good Politician would plot, as long as he would against Despotism. Empire, Monarchy, Aristocracy, Oligarchy, or Ochlocracy.—A fine Story indeed. I begin to think the Ministry as deep as they are wicked. After stirring up Tories, Landjobbers, Trimmers, Bigots, Canadians, Indians, Negroes, Hanoverians, Hessians, Russians, Irish Woman Catholicks, Scotch Renegadoes, at last they have stimulated the [Ladies] to demand new Priviledges and threaten to rebell.

Source: Adams, Abigail. <u>Familiar Letters of John Adams and his Wife Abigail Adams</u>. (Boston: Houghton, Mifflin & Co., 1875).

A Plea for Race Rights, and Gender Equity

"Ain't I A Woman?"

Well, children, where there is so much racket there must be something out of kilter. I think that 'twixt the negroes of the South and the women at the North, all talking about rights, the white men will be in a fix pretty soon. But what's all this here talking about?

That man over there says that women need to be helped into carriages, and lifted over ditches, and to have the best place everywhere. Nobody ever helps me into carriages, or over mud-puddles, or gives me any best place! And ain't I a woman? Look at me! Look at my arm! I have ploughed and planted, and gathered into barns, and no man could head me! And ain't I a woman? I could work as much and eat as much as a man - when I could get it - and bear the lash as well! And ain't I a woman? I have borne thirteen children, and seen most all sold off to slavery, and when I cried out with my mother's grief, none but Jesus heard me! And ain't I a woman?

Then they talk about this thing in the head; what's this they call it? [member of audience whispers, "intellect"] That's it, honey. What's that got to do with women's rights or negroes' rights? If my cup won't hold but a pint, and yours holds a quart, wouldn't you be mean not to let me have my little half measure full?

Then that little man in black there, he says women can't have as much rights as men, 'cause Christ wasn't a woman! Where did your Christ come from? Where did your Christ come from? From God and a woman! Man had nothing to do with Him.

If the first woman God ever made was strong enough to turn the world upside down all alone, these women together ought to be able to turn it back , and get it right side up again! And now they is asking to do it, the men better let them.

Obliged to you for hearing me, and now old Sojourner ain't got nothing more to say.

Source: Truth, Sojourner. Elizabeth C. Stanton, S. B. Anthony, and M. J. Gage, eds. "Address to the Ohio Women's Rights Convention." From History of Woman Suffrage. Rochester, NY: Susan B. Anthony. 1887.

Black Women Shaping Feminist Theory

Feminism in the United States has never emerged from the women who are most victimized by sexist oppression; women who are daily beaten down, mentally, physically, and spiritually-women who are powerless to change their condition in life. They are a silent majority. A mark of their victimization is that they accept their lot in life without visible question, without organized protest, without collective anger or rage. Betty Friedan's The Feminine Mystique is still heralded as having paved the way for contemporary feminist movement-it was written as if these women did not exist. Friedan's famous phrase, "the problem that has no name," often quoted to describe the condition of women in this society, actually referred to the plight of a select group of college-educated, middle and upper class, married white women-housewives bored with leisure, with the home, with children, with buying products, who wanted more out of life. Friedan concludes her first chapter by stating: "We can no longer ignore that voice within women that says: 'I want something more than my husband and my children and my house.'" That "more" she defined as careers. She did not discuss who would be called in to take care of the children and maintain the home if more women like herself were freed from their house labor and given equal access with white men to the professions. She did not speak of the needs of women without men, without children, without homes. She ignored the existence of all non-white women and poor white women. She did not tell readers whether it was more fulfilling to be a maid, a babysitter, a factory worker, a clerk, or a prostitute, than to be a leisure class housewife.

She made her plight and the plight of white women like herself synonymous with a condition affecting all

American women. In so doing, she deflected attention away from her classism, her racism, her sexist attitudes towards the masses of American women. In the context of her book, Friedan makes clear that the women she saw as victimized by sexism were college-educated, white women who were compelled by sexist conditioning to remain in the home. She contends:

It is urgent to understand how the very condition of being a housewife can create a sense of emptiness, non-existence, nothingness in women. There are aspects of the housewife role that make it almost impossible for a woman of adult intelligence to retain a sense of human identity, the firm core of self or "I" without which a human being, man or woman, is not truly alive. For women of ability, in America today, I am convinced that there is something about the housewife state itself that is dangerous.1

Specific problems and dilemmas of leisure class white housewives were real concerns that merited consideration and change but they were not the pressing political concerns of masses of women. Masses of women were concerned about economic survival, ethnic and racial discrimination, etc. When Friedan wrote The Feminine Mystique, more than one third of all women were in the work force. Although many women longed to be housewives, only women with leisure time and money could actually shape their identities on the model of the feminine mystique. They were women who, in Friedan's words, were "told by the most advanced thinkers of our time to go back and live their lives as if they were Noras, restricted to the doll's house by Victorian prejudices."2

From her early writing, it appears that Friedan never wondered whether or not the plight of college-educated, white housewives was an adequate reference point by which to gauge the impact of sexism or sexist oppression on the lives of women in American society. Nor did she move beyond her own life experience to acquire an expanded perspective on the lives of women in the United States. I say this not to discredit her work. It remains a useful discussion of the impact of sexist discrimination on a select group of women. Examined from a different perspective, it can also be seen as a case study of narcissism, insensitivity, sentimentality, and self-indulgence which reaches its peak when Friedan, in a chapter titled "Progressive Dehumanization," makes a comparison between the psychological effects of isolation on white housewives and the impact of confinement on the self-concept of prisoners in Nazi concentration camps.3

Friedan was a principal shaper of contemporary feminist thought. Significantly, the one-dimensional perspective on women's reality presented in her book became a marked feature of the contemporary feminist movement. Like Friedan before them, white women who dominate feminist discourse today rarely question whether or not their perspective on women's reality is true to the lived experiences of women as a collective group. Nor are they aware of the extent to which their perspectives reflect race and class biases, although there has been a greater awareness of biases in recent years. Racism abounds in the writings of white feminists, reinforcing white supremacy and negating the possibility that women will bond politically across ethnic and racial boundaries. Past feminist refusal to draw attention to and attack racial hierarchies suppressed the link between race and class. Yet class structure in American society has been shaped by the racial politic of white supremacy; it is only by analyzing racism and its function in capitalist society that a thorough understanding of class relationships can emerge. Class struggle is inextricably bound to the struggle to end racism. Urging women to explore the full implication of class in an early essay, "The Last Straw," Rita Mae Brown explained:

Class is much more than Marx's definition of relationship to the means of production. Class involves your behavior, your basic assumptions about life. Your experience (determined by your class) validates those assumptions, how you are taught to behave, what you expect from yourself and from others, your concept of a future, how you understand problems and solve them, how you think, feel, act. It is these behavioral patterns that middle class women resist recognizing although they may be perfectly willing to accept class in Marxist terms, a neat trick that helps them avoid really dealing with class behavior and changing that behavior in themselves. It is these behavioral patterns which must be recognized, understood, and changed.4

White women who dominate feminist discourse, who for the most part make and articulate feminist theory, have little or no understanding of white supremacy as a racial politic, of the psychological impact of class, of their political status within a racist, sexist, capitalist state.

It is this lack of awareness that, for example, leads Leah Fritz to write in Dreamers and Dealers, a discussion of the current women's movement published in 1979:

Women's suffering under sexist tyranny is a common bond among all women, transcending the particulars of the different forms that tyranny takes. Suffering cannot be measured and compared quantitatively. Is the enforced idleness and vacuity of a "rich" woman, which leads her to madness and/or suicide, greater or less than the suffering of a poor woman who barely survives on welfare but retains some-how her spirit? There is no way to measure such difference, but should these two women survey each other without the screen of patriarchal class, they may find a commonality in the fact that they are both oppressed, both miserable.5

Fritz's statement is another example of wishful thinking, as well as the conscious mystification of social divisions between women, that has characterized much feminist expression. While it is evident that many women suffer from sexist tyranny, there is little indication that this forges "a common bond among all women." There is much evidence substantiating the reality that race and class identity creates differences in quality of life, social status, and lifestyle that take precedence over the common experience women share-differences which are rarely transcended. The motives of materially privileged, educated, white women with a variety of career and lifestyle options available to them must be questioned when they insist that "suffering cannot be measured." Fritz is by no means the first white feminist to make this statement. It is a statement that I have never heard a poor woman of any race make. Although there is much I would take issue with in Benjamin Barber's critique of the women's movement, Liberating Feminism, I agree with his assertion:

Suffering is not necessarily a fixed and universal experience that can be measured by a single rod: it is related to situations, needs, and aspirations. But there must be some historical and political parameters for the use of the term so that political priorities can be established and different forms and degrees of suffering can be given the most attention.6

A central tenet of modern feminist thought has been the assertion that "all women are oppressed." This assertion implies that women share a common lot, that factors like class, race, religion, sexual preference, etc. do not create a diversity of experience that determines the extent to which sexism will be an oppressive force in the lives of individual women. Sexism as a system of domination is institutionalized but it has never determined in an absolute way the fate of all women in this society. Being oppressed means the absence of choices. It is the primary point of contact between the oppressed and the oppressor. Many women in this society do have choices, (as inadequate as they are) therefore exploitation and discrimination are words that more accurately describe the lot of women collectively in the United States. Many women do not join organized resistance against sexism precisely because sexism has not meant an absolute lack of choices. They may know they are discriminated against on the basis of sex, but they do not equate this with oppression. Under capitalism, patriarchy is structured so that sexism restricts women's behavior in some realms even as freedom from limitations is allowed in other spheres. The absence of extreme restrictions leads many women to ignore the areas in which they are exploited or discriminated against; it may even lead them to imagine that no women are oppressed.

There are oppressed women in the United States, and it is both appropriate and necessary that we speak against such oppression. French feminist Christine Delphy makes the point in her essay, "For a Materialist Feminism," that the use of the term oppression is important because it places feminist struggle in a radical political framework:

The rebirth of feminism coincided with the use of the term "oppression." The ruling ideology, i.e. common sense, daily speech, does not speak about oppression but about a "feminine condition." It refers back to a naturalist explanation: to a constraint of nature, exterior reality out of reach and not modifiable by human action. The term "oppression," on the contrary, refers back to a choice, an explanation, a situation that is political. "Oppression" and "social oppression" are therefore synonyms or rather social oppression is a redundancy: the notion of a political origin, i.e. social, is an integral part of the concept of oppression.7

However, feminist emphasis on "common oppression" in the United States was less a strategy for politicization than an appropriation by conservative and liberal women of a radical political vocabulary that masked the extent to which they shaped the movement so that it addressed and promoted their class interests.

Although the impulse towards unity and empathy that informed the notion of common oppression was directed at building solidarity, slogans like "organize around your own oppression" provided the excuse many privileged women needed to ignore the differences between their social status and the status of masses of women. It was a mark of race and class privilege, as well as the expression of freedom from the many constraints sexism places on working class women, that middle class white women were able to make their interests the primary focus of feminist movement and employ a rhetoric of commonality that made their condition synonymous with "oppression." Who was there to demand a change in vocabulary? What other group of women in the United States had the same access to universities, publishing houses, mass media, money? Had middle class black women begun a movement in which they had labeled themselves "oppressed," no one would have taken them seriously. Had they established public forums and given speeches about their "oppression," they would have been criticized and attacked from all sides. This was not the case with white bourgeois feminists for they could appeal to a large audience of women, like themselves, who were eager to change their lot in life. Their isolation from women of other class and race groups provided no immediate comparative base by which to test their assumptions of common oppression.

Initially, radical participants in women's movement demanded that women penetrate that isolation and create a space for contact. Anthologies like Liberation Now, Women's Liberation: Blueprint for the Future, Class and Feminism, Radical Feminism, and Sisterhood Is Powerful, all published in the early 1970s, contain articles that attempted to address a wide audience of women, an audience that was not exclusively white, middle class, college-educated, and adult (many have articles on teenagers). Sookie Stambler articulated this radical spirit in her introduction to Women's Liberation: Blueprint for the Future:

Movement women have always been turned off by the media's necessity to create celebrities and superstars. This goes against our basic philosophy. We cannot relate to women in our ranks towering over us with prestige and fame. We are not struggling for the benefit of the one woman or for one group of women. We are dealing with issues that concern all women.8

These sentiments, shared by many feminists early in the movement, were not sustained. As more and more women acquired prestige, fame, or money from feminist writings or from gains from feminist movement for equality in the workforce, individual opportunism undermined appeals for collective struggle. Women who were not opposed to patriarchy, capitalism, classism, or racism labeled themselves "feminist." Their expectations were varied. Privileged women wanted social equality with men of their class; some women wanted equal pay for equal work; others wanted an alternative lifestyle. Many of these legitimate concerns were easily co-opted by the ruling capitalist patriarchy. French feminist Antoinette Fouque states:

The actions proposed by the feminist groups are spectacular, provoking. But provocation only brings to light a certain number of social contradictions. It does not reveal radical contradictions within society. The feminists claim that they do not seek equality with men, but their practice proves the contrary to be true. Feminists are a bourgeois avant-garde that maintains, in an inverted form, the dominant values. Inversion does not facilitate the passage to another kind of structure. Reformism suits everyone! Bourgeois order, capitalism, phallocentrism are ready to integrate as many feminists, as will be necessary. Since these women are becoming men, in the end it will only mean a few more men. The difference between the sexes is not whether one does or doesn't have a penis, it is whether or not one is an integral part of a phallic masculine economy.9

Feminists in the United States are aware of the contradictions. Carol Ehrlich makes the point in her essay, "The Unhappy Marriage of Marxism and Feminism: Can It Be Saved?," that "feminism seems more and more to have taken on a blind, safe, nonrevolutionary outlook" as "feminist radicalism loses ground to bourgeois feminism," stressing that "we cannot let this continue":

Women need to know (and are increasingly prevented from finding out) that feminism is not about dressing for success, or becoming a corporate executive, or gaining elective office; it is not being able to share a two career marriage and take skiing vacations and spend huge amounts of time with your husband and two lovely children because you have a domestic worker who makes all this possible for you, but who hasn't the time or money to do it for herself, it is not opening a Women's Bank, or spending a weekend in an expensive workshop that guarantees to teach you how to become assertive (but not aggressive); it is most emphatically not about becoming a police detective or CIA agent or marine corps general.

But if these distorted images of feminism have more reality than ours do, it is partly our own fault. We have not worked as hard as we should have at providing clear and meaningful alternative analyses which relate to people's lives, and at providing active, accessible groups in which to work.10

It is no accident that feminist struggle has been so easily co-opted to serve the interests of conservative and liberal feminists since feminism in the United States has so far been a bourgeois ideology. Zillah Eisenstein discusses the liberal roots of North American feminism in The Radical Future of Liberal Feminism, explaining in the introduction:

One of the major contributions to be found in this study is the role of the ideology of liberal individualism in the construction of feminist theory. Today's feminists either do not discuss a theory of individuality or they unselfconsciously adopt the competitive, atomistic ideology of liberal individualism. There is much confusion on this issue in the feminist theory we discuss here. Until a conscious differentiation is made between a theory of individuality that recognizes the importance of the individual within the social collectivity and the ideology of individualism that assumes a competitive view of the individual, there will not be a full accounting of what a feminist theory of liberation must look like our Western society.11

The ideology of "competitive, atomistic liberal individualism" has permeated feminist thought to such an extent that it undermines the potential radicalism of feminist struggle. The usurpation of feminism by bourgeois women to support their class interests has been to a very grave extent justified by feminist theory as it has so far been conceived. (For example, the ideology of "common oppression.") Any movement to resist the co-optation of feminist struggle must begin by introducing a different feminist perspectives new theory-one that is not informed by the ideology of liberal individualism.

The exclusionary practices of women who dominate feminist discourse have made it practically impossible for new and varied theories to emerge. Feminism has its party line and women who feel a need for a different strategy, a different foundation, often find themselves ostracized and silenced. Criticisms of or alternatives to established feminist ideas are not encouraged, e.g. recent controversies about expanding feminist discussions of sexuality. Yet groups of women who feel excluded from feminist discourse and praxis can make a place for themselves only if they first create, via critiques, an awareness of the factors that alienate them. Many individual white women found in the women's movement a liberatory solution to personal dilemmas. Having directly benefited from the movement, they are less inclined to criticize it or to engage in rigorous examination of its structure than those who feel it has not had a revolutionary impact on their lives or the lives of masses of women in our society. Non-white women who feel affirmed within the current structure of feminist movement (even though they may form autonomous groups) seem to also feel that their definitions of the party line, whether on the issue of black feminism or on other issues, is the only legitimate discourse. Rather than encourage a diversity of voices, critical dialogue, and controversy, they, like some white women, seek to stifle dissent. As activists and writers whose work is widely known, they act as if they are best able to judge whether other women's voices should be heard. Susan Griffin warns against this overall tendency towards dogmatism in her essay, "The Way of All Ideology":

... when a theory is transformed into an ideology, it begins to destroy the self and self-knowledge. Originally born of feeling, it pretends to float above and around feeling. Above sensation. It organizes experience according to itself, without touching experience. By virtue of being itself, it is supposed to know. To invoke the name of this ideology is to confer truthfulness. No one can tell it anything new. Experience ceases to surprise it, inform it, transform it. It is annoyed by any detail which does not fit into its world view. Begun as a cry against the denial of truth, now it denies any truth which does not fit into its scheme. Begun as a way to restore one's sense of reality, now it attempts to discipline real people, to remake natural beings after its own image. All that it fails to explain it records as its enemy. Begun as a theory of liberation, it is threatened by new theories of liberation; it builds a prison for the mind.12

We resist hegemonic dominance of feminist thought by insisting that it is a theory in the making, that we must necessarily criticize, question, re-examine, and explore new possibilities. My persistent critique has been informed by my status as a member of an oppressed group, experience of sexist exploitation and discrimination, and the sense that prevailing feminist analysis has not been the force shaping my feminist consciousness. This is true for many women. There are white women who had never considered resisting male dominance until the feminist movement created an awareness that they could and should. My awareness of feminist struggle was stimulated by social circumstance. Growing up in a Southern, black, father-dominated, working class household, I experienced (as did my mother, my sisters, and my brother) varying degrees of patriarchal tyranny and it made me angry-it made us all angry. Anger led me to question the politics of male dominance and enabled me to resist sexist socialization. Frequently, white feminists act as if black women did not know sexist oppression existed until they voiced feminist sentiment. They believe they are providing black women with "the" analysis and "the" program for liberation. They do not understand, cannot even imagine, that black women, as well as other groups of women who live daily in oppressive situations, often acquire an awareness of patriarchal politics from their lived experience, just as they develop strategies of resistance (even though they may not resist on a sustained or organized basis).

These black women observed white feminist focus on male tyranny and women's oppression as if it were a "new" revelation and felt such a focus had little impact on their lives. To them it was just another indication of the privileged living conditions of middle and upper class white women that they would need a theory to inform them that they were "oppressed." The implication being that people who are truly oppressed know it even though they may not be engaged in organized resistance or are unable to articulate in written form the nature of their oppression. These black women saw nothing liberatory in party line analyses of women's oppression. Neither the fact that black women have not organized collectively in huge numbers around the issues of "feminism" (many of us do not know or use the term) nor the fact that we have not had access to the machinery of power that would allow us to share our analyses or theories about gender with the American public negate its presence in our lives or place us in a position of dependency in relationship to those white and non-white feminists who address a larger audience. The understanding I had by age thirteen of patriarchal politics created in me expectations of the feminist movement that were quite different from those of young, middle class, white women. When I entered my first women's studies class at Stanford University in the early 1970s, white women were revelling in the joy of being together -- to them it was an important, momentous occasion. I had not known a life where women had not been together, where women had not helped, protected, and loved one another deeply. I had not known white women who were ignorant of the impact of race and class on their social status and consciousness (Southern white women often have a more realistic perspective on racism and classism than white women in other areas of the United States.) I did not feel sympathetic to white peers who maintained that I could not expect them to have knowledge of or understand the life experiences of black women. Despite my background (living in racially segregated communities) I knew about the lives of white women, and certainly no white women lived in our neighborhood, attended our schools, or worked in our homes.

When I participated in feminist groups, I found that white women adopted a condescending attitude towards me and other non-white participants. The condescension they directed at black women was one of the means they employed to remind us that the women's movement was "theirs" -- that we were able to participate because they allowed it, even encouraged it; I after all, we were needed to legitimate the process. They did not see us as equals. They did not treat us as equals. And though they expected us to provide first hand accounts of black experience, they felt it was their role to decide if these experiences were authentic. Frequently, college-educated black women (even those from poor and working class backgrounds) were dismissed as mere imitators. Our presence in movement activities did not count, as white women were convinced that "real" blackness meant speaking the patois of poor black people, being uneducated, streetwise, and a variety of other stereotypes. If we dared to criticize the movement or to assume responsibility for reshaping feminist ideas and introducing new ideas, our voices were tuned out, dismissed, silenced. We could be heard only if our statements echoed the sentiments of the dominant discourse.13

Attempts by white feminists to silence black women are rarely written about. All too often they have taken place in conference rooms, classrooms, or the privacy of cozy living room settings, where one lone black woman faces the racist hostility of a group of white women. From the time the women's liberation movement began, individual black women went to groups. Many never returned after a first meeting. Anita Cornwall is correct in "Three for the Price of One: Notes from a Gay Black Feminist," when she states, "... sadly enough, fear of encountering racism seems to be one of the main reasons that so many black womyn refuse to join the women's movement. "13 Recent focus on the issue of racism has generated discourse but has had little impact on the behavior of white feminists towards black women. Often the white women who are busy publishing papers and books on "unlearning racism" remain patronizing and condescending when they relate to black women. This is not surprising given that frequently their discourse is aimed solely in the direction of a white audience and the focus solely on changing attitudes rather than addressing racism in a historical and political context. They make us the "objects" of their privileged discourse on race. As "objects," we remain unequals, inferiors. Even though they may be sincerely concerned about racism, their methodology suggests they are not yet free of the type of paternalism endemic to white supremacist ideology. Some of these women place themselves in the position of "authorities" who must mediate communication between racist white women (naturally they see themselves as having come to terms with their racism) and angry black women whom they believe are incapable of rational discourse. Of course, the system of racism, classism, and educational elitism remain intact if they are to maintain their authoritative positions.

In 1981, I enrolled in a graduate class on feminist theory where we were given a course reading list that had writings by white women and men, one black man, but no material by or about black, Native American Indian, Hispanic, or Asian women. When I criticized this oversight, white women directed an anger and hostility at me that was so intense I found it difficult to attend the class. When I suggested that the purpose of this collective anger was to create an atmosphere in which it would be psychologically unbearable for me to speak in class discussions or even attend class, I was told that they were not angry. I was the one who was angry. Weeks after class ended, I received an open letter from one white female student acknowledging her anger and expressing regret for her attacks. She wrote:

I didn't know you. You were black. In class after a while I noticed myself, that I would always be the one to respond to whatever you said. And usually it was to contradict. Not that the argument was always about racism by any means. But I think the hidden logic was that if I could prove you wrong about one thing, then you might not be right about anything at all.

And in another paragraph:

I said in class one day that there were some people less entrapped than others by Plato's picture of the world. I said I thought we, after fifteen years of education, courtesy of the ruling class, might be more entrapped than others who had not received a start in life so close to the heart of the monster. My classmate, once a close friend, sister, colleague, has not spoken to me since then. I think the possibility that we were not the best spokespeople for all women made her fear for her self-worth and for her Ph.D.

Often in situations where white feminists aggressively attacked individual black women, they saw themselves as the ones who were under attack, who were the victims. During a heated discussion with another white female student in a racially mixed women's group I had organized, I was told that she had heard how I had "wiped out" people in the feminist theory class, that she was afraid of being "wiped out" too. I reminded her that I was one person speaking to a large group of angry, aggressive people; I was hardly dominating the situation. It was I who left the class in tears, not any of the people I had supposedly "wiped out."

Racist stereotypes of the strong, superhuman black woman are operative myths in the minds of many white women, allowing them to ignore the extent to which black women are likely to be victimized in this society and the role white women may play in the maintenance and perpetuation of that victimization. In Lillian Hellman's autobiographical work Pentimento, she writes, "All my life, beginning at birth, I have taken orders from black women, wanting them and resenting them, being superstitious the few times I disobeyed." The black women Hellman describes worked in her household as family servants and their status was never that of an equal. Even as a child, she was always in the dominant position as they questioned, advised, or guided her; they were free to exercise these rights because she or another white authority figure allowed it. Hellman places power in the hands of these black women rather than acknowledge her own power over them; hence she mystifies the true nature of their relationship. By projecting onto black women a mythical power and strength, white women both promote a false image of themselves as powerless, passive, victims and deflect attention away from their aggressiveness, their power, (however limited in a white supremacist, male-dominated state) their willingness to dominate and control others. These unacknowledged aspects of the social status of many white women prevent them from transcending racism and limit the scope of their understanding of women's overall social status in the United States.

Privileged feminists have largely been unable to speak to, with, and for diverse groups of women because they either do not understand fully the inter-relatedness of sex, race, and class oppression or refuse to take this inter-relatedness seriously. Feminist analyses of woman's lot tend to focus exclusively on gender and do not provide a solid foundation on which to construct feminist theory. They reflect the dominant tendency in Western patriarchal minds to mystify woman's reality by insisting that gender is the sole determinant of woman's fate. Certainly it has been easier for women who do not experience race or class oppression to focus exclusively on gender. Although socialist feminists focus on class and gender, they tend to dismiss race or they make a point of acknowledging that race is important and then proceed to offer an analysis in which race is not considered.

As a group, black women are in an unusual position in this society, for not only are we collectively at the bottom of the occupational ladder, but our overall social status is lower than that of any other group. Occupying such a position, we bear the brunt of sexist, racist, and classist oppression. At the same time, we are the group that has not been socialized to assume the role of exploiter/oppressor in that we are allowed no institutionalized "other" that we can exploit or oppress. (Children do not represent an institutionalized other even though they may be oppressed by parents.) White women and black men have it both ways. They can act as oppressor or be oppressed. Black men may be victimized by racism, but sexism allows them to act as exploiters and oppressors of women. White women may be victimized by sexism, but racism enables them to act as exploiters and oppressors of black people. Both groups have led liberation movements that favor their interests and support the continued oppression of other groups. Black male sexism has undermined struggles to eradicate racism just as white female racism undermines feminist struggle. As long as these two groups or any group defines liberation as gaining social equality with ruling class white men, they have a vested interest in the continued exploitation and oppression of others.

Black women with no institutionalized "other" that we may discriminate against, exploit, or oppress often have a lived experience that directly challenges the prevailing classist, sexist, racist social structure and its concomitant ideology. This lived experience may shape our consciousness in such away that our world-view differs from those who have a degree of privilege (however relative within the existing system). It is essential for continued feminist struggle that black women recognize the special vantage point our marginality gives us and make use of this perspective to criticize the dominant racist, classist, sexist hegemony as well as to envision and create a counter-hegemony. I am suggesting that we have a central role to play in the making of feminist theory and a contribution to offer that is unique and valuable. The formation of a liberatory feminist theory and praxis is a collective responsibility, one that must be shared. Though I criticize aspects of

feminist movement as we have known it so far, a critique which is sometimes harsh and unrelenting, I do so not in an attempt to diminish feminist struggle but to enrich, to share in the work of making a liberatory ideology and a liberatory movement.
Source: hooks, bell, "Black Women Shaping Feminist Thought". In: Feminist Theory: From the Margin to Center. Boston: South End Press. 1984.

Men As Success Objects

The Draft
"95% of women's experiences are about being a victim. Or about being an underdog, or having to survive... women didn't go to Vietnam and blow things up. They are not Rambo." --Jodie Foster, The New York Times Magazine.

Muhammad Ali's refusal to participate in what he felt was the criminal nature of the Vietnam War forced him into prison during the height of his career and deprived him of four years that could never be recovered. At the same time Jodie Foster was safe at home, becoming wealthy and famous and cashing in on her sex appeal.

What would Jodie Foster have said if a sexist law kept her in prison when she was 24, 25, 26, and 27? Or if her body was valued so minimally that the only way she felt she could make millions was to subject herself to batterings that could eventually lead to brain damage and Parkinson's disease?

By the 1970's, the American woman was being called "liberated" or "superwoman" while the American man was being called "baby killer" if he fought in Vietnam, "traitor" if he protested, or "apathetic" if he did neither. It saddened men who watched women their age get a

head start on their careers while they fought in a war that tore their apart
their souls, to return from that war to hear a woman call herself the only victim of sexism because she was asked to make coffee at a job that no law required her to take.

The "Work Obligation Gap"

Women interpret men's tendency to earn more for different work as an outcome of male dominance rather that male subservience: they did not see it as outcome of male obligation -- obligation to go where the money is, not where fulfillment is.

Feminists focused on the fact that women as a whole earn less without focusing on why women earn less: full-time working men work 9 hours per week more (in the workplace) than full-time working women (Martha Hill, Univ. of Michigan)*;

Men are more willing to relocate to undesirable locations, work the less desirable hours (doctor vs. nurse), take jobs that are: dangerous (firefighter vs. receptionist), high risk (venture capitalist vs. file clerk)...

Women more than men can afford to take jobs that provide: high fulfillment relative to training (child-care professional vs. coal miner), contact with people in a pleasant environment (restaurant hostess vs. long distance trucker), the ability to psychologically check out at end of day (department store clerk vs. lawyer) and jobs that are indoors (secretary vs. garbage collector) and jobs with no demands to relocate (corporate secretary vs. corporate executive).

Desirable jobs pay less because they get plenty of qualified applicants. Instead of calling their refusal to take these undesirable jobs sexism, women could take the higher paying jobs (making the necessary sacrifices) that men took to allow women to stay home, and return the favor (don't marry for money; marry someone with a lower income, like men do.

With men taking time off from work as much as women, there goes their advantage in being hired and promoted. By eliminating the glass cellar, women would eliminate the glass ceiling. By allowing men equal access to his children, women would gain equal access in the job market. Giving up her advantages in the home-front, annihilates his in the workplace. To get equality, she merely had to give it. But while demanding that men give up their advantages, feminists are unwilling to give up theirs and instead are forcing everything and everyone to adapt to them. Sooner or later this is going to backfire.

*When you combine hours worked inside the home with hours worked outside the home the average man works 61 hours per week, the average woman 56 -- University of Michigan study reported in the Journal of Economic Literature in 1991.
Source: The preceding was paraphrased or quoted from: Farrell, Warren. The Myth of Male Power: Why Men Are The Disposable Sex. New York: Simon & Schuster. 1993.

Gay Cultures, Gay Communities & Social Organization

Academic research and popular depictions would have us believe that sexual identities are simply about sex. Much of the research literature focuses, for example, on the role of sexuality, especially its physiological components, in defining a lesbian, gay, or bisexual identity; other research is concerned with the etiology, or "causes" of homosexuality. While studies that examine lesbian, gay, and, to a much lesser extent, bisexual life in a much larger context are becoming increasingly common, sexology's stamp on lesbian and gay research, which stresses the sexual aspects of lesbian and gay life, is far more apparent. Popular accounts have also assumed that lesbians, gays, and bisexuals are primarily sexual beings. Unlike heterosexuals, who are defined by their family structures, communities, occupations, or other aspects of their lives, lesbians, gay men, and bisexuals are often defined primarily by what they do in bed. Many lesbians, gay men, and bisexuals, however, view their identity as social and political as well as sexual. For this reason, it is important to study the social contexts of lesbian, gay, and bisexual lives and the communities they create.

The term community has experienced a resurgence in recent years. In common conversation, people speak of all types of communities: workplace or occupational communities, recreational communities ("the running community"), racial/ethnic communities ("the African American community," "the Italian American community"), and so forth. Lesbians, gay men, and, increasingly, bisexuals use the same language to refer to their social groupings. Unlike earlier views, contemporary notions of community do not necessarily imply a geographically bounded, physical location. Instead of an actual place, people often speak of an identification or sense of connection with a social category or group (di Leonardo, 1984; Herrell, 1992). People are members of a community-whether a lesbian or gay community, an ethnic community, or some other type of community-because they feel a sense of kinship and belonging. Geographical proximity and face-to-face interaction help community members maintain contact and develop institutions that facilitate the growth of communities, but proximity and intimacy are by no means strictly necessary for maintaining the sense of shared identity that predicates contemporary notions of community. Some speak, for example, of a national or even an international lesbian and gay community, connected by books and periodicals, national political institutions, and other signs of a cultural life that allow even isolated lesbians, gay men, and bisexuals to feel part of a much larger social grouping.

Lesbian and gay communities are in some respects similar to racial and ethnic communities in that both are based on a shared identity defined as "other" in relation to the majority. For both groups, community provides the terrain on which social identities are enacted. They provide shared meanings for behavior and a means for ongoing interactions of group members-whether face-to-face, long distance, or media-based (Esterberg, 1991). There are also differences between lesbian/gay and racial/ethnic communities (Epstein, 1992; Esterberg, 1994). As Herrell (1992) noted, "The difference between the gay and other American 'subcultural' communities is that, for gays and lesbians, the experience of community derives, not from parents and peers during childhood, but from adult participation in a network of institutions and from shared responses to the pervasive denial of social personality itself" (p. 248).

Lesbians, gay men, and bisexuals are racially and ethnically diverse. We are divided by class, gender, and all the social cleavages that characterize American life. Unlike some others, gay and lesbian communities attempt to fashion commonalities out of a much larger set of disparate experiences, and gay and lesbian communities attempt to socialize diverse adult members into a shared community life.

Mirroring lesbian and gay social life during the twentieth century, research on lesbian and gay communities has, by and large, been separated along gender lines. One body of research focuses on gay men's communities, often seen primarily in sexual and social terms, and the other on lesbian communities, often considered in conjunction with the feminist movement and in political terms. Despite the emphasis on separation, gay men, lesbians, and bisexuals have certainly participated in shared activities and institution building, and some participants and scholars alike refer to shared lesbian and gay men' s communities, which sometimes include bisexuals.

I focus primarily on the two communities as distinct though certainly overlap- ping. In recent years, lesbian and gay communities have moved closer together. The AIDS epidemic has inexorably changed the nature of gay men' s communities, and the "lesbian sex wars" of the early 1980s-in which lesbians vigorously debated the nature of lesbian sexuality and the place of woman-made pornography and other graphic representations of sexuality-have fundamentally shaken the myth of a uniform lesbian community. As gay men and lesbians alike have responded to the AIDS epidemic and the threats of the radical right in the 1980s and 1990s, they have increasingly participated in common pursuits. In the 1990s, at least for some areas of the United States, it may well make sense to begin speaking of a shared lesbian and gay community.

In the same way that lesbians and gay men have developed communities apart from one another and lesbian lives have often been ignored by gay men, communities and networks of ethnic-minority gay men and lesbians have, with few exceptions, been rendered largely invisible both by White lesbian and gay community participants and by researchers of lesbian and gay social life. Although there are a few outstanding works that detail the lives and social relationships of ethnic-minority gay men and lesbians, much more work needs to be done (see, for example, Anzaldua, 1987; Beam, 1986; Garber, 1989; Hemphill, 1991; Lorde, 1982; Moraga & Anzaldua, 1981). Similarly, although working-class men and women have long participated in an active bar culture, only recently have discussions of working-class gay and lesbian life been published (see especially Kennedy & Davis's [1993] lovingly researched oral history of Buffalo's lesbian bar community, as well as the writings of Nestle [1987,1992].

Historical Perspectives on Gay and Lesbian Communities

In the last few years, a number of remarkable books have chronicled the recent history of lesbian and gay communities in the United States and their movements for social change (Berube, 1990; D'Emilio, 1983b; Duberman, 1993; Faderman, 1991; Kennedy & Davis, 1993; Newton, 1993). These works provide extraordinary insights into the social organization of lesbians and gay men: the friendships they nurtured, the erotic relationships they celebrated, and the communities they created. As outlined by Berube (1990) and D'Emilio (1983a), contemporary gay and lesbian communities gained shape during and after World War II. Prior to the war, a few bars and public places existed where men found other men for erotic encounters and, much less frequently, where women found other women. The large-scale mobilization of men and women into the military and women's entrance into the wartime labor force enabled those with erotic desires for others of the same gender to find each other. At the same time, the mass movement of people into cities across the United States enabled a degree of anonymity and independent living hitherto unavailable, especially for women, many of whom had not previously lived outside of a family setting. In his book Coming Out Under Fire, Berube (1990) described the vibrant social life for gay men and women that developed during World War II. Bars and other public gathering places, such as the Black Cat Cafe in San Francisco and the If Club in Los Angeles, appeared in large- and medium-sized cities to cater to gay men and, to a lesser extent, lesbians. At war's end, this gay life did not stop. Many of the returning service men and women stayed in the cities where they had begun to form networks of gay men and women. Further, many of those who were purged from the military with undesirable discharges felt they could not return to their rural homes. They migrated to the cities-such as San Francisco and New York-where they knew a gay and lesbian life existed.

Gay and lesbian life, which continued to develop after the war, flourished mainly in the bars. Public communities were slow to develop because of the stigma attached to homosexuality and the dangers of going to the bars, which were frequent targets of police raids and harassment. Openly gay men and women, many of whom were working class, were assaulted on the streets and in the bars (for an excellent fictional account of the rigors of 1950s and 19609- gay life, see Feinberg, 1993; see also Kennedy & Davis, 1993; Nestle, 1987). For working-class "butch" lesbians, who could not hide their sexual orientation, job security was certainly difficult to find. In the cold years of the McCarthy era, gays and lesbians and those suspected of homo- sexuality were purged in large numbers from government and military jobs. Even those willing or able to hide their sexual orientation feared losing a job; being evicted from a house or apartment; or losing the approbation of heterosexual friends, coworkers, and neighbors. These fears of public disclosure made participating in an open and public gay and lesbian community difficult. Despite these obstacles, communities grew in the bars and bathhouses; in the personal friendship networks; in a few resort communities, such as Cherry Grove on Fire Island (Newton, 1993); and in the nascent homophile movement's attempts to organize politically.

The Homophile Movement

D'Emilio (1992) argued that the history of lesbian and gay politics is intricately entwined with the history of lesbian and gay community building and social movement activity: "The structure of the community marks the terrain on which the movement can operate, and the actions of the movement are continually reshaping the life of the community" (p. 237). The 1969 Stonewall Rebellion, in which working- class gay men and lesbians fought back against police raids at the Stonewall Inn in New York City, is commonly viewed as marking the birth of the lesbian and gay liberation movement. Yet lesbian and gay historians have revealed a much longer history of organizing for social change by lesbians and gay men in the homophile movement of the 1950s and 1960s (Adam, 1987; D'Emilio, 1983b; Duberman, 1993; Marcus, 1992). This earlier movement is also chronicled in the film Before Stonewall and in community oral history projects such as those in Boston and San Francisco.

The homophile movement, although small, signaled the beginning of continuous social movement activity on behalf of lesbians and gay men in the United States. Their goals were primarily integrationist; that is, rather than developing a self-conscious, organized "homophile" community, their aim was to integrate gay men and lesbians into the mainstream of heterosexual life. The original goals of the Daughters of Bilitis, the only homophile organization exclusively for women, were reprinted on the inside front cover of every issue of their publication, The Ladder. These included "education of the variant. ..to enable her to understand herself and make her adjustment to society in all its social, civic and economic implications." This was to be accomplished by, among other things, establishing a library "on the sex deviant theme" and "by advocating a mode of behavior and dress acceptable to society." Despite these accommodationist goals, a by-product of homophile organizing was to increase the visibility of lesbians and gay men and to make more salient, rather than less, lesbian and gay sexual identity (Esterberg, 1994).

Organizing by the homophile movement highlights several features of lesbian and gay community life. First, organizing was segregated by gender and class: The homophile movement was predominantly White and middle class. Although in their social and sexual activities gay men were more likely to mix with others of different classes and, in certain situations, different race and ethnic groups, women' s bars were separated by class. In accordance with the rigid gender roles of the 1950s and early 1960s and fearful of losing their jobs, middle-class women tended not to socialize in bars. Daughters of Bilitis, in fact, originally formed as an alternative to lesbian bars; members were actively discouraged from participating in the butch-femme bar life. Instead, they were encouraged to dress "femininely" and to "adjust" to the feminine role. Other homophile organizations, such as the Mattachine Society and One, Inc., although technically open to women, were dominated by middle-class White men; after a short, more radical founding period, they too moved toward a similar integrationist stance. As a whole, homophile organizations did not encourage lesbians and gay men to develop strong and active autonomous communities. Instead, in the repressive years of the McCarthy era, homophile leaders encouraged participation in the broader heterosexual community, considering that a more secure route to acceptance. By their very efforts at building organizations, however, the homophile movement helped strengthen lesbian and gay life and paved the way for a more radical social movement in the 1970s, one which actively sought to create a distinctive lesbian and gay life.

Gay Liberation
The gay liberation movement was sparked by the increasing militancy of the homophile movement and the other radical movements for social change during the latter part of the 1960s. The precipitating event was the 1969 Stonewall Rebellion, in which working-class gay men and lesbians, including drag queens and butch lesbians, fought back when police raided the Stonewall Inn in New York City (Duberman, 1993).

Gay liberation, along with the resurgence of feminism in the 1970s, brought radical changes to gay, lesbian, and bisexual life. Gay men saw the birth of a highly commercialized sexual culture, and women saw the emergence of a "lesbian nation." The term ".clone culture" has been used by some participants and observers to describe urban gay men' s communities in the 1970s (Levine, 1990). Many gay men in urban areas cultivated a homogeneous style, consisting of masculine attire, such as tight jeans and leather jackets, that emphasized gay male sexuality. Some used the term "clone" to refer to those who adopted the style and participated in the vibrant social and sexual scene of urban gay men. "Lesbian nation" refers to the title of a book by Johnston (1973). Many lesbians in the 1970s focused on building autonomous, separatist lesbian communities as a response to society's pervasive sexism and heterosexism.

The life that developed in the gay meccas 'of New York and San Francisco and in smaller lesbian communities, such as Amherst/Northampton, Massachusetts, and Madison, Wisconsin, was not replicated uniformly across the nation. Nonetheless, gay and lesbian culture and community spread from the centers in the forms of periodicals, such as The Advocate, Gay Community News, Lavender Tide, and Lesbian Connection; books published by small presses, including Daughters, Inc., and Alyson Publications; music by "women's" music performers such as Linda Tillery, Alix Dobkin, and Holly Near; and other cultural productions, including art shows and oral history projects.

Especially among feminist lesbians in the 1970s, culture and community building were explicit aims. In their attempts to build a "lesbian nation," where lesbian life could flourish free from heterosexist and sexist oppression, many chose to separate themselves from the sexism they found in working politically and socially with gay men. But in creating these communities, their aims to be truly inclusive often fell short when confronted with the very real and persistent differences of class, race, and ethnicity among women. At the same time that lesbians were creating an explicitly antimaterialist political and cultural life, many gay men were actively creating a distinctive sexual and social life. Men developed an extensive community network, centered in bars, bathhouses, and a highly commercialized sexual culture. Although many women and 'men did not feel at home in the segregated lesbian and gay subcultures growing up around them and wished to create a more integrated community, the two communities could not have been more distinct.

Gay Men's Communities

In a recent anthology focusing on gay men's culture in America, Herdt and Boxer (1992) made a clear distinction between early gay men's culture (which they referred to as "homosexual"), rooted in a furtive bar life, and today's contrasting "gay" culture, anchored by more positive cultural images and shared community institutions such as gay pride parades. Herdt argued, "The secret world of the gay bar and covert social networks made homosexuality an individualized sort of puberty rite into a secret oppressed society. There was no manifest gay culture at the time. Today, the political power of the gay and lesbian community suggests that coming out is more of a collective initiation rite, a public coming-of-age status-adjustment transition into the adult gay community" (Herdt, 1992, p. 31). Since the 1960s, the gay men's community has grown dramatically.

Martin Levine noted in his study of the 1970s' West Village (New York) "clone culture" that the gay liberation movement of the 1970s fundamentally altered forms of gay men's social and sexual lives. Gay liberationists and activists worked to reduce police harassment of bars and other gay institutions; at the same time, they sought to decrease the stigma of gender deviance attached to gay men. As a result, urban gay neighborhoods thrived, complete with gay-owned bars, bathhouses, shops, book- stores, professional services, and a wide variety of political, recreational, and cultural organizations. As Levine (1992) explains:

Certainly, coming out into the flourishing gay social and community life during the height of the 1970s was dramatically different from coming out during the 1950s. Urban men's communities saw an increased emphasis on sexual freedom and self-expression, and the "clone culture" that developed in major cities in the 1970s trans- formed earlier stereotypes of gay men. Replacing the image of gay male effeminacy with a hypermasculine sensibility, "butch " presentational strategies highlighting men's erotic features and sexual availability were a major feature of clone culture. In the pre-AIDS 1970s, many urban gay men's social lives centered around cruising and tricking; a wide variety of businesses and social institutions catering to gay men's erotic desires prospered. For some, the essence of gay liberation and community of the 1970s was its exuberant celebration of male sexuality.

While a highly sexualized gay male subculture flourished, gay rights activists of the 1970s also expressed frustration with the apolitical stance of the "new gay man" and his emphasis on gay sociability. As D'Emilio wryly noted:

Reformers fought for the right to be gay, free from harassment and punishment. Since the sexual subculture had been the location where gay men most acutely experienced both their gayness and their vulnerability, the fading police presence seemed incontrovertible evidence that they were free. As far as they could tell, gay liberation had succeeded. ...Activist harangues about the persistence of job discrimination, about media invisibility, about the role of the churches and the military in excluding homosexuals from equal participation in American life seemed like the ravings of grim politicos who just didn't know how to have fun (1992, p. 251).

Thus, while many men made the social rounds of parties, bars, bathhouses, and restaurants, creating a sexual subculture of liberation, others worked in overtly political venues for increased freedoms for lesbians and gay men.

If gay men experienced their subordination primarily in terms of their sexual lives, lesbians experienced gender as at least as important in limiting their opportunities for self-determination. And if gay men set out to create communities based on sexual ties, lesbians set out to create communities based not on sex but on relationships. Although lesbians certainly participated with gay men in activist organizations and the establishment of urban gay and lesbian communities, they worked in far greater numbers to create an autonomous lesbian-feminist movement and separate lesbian communities and cultures, Lesbian feminists were influenced by radical critiques of gender and women' s position in a male-dominated society. Rather than understanding their oppression as rooted solely in a denial or repression of their lesbian sexuality, lesbian feminists sought to understand women' s oppression in broader terms, rooted in the institutions of family, church, and state, In solidarity with other women, some lesbian feminists sought to redefine lesbian- ism in primarily homosocial ways: as women bonding with other women. "Feminism is the theory, lesbianism is the practice" was the slogan championed by some. Radicalesbians, for example, in a much-cited position paper, asked: "What is a lesbian?" And they responded, " A lesbian is the rage of all women condensed to the point of explosion. She is the woman who, often beginning at an extremely early age, acts in accordance with her inner compulsion to be a more complete and freer human being than her society. ..cares to allow her"

(Radicalesbians, 1970/1988, p. 17). Similarly, in a controversial essay, the poet Adrienne Rich outlined the notion of a lesbian continuum; defined thus, lesbianism included a range of "woman-identified experience; not simply the fact that a woman has had or consciously desired genital sexual experience with another woman" (1980/1983, p. 192). If some gay men in the 1970s were furiously attempting to define them- selves and their communities by their sexual experiences with other men, some lesbians were just as furiously attempting to de-sex lesbian identity and community (Snitow, Stansell, & Thompson, 1983).

Lesbian feminism was never the predominant form of lesbian self-definition (Whisman, 1991). Many women felt an allegiance to working with their gay brothers, and others felt little connection with the primarily White and middle-class feminist movement. Yet lesbian feminism was enormously influential in the creation of a vibrant and visible lesbian culture and community. Throughout the 1970s, lesbians created "women's" (lesbian) music festivals, feminist books and bookstores, coffee- houses, support groups, and a wide variety of cultural, political, and social organizations and institutions. (For descriptions of lesbian-feminist communities, see Fader- man, 1991, chapter 9; Krieger, 1983; Wolf, 1979.). Yet lesbian-feminist communities were often narrow and intolerant of those who diverged from community ideals, including women who had been openly lesbian in the pre-Stonewall butch-femme bar life. Nestle (1987) recalled:

Many of us were active in political change struggles, fed by the energy of our hidden butch-femme lives, which even our most liberal-left friends could not tolerate. Articulated feminism added another layer of analysis and understanding, a profound one, one that felt so good and made such won- derful allies that for me it was a gateway to another world-until I realized I was saying radical feminist when! could not say Lesbian (p. 107).

Zita (1981) called the attempt to define just who "belonged" in lesbian community as the Lesbian Olympics, "where competing lesbians are ranked, categorized, accepted, and rejected" (p. 173; see also Krieger, 1983; Whisman; 1993). Yet despite the problems involved, lesbian communities also served as the basis for an autonomous lesbian life.

From Lesbian Nation to Lesbian Sex/ From Clone Culture to Queer Nation

In the 1970s, gay men and lesbians alike moved away from creating a social movement and toward creating a community and culture. Yet the cultures they created could not have been more distinct, and attempts at mixed lesbian and gay organizations were fraught with tension. The 1980s brought major changes to lesbian and gay men' s communities, changes that, perhaps, moved their experiences closer to one another and may have served to re-ground lesbian and gay identity and community within a combined social movement for change.

A more openly sexual lesbian scene, with its own woman-made pornography, go-go bars, and frankly sexual style, more akin to gay men's culture than to lesbian feminism, developed in some large urban centers in the 1980s. The lesbian "sex wars" generated by the diverging styles made apparent the deep disagreements about the nature of lesbian sexuality, the place of fantasy and graphic representations of women's sexuality, and the ambiguous place of bisexual women within the "lesbian nation." Lesbian community, long painted in rosy hues by its participants, could no longer be seen as a place of harmony, where women's perceived essential sameness as women could override all disagreements and conflicts based on difference. As butches and femmes, working-class women and ethnic-minority women demanded a widening of the boundaries of the lesbian nation, lesbian community life changed dramatically. Lesbian feminism had been decentered, as Stein (among others) argued (1992). As a result, lesbian culture in the 1990s is far more diverse than that imagined in the 1970s.

At the same time, the AIDS epidemic has shaped gay men' s sexual and social lives in ways previously unimaginable. With the spread of AIDS and HIV through- out gay men' s communities, gay men, along with lesbians and bisexuals, have mobilized to stop the spread of the epidemic, to provide services to their ill and dying brothers (and sisters, though women, especially lesbians, with AIDS have yet to be fully recognized), and to change an intransigent political and medical system that treats gay men' s lives as hardly worth saving. The AIDS epidemic challenged the complacency of many formerly apolitical gay men; their beliefs that full societal acceptance was at hand were badly shaken by the treatment they received by the medical and political establishment. As gay men organized to stop the spread of AIDS and to care for their ill friends and lovers, the social institutions that kept alive a vigorous sexual social life changed. Bathhouses and back rooms of bars were shut down, and social cliques and networks were torn apart by death and illness. At the same time, the number of AIDS and HIV political action and service-providing groups grew rapidly. The diffusion of information about safer sex practices and ways to decrease transmission of HIV led to an increased emphasis on relationships, love, and dating. At the same time that some lesbians have moved closer to the frank and expressive sexuality of gay men, gay men have moved closer to the relationship ideals expressed by many lesbians. As Gorman expressed it, "The [gay men's] community finds itself no longer in adolescence but rather increasingly taking on the roles and tasks of adulthood. This transformation is reflected politically, economically, demographically, sociologically, culturally, and with respect to gender issues" (1992, p. 103).

Perhaps it is this shift toward a middle ground by lesbians and gay men, or the resurgence of a radical right threatening the political gains made in the 1970s and early 1980s, that has sparked the beginnings of joint social-movement activity and a tentative shared community of lesbians and gay men. Many younger lesbians are more likely to embrace a queer identity in ACT UP and Queer Nation than a feminist lesbian identity. Although all is not well in those groups and some feminists (young and old) have decried their sexism, Queer Nation and ACT UP actively seek to create a combined queer community (Elliott, 1992; Whisman, 1991; see also Maggenti, 1993). Whether the future holds increased mixed-gender organizing and community building remains to be seen. At the same time, groups such as the National Latino/a Lesbian and Gay Organization, the National Coalition for Black Lesbians and Gays, and Asian Pacifica Lesbian Network have provided autonomous organizations for ethnic/sexual minorities and have highlighted the race and class divisions within lesbian and gay communities. Whether, and how, their challenges to broaden the leadership and visions of gay communities to include ethnic minorities will be met, or whether ethnic communities will remain largely autonomous, remains to be seen.

An Emerging Bisexual Community

Bisexual people have largely been invisible-and, when visible, maligned- within lesbian and gay communities. Stereotyped as fence-sitters or undecided, as people in transition to a "true" lesbian or gay identity, or as traitors, bisexuals have been made to feel less than welcome in lesbian and gay communities. Bisexuality calls into question the very dualistic categories we use to define sexuality; by its nature, bisexuality highlights the fluidity of sexual experience and the continuous nature of sexuality. Many have argued that underneath the categories, everyone (or almost everyone) is essentially bisexual; in fact, one of the goals of the early gay liberationists was to unleash "the homosexual in everyone" and smash rigid sexual categories. This goal has long been abandoned, however, and holding a proud and open bisexual identity is a relatively recent phenomenon (see Hutchins & Kaahumanu, 1991, and Weise, 1992).

It is only since the 1980s that bisexual groups have become active in major cities. Even in the early 1990s, many bisexuals still feel isolated. Yet bisexuals' attempts to assert an autonomous identity and to openly express attractions to both genders have been met with resistance in gay and, especially, lesbian communities. Rust (1992) recently noted that many lesbians' experience is essentially similar to the experience of bisexual women; lesbians have often had significant sexual or affectional relation- ships with men, but they prefer to label themselves lesbian. Lesbian-feminist singer Holly Near is one of the most famous lesbians to speak openly about her relationships with men, and she has been criticized both by lesbians, for relating to men, and by bisexuals, for not claiming a bisexual identity. Lesbian communities, Rust argued, are threatened by the emergence of a vigorous bisexual women's contingent because lesbians and bisexual women may be staking a claim to the very same territory.

Despite the arguments about bisexuality within lesbian and gay communities, many bisexual men and women have worked hard to help build the very communities from which they feel excluded. Some continue to work within lesbian and gay communities, pushing the boundaries to include an open bisexual presence. Others feel included within Queer Nation an-d its in-your-face politics and inclusion of all sexual minorities. Still others work to create a distinct bisexual movement and bisexual community. Where this movement will go-whether autonomous bisexual communities will flourish, or whether bisexual men and women will continue to push lesbian, gay, and heterosexual communities to expand their boundaries-remains to be seen.

The Future of Community

What is the future of lesbian, gay, and bisexual community? And why does it matter? Why bother with creating communities? Why stress that which is different- sexual identity-when that is what serves to exclude lesbians, gay men, and bisexuals from heterosexual society? Despite the gains of the homophile movement of the 1950s and 1960s and the lesbian and gay movements of the 1970s and 1980s, lesbians, gay men, and bisexuals still have a long way to go in attaining full acceptance in a heterosexist society. The indifferent response by the American public to the AIDS epidemic galvanized many formerly apolitical gay men into action (see Shilts, 1987, for a chronicle of the early years of the AIDS epidemic). Recent attacks by the radical right, including attempts to pass state constitutional amendments that would legalize discrimination against lesbians, gay men, and bisexuals, have provided a similar impetus to coordinated activism in the 1990s.

Although communities clearly provide a basis for social movement activity, they also serve other purposes. In fact, the vast majority of lesbians, gays, and bisexuals do not participate in the political aspects of community life. From a developmental perspective, communities provide a way to socialize gay, lesbian, and bisexual youth-and those who come to claim these identities in later life-into a larger community. As Herdt described in his study of a Chicago "coming out" group for adolescents, coming out is a rite of passage-"a category change of the most profound sort in self and other representations and relationships" (1992, p. 59). Communities offer a set of shared meanings for interpreting the experiences of those who desire same-sex lovers and partners and a mechanism for valuing those desires instead of denigrating them. Lesbian, gay, and bisexual communities can provide a set of positive, prideful images that offset heterosexist images of lesbians, gay men, and bisexual people as perverse and perverted, sick and sinful. For young people who are just coming into their sexual identities, for those who are isolated, communities can furnish a lifeline.

Certainly, lesbian, gay, and bisexual communities have their share of problems of exclusion, intolerance, sexism, racism, and class ism. But communities can also provide a link to other lesbians, gay men, and bisexuals and a means to assert a vivid queer presence in the world. At their very best, communities offer a model of compassion, support, and commitment, as evidenced by the way in which the AIDS crisis has brought together gay men, bisexuals, and lesbians in caring for the dying, sick, and well in our communities. As our movements and our communities shift and grow in response to changing social and historical circumstances, they help shape what it means to be a lesbian, a gay man, or a bisexual person. ~

Source: Esterberg, Kristen Gay. "Gay Cultures, Gay Communities: The Social Organization of Lesbians, Gay men, and Bisexuals". in Savin-Williams, Ritch C., & Kenneth M. Cohen. The Lives of Lesbians, Gays, and Bisexuals. New York: Harcourt Brace Publishers. 1996.

Ellen Goodman, When A Woman Says No

There are a few times when, if you watch closely, you can actually see a change of public mind. This is one of those times.

For as long as I can remember, a conviction for rape depended as much on the character of the woman involved as on the action of the man. Most often the job of the defense lawyer was to prove that the woman had provoked or consented to the act, 'to prove that it was sex, not assault.

In the normal course of events the smallest blemish, misjudgment, misstep by the woman became proof that she had invited the man's attentions. Did she wear a tight sweater? Was she a "loose" woman? Was she in the wrong part of town at the wrong hour? A woman could waive her right to say no in an astonishing number of ways.

But in the past few weeks, in Massachusetts, three cases of multiple rape have come into court and three sets of convictions have come out of juries. These verdicts point to a sea change in attitudes. A simple definition seems to have seeped into the public consciousness. If she says no, it's rape.

The most famous of these cases is the New Bedford barroom rape. There, in two separate trials, juries cut through complicated testimony to decide the central issue within hours. Had the woman been drinking? Had she lied about that in testimony? Had she kissed one of the men? In the end none of these points were relevant. What mattered to the juries that found four of these six men guilty was that they had forced her. If she said no, it was rape.

The second of these cases involved a young woman soldier from Ft. Devens who accepted a ride with members of a rock band, the Grand Slamm. She was raped in the bus and left in a field hours later. Had she flirted with the band members? Had she told a friend that she intended to seduce one of the men? Had she boarded the bus willingly? The judge sentencing three of the men to jail said, "No longer will society accept the fact that a woman, even if she may initially act in a seductive or compromising manner, has waived her right to say no at any further time." If she said no, it was rape.

The third of these cases was in some ways the most notable. An Abington woman was driven from a bar to a parking lot where she was raped by four men, scratched with a knife, had her hair singed with a cigarette lighter and was left half-naked in the snow. The trial testimony showed that she previously had sex with three of the men, and with two of them in a group setting. Still, the jury was able to agree with the district attorney: "Sexual consent between a woman and a man on one occasion does not mean the man has access to her whenever it strikes his fancy." If she said no, it was rape.

Not every community, courtroom or jury today accepts this simple standard of justice. But ten years ago, five years ago, even three years ago these women might not have even dared press charges.

It was the change of climate that enabled, even encouraged, the women to come forward. It was the change of attitude that framed the arguments in the courtroom. It was the change of consciousness that infiltrated the jury chambers.

The question now is whether that change of consciousness has become part of our own day-to-day lives. In some ways rape is the brutal, repugnant extension of an ancient ritual of pursuit and capture. It isn't just rapists who refuse to take no for an answer. It isn't just rapists who believe that a woman says one thing and means another .

In the confusion of adolescence, in the chase of young adulthood, the sexes were often set up to persist and to resist. Many young men were taught that "no" means "try again." Many young women were allowed to excuse their sexuality only when they were "swept away," overwhelmed.

The confused messages, the yes-no-maybes, the overpowered heroines and over- whelming heroes, are still common to supermarket gothic novels and Hustler magazine. It isn't just X-rated movies that star a resistant woman who falls in love with her sexual aggressor. It isn't just pornographic cable- TV that features the woman who really "wanted it." In as spritely a sitcom as "Cheers," Sam blithely locked a coyly ambivalent Diane into his apartment.

I know how many steps it is from that hint of sexual pressure to the brutality of rape. I know how far it is from lessons of sexual power plays to the violence of rape. But it's time that the verdict of those juries was fully transmitted to the culture from which violence emerges. If she says no, it means no. ~

Source: Goodman, Ellen. "When A Woman Says No". Copyright 1993, The Boston Globe Company.

CLASS IN AMERICA

KEY CONCEPTS

Economic access and opportunity for economic success are key to power, privilege and identity in a capitalist society. America is a capitalist society. Diversity in America has always produced a margin for profit. Class has historically been used as a device to separate otherwise cohesive cultural groups, and has been a mask for ethnocentrism as well as racism. Historically, most groups who have immigrated to the United States have spent a period of time socially restricted into working class occupations. Indeed some ethnic groups -- Blacks and Latinos - are still under considerable social pressure to form a permanent underclass of working poor in America. Women regardless of ethnicity are still denied the same access to social class mobility as males. There is a judgmental undercurrent to class in a capitalist society. Poor is bad, rich is good - morally. The more "things" you have, the better person you are assumed to be. Material goods and things can and have become accepted as more worthwhile than individuals or experiences. Poor people are assumed to be somehow implicated in their own poverty, as though they would willfully perpetuate their own disadvantage. People are allowed to sicken and die because their lack of money devalues their humanity. Class is life at a premium.

Class Conflict in Capitalist Agriculture

In February 1903 over 1,200 Mexican and Japanese farm workers organized the Japanese-Mexican Labor Association (JMLA) in the southern California community of Oxnard. The JMLA was the first major agricultural workers' union in the state comprised of different minority workers and the first to strike successfully against capitalist interests. ...Emerging as one of the many "boom towns" in California at the turn of the century, Oxnard owed its existence to the passage of the 1897 Dingley Tariff Bill, which imposed a heavy duty on imported sugar, and the introduction of the sugar beet industry to Ventura County. The construction of an immense sugar beet factory in Ventura County by Henry, James, and Robert Oxnard, prominent sugar refiners from New York, drew hundreds into the area and led to the founding of the new community. The sugar beet factory quickly became a major processing center for the emerging u.s. sugar beet industry, refining nearly 200,000 tons of beets and employing 700 people by 1903.

The developing Ventura County sugar beet Industry had an important social impact on the new community. One major repercussion was the racial segregation of Oxnard into clearly discernible white and non-white social worlds. The tremendous influx of numerous agricultural workers quickly led to the development of segregated minority enclaves on the east side of town. The Mexican section of Oxnard, referred to as "Sonoratown," was settled by Mexican workers who migrated into the area seeking employment. Arriving in the early 1900s, the Mexican population was viewed by the Anglo population with disdain. ...

Also segregated on the east side of town, adjacent to the Mexican colonia, was the "Chinatown" section of Oxnard. This segregated ethnic enclave was even more despised by the local Anglo population than "Sonoratown." ...Despite widespread anti-Oriental sentiment in the local community, the Asian population grew to an estimated 1,000 to 1,500 people in less than a decade after the founding of Oxnard...

...The Anglo residents on the west side of town, in contrast, were comprised of "upstanding" German and Irish farmers and several Jewish families. "While the east side of town was a rip-roaring slum," according to one local historian, "the west side was listening to lecture courses, hearing WCTU [Women ' s Christian Temperance Union] speakers, having gay times at the skating rink in the opera house, [and] putting on minstrel shows ...

The development of the sugar beet industry in Ventura County led to a precipitous increase in the demand for seasonal farm laborers in Oxnard. Initially, sugar beet farmers in Oxnard relied upon Mexican and Chinese contracted laborers. The decline in the local Chinese population and the utilization of Mexicans in other sectors of agriculture, however, led to the recruitment of Japanese farm laborers to fill this labor shortage. Japanese farm laborers were first employed in the Oxnard sugar beet industry in 1899. By 1902 there were nine Japanese labor contractors meeting nearly all the seasonal need for farm laborers in the area.

In the spring of 1902, however, a number of prominent Jewish businessmen and bankers in Oxnard organized a new contracting company, the Western Agricultural Contracting Company (WACC). [Its] initial purpose. ..was to provide local farmers with an alternative to the Japanese labor contractors in the area. Anglo farmers and the American Beet Sugar Company feared that these contractors would use their control of the local labor market to press for wage increases and improvements in working conditions. Under the leadership of Japanese contractors, Japanese farm laborers had already engaged in work slowdowns and strikes to secure concessions from Anglo farmers elsewhere in the state. ...

Undermining the position of Japanese labor contractors and gaining control of approximately 90% of the contracting business by February 1903, the WACC forced all minority labor contractors to subcontract through their company or go out of business. Through this arrangement, minority contractors and their employees were both forced to work on terms dictated by the W ACC. The commission formerly received by minority contractors was reduced severely through this subcontracting arrangement and they could no longer negotiate wages directly with local farmers. The minority farm laborers employed on this basis also were affected negatively. In addition to paying a percentage of their wages to the minority contractor who directly supervised them, they also paid a fee to the W ACC for its role in arranging employment. Furthermore, the W ACC routinely required minority workers to accept store orders from its company-owned stores instead of cash payment for wages. Overcharging for merchandise at these stores was common. ...

Most of the Japanese farm laborers and labor contractors working in Oxnard were extremely dissatisfied with having to subcontract through the W ACC. Mexican farm laborers in the area and the other numerous minority laborers recruited from other parts of the state also expressed displeasure with the new system. ...

The grievances of these disgruntled workers provided the key impetus for forming a union comprised of Japanese and Mexican farm workers and contractors in Oxnard. At a. ..meeting held on February II, 1903, approximately 800 Japanese and Mexican workers organized the Japanese-Mexican Labor Association, electing as officers Kosaburo Baba (president), Y. Yamaguchi (secretary of the Japanese branch), and J. M. Lizarras (secretary of the Mexican branch). Among the charter members of the JMLA were approximately 500 Japanese and 200 Mexican workers. The decision to form this union and challenge the W ACC marked the first time the two minority groups successfully joined forces to organize an agricultural workers' union in the state. This was no minor achievement, as the JMLA' s membership had to overcome formidable cultural and linguistic barriers. At their meetings, for example, all discussions were carried out in both Spanish and Japanese, with English serving as a common medium of communication. ...

The major purpose of the Japanese-Mexican Labor Association was to end the W ACC' s monopoly of the contract labor system in Oxnard. By eliminating the W ACC's control, the JMLA sought to negotiate directly with local farmers and to secure better wages. Since the formation of the W ACC, the prevailing rate of $5.00 to $6.00 per acre of beets thinned had been reduced to as low as $2.50 per acre. The new union wanted to return to the "old prices" paid for seasonal labor. By eliminating the W ACC from the contracting business, the JMLA also sought to end the policy of enforced patronage. In order to secure their demands the JMLA membership agreed to cease working through the W ACC and their subcontractors. This decision was tantamount to call for a strike. In striking the JMLA threatened seriously the success of the local sugar beet crop because its profitability rested on the immediate completion of the thinning operation. This labor-intensive process required that workers carefully space beet seedlings and allow only the strongest beet plants to remain. Unlike the harvest, where timeliness was not as crucial, beet thinning required immediate attention in order to ensure a high-yield crop.

Although the JMLA was largely concerned with wages and the policy of enforced patronage, there is evidence that the leadership of the union saw their struggle in broad class terms. ...Eloquent testimony of the JMLA 's position is captured vividly in one
news release issued by the Japanese and Mexican secretaries of the union. In putting forth the union's demands, Y. Yamaguchi and J. M. Lizaffas wrote:

Many of us have families, were born in the country, and are lawfully seeking to protect the only property that we have-our labor. It is just as necessary for the welfare of the valley that we get a decent living wage, as it is that the machines in the great sugar factory be properly oiled-if the machines stop, the wealth of the valley stops, and likewise if the laborers are not given a decent wage, they too, must stop work and the whole people of this country suffer with them. ...

Reacting to the organization of the JMLA, the American Beet Sugar Company made clear that it would do everything in its power to insure that the new union did not disrupt the smooth operation of the sugar beet industry in Oxnard. It immediately informed the union that the company was fully in support of the WACC. ...

By the first week in March, the JMLA had successfully recruited a membership exceeding 1,200 workers or over 90% of the total beet workforce in the county. The JMLA's recruitment drive resulted in the W ACC losing nearly all of the laborers it had formerly contracted. The growing strength of the JMLA greatly alarmed beet farmers in the area, for nothing like the new union had been organized in Ventura County or, for that matter, anywhere else in southern California.

One of the first public displays of the JMLA's strength was exhibited at a mass demonstration and parade held in Oxnard on March 6, 1903. ...Unwilling to allow this exhibition of strength to go unchallenged, the W ACC initiated an effort to undercut the solidarity of the JMLA and regain its position as the major supplier of contracted labor in Oxnard. During the second and third week of March, the W ACC helped form an alternative, minority-led union. In supporting the organization of the Independent Agricultural Labor.Union (IALU), the WACC sought to undercut the organizational successes of the JMLA and use the IALU to help regain its former dominance. ...

Immediately after its foundation, the IALU began working in conjunction with the W ACC to meet the pressing labor needs of local farmers. These efforts were, of course, seen by the JMLA as a strikebreaking tactic. ...[A]n outburst of violence occurred a few days after the IALU was organized.

Occurring on March 23, 1903, in the Chinatown section of Oxnard the violent confrontation was triggered when members of the JMLA attempted to place their union banner on a wagon loaded with IALU strikebreakers being taken to a ranch of a local farmer. ...One newspaper described the ensuing confrontation in the following way: ". ..[A] fusillage of shots was fired from all directions. They seemed to come from every window and door in Chinatown. The streets were filled with people, and the wonder is that only five persons were shot." When the shooting subsided, two Mexican and two Japanese members of the JMLA lay wounded from the erupting gunfire. ...Another Mexican, Luis Vasquez, was dead, shot in the back.

Responsibility for the violent confrontation was placed on the JMLA. The Los Angeles Times, for example, reported that "agitation-crazed striking Mexicans and Japanese" had attacked "independent workmen" and precipitated a "pitched battle" in which dozens had been wounded and "thousands gone wild." ...Although more restrained than the Times, the Oxnard Courier also blamed the union for precipitating the confrontation. ...The only weekly that did not directly blame the JMLA was the Ventura Independent. ...

Outraged over the biased coverage of the March 23rd confrontation the JMLA issued its own public statement. It was subsequently published in only two newspapers: the Los Angeles Herald and the Oxnard Courier. The newspaper that the JMLA was principally responding to, the Los Angeles Times, refused to publish the following release:

.
..[W]e assert, and are ready to prove, that Monday afternoon and at all times during the shooting, the Union men are unarmed, while the nonunion men sent out by the Western Agricultural Contracting Company were prepared for a bloody fight with arms purchased, in many cases, recently from hardware stores in this town. As proof of the fact that the union men were not guilty of violence, we point to the fact that the authorities have not arrested a single union man-the only man actually put under bonds, or arrested, being deputy Constable Charles Arnold. Our union has always been law abiding and has in its ranks at least nine-tenths of all the beet thinners in this section, who have not asked for a raise in wages, but only that the wages be not lowered, as was demanded by the beet growers. ...

Shortly after the shooting, Charles Arnold was arrested for the murder of Vasquez, and a coroner's inquest held to determine his guilt or innocence. The conflicting testimony of 50 eyewitnesses was heard at the inquest. ...Testifying against Arnold were a number of Mexican witnesses claiming to have seen Arnold fire at JMLA members. Among these witnesses was Manuel Ramirez, a victim of the shooting, who testified that it was a Japanese strikebreaker in the W ACC wagon who had shot him in the leg. Despite the evidence presented to the all male Anglo jury. ...Arnold was cleared of any complicity in the death of Luis Vasquez.

Outraged at what they believed to be a gross miscarriage of justice, members of the JMLA stepped up their efforts to win the strike. Following the March 23rd confrontation, the union took the offensive and escalated militant organizing activities. ...

...[T]he JMLA organized laborers being brought to Oxnard and succeeded in winning them over to the union' s side. In doing so, the union stationed men at the nearby Montalvo railroad depot and met the newly recruited laborers as they arrived in the county. In one incident reported by the Ventura Free Press, a local rancher attempted to circumvent JMLA organizers by personally meeting incoming laborers and scurrying them off to his ranch. Before arriving at his ranch, however, the farmer was intercepted by a group of JMLA members who unloaded the strikebreakers and convinced them to join the union. ...

The success of the JMLA in maintaining their strike lead to a clearcut union victory. In the aftermath of the violent confrontation in Chinatown, representatives of local farmers, the W ACC, and the JMLA met at the latter's headquarters in Oxnard to negotiate a strike settlement. ...The JMLA negotiating team was led by J. M. Lizarras, Kosaburo Baba, Y. Yamaguchi, J. Espinosa, and their counsel, W. E. Shepherd. Also representing the union were Fred C. Wheeler and John Murray, socialist union organizers affiliated with the Los Angeles County Council of Labor, the California State Federation of Labor, and the AFL.

J. M. Lizarras forcefully presented the JMLA' s demands at the initial meeting. Insisting that the union wanted to bargain directly with local farmers, Lizarras threatened that the union would take all of their members out of the county, thereby ensuring the loss of the entire beet crop, if their demands were not met. ...

...[T]he WACC partially acceded to the JMLA 's demand to negotiate contracts directly with local farmers. The WACC offered the JMLA the right to provide labor on 2,000 of the 7,000 acres of farm land it had under contract. In return, the W ACC requested that the JMLA order its men back to work and agree not to unionize men working for the WACC on the remaining farm land. This offer was flatly rejected by JMLA negotiators, who insisted that they would not end their strike until the W ACC's monopoly was broken and all farmers agreed to contract directly with them. ...

..[T]he union firmly stood by its demand and gained the first important concession in the negotiations. It was an agreement from the farmers' committee to establish a minimum wage scale of$5.00, and a high of$6.00, per acre for the thinning of beets by union laborers. This was nearly double what the W ACC was paying laborers before the strike.

On March 30, 1903, the tumultuous Oxnard sugar beet workers' strike ended with the JMLA winning a major victory. The agreement reached included a provision forcing the W ACC to cancel all existing contracts with local sugar beet growers. The only exception to this was the 1,800 acre Patterson ranch. ...[T]he WACC relinquished the right to provide labor to farmers owning over 5,000 acres of county farm land. ...

The issue of admitting Mexican and Japanese workers to the trade union movement became an important issue in both northern and southern California after the JMLA victory. ...The official attitude of organized labor toward the JMLA was, from the very beginning, mixed and often contradictory. Certain local councils, for example, supported the JMLA and further organizing of Japanese and Mexican workers. This tendency, led by prominent union socialists, also supported organizing all agricultural workers and including farm labor unions in the AFL. Most union councils and high-ranking AFL officials were, on the other hand, opposed to any formal affiliation with the JMLA. This position was based, in part, on organized labor's anti-Asian sentiment and its general opposition to organizing agricultural laborers. ...

In refusing to join the AFL without the Japanese branch of the union, the JMLA ultimately closed the door to any hopes of continuing its union activities in Oxnard. The AFL decision not to admit all members of the JMLA undoubtedly contributed to the union eventually passing out of existence. ...For years after the Oxnard strike, AFL hostility towards organizing Japanese workers and farm laborers persisted. Not until 1910 did the AFL Executive Council attempt to organize farm workers as an element of the Federation. These efforts, however, accomplished very little. ~

Source: Almaguer, Tomas. "Racial Domination and Class Conflict in Capitalist Agriculture: The Oxnard Sugar Beet Worker's Strike of 1903." Labor History. Vol. 25. 1984.

Okies in California: the Migration of Destitute Citizens

But migrant families do not gather about soup kitchens, nor do they travel in boxcars or form improvised armies for protest demonstrations. They have, in fact, an extraordinary faculty for making themselves inconspicuous; they are the least noticeable of people and the most difficult to locate. Nor is their inconspicuousness accidental. They are forced, by circumstance, to be inconspicuous. Many of them travel by night, not because they prefer to do so, but because they have old license plates on their cars and are anxious to avoid highway patrolmen. For the same reason, they frequently travel along minor highways and make many detours and pursue zigzag routes. Occasionally travelers will be amused at the sight of an overloaded jalopy puffing up a grade or stalled in a gas station. But, at the pace most people travel nowadays, they seldom notice the numberless migrant cars they pass on the road.

When migrants stop overnight, it is usually in the cheaper auto and tourist camps or in some squatters' camp off the main highway. If they were deliberately avoiding detection, they could scarcely do a better job of concealing themselves. When they camp along the way, it is usually in a clump of trees or under a bridge or around the bend of a stream out of sight. Good-sized camps of this character may exist under bridges over which thousands of motorists pass every day utterly unaware of their presence. Each spring for nearly twenty years, some ten or fifteen thousand Mexicans have journeyed from Texas to Michigan to work in the sugar-beet fields. In getting to their destination, they pass through a number of states and innumerable cities and towns. Yet so quietly, one is almost tempted to say so mysteriously, is this migration effected that few, if any, people along the line of march have ever noticed the presence of the Mexicans passing north or returning south. Nor are these Mexicans generally observed in Michigan, for they work in the fields, not in the towns; in small family groups, not in one mass.

Migrants do not arrive in a community to the sound of blaring trumpets or noisy fanfares. It is not that they sneak in or that they hide once there. It is rather that they drift into the community, not as a procession, but in single families, car by car, at different hours and by different routes. They do not migrate, like geese, in well-organized squadrons. Today, a community may not have a single migrant family in its environs; tomorrow, several hundred migrant families may have arrived. They do not congregate in the center of town; they linger about the outskirts. They make their purchases, such as they are, not in the downtown shopping districts, but in the cheaper roadside stores. Many communities throughout the country, at the height of the season, are often wholly unaware of the presence in their midst of several thousand migrants.

It is also difficult to see these shadowy figures at work in a field. It is hard to distinguish them, sometimes, from the land. They never work twice in the same place; no matter how many times you may return to the same field, they are not likely to be there. Workers in a garment factory can be located; they can be interviewed and their earnings can be tabulated and analyzed. But the agricultural migrant generally has neither home nor address. In the vast majority of cases, his employer does not even know his name. He works not for a single employer in one area, but for many employers who are frequently scattered over several counties or, for that matter, several states. In California there are 5474 private labor camps in agriculture, yet you can drive the main highways of the state, from one end to the other, and never see a labor camp. The owners who built these camps did not want them located near highways. Even during the peak of the season, the traveler scarcely gets a passing impression of the fact that 150,000 migrants are at work in the San Joaquin Valley alone. You do not see them in the fields, on the highways, or in the towns. You do not feel that impact of thousands of workers which you do, for example, in visiting a large factory. Even when you notice a crew at work in the fields, you can be completely misled as to the number involved. From the highway, it may look as though a dozen or so hands were stooping over at work in the fields. But get out of your car, go into the fields, and count them. And don't be surprised if you count several hundred.

Source: U.S. Congress, House Select Committee to Investigate the Interstate Migration of Destitute Citizens.
McWilliams, Carey. "Okies in California." Hearings. 76th Congress, 3rd Session. 1941.

The Bracero Program

Before 1944, the illegal traffic on the Mexican border, though always going on, was never overwhelming in numbers. Apprehensions by immigration officials leading to deportations or voluntary departures before 1944 were fairly stable and under ten thousand per year....
The magnitude of the wetback traffic has reached entirely new levels in the past seven years. The number of deportations and voluntary departures has continuously mounted each year, from twenty-nine thousand in 1944 to 565,000 in 1950. In its newly achieved proportions, it is virtually an invasion. It is

estimated that at least 400,000 of our migratory farm labor force of 1 million in 1949 were wetbacks....

Farmers in the northern areas of Mexico require seasonal labor for the cotton harvest just as do the farmers on our side of the Rio Grande. There is, accordingly, an internal northward migration for this employment. American farm employers in need of seasonal labor encourage northward migratory movements within Mexico.

This rapid economic development in the areas immediately south of the border has accelerated the wetback traffic in several ways. An official in Matamoros estimates that twenty-five thousand transient cotton pickers were needed in the 1950 season, whereas the number coming from interior Mexico was estimated at sixty thousand. It is to be expected that many Mexican workers coming north with the anticipation of working in northern Mexico do not find employment there and ultimately spill over the border and become wetbacks....

Although smuggling of wetbacks is widespread, the majority of wetbacks apparently enter alone or in small groups without a smuggler's assistance. In a group moving without the aid of a smuggler, there usually is one who has made the trip before and who is willing to show the way. Not infrequently the same individual knows the farm to which the group intends to go and sometimes he has made advance arrangements with the farm employer to return at an appointed date with his group. Such wetbacks stream into the United States by the thousands through the deserts near El Paso and Calexico or across the Rio Grande between Rio Grande City and Brownsville....

Well-established practices to facilitate and encourage the entrance of wetbacks...range from spreading news of employment in the plazas [of Mexican towns and cities] and over the radio to the withholding from wages of what is called a "deposit" which is intended to urge, if not guarantee, the return to the same farm as quickly as possible of a wetback employee who may be apprehended and taken back to Mexico.

The term "deposit" requires some explanation. Members of this commission personally interviewed wetback workers apprehended by immigration officers in the lower Rio Grande Valley. These workers had been paid for the cotton they had picked during the preceding two or three weeks. However, there employers had withheld $10 to $15 from their pay. Such sums, we discovered, are known as deposits. To redeem this deposit, the wetback was required to re-enter illegally and to reappear on the farm employer's premises within ten days.

Once on the United States side of the border and on the farm, numerous devices are employed to keep the wetback on the job. Basic to all these devices is the fact that the wetback is a person of legal disability who is under jeopardy of immediate deportation if caught. He is told that if he leaves the farm, he will be reported to the Immigration Service or that, equally unfortunate to him, the Immigration Service will surely find him if he ventures into town or out onto the roads. To assure that he will stay until his services are no longer needed, his pay, or some portion thereof, frequently is held back. Sometimes, he is deliberately kept indebted to the farmer's store or commissary until the end of the season, at which time he may be given enough to buy shoes or clothing and encouraged to return the following season.

When the work is done, neither the farmer nor the community wants the wetback around. The number of apprehensions and deportations tends to rise very rapidly at the close of the seasonal work period. This can be interpreted not alone to mean that the immigration officer suddenly goes about his work with renewed zeal and vigor, but rather that at this time of the year "cooperation" in law enforcement by farm employers and townspeople undergoes considerable improvement....

Wages for common hand labor in the lower Rio Grande Valley, according to the testimony, were as low as 15 to 25 cents per hour.

Source: Migratory Labor in American Agriculture: Report of the President's Commission on Migratory Labor. Washington: U.S. Government Printing Office, 1951.

Shouts and Whispers, The Rage Of A Privileged Class

Despite its very evident prosperity, much of America's black middle class is in excruciating pain. And that distress-although most of the country does not see it-illuminates a serious American problem: the problem of the broken covenant, of the pact ensuring that if you work hard, get a good education, and play by the rules, you will be allowed to advance and achieve to the limits of your ability.

Again and again, as I spoke with people who had every accouterment of success, I heard the same plaintive declaration-always followed by various versions of an unchanging and urgently put question. "1 have done everything I was supposed to do. I have stayed out of trouble with the law, gone to the right schools, and worked myself nearly to death. What more do they want? Why in God's name won't they accept me as a full human being? Why am I pigeonholed in a 'black job'? Why am I constantly treated as if I were a drug addict, a thief, or a thug? Why am I still not allowed to aspire to the same things every white person in America takes as a birthright? Why, when I most want to be seen, am I suddenly rendered invisible?"

What exactly do such questions mean? Could their underlying premise conceivably be correct? Why, a full generation after the most celebrated civil rights battles were fought and won, are Americans still struggling with basic issues of racial fairness? This book attempts to provide some possible answers. And in exploring why so many of those who have invested most deeply in the American dream are consumed with anger and pain, I hope to show how certain widespread and amiable assumptions held by whites-specifically about the black middle class but also about race relations in general-are utterly at odds with the reality many Americans confront daily.

That the black middle class (and I use the term very loosely, essentially meaning those whose standard of living is comfortable, even lavish, by most reasonable measures) should have any gripes at all undoubtedl':1 strikes many as strange. The civil rights revolution, after all, not only killed Jim Crow but brought blacks more money, more latitude, and more access to power than enjoyed by any previous generation of African Americans. Some blacks in this new era of opportunity have amassed fortunes that would put Croesus to shame. If ever there was a time to celebrate the achievements of the color-blind society, now should be that time.

Joe Feagin, a sociologist at the University of Florida, observed in a paper prepared for the U.S. Commission on Civil Rights that most whites believe that blacks no longer face significant racial barriers. "From this white perspective employment discrimination targeting black Americans is no longer a serious problem in the United States. The black middle class, in particular, has largely overcome job discrimination and is thriving economically. Only the black underclass is in serious trouble, and that has little to do with discrimination." Indeed, many people "believe the tables have turned so far that whites are more likely to be victimized by discrimination than blacks.

At an early stage of my work, I outlined the thesis of this book to Daniel Patrick Moynihan, senior senator from New York and celebrated scholar of ethnicity .Moynihan made the counterargument succinctly. The black middle class, he noted, was "moving along very well." And he had every expectation that it would continue to do so. Indeed, with so many black mayors and black police chiefs in place, blacks represented, to many new arrivals, America's power establishment. "The big problem," added Moynihan, "is, 'What are we going to do about the underclass?' And a particular problem is that [the] black group you're talking about [the middle class] doesn't want to have anything to do with them."

Certainly one can show statistically that black "married-couple families" with wives in the paid labor force (as categorized by the U.S. Census Bureau) do not make that much less than comparably stratified whites. Such households, which earn slightly over 80 percent as much as similar white households, are arguably within striking distance of economic parity. One can empathize with Moynihan' s pique when he reflects on the public reaction to his famous 1970 memorandum to Richard Nixon pointing out that young two-parent black families in the Northeast were progressing nicely and suggesting that perhaps race could benefit from a period of "benign neglect." "I went through hell's own time," recalls Moynihan.

But whatever such aggregate statistics may show, they do not demonstrate-and cannot-that hiring has become color-blind. As Andrew Hacker observes in Two Nations, "While there is now a much larger black middle class, more typically, the husband is likely to be a bus driver earning $32,000, while his wife brings home$28,000 as a teacher or a nurse. A white middle-class family is three to four times more likely to contain a husband earning $75,000 in a managerial position." Feagin notes that he has found "no [emphasis his] research study with empirical data supporting the widespread white perspective that employment discrimination is no longer serious in the u.s. workplace."

In lieu of scientific research, we are offered speculation and conjecture, self-con- gratulatory theories from whites who have never been forced to confront the racial stereotypes routinely encountered by blacks, and who-judging themselves decent people, and judging most of their acquaintances decent as well-find it impossible to believe that serious discrimination still exists. Whatever comfort such conjecture may bring some whites, it has absolutely no relevance to the experiences of blacks in America.

I am not suggesting that most whites are "racist." The majority emphatically are not-at least not in any meaningful sense of the word. If a racist is defined as one who hates blacks (or members of any other racial group, for that matter), the number of true racists is very small, and a substantial portion of them are the pathetic sorts of people who call themselves Nazis and glorify the Ku Klux Klan. Even those fanatics tend to be motivated less by racism than by some pathology expressed in racial terms. The point here, however, is that people do not have to be racist-or have any malicious intent-in order to make decisions that unfairly harm members of another race. They simply have to do what comes naturally.

In 1991, ABC's "Primetime Live" attempted to gauge the effect of race on average black and white Americans. Over a period of two and a half weeks, the program followed two "testers," one black and one white, both trained to present themselves in an identical manner in a variety of situations. At times, host Diane Sawyer acknowledged, the two men were treated equally, but over and over-"every single day," she said-they were not.

The white tester, John, got instant service at an electronics counter; the black one, Glenn, was ignored. Glenn was tailed, not helped, by the salesman in a record store, while John was allowed to shop on his own. Passersby totally ignored Glenn when he was locked out of his car; John was showered with offers of help. In an automobile showroom, Glenn was quoted a price of $9,500 (with a 20 to 25 percent down payment) for the same red convertible offered to John for $9,000 (with a 10 to 20 percent down payment). In an apartment complex, John was given the keys to look around, while Glenn was told that the apartment was rented. At an employment agency, Glenn was lectured on laziness and told he would be monitored "real close," while John was treated with consideration and kindness. At a dry cleaners, Glenn was turned down flat for a job and John was encouraged to apply. In encounter after encounter, the subtle insults and rejections that Glenn had to swallow mounted, to the extent that even the two professional testers said their eyes had been opened. "Primetime Live" did its experiment in St. Louis, Missouri. Yet throughout America, black and white Johns and Glenns, no matter how equivalent their backgrounds and personal attributes, live fundamentally different lives. And because the experiences are so immensely different, even for those who walk through the same institutions, it is all but impossible for members of one group to see the world through the other's eyes. That lack of a common perspective often translates into a lack of empathy, and an inability on the part of most whites to perceive, much less under- stand, the soul-destroying slights at the heart of black middle-class discontent.

This is not to say that white Americans are intent on persecuting black people, or that blacks are utterly helpless and fault-free victims of society. Nothing could be further from the truth. Nonetheless, America is filled with attitudes, assumptions, stereotypes, and behaviors that make it virtually impossible for blacks to believe that the nation is serious about its promise of equality-even (perhaps especially) for those who have been blessed with material success.

Donald McHenry, former U.S. permanent representative to the United Nations, told me that though he felt no sense of estrangement himself, he witnessed it often in other blacks who had done exceptionally well: "It's sort of the in talk, the in joke, within the club, an acknowledgment of and not an acceptance. ..of the effect of race on one's life, on where one lives, on the kinds of jobs that one has available. I think that's always been there. I think it's going to be there for some time." Dorothy Gilliam, a columnist for the Washington Post, expressed a similar thought in much stronger terms. "You feel the rage of people, [of] your group. ..just being the dogs of society."

Upon declaring her intention to leave a cushy job with a Fortune 500 company to go into the nonprofit sector, a young black woman, a Harvard graduate, was pulled aside by her vice president. Why, the executive wanted to know, was the company having such a difficult time retaining young minority professionals? The young woman's frustrations were numerous: she felt herself surrounded by mediocrity, by people trying to advance on the basis of personal influence and cronyism rather than merit; she was weary of racial insensitivity, of people who saw nothing about her except her color, or conversely of those who, in acknowledging her talents, in effect gave her credit for not really being black; she deemed it unlikely, given her perceptions of the corporate culture, that she would be allowed to make it to the top, and feared waking up in a rut several years hence to find that opportunities (and much of life) had passed her by; and she was tired of having to bite her tongue, tired of feeling that she could only speak out about the wrongs she perceived at the risk of being labeled a malcontent and damaging her career. Rather than try to explain, the woman finally blurted out that there was "no one who looks like me" in all of senior management-by which she meant there were no blacks, and certainly no black women. "What reason do I have to believe," she added, "that I can make it to the top?" When she related the incident to me several years later, she remained discouraged by

what seemed a simple reality of her existence. "The bottom line is you're black. And that's still a negative in this society."

Ulric Haynes, dean of the Hofstra University School of Business and a former corporate executive who served as President Carter's ambassador to Algeria, is one of many blacks who have given up hope that racial parity will arrive this-or even next-millennium: "During our lifetimes, my children's lifetimes, my grandchildren' s lifetimes, I expect that race will matter. And perhaps race will always matter, given the historical circumstances under which we came to this country." But even as he recognizes that possibility, Haynes is far from sanguine about it. In fact, he is angry. "Not for myself. I'm over the hill. I've reached the zenith," he says. "I'm angry for the deception that this has perpetrated on my children and grandchildren." Though his children have traveled the world and received an elite education, they "in a very real sense are not the children of privilege. They are dysfunctional, because I didn't prepare them, in all the years we lived overseas, to deal with the climate of racism they are encountering right now. "

In 1992, a research team at UCLA's Center for the Study of Urban Poverty benefited from a fortuitous accident of timing. They were midway through the field work for a survey of racial attitudes in Los Angeles County when a jury exonerated four white policemen of the most serious charges in the videotaped beating of a black man named Rodney King. The riot that erupted in South Central Los Angeles in the aftermath of the verdict delayed the researchers' work, so they ended up, in effect, with two surveys: one of attitudes before the riot, and one of attitudes after.

The questionnaire they used included four statements thought to be helpful in measuring "ethnic alienation from American Society": " American Society owes people of my ethnic group a better chance in life than we currently have." " American society has provided people of my ethnic group a fair opportunity to get ahead in life." "I am grateful for the special opportunities people of my ethnic group have found in America." " American society just hasn't dealt fairly with people from my back- ground. "

Responses to the statements were merged into a single score, cataloged by income level and ethnic group. The responses of blacks with a household income of $50,000 and more were especially intriguing. Even before the riot, that group, on average, appeared to be more alienated than poorer blacks. But what stunned the researchers was that after the riot, alienation among the most affluent group of African Americans skyrocketed, rising nearly a full "standard deviation"- much more than it did for those who were less well off. In reporting the findings, the UCLA team wrote: "This strong and uniform rise in black alienation from American social institutions is the single clearest and most consistent change observed from any of the items we have examined. Careful inspection of responses shows that this rising discontent occurred among black men and women, as well as across educational and income levels. With respect to the effects of income level, however, there is an unexpected

conducted in 1991 by Peter Hart Research Associates found whites more likely to believe that "qualified whites" were hurt by affirmative action than that "qualified minorities" were harmed by racial discrimination.) The histories and current experiences of all these groups differ too much to lump them together in one coherent analysis. In focusing on the predicament of blacks, and specifically of those who belong to the middle class, I do not intend to imply that the concerns of others are trivial, or that there are no similarities between their situation and that of blacks, or no common lessons to be divined. In reality, the opposite is true.

Yet even in this age of "diversity" and multiculturalism, the status of blacks in American society rates special attention. No other racial group in America's history has endured as much rejection on the path to acceptance. No other group has stared so longingly and for so long at what Sharon Coffins, a University of Illinois sociologist, calls "the final door." And no other group remains so uncertain of admittance.

Racial discussions tend to be conducted at one of two levels-either in shouts or in whispers. The shouters are generally so twisted by pain or ignorance that spectators tune them out. The whisperers are so afraid of the sting of truth that they avoid saying much of anything at all.

Those profiled in the following pages are neither shouting nor whispering. They are trying, in a more honest manner than is generally encouraged, to explain how race affects their lives and the lives of those they care about. They are passionately, often eloquently, sometimes anonymously bearing witness. Their hope-and mine-is that their voices will be heard. ~
Source: Cose, Ellis. The Rage Of A Privileged Class. New York: Harper Perennial/HarperCollins. 1993.

A New Social Contract — Five Years Later

IN THE FIVE YEARS that have elapsed since I published The End of Work, structural unemployment has remained dangerously high in Europe and countries around the world, despite gains in both global productivity and gross domestic product. In 1995, 800 million people were unemployed or underemployed. Today, more than a billion people fall in one of these two categories. Only the United States, of the major industrial nations, has significantly lowered its unemployment to a record 4 percent, raising the question of whether it alone has found a formula for success in the new economy. The fact of the matter is, U.S. gains in employment have less to do with a new economic vision and more with a combination of short-term fixes that give the appearance of a robust economy, but hide a darker reality.

To begin with, the U.S. counts its unemployed workers in a very narrow way, allowing it to hide structural unemployment in its official reporting figures. If a worker's unemployment benefits runs out and he or she gives up looking for work, they are reclassified as "discouraged" workers and not counted in the official tally of the unemployed. One can walk the streets of any city in the U.S. and encounter large numbers of unemployed men and women. Yet, few of these men and women are deemed "unemployed" by the U.S. Labor Department. Second, as incredible as it may seem, 2 percent of the adult male workforce in the U.S. is currently incarcerated, by far the largest percentage of imprisoned workers of any country in the world. Third, the U.S. economy did bring record numbers of unemployed Americans back to work over the past eight years, by creating an unprecedented "just in time" work force. Today, millions of American workers are leased out to employers by temporary and professional employment organizations. Millions of others who once enjoyed full time jobs with benefits are now working under short-term contracts or as consultants and freelancers. While the ranks of the unemployed have shrunk, the number of underemployed workers has increased significantly.

Finally, and most significantly, the American miracle has, to a great extent, been bought on credit. It is impossible to understand the dramatic reduction in U.S. unemployment in recent years without examining the close relationship that has developed between job creation and the amassing of record consumer debt. Consumer credit has been growing for nearly a decade. Credit card companies are extending credit at unprecedented levels. Millions of American consumers are buying on credit — and because they are, millions of other Americans have gone back to work to make the goods and perform the services being purchased.

Today, according to the Federal Reserve, Americans are literally spending as much as they are taking in, marking the first time since the Great Depression that the country has experienced a near-zero savings rate. Recall that just eight years ago the average family savings rate in the U.S. was 6 percent of after-tax income.

An analogous situation occurred in the mid to late 192Os. Like today, the 192Os was a period of great economic change. Electricity replaced steam power across every major industry, greatly increasing the productive capacity of the country. Productivity gains, however, were not matched by a significant increase in worker compensation. Instead, wages remained relatively flat, while many marginal workers were let go in the wake of cheaper, more efficient technology substitutions. By the late 192Os, American industry was running at only 75 percent of capacity in most key sectors of the economy. The fruits of the new productivity gains were not being distributed broadly enough among workers to sustain increased consumption and empty the inventories. Concerned over ineffective consumer demand, the banking community and retail trade extended cheap credit in the form of installment buying to encourage workers to buy more and keep the economy growing. By late 1929, consumer debt was so high, it could no longer be sustained. Even the bull market was being stoked by record purchases of stocks on margin (i.e., the amount paid by the customer when using a broker's credit to buy or sell a security). Finally, the entire house of cards collapsed.

The short-term substitution of cheap credit in lieu of a broad redistribution of the fruits of new productivity gains in the form of increases in income and benefits is a subject that has received little, if any, attention among economists. Still, the fact remains that great technology revolutions — like the substitution of electricity for steam power — generally spread quickly, once all of the critical elements are in place. (It should be noted that it took several decades for the electro-dynamo to finally kick in and become a tour de force. Once, however, all the necessary conditions were finally realized, the new technology paradigm swept through every industry in less than a decade or so.) The problem is that it generally takes at least a generation or more after a defining new technology finally comes on line, for social movements to build enough coherence and momentum to demand a fair share of the vast productivity gains made possible by the new technologies. In the 1920s the interim crisis of increased productive capacity and ineffective consumer purchasing power was met by the extension of consumer credit to unprecedented levels.

The same phenomenon is occurring today. The productivity gains brought on by the information and telecommunication revolutions are finally being felt and, in the process, virtually every main industry is facing global underutilisation of capacity and insufficient consumer demand. Once again, in the United States, consumer credit has become the palliative of sorts, a way to keep the economic engines throttled up, at least for a time.

Today, consumer credit is growing by a staggering 9 percent annual rate and personal bankruptcies are increasing. In 1994, 780,000 Americans filed for bankruptcy. By 1999 the number of bankruptcies had soared to 1,281,000. Some economists argue that the zero savings rate is not really as bad as the figures might suggest, because millions of Americans have experienced record gains in the stock market, making their equity portfolios a substitute for traditional bank savings. Still, it should be pointed out that even here, many of the high-tech stocks Americans hold are over-valued and likely to be the subject of significant "readjustment" in the months ahead. Moreover, it should be noted that 90 percent of the gains of the stock market have gone to the top 10 percent of households while the bottom 60 percent of Americans have not benefited at all from the bull market, as they own no stock.

The point is, if countries of the European Union were to lower their current family savings rate from 8.8 percent to near zero, as the United States has, they could likely reduce their unemployment rate from 8.5 percent to under 4 percent. Millions of people spending money — on credit — would assuredly bring millions of additional European workers back to work to make the goods and perform the services being purchased on credit. But, following the U.S. lead would only result in a short-term fix and create the conditions for an even more profound long-term period of economic instability when the extension of credit reached its limits, pushing consumers into default and the economy into a downward spiral, as occurred in the late 1920S and early 1930s.

Hiding unemployment figures, incarcerating large numbers of male workers, creating a "just in time" work force, and extending consumer credit to grease the economic engine are all weak, temporary measures that, in the final analysis, will prove ineffective at dealing with the long-term rising structural unemployment brought on by increasing technological and organizational displacement of workers in the new economy. The twenty-first century will increasingly be characterized by a transition from mass to elite employment as more and more agricultural, manufacturing and service work is performed by intelligent technology. The bottom line is that the cheapest workers in the world — from the factory floor to the professional suites- will not be as cheap and efficient as the intelligent software and wet-ware coming on line to replace them. By the mid decades of the twenty-first century, computers, robotics, biotechnologies, and nano-technologies will be able to produce cheap and abundant basic goods and services for the world's human population, employing a fraction of the world's human labour in the process. Based on current and projected trends in the agriculture, manufacturing, and service sectors, in the year 2050, less than five percent of the human population on earth -working with and alongside intelligent technology-will be required to produce all the goods and basic services needed by the human race. Few of the CEOs I talk to believe that mass amounts of human labour will be needed to produce conventional goods and services in fifty years from now. Virtually all believe that intelligent technology will be the workforce of the future.

The great issue at hand is how to redefine the role of the human being in a world where less human physical and mental labour will be required in the commercial arena. We have yet to create a new social vision and a new social contract powerful enough to match the potential of the new technologies being introduced into our lives. The extent to which we are able to do so, will largely determine whether we experience a new renaissance or a period of great social upheaval in the coming century.

Source
Rifkin, Jeremy. (Introduction to the 2000 Penguin edition). The End of Work: The Decline of the Global Labor Force and the Dawn of the Post-Market Era. New York: G.P. Putnam's Sons. 1996.

AFTERWORD:
THE FUTURE OF OUR PAST

We have seen the tip of the iceberg only. So much of American social and cultural history surrounds us that we could write volumes and not just one text. What it means to be an American continues to change, morph, and develop. We have not looked at the institutions of health care. We have not spent time on environmental concerns. We have not discussed the post 9/11 posture of American culture nor have we examined profound changes in American social institutions as a result of the War on Terrorism. Partly, at least in the case of the Patriot Act for instance, this is because there has been no significant historical distance. Historians are still working on the Bush legacy. And this is more of a book on how we got to where we are – a diverse multiethnic social and cultural complex with serious unresolved issues than it is about current events. Anthropologists and sociologists have produced copious amounts of data on changes in American culture in the 21st century, but all of this can and will be synthesized into future texts.

What remains for this book is to look back and examine the implications of a newer understanding of who we all are and how we can apply that individual and collective identity to the ongoing challenges of diversity. To do this requires deeper self knowledge a keen awareness of the realities those around us face. Race, class, and gender matter. The United States that calls itself America is always on the edge of becoming. If we are to live up to the highest possible potential of the American philosophy, then each person must be aware of the ways our institutions work and what others have done in our past to positively direct institutional change. This is intellectual activism. Its goal – our goal – is social transformation. The objective is justice – social and economic justice. Then we may all celebrate a future collective culture of freedom and self-determination.

ADDITIONAL BIBLIOGRAPHY

Acuna, Rodolfo. Occupied America: A History of Chicanos, 3rd ed. New York: Harper and Row, 1988.

Adams, Abigail. Familiar Letters of John Adams and his Wife Abigail Adams. Boston: Houghton, Mifflin & Co., 1875.

Aldrich, Thomas Bailey. The Poems of Thomas Bailey Aldrich. 1907.

Almaguer, Tomas. "Racial Domination and Class Conflict in Capitalist Agriculture: The Oxnard Sugar Beet Worker's Strike of 1903." Labor History. Vol. 25. 1984.

Archdeacon, Thomas J. Becoming American: An Ethnic History. New York: The Free Press, a division of Macmillan, Inc. 1983.

Asante, Molefi Kete, & Abu S. Abarry. African Intellectual Heritage: A Book of Sources. Philadelphia: Temple University Press. 1996.

Bachmann, Susan & Melinda Barth. Between Worlds, A Reader, Rhetoric, and Handbook. New York: HarperCollins College Publishers. 1995.

Bennett, Jr., Lerone. Before the Mayflower: A History of Black America, 6th ed. New York: Penguin, 1988.

Beverly, Robert. The History of Virginia in Four Parts. (London, 1722).

Blumenthal, Sidney & Thomas B. Edsall, eds. The Reagan Legacy. Pantheon. 1988.

Boyd, Herb. Down the Glory Road: Contributions of African Americans in United States History and Culture. New York: Avon, 1995.

Brown, Tony. Black Lies, White Lies. New York: William Morrow, 1997.

Browne, William H., ed. Archives of Maryland. (Baltimore: Maryland Historical Society, 1883).

Cabral, Amilcar. "Identity and Dignity in the Context of Struggle". Text of a speech delivered at Syracuse University, 02/20/70. Copyright African Information Service, Guinea Bissau, 1973.

Carmichael, Stokely. Excerpt from "What We Want." As appeared in New York Review of Books, September 22, 1966.

Chan, Sucheng. Asian Americans: An Interpretive History. New York: Twayne Publishers, an imprint of Macmillan Publishing Company. 1991.

Chan, Sucheng, & D. H. Daniels, M. T. Garcia, T.P. Wilson, eds. Peoples Of Color in the American West. Lexington Massachusetts: D.C. Heath and Company. 1994

Champagne, Duane. Native America: Portrait of the Peoples. Detroit: Visible Ink Press, 1994.

Chew, Lee. "Experiences of a Chinese Immigrant, 1903." Independent 55 February 19, 1903, 417-423.

Chideya, Farai. Don't Believe the Hype. New York: Plume, 1995.

Commager, Henry Steele. "Black Codes Of Mississippi, 1865." From Documents in American History (1973): Laws of Mississippi, 1865, p. 82ff.

Cose, Ellis. The Rage Of A Privileged Class. New York: Harper Perennial/HarperCollins.1993.

Daniels, Roger. Concentration Camps, North America: Japanese in the United States and Canada during World War II. Robert E. Krieger Pub. Co., Inc. 1981.

Davis, Angela. Angela Davis: An Autobiography. International Publishers Co., Inc. 1974.

Davis, Angela Y. "Masked Racism: Reflections on the Prison Industrial Complex". Color Lines magazine. Oakland, CA: Applied Research Center. Vol. 1, Number 2, Fall 1998.

Dees, Morris with James Corcoran. Gathering Storm: America's Militia Threat. New York: HarperCollins Publishers, Inc. 1996.

De las Casas, Bartolome. "An Early Proponent for Native Rights Condemns the Torture of the Indians in 1565." From The Devastation of the Indies. The Crossroad Publishing Company. English Translation Copyright 1974.

Dorenkamp, Angela et al. Images of Women in American Popular Culture. San Diego: Harcourt Brace Jovanovich, 1985.

Douglass, Frederick. "What to a Slave is the Fourth of July?" Rochester, NY: Frederick Douglass. 1852.

Douglass, Frederick. A Narrative of the Life of Frederick Douglass, An American Slave. 1845.

Drake, Samuel G. Biography and History of the Indians of North America. Boston: O.L. Perkin, 1834.

Dreyfuss, Joel. "Then Invisible Immigrants: Haitians in America Are Industrious, Upwardly Mobile, and Vastly Misunderstood." New York: New York Times magazine section of May 23rd, 1993.

Du Bois, Ellen and Ruiz, Vicki eds. Unequal Sisters: A Multicultural Reader In U.S. Women's History. New York: Routledge, 1990.

DuBois, W.E.B. The Souls Of Black Folk. Viking Penguin, a division of Penguin Books USA, Inc. 1989.

Du Bois, W.E.B., et al. The Niagara Movement Declaration of Principles. 1905.

Duncan, D. W. C. How the Allotment Impoverishes the Indian, 1906 Burke Act. Senate Report 5013, 59th Congress, Second Session, Part 1.

Dyson, Michael Eric. Making Malcolm: The Myth & Meaning of Malcolm X. New York: Oxford University Press, Inc. 1995.

Emerson, Ralph, Waldo. Emerson's Complete Works. Cambridge, Massachusetts: The Riverside Press. 1883-1893.

Equiano, Olaudah. The Interesting Narrative of the Life of Olaudah Equiano or Gustavus Vasa, The African. (New York: n.p., 1791).

Farrell, Warren. "Men A Success Objects". Reprinted by permission of Warren Farrell, Ph.D. (in Bachmann, Susan & Melinda Barth. Between Worlds, A Reader, Rhetoric, and Handbook. New York: HarperCollins College Publishers. 1995.

Flacks, Richard. Making History: The American Left and the American Mind. New York: Columbia University Press. 1988.

Garrow, David J. The FBI and Martin Luther King, Jr. Harrisonburg, VA: R.R. Donnelly & Sons Company. 1981.

Giovanni, Nikki. Black Feeling, Black Talk, Black Judgement. William Morrow & Company, Inc. 1968.

Glick, Clarence E. Sojourners and Settlers: Chinese Migrants in Hawaii. Hawaii: University of Hawaii Press. 1980.

"Gloria Steinhem in Support of the Equal Rights Amendment, 1970." U.S. Congress, Senate Committee on the Judiciary, Subcommittee on Constitutional Amendments. Hearings. The Equal Rights Amendment, 91st Congress, 2nd Session, 1970.

Goodman, Ellen. "When A Woman Says No". The Boston Globe Company. 1993.

Gregory, James. American Exodus: The Dustbowl Migration and Okie Culture In California. New York: Oxford University Press, 1989.

Griffin, John Howard. Black Like Me, Houghton Mifflin Co. 1977.

Grinde, Jr., Donald A., and Quintard Taylor "Red vs. Black: Conflict and Accomodation in the Post Civil War Indian

Territory, 1865-1907." <u>American Indian Quarterly</u>. Vol. 8.1984.

Guevara, Ernesto "Che". <u>Guerrilla Warfare</u>. Lincoln and London: University of Nebraska, 1985.

Haley, Alex. <u>The Autobiography of Malcom X: as told to Alex Haley</u>. New York: Ballantine Books. 1982.

Handlin, Oscar. "The Ghettos." Excerpted from chapter 6 in <u>The Uprooted: The Epic Story of the Great Migrations That Made the American People</u>. Little, Brown, & Company. 1951.

Harris, Marvin. <u>Why Nothing Works</u>. New York: Simon & Schuster, Inc. 1981.

Heizer, Robert F., ed. <u>The Destruction Of California Indians</u>. Lincoln, NA: the University of Nebraska Press & Bison Books. 1993.

Hoar, George F. "Against Imperialism." <u>Congressional Record</u>, 57th Congress, 1st Session (1902).

Hughes, Langston. "Let America Be America Again." Published by International Workers Order, copyright 1965 by Langston Hughes. Reprinted by permission of Harold Ober Associates Incorporated.

Ibieta , Gabriella, & James Orvell, eds., <u>Inventing America: Readings in Identity and Culture</u>. New York: St. Martin's Press. 1996.

Jacobs, Harriet. <u>Incidents in the Life of a Slave Girl</u>. Boston. 1861.

Johnson, Broderick H. Navajo and World War II. Navajo Community College Press. 1977.

Johnson, Charles S. The New Negro, Alain Locke, ed., 1925.

Khapoya, Vincent. The African Experience, 2nd ed. New Jersey: Prentice Hall, 1998.

King, Jr., Martin Luther. "Letter From A Birmingham Jail," From Why We Wait. Copyright Coretta Scott King, 1991.

Kozol, Jonathan. Savage Inequalities: Children in America's Schools. New York: Harper Perennial, 1992.

Leonard, Karen. "California's Punjabi-Mexican-Americans." The World and I. The Washington Times Corporation. 1989.

Leon-Portilla, Miguel. "An Aztec Remembers the Conquest of Mexico a Quarter of a Century Afterwards, in 1550." From The Broken Spears. Beacon Press. Copyright 1962 & 1990.

Lincoln, Abraham. The Life and Writings of Abraham Lincoln, Philip Van Doren Stern, ed. New York: The Modern Library. 1940.

Lincoln, Abraham. United States Statutes At Large 12:1268-69.

Mayfield, Thomas Jefferson. Indian Summer. Berkeley, CA: Heyday Books & the California Historical Society. 1993.

Mc Cloud. African American Islam. New York: Routledge, 1995.

McIntosh, Peggy. "White Privilege: Unpacking the Invisible Knapsack". From Working Paper 189. "White Privilege and

Male Privilege: A Personal Account of Coming To See Correspondences Through Work In Women's Studies" (1988), Wellesley College Center for Research on Women, Wellesley MA 02181.

McWilliams, Carey. "Okies in California." From Testimony before U.S. Congress, House Select Committee to Investigate the Interstate Migration of Destitute Citizens. Hearings. 76th Congress, 3rd Session. 1941.

McWilliams, Carey. "The Zoot Suit Riots." New Republic. Volume 108. June 21, 1943.

Meredith, James. "A Challenge to Change", Newsweek, Oct 6th, 1997.

Moody, Anne. Coming of Age in Mississippi. New York: Laurel (Dell), 1997.

Munoz, Jr., Carlos. Youth, Identity, Power: The Chicano Movement. Verso Publishers. 1989.

Naylor, Gloria. "Mommy, What Does "Nigger" Mean?" New York Times Magazine, 1986.

Ni, Preston. With Dignity and Honor: Social Justice and Personal Responsibility In Multicultural America. Burgess International Publishing, 1997.

Njeri, Itabari. Lure and Loathing: Essays on Race, Identity and the Ambivalence of Assimilation, Gerald Early, ed. Penguin Group. 1993.

Olds, Sharon. The Gold Cell. Alfred A. Knopf, Inc. 1987.

Olson, Steve. "Year of the Blue Collar Guy". Pp. 251-253 in Across Cultures. Sheena Gillespie, & R. Singleton, eds. Boston: Allyn and Bacon, A division of Simon & Schuster, Inc. 1991.

O'Neill, Teresa, ed. Immigration: Opposing Viewpoints. San Diego: Greenhaven Press, Inc., 1992.

O'Sullivan, John L. Democratic Review, July 1845.

Porter, Kenneth W. "Negro Labor in the Western Cattle Industry, 1866-1900". Labor History. Vol. 10. 1969.

Quinsaat, Jesse, et al. Letters in Exile: An Introductory Reader on the History of Pilipinos in America. Los Angeles: UCLA Asian American Studies Center. 1976.

"Ronald Reagan and Albert Maltz, Testimony Before HUAC, 1947." U.S. Congress, House Committee on Un-American Activities. Hearings. 1947.

Reed, Ishmael. "America: The Multicultural Society". Pp. 431-434. (in Across Cultures. Sheena Gillespie, & R. Singleton, eds. Boston: Allyn and Bacon, A division of Simon & Schuster, Inc. 1991.)

Rifkin, Jeremy. The End of Work: The Decline of the Global Labor Force and the Dawn of the Post-Market Era. New York: G.P. Putnam's Sons. 1996.

Riordan, William. Plunkitt of Tammany Hall. E.P. Dutton. 1905.

Roosevelt, Theodore. "The Corollary to the Monroe Doctrine." Annual Message to the United States Congress, December 1904 and December 1905.

Sanger, Margaret. The Case for Birth Control. New York. 1917.

Savin-Williams, Ritch C., & Kenneth M. Cohen. The Lives of Lesbians, Gays, and Bisexuals. New York: Harcourt Brace Publishers. 1996.

Sedgwick, Jr., Theodore, ed. A Collection of the Political Writings of Willian Leggett. New York: Taylor & Dodd, 1840.

Shakur, Assata. Assata: The Autobiography of Assata Shakur. New York: Lawrence Hill & Co. 2001.

Sinclair, Upton. The Jungle. 1906.
Smith, A., et al., eds. Document Set for Out Of Many: A History of the American People, by J. M. Faragher, et al. New Jersey: Prentice-Hall, Inc. 1994.

Smith, Venture. A Narrative of the Life and Adventures of Venture. (New London: n.p., 1798).

Soto, Gary. "Like Mexicans." Small Faces. Copyright 1986 by Gary Soto. Delacorte Press, a division of Bantam Doubleday Dell Publishing Group, Inc.

Stanton, Elizabeth C., S. B. Anthony, and M. J. Gage, eds. History of Woman Suffrage. Rochester, NY: Susan B. Anthony. 1887.

Staples, Brent. "Just Walk On By: A Black Man Ponders His Power To Alter Public Space", Ms. Magazine, Sept. 1986.

Strong, Josiah. Our Country: It's Possible Future and It's Present Crisis. 1885.

Takaki, Ronald. A Different Mirror: A History of Multicultural America. Boston: Little, Brown and Company, 1993.

Takaki, Ronald. Strangers From A Different Shore: A History of Asian Americans. Boston: Little, Brown, & Company (&Viking Penguin), 1989.

Tenhula, John. Voices From Southeast Asia: The Refugee Experience in the United States. New York: Holmes & Meier Publishers. 1991.

Terkel, Studs. "Earl B. Dickerson, The Fair Employment Practices Committee, 1941-43." From The Good War: An Oral History of World War II. Pantheon Books, a Division of Random House, Inc. 1984.

Turner, Frederick Jackson. The Significance of the Frontier in American History. (1893).

Vizenor, Gerald. Native American Literature: A Brief Introduction and Anthology. New York: Harper Collins, 1995.

Walker, Cheryl, ed. American Women Poets of the Nineteenth Century. Rutgers State University Press. 1992.

Walker, David. Walker's Appeal, In Four Articles. Boston: D. Walker. 1830.

Washington, Booker T. Up From Slavery. 1901.

Wells-Barnett, Ida B. A Red Record. 1895.

West, Cornell. Race Matters. Beacon Press. 1993.

Wicker, Tom. Report of the National Advisory Committee on Civil Disorders. New York: Bantam Books. 1968.

Wilkinson, Virginia Snow. "From Housewife to Shipfitter." Harper's Magazine. September,1943.

Wilson, Woodrow. "The Fourteen Points". Address to Congress, January 8, 1918.

X, Malcolm. "Malcolm X Speech. 1964" excerpted from "The Black Revolution." From Two Speeches by Malcolm X. Pathfinder Press & Betty Shabazz. 1969 & 1990.

Young, Al. African American Literature: A Brief Introduction and Anthology. New York: Harper Collins, 1996.

Zinn, Howard. A People's History of the United States 1492-Present, revised and Updated. New York: Harper Perennial, 1995.

Zinn, Howard. The Twentieth Century: A People's History. New York: Harper Perennial/ HarperCollins. 1998.

SUGGESTED GOVERNMENT DOCUMENTS

Jefferson, Thomas. The Declaration of Independence. 1776.

The Constitution of the United States of America

The Bill Of Rights (1st Ten Amendments to the Constitution).

The 13th, 14th, and 15th Amendments to the Constitution of the United States.

Taney, Roger. Cases Argued and Adjudged in the Supreme Court. 1857.

Plessy v. Ferguson, 1896. 163 U.S. 537 (1896).

The National Origins Act of 1924.

"Brown v. Board of Education, 1954." 347 U.S. 483. 1954.

The Civil Rights Act, 1964. 78 U.S. Statutes At Large 241 ff Public Law 88-352.

The Civil Rights Act, 1965.

Roe v. Wade. 410 U.S. 113. 1973.

MANY MORE SUGGESTED READINGS ARE AVAILABLE THROUGH THE VARIOUS SOURCES.